CH00924356

Henry Maudslay: Dam Buster

John de Hoop
75 (NZ)

Geo Dunn DFC
10 76 60B 1409 Met Fll

Hal A. Gardner
106 589 Sqan

Terry Mason DSO
91 0 96 Sqdn

Lucas S/Ldr)FC
9.15.162,139.

Geoff Packham   550 Sqn
Daphne - widow of Ian Brownlie D.F.C.
77 & 35 Sq.

HENRY MAUDSLAY
DAM BUSTER
ROBERT OWEN

Robert C

Dave Fellowes
460 ESN RAAF

Jo Lancaster DFC
40 & 12 Sqdn.

G/L (Johny Johnson DFM
97 V 617 Sqn

Harry Mackie
P/F / 460 Sqdn

Mary Stopes-Roe
daughter of Barnes Wallis

Published in 2014 by Fighting High Ltd,
www.fightinghigh.com

Copyright © Fighting High Ltd, 2014
Copyright text © Robert Owen, 2014

The rights of Robert Owen to be identified as the
author of this book are asserted in accordance with the
Copyright, Patents and Designs Act 1988.

British Library Cataloguing-in-Publication data.
A CIP record for this title is available from the
British Library.

ISBN – 13: 978-0992620707

Designed and typeset in Adobe Minion
10/14pt by Michael Lindley www.truthstudio.co.uk

Printed and bound in China by Toppan Leefung.
Front cover design by Michael Lindley.

For Annette, Henrietta and Victoria

Contents

Acknowledgements

The greatest acknowledgement must be accorded to members of the Maudslay family who made available, with unconstrained generosity, their private collection of documentation and memorabilia: Annette Parrott, Victoria Trevelyan and Henrietta MacCurrach, together with Christopher Blount and Richard Maudslay.

A great debt is also owed to the many organizations consulted, in particular the Air Historical Branch – Sebastian Cox, Mike Hatch, Alan Thomas and Clive Richards, the Royal Air Force Museum – Peter Elliott and the Staff of DoRIS, Eton College – Annabel Casey, Penny Hatfield and Patricia Wood, and St Hugh's College, Oxford – Deborah Quare. Also the staff of The National Archives, Kew, Birmingham Public Libraries, Warwickshire County Records Office, The British Library Newspaper Library, Colindale, 617 Squadron Association – Les Munro, Fred Sutherland, the late Edward Johnson and the late Tom Bennett.

To the following individuals I also express my gratitude: Dr John Sweetman and Richard Morris, who offered their scholarship, encouragement and advice, reading drafts of the manuscript and offering constructive observations, Robert Beresford-Peirse, Derek Brumhead, the late Lucian Ercolani, Robert W. Evans, Ray Hepner, the late Enid Keyte, Rachel Loraine-Smith, Peter Remagen, Virginia Richardson, the late J Philip Sorenson, David Stephens, Virginia Wells and David Wentworth-Stanley.

I also extend my debt of gratitude and thanks to Air Commodore John Langston, Group Captain David Robertson, the Committee and all members of the 617 Squadron Association for the privilege of many years of enthusiastic support, encouragement and fellowship.

Introduction

On the wall of the small rural parish church of St Andrew at Sherbourne, Warwickshire, a bronze plaque commemorates the life of a young airman killed in the service of his country during the conflict of 1939–45. Such memorials are not uncommon, but each is a reminder that the greatest military forces comprise individuals, each one with a unique life story and family connections.

In the broad context, Squadron Leader Henry Maudslay, DFC, was no different from so many of his comrades. Born three years after the end of the 'war to end all wars', he was one of a generation whose families had been extremely fortunate if they had been untouched by the carnage that had littered the fields of France with the corpses of those who should have contributed to the prosperity of early twentieth-century Britain. Despite the lessons learned, hopes of a peaceful future had evaporated gradually with the growing antagonism of Hitler's Germany. By the time Henry's education was complete, the wheel had turned full circle and, after twenty years of peace, he and his peers found themselves committed to defending their country again against the German aggressor.

However, in detail there was much to distinguish him. In recording the life of Henry Maudslay, it is necessary to set it in the context of his family's earlier achievements. Successive generations had exhibited similar traits: the desire to achieve the best possible results through both application and innovation, combined with loyalty and consideration both for family and for those in their employ. The Maudslay family were the inheritors of an outstanding engineering pedigree, instrumental in forging the Industrial Revolution, which was echoed and rekindled by Henry's father during the birth of the Midlands motor industry. In keeping with his family background, Henry had a scientific bent and a natural aptitude for things mechanical. He was a pioneer himself, being among the first RAF aircrew to train in Canada, an event not without its trying moments, and he was selected as one of those who would introduce into service the aircraft that would become the mainstay of Bomber Command and the harbinger of victory – the Avro Lancaster.

Educated at Eton, he might have been expected either to progress into business or to seek the opportunity of a university education, where he would have furthered his scientific studies, most probably in a practical discipline. But the declaration of war a year before he left school curtailed these aspirations, and he voluntarily applied himself to service in the RAF, following an aeronautical interest that had been developing over several years. In doing so he became one of many destined never to see a peacetime adulthood.

After training as a pilot, he was posted to an operational bomber squadron, where he survived for six months, completing a tour of operations, before being posted to a training unit, where his experience of battle would be a valued commodity. Engineering a return to a second tour of operations at the start of 1943, he reapplied himself to the onslaught against the enemy. Some two months later his skills as both a pilot and a leader were acknowledged by his transfer to a newly formed unit training to perform the unique operation against the German dams. It was from this operation that he and his crew failed to return, shot down on the return flight near the banks of the Rhine.

Previously published accounts of the Dams Raid have, of necessity, glossed over details of this officer's life, summarizing him briefly as an ex-Etonian athlete. Despite the fact that he was a flight commander, his contribution to the development of equipment and technique has been recorded but fleetingly. For a long time the facts surrounding his death were unclear, leading to a general belief that he and his crew simply disappeared into the night sky over the Eder Dam, destroyed by their own weapon. Other accounts contribute a tapestry of errors, creating a mantle of myths and further adding to the enigma. One states that he came from Nottingham, another from a wealthy West Country family – yet the family roots lie on the Pennine borders of Lancashire and Yorkshire before moves to London and the Midlands. It was only after his father's death that Henry Maudslay's family home migrated westwards, but then only as far as the rolling hills of the Cotswolds. Others have suggested that he served at one time with the 'Kipper Fleet' – Coastal Command – another fallacy, stemming presumably from a misinterpretation of the citation for his Distinguished Flying Cross.

Readers of these accounts may be forgiven for presuming that Henry Maudslay enjoyed a carefree life full of privilege and effortless ease; that his education at one of the country's leading public schools had at best engendered a sporting 'Boy's Own Hero' attitude to the risks of war, or at worst developed the brash arrogance often attributed to young men with wealth and social status. Such assumptions will be seen to be far wide of the mark.

In looks he was very much the epitome of a young Englishman. Long boned, but of average height, Henry was of sinewy build and fair complexion. He had an open face, with even, slightly aquiline features and a long ridged nose. Brown almond eyes complemented a wide mouth, ever ready to break into a grin expressing a purposeful vitality. His short, dark brown wavy hair was kept in place with oil, as was the fashion of the day, fortuitously since it had a tendency to frizz when dry.

Sports training had kept him physically fit, and he appears to have suffered few ailments when young other than those traditionally associated with childhood. He was never a heavy drinker, although he smoked regularly, occasionally using a short cigarette holder, a habit seemingly acquired during his latter days at Eton. By nature he had inherited his father's temperament, being quiet and modest, almost to the point of apparent shyness at times, and his mother's charm. Although his background enabled him to be at ease in most social situations, he was not a great party goer and avoided the dance floor whenever possible, preferring instead smaller gatherings among a wide circle of friends.

Although tolerant of most things, he could be strong-willed and knew his own mind. Seeking perfection, he was a thorough planner, setting his own high standards and rebuking himself when he considered that he had failed to achieve them. Academically, although intelligent, he was not naturally gifted in many fields. As a boy he was not a great reader for pleasure and his results suggest that they were not effortless, but the outcome of diligent application. He was determined to make the utmost of his ability and drove himself to do so.

His focused energy brought commendation as an airman, and his determination placed him high among the 'press on' ranks of bomber captains. Henry's Group Commander, Air Vice-Marshal Sir John Slessor, was later to recall:

> There were always the few ultra-conscious captains who gave one horribly anxious moments in those bleak dawns. One such who remains vividly in my memory was Henry Maudslay, courteous, diffident and strikingly good looking, whom my schoolboy son not so many years his junior remembered with respect as an Olympian swell at Eton. Time and time again one would have almost given him up for lost when the welcome sound of engines would be heard overhead and the control tower would come through to say that D-Donald was in the circuit. He would always go to the limits of safe endurance to make sure of finding and hitting his targets. I never remember being more impressed by the quality of any young officer and sometimes had a horrid premonition that he was one of the dedicated sort who sooner or later would tempt providence too far.[1]

Henry had no time for inefficiency and poor organization, especially among his superiors. He did not suffer fools gladly but would willingly help those who demonstrated a desire to improve their performance, leading them by example. Providing they made the required effort, he could be a strong mentor, generous with praise and encouragement, showing qualities of leadership that did not go unrecognized by Eton masters. A younger boy[2] remembers his openness and friendliness towards new arrivals. His quiet yet confident, easygoing manner and sense of justice and fair play gained the respect of both his elders and peers. At school he became Captain of Boats and Captain of Athletics and was elected to an elite body of senior boys. These attributes continued into Service life. In the words of one who had served in a flight under Henry's command: 'He was a true gentleman' – an astute recollection by one then in his late eighties reflecting on a contemporary of his youth.[3] Another comments: 'I think Henry Maudslay was one of the most popular officers on the Squadron. He was down to earth, no frills, no airs, but lots of courage.'[4]

It is perhaps these traits, combined with a natural modesty and inherent consideration for others, that shaped Henry's personality. He did not demand adulation, nor was he disparaging of those from less prosperous backgrounds. (Despite his coming from a successful family, among those at Eton he was relatively speaking not particularly wealthy, and may have been seen by some as being nouveau riche, his family being in trade rather than inherent landowners and members of the Establishment). Nevertheless, he found the experience of Initial Training revealing, as it introduced him to a wider social circle; to his surprise he found these colleagues reasonably conducive, despite the often somewhat limited nature of their initial conversation.

Henry's schooling instilled in him a strong sense of self-reliance, fortitude, loyalty and sense of responsibility. The latter may have been fostered further by the death of his father relatively early in Henry's life. His letters are evidence of a strong relationship with his mother, although in no sense could he be considered to be tied to her apron strings. When required, he was more than able to stand up for himself and for principles in which he believed. As with most young men, he seems to have tried her patience at times, with moderate demands and minor misdemeanours. As time passed he sought to provide her with advice on issues, in addition to seeking her counsel. His desire for independence was tempered with a concern for other members of the family. He was close to his elder sister, although contact with his brother, nine years his senior, appears to have been more remote. A great affection was shown also to his childhood governess, with whom the family retained close links until her death only a few weeks before Henry was killed.

The possibility of his own death had not escaped him. Three members of his course died before ever reaching an operational unit, and with typical preparation Henry organized his affairs, making his will within a short time of confronting the enemy. There was nothing morbid in this; if anything he was an optimistic realist. He knew that he might be killed, or taken prisoner, and tried to ensure that eventualities were covered, thereby avoiding unnecessary hardship to those for whom he cared.

As will be seen, in many respects he was an 'old head on young shoulders', but in others a certain naivety emerges, a conflict not surprising in times when circumstances caused boys to become men overnight. It is meaningless to speculate what he might have achieved had he survived the war. More appropriate is the acknowledgement of his attainments and his commitment to execute his duty, regardless of personal risk.

The following account does not seek to be an in-depth character study, nor a comprehensive psychological profile. Instead, it is very much a narrative of the events that shaped the life of Henry Maudslay, combining material from official records, the family archive, personal recollections and other disparate sources. Where appropriate, Henry's own words are used, taking extracts from letters to his mother. When known, the achievements and fates of his contemporaries have been included for comparison. In many respects the rigours of boarding school and military establishment conferred on the majority of these young men a degree of homogeneity, as did the forced circumstances of war, yet beneath this veneer each had his own individual likes and dislikes, pleasures and concerns. To each and every family, they were someone special.

Prologue

Henry Maudslay came from a family of engineers. His great, great grandfather, whose name he shared, had been one of the founding fathers of Britain's industrial heritage. The engineering company he established at the beginning of the nineteenthth century produced innovatory stationary engines, marine engines, and other technical products, including production tools enabling accurate and consistent manufacturing essential for mass production. Maudslay, Sons and Field, managed by future family generations, survived until 1900. By that time other family descendants were turning their engineering skills to the manufacture of new forms of transport and replacing steam with the emerging internal combustion engine.

Henry's father, Reginald Walter Maudslay, had trained as a civil engineer, but in 1902 moved from London to Coventry to establish what was to become the Standard Motor Company. In 1908, aged 36, he married 26-year-old Susan Gwendolen Herbert – reputedly the first lady to be seen riding a bicycle in Coventry. The next few years saw the arrival of a daughter, Margaret Kate, born in 1910, followed two years later by a son, John Richard. Soon the young family would be joined by a governess for the children, Miss Emily Walton Kellaway, known to the family as Kelly.

The Standard Motor Company would develop into one of Britain's major motor manufacturers. As Managing Director and later Chairman, Reginald became a leading spokesman for the British motor industry. Seen as an innovator in design, the company's cars had a reputation for reliability, produced by a skilled workforce managed by a philanthropic employer.

By 1921 the family were comfortably established in a substantial Victorian house at Lillington, a respectable village on the fringes of Leamington Spa, and Gwen was expecting their third child.

Part 1

Henry Maudslay – Schoolboy and Sportsman

Chapter 1

Boyhood

Then the whining school-boy, with his satchel,
And shining morning face, creeping like a snail
Unwillingly to school.
(William Shakespeare, *As You Like It*, Act 2, Scene 7)

A celebratory air pervaded Leamington Spa on Thursday, 28 July 1921. Captain C. F. Scrope had just taken victory in the Men's Finals of the town's annual tennis tournament and the population was looking forward to enjoying the following Monday's August Bank Holiday. At 1 Vicarage Road in the north-eastern district of Lillington there was even greater cause to rejoice as Gwen Maudslay was delivered safely of her third child, a brother for Margaret and John. He was to be christened Henry Eric by the Revd Charles Bernard McNulty, vicar of Holy Trinity church, Leamington, in a baptism conducted at the family's parish church of St Mary Magdalene, Lillington, on 11 September 1921.[5] Within a few years the family had moved to a more rural location at Sherbourne, near Warwick, where they established themselves in the former Victorian vicarage.[6]

Little is recorded of Henry's early years at Lillington and Sherbourne. He would have been supervised and cared for initially by Kelly, the family governess, assisted perhaps by his elder sister Margaret (by now known to members of the family as 'Tita'). (His elder brother John, away at school, would have been seen only during his holidays.[7]) In keeping with many middle-class children of the period, he may also have received his early education from Kelly, rather than attending the local village school. Nevertheless he still mixed with the village children and was a member of the local wolf cub pack run by Lady Howard, assisted on occasion by Tita.

By 1930 it was time for Henry to receive more formal tuition among peers of his own age and social standing. His parents had selected a suitable preparatory school, and at the age of 9 Henry was enrolled as a boarder at Beaudesert Park School, Minchinhampton, near Amberley, a few miles south of Stroud,

Gloucestershire. Housed in 'Highlands', an imposing Victorian Tudor building resplendent with its black-and-white 'half timbering' and jutting gables, it was set in thirty acres of attractively wooded grounds on a terraced south-facing slope overlooking a lake at the edge of Minchinhampton Common. With an expanding roll, currently of thirty boys aged between 8 and 14, fees approached 50 guineas (£52.50) a term, plus a further fee for laundry (£1.05). Pocket money was fixed at a guinea (£1.05) per term and also covered stamps, school books and stationery. Extra subjects could be accommodated on payment of additional fees: Music (£2.10), Carpentry, Dancing, Drawing (each £1.05) and Riding (£4.20).

Winter uniform comprised a navy blue serge suit, with a waistcoat over a shirt with an Eton collar, and footwear of stout cross-laced boots. For outdoor wear, including the Sunday walk to Amberley church, boys donned a stout grey overcoat of herringbone tweed, wrapped a long grey woollen scarf around their necks, with matching gloves, and on their heads placed their newly acquired bowler hat. (By the end of Henry's time at Beaudesert, black brogues replaced the boots, and the bowler gave way to a grey herringbone 'burglar Bill' tweed cap.) During the summer season lighter-weight materials would prevail, a grey flannel suit and straw boater, with white shirt and shorts for sports, not forgetting the compulsory cloche-style sun hat.

Beaudesert had established a strong record for attainment, with an emphasis on Classics. There was almost 100 per cent success in the Common Entrance Examination, and during the 1930s twenty-eight boys would win scholarships to the leading public schools, or naval cadetships to the Royal Naval College at Dartmouth. The school was very much a family affair. The founder Arthur Richardson – 'Big Sir' – was assisted by his elder son, Austin Richardson and the staff already included Maurice Richardson, the founder's nephew, who was joined in 1930 by Barton Richardson the headmaster's second son, while his third son, Colin Richardson, was a pupil (and subsequently head boy). The headmaster's wife, Margaret Richardson, administered the domestic, health and social issues. Lower School was run by Miss Simpson and Miss Butterfield, into whose charge Henry was transferred at the beginning of the autumn term 1930, along with eight other new arrivals.[8]

Pupils were taught in a number of converted family rooms, masters each covering a wide variety of subjects. The 'Big Room', next to the headmaster's study adjacent to the entrance hall was typical. Wide bay windows presented vistas of the wooded landscape beyond, but despite their size the interior was often dull, the gloom being in part caused by the heavy dark wooden-panelled ceiling with gilt embellished beams. The dark bare boards of the polished wooden floors were relieved by a single runner of carpet. A stencilled dado frieze ran at waist height around the plain painted walls. There was an upright piano against one wall, and the blackboard was perched precariously on the marble mantle of a tall Victorian fireplace. Pupils sat on long wooden benches running along the length of a long refectory-style table, upon which were placed sloping writing boards with glass ink bottles for the dip pens. Lessons lasted approximately forty minutes, with Latin taking precedence over most other subjects. The prospectus proclaimed proudly: 'There is no preparation. All the boys are carefully taught how to play cricket and other games, and there is a daily class of Physical Drill and Swedish Exercises. Singing, Boxing, Shooting and Swimming are also thoroughly encouraged.'

Sergeant Major Miller, fearsomely Irish, ex-Army and a national exponent of athletics, encouraged physical fitness among the boys. Boxing, PT, athletics and drill came within his remit. For the latter the boys were divided into platoons, each with its leader, and taught the rudiments of physical discipline preparing them for enrolment in their subsequent school Officer Training Corps. Lower and upper classes trained separately every day, except on Wednesdays and Fridays, when they combined. The boys also learned scouting, tracking and sema-phore. On wet days Sergeant Major Miller gave lectures on games and fitness-related subjects. Team points were given for discipline, marks being deducted from any team whose member was seen with hands in pockets or other unfavourable behaviour. The *pièce de résistance* each year was a torchlight drill and formation marching display that was held in front of assembled parents attending the autumn half-term function at the beginning of November. Some twenty-four boys marched and counter-marched, each with a yellow, green, red or mauve torch carried on the end of a stick. The event was part of a Parents' Day, which included a performance of the school play and culminated in a Guy Fawkes display. Parents and younger boys watched from the terrace, as masters, prefects and team captains set off fireworks (supplied by generous parents) and ignited the large bonfire, which had been built by the gardeners, and around which the older boys danced, singing 'Auld Lang Syne'.

An outdoor swimming pool had been completed shortly before Henry's arrival at Beaudesert, and all boys were expected to be able to swim. Austin Richardson taught those who could not. His prime aid was a pole, to which a thick belt was attached, passing beneath the pupil. Austin would use this to keep the unfortunate pupil's head above water while he exhorted, 'Swim, boy. Swim!' Occasionally the master would be distracted and the pole would lower, allowing a non-swimmer gently to submerge, much to the delight of onlookers. Never-theless the method was demonstrably successful, for by 1933 eighty-one out of the ninety boys then on the roll were classed as swimmers.

Life was not all academia and physical exertion. Every Sunday, having marched to and from the service at Amberley church and written their compulsory weekly letter home, the younger boys were rewarded with a lollipop when they presented themselves at Mrs Richardson's room. The fragrance of many a fine summer evening would be enhanced by the smell of cooking over an outdoor fire. Boys would help carry provisions down to the lakeside in wicker baskets before being despatched to find kindling. Duty done, and supervised by Enid Richardson, the headmaster's 24-year-old daughter,[9] they would then enjoy sausages and bread rolls washed down with 'gallons' of orange juice. If time permitted they might then play wild Red Indian games or a junior cricket match, before retiring to bed by seven o'clock.[10]

The dormitories were typical of their period. A dozen or so white-painted iron beds, covered by embroidered counterpanes, lined the walls, leaving a gangway down the middle of the room. Next to each was a double cabinet (half per boy) with a towel rail. On top was placed the boy's wash bowl, to be filled each morning with warm (if you were lucky) water for washing. A small rug alongside each bed alleviated freshly woken feet from the cold bare floorboards. At the far end a plain tiled, high-mantled fireplace provided a source of warmth, although restricted only to the bitterest weather. Personal items were kept to a minimum, and a spartan atmosphere prevailed. A senior boy served as dormitory captain to supervise the younger members.

Sports days, with their garden-party atmosphere, combined with the headmaster's annual review to create the big social event of the school calendar. Events were held on the Lower Field to a background of music provided by the Nailsworth Band. The competition over, tea would be taken by parents and visitors in the dining room before they strolled out on to the terrace to hear the speeches and applaud the day's victors as they received prizes for their sporting prowess.

During his time at Beaudesert Henry appears to have been an average pupil, neither gaining a scholarship, nor becoming a prefect. He was absent from the team lists for football and cricket, and the records for school sports days show little sign of the athletic ability that was to distinguish him in his subsequent school career. Peter Giffard, John Stewart Robinson, Parker and Maude were all budding runners at this time, but Henry is not mentioned.[11] Photographs in his album show football, cricket and tennis matches, together with general shots of track and tug-of-war events at sports days, perhaps indicating a greater interest in photography than physical activity. The sole exception was his prowess at shooting. The school had a range where boys could learn the safe handling of smallbore weapons under the watchful eye of Mr Rundle. In 1933 Henry began to show promise, assisted by a parent's presentation of a recoilless rifle to the school. An article in the school magazine noted that Henry showed above-average ability and predicted he would do well the following year. The author was correct, for, partnered by Habershon, Atherton and Workman, Henry was a member of the successful 'B' Team,[12] which won the school's inter-team contest held at the end of summer term 1934. Henry's own superior performance in this event earned him the Russell Cup, awarded for the best individual shot in the competition.

Henry's qualities of leadership and organization began to manifest themselves in late 1932, when he and George Graham mooted the formation of the Beaudesert Park Model Automobile Club with the objective 'to enable those who possess model cars to join together in a spirit of friendly rivalry'.[13] The club proper, with a committee of five boys, a chairman, treasurer and two vice-presidents, held its first meeting during the spring term of the following year. In keeping with his position as son of one of the country's leading motor manufacturers, Henry became the club's first president and provided two notebooks in which the club's events would be recorded. Writing the club's first report in the school magazine, Henry stated that races were organized as frequently as possible:

> These are really thrilling, as crashes occur frequently. To give an instance of the speeds obtained from some of these cars – let us suppose that a magician could wave his wand over one of the models while it was travelling at full speed and make it the same size as a real car travelling at a comparative speed. The result would be a super sports motor car travelling in the neighbourhood of one hundred miles per hour!

There was a range of models, many of them being scale replicas of contemporary cars or record-breakers such as the Golden Arrow, which had gained the world land speed record for Britain in 1931. They were either commercially purchased, or built by the boys from construction sets, those from Meccano being the most popular. Some of the more technically minded boys built their own from locally available materials. An account written in 1937 records that the club was still racing an excellent model built by Henry from three-ply wood and powered by twenty-four strands of elastic.

To encourage members and boost its growth, membership was originally free to those interested, but by the beginning of the autumn term 1934 a subscription charge of 3*d* (2p) per term would be charged. This would permit free entrance for members to the various events, rallies and trials organized by the club and the purchase of prizes. The first such event of the new regime was a model 'Olympia' motor show, echoing that providing a showcase for the products of his father's company. The exhibition was held in 'The End Room', an area attached to the dining room that provided accommodation for school plays and other gatherings.

An article written by Henry in the school magazine described the event. Opened by Mrs Prichard, mother of one of the members,

> the exhibition was an almost complete miniature reproduction of the real Olympia... The cars were exhibited on specially constructed stands, each stand having a salesman and assistant. The cars were demonstrated in a partitioned off space in the middle of the room and all orders for cars were taken at the enquiry office.

Among Henry's other hobbies developing at this time was an interest in lead toy soldiers, of which he built up a considerable collection, and rubber-powered model aircraft. One Sunday afternoon, shortly after arriving at the school, Henry was flying his latest model, a 'ready to fly' 19-inch-wingspan rubber-powered Warneford monoplane, on the field below the school buildings. After a few flights requiring minor adjustments, Henry succeeded in getting the aircraft to complete some 20 yards of powered flight before it glided down for a perfect landing. Conscious that the activity was being watched by a solitary new boy, Henry commented to him on the smoothness of the landing. Striking up a conversation Henry learned that the spectator was Tim Vigors,[14] a new boy who was finding it difficult to adjust to the new regime of life away from home. After hearing how much the boy hated it, Henry commented that 'it's not so bad particularly if you have a friend', thus striking up a friendship that was to continue for the remainder of his schooldays.

In his memoirs *Life's too Short to Cry*, Tim Vigors recounts that he had been offered a ticket in the Irish Hospital Sweepstake by Sergeant Major Miller (at a time when betting on such events was illegal in England) and persuaded Henry to go halves on the necessary five shillings for its purchase. Boys' funds were controlled by the headmaster, and Henry made the necessary application for the withdrawal of five shillings. Innocently the headmaster asked Henry if he were buying another model aircraft, and, equally innocently, Henry told him the truth – that he was buying a sweepstake ticket with Vigors! Although there was a minor eruption from Richardson, no further action was taken against the boys.[15]

Austin Richardson fostered an interest in natural history. A keen entomologist, he took boys on field trips to the Forest of Dean and other suitable locations at weekends, in addition to a regular school trip to Norway. At 8.45 a.m. one Sunday in July 1934, Henry, along with Vigors, Taylor, Giffard and Williams, laden with nets, killing bottles and pill boxes, set off with the master in his Humber in search of additions to their butterfly and moth collection. Crossing Salisbury Plain and passing through Corfe Castle, they arrived near Swanage, where they caught fine specimens of silver-studded blues, humming-bird hawks, and Lulworth skippers. On one notable occasion Henry's keen eye and coordination enabled him to catch two in one stroke. After bathing at Studland and enjoying a picnic lunch, the party travelled on the ferry across the mouth of Poole Harbour to the New Forest and Lyndhurst, where they collected copious white admirals. Following tea, another stop netted grass emeralds and yellow underwings, before setting off for home, pausing again for supper near Stonehenge, to arrive back at Beaudesert by a quarter to ten.

Austin Richardson also encouraged the boys' character development in his role as President of the Debating Society. This met on Sunday evenings and comprised forty-eight senior boys (known as 'eight o'clocks', since they were permitted to stay up an hour or so later than the younger boys), who were encouraged to speak on a wide variety of subjects. The second meeting of 1933 saw a debate on the relative merits of road and rail transport. Henry – 'our resident car expert' – expounded on the power–weight ratio of the car compared with that of a train, being opposed by Beor-Roberts, who maintained that the aeroplane would replace the car, but that trains would remain. Adding variety to meetings, a mock trial was held, determining the case of a defendant who had won £100 from a bookmaker and bought a necklace for his wife. On the way home he was attacked, knocked unconscious and robbed. The bookmaker stood trial as the accused. Austin Richardson, in the chair, acted as judge, the other roles being played by the boys. Henry appeared as a witness for the prosecution, claiming that he had seen the accused hanging around his car and had then missed a spanner that subsequently had been found in the woods near the scene of 'the attack'. The accused was found guilty, his punishment being 'to come into meals with clean hands and face for a whole fortnight'! In 1934 topics included the advantages of a Channel tunnel, whether democracy was the best form of government, the existence of ghosts and the validity that 'The Lion is the King of Beasts'. The second meeting of the 1934 autumn term raised the subject of the possibility of machinery proving to be man's undoing. The motion was proposed by Atherton, saying that unemployment created by increased automation supported the premiss. Griffith said that it was man who made the machinery, and that without man this would not be possible. Henry supported this view, venturing that man would not be mastered by machine until the latter had a superior brain. The president steered the debate by suggesting that machinery could master man in warfare, or by creating unemployment, and the headmaster pointed out that, in his view, 'man on the dole is now better off than the man of olden times'. When put to the vote, the motion was carried by thirty-four votes to fourteen.

Starting the year before Henry's arrival, a new form of entertainment for the boys was the school cinema, also run by Austin Richardson. The films were shown during autumn and easter terms, when the early onset of darkness eased the problems of blacking out a suitable room. Screened using a Kodascope projector, they were a mixture of adventure, such as *Hands Up* (a tale of the American Civil War) and the *Western Wagon Master*, comedy with Laurel and Hardy and Harold Lloyd and informative documentaries illustrating mineral extraction, natural history and *The Birth of an Aeroplane* – the latter of interest to several boys, including Tim Vigors and Henry, who both built and flew their own model aircraft. Further interest in aviation was aroused one day when a de Havilland Gipsy Moth (G-AAAS) landed on Minchinhampton Common. (This may have been the occasion in 1931 when a pupil's father came to visit his son. Landing on the Common, the pilot omitted to notice the sunken roadway, causing the aircraft to drop on to it and bounce out again, fortunately without serious damage.)

Holidays at home provided opportunities for riding (although this had limited appeal to Henry) or taking the family's numerous dogs for a walk. Carefree summers were spent with family and friends at the family's sporting estate at Shinness in the Scottish Highlands. There the frequent stream of visitors provided a range of entertainment, while for solitude Henry could go for a walk or cross the fields below the house and take a boat out on Loch Bhanabhaidh, perhaps fostering his latent talent as an oarsman. Sometimes he would venture further to Loch Shin. On occasion Henry would ask a school friend to join the family. When Colin Richardson, the headmaster's son, was invited, he told his parents that he would have to take a pair of new plus fours because all the Maudslay party would be so dressed. At the same time Henry was telling his parents that he required a pair of plus fours since Colin would be wearing his. As a result both boys obtained their much-desired clothing, most probably against their parents' wishes and better judgement![16] Picnics would be organized. Gentlemen in plus fours, accompanied by ladies in tweed skirts and capes, together with children and dogs, would motor out into the countryside to a suitable location, where they would sit among the heather and enjoy the contents of the hampers they had brought with them. The more adventurous made excursions farther afield, taking the form of motoring expeditions spread over several days.[17] There was trout fishing in the lochs and River Fiag, the children serving as ghillies to the adults. Sometimes on Sundays, when fishing was not allowed, Henry would go down to the loch and sail his model yacht, to which he had surreptitiously attached a length of line with a baited hook. Come August and the 'Glorious 12th', the shooting parties would arrive, and the surroundings would echo to the sound of their guns and dogs. Henry's own shooting prowess in the field was celebrated when on 3 August 1933 he shot his first rabbit. After this inauguration he would become a regular gun, both at Shinness and at home in Warwickshire.[18]

By 1934 the rapid growth of the school's intake resulted in two-thirds of the roll being aged under 12, Henry being in the minority of older boys. Already a number of his friends were moving on. Colin Richardson had taken up his scholarship to Eton.[19] William Spooner had already left to attend a school nearer his home in Yorkshire. Tim, one of three Vigors brothers attending the school, a keen rugger and cricket player, captain of 'A' Team and prefect, went up to Eton at the end of the Easter term 1934. John Stewart Robinson, another promising but temperamental cricketer, left at the end of summer term 1934 to attend Shrewsbury School.

Henry had one more term to complete and bade farewell to Beaudesert shortly before Christmas 1934. He had enjoyed his time at the school and would return at least once a year during 1936–38 to revisit friends and staff. Although he passed the Common Entrance Examination, essential for entrance to public school, Henry seems never to have excelled at either academics or sport. He was seen as a pleasant boy, considerate and a hard worker, although he had yet to display many of the characteristics that would shape him in the future. As the door closed on what was otherwise an enjoyable period of Henry's life, he became an 'Old Beaudeserter', qualifying for his Old Boy tie in the school colours of grey on a green ground. Almost immediately, however, other external influences were at work accelerating his progress from boyhood to man. Throughout the year his father's health had been deteriorating, causing increased concern. On 14 December 1934, ten weeks after being admitted to a London private hospital, Reginald Maudslay died, aged 63.

Chapter 2

Oppidan Schooldays

Alas regardless of their doom
The little victims play!
No sense they have of ills to come,
Nor care beyond today:
Yet see how all around them wait
The ministers of human fate,
And black Misfortune's baleful train!
Ah, show them where in ambush stand
To seize their prey the murderous band!
Ah, tell them they are men!
(Thomas Gray, 'Ode on a Distant Prospect of Eton College')

It was intended that Henry should follow in his brother's academic footsteps and his name had been entered for Eton, now under the new headship of Claude Elliott, an ex-Etonian and Cambridge medieval historian. In doing so he would accompany fellow Beaudeserter Michael Kemble and rejoin near contemporaries Tim Vigors, Thomas Bowen, Peter Giffard and Robert Williams, who had preceded him during the previous two terms.

During the 1930s all secondary education, even within the state system, required the payment of fees, unless a rare scholarship could be obtained. As part of an established middle-class family and without the need to start work to help support the family, there could be no doubt that Henry would continue his education at an independent fee-paying school. Education was not only a means of obtaining qualifications, but also ensured the correct social background and the cultivation of an appropriate mix of friends who would ease progress through adult life. Public schools were seen as the gateway to the universities, notably Oxbridge, or Sandhurst, and nearly all members of the ruling strata, be they politicians, senior civil servants, high-ranking military officers, senior members of the clergy or influential industrialists or financiers, were part of the 'Old Boy' network.

Although they were greatly sought after, the high cost of sending a boy to an independent public school effectively reduced the competition for places.[20] The fees for Eton exceeded £300 per annum.[21] First, an entrance fee of £21 had to be paid to the School Fund four years before the boy's scheduled arrival. Then there was an inclusive fee of £230 p.a. that covered board, tuition and the School Fund, after which came other charges for the River Subscription, Laboratory Fees, Gymnasium Fee and Sanatorium Fee. An inclusive games subscription of £5 was charged for athletics, fives, football and cricket. Amounting to £78 6s 8d (£78.34), the inclusive fee and games subscription had to be paid fully in advance before the commencement of the school year. On top of these there were the additional costs of providing uniform, books, sports kit and a private allowance.

Ability to meet the cost of fees was a necessary, but not sufficient factor in a boy being accepted. Academic criteria also had to be met. Boys were admitted at ages ranging between 10 and 14 years, dependent upon their gaining a King's Scholarship or passing the Oppidan Entrance Examination for fee-paying scholars. Henry was entered for admission as an Oppidan. The examinations were exacting for a 13-year-old and reflected the classical emphasis of the curriculum: the translation of easy Latin into English, Latin parsing and grammar, Latin composition (prose and verse), French grammar, parsing and easy translation, elementary Arithmetic, Algebra and Geometry, outlines of English History and Geography. In addition to passing the Common Entrance Exam, an aspiring Oppidan was required to secure a place in one of the twenty-five boarding houses run by Masters and Dames (either their wives, or substitute matrons) throughout the town. This could be achieved either by entering the boy's name at birth on the provisional list of the Master making the list, or by putting his name on the general list before his 12th birthday. The Housemaster would be approached directly and a personal meeting arranged, at which he would assess the boy's character as well as his academic requirements. On average each Housemaster found himself able to offer eight places a year for the new intake.

Henry was successful and granted admission as an Oppidan. 'Archie' McNeile had given up his House at Easter 1933, preventing Henry from lodging with his brother's mentor.[22] Instead he was to board at a house known as the Hopgarden, a three-storey yellow-brick building with Georgian sash windows and two incongruously tall chimneys situated in Common Lane, across from the main entrance to School Yard. The building itself comprised three blocks of different periods, melded together as one; an earlier cottage had been developed into a boarding house about 1823 by the Revd T. Carter and further extended at the turn of the century by Ernest Lee 'Jelly' Churchill, then Housemaster, who added a north range. The result was a rabbit warren of a building, with a central open area, 'The

Well', enclosed by the various extensions. In a corner of the garden was a hop-drying store, which had been converted into a seventeenth-century music room. Two Homeric quotes adorned its painted ceiling, dated 1732: 'The glorious gifts of the gods are not to be rejected' (Iliad III. 65) and 'Singers deserve honour and respect' (Odyssey VIII. 480). House colours, when awarded, were dark blue and white, shirts and caps being quartered, one sock being blue, the other grey, with alternate turnovers.

Boys entered the House from the brick-paved drive leading off Common Lane, dividing the Hopgarden from the adjacent House, 'Angelo's'. A large pale green door led into a concrete-floored entrance hall from which a door led off down a dark passageway to the Housemaster's private quarters and his study, from which access to the garden was gained through a large sash window. Another doorway led to the lavatories, with their ubiquitous aroma of Jeyes fluid, and another gave access from the entrance hall to the boot room and an area containing a large multiple toaster upon which fags would prepare fare for their masters. Beyond this lay the boy's dining hall, adjacent to which was the tutor's private dining room. A staircase on the right-hand side of the entrance hall gave access to the first floor. With rooms at one end overlooking either Common Lane or the yard, a corridor led past a small cooking area to a WC at the far end, past five study bed-rooms, those overlooking the garden usually occupied by senior boys. The upper floor was of similar layout. A further few steps led up to 'The Library' – a common room for selected senior boys. Another set of stairs led off to the boys' maid's room and a rather scruffy bathroom, before descending again, providing access to number of small but cosy rooms overlooking the driveway.[23]

In early 1935 the Hopgarden was run by a Classics master, Henry Grey Champion Streatfeild, himself an Old Etonian, and was home to some forty boys of varying ages from 14 to 19. The Dame acted as intermediary between the boys and the Housemaster, supervising administration, catering, finances and medical problems, while much of the authority of the House resided in 'The Library', a select self-elected group of half a dozen or so senior boys, including the Captain of the House and Captain of Games. These advised the House Tutor on House politics, and maintained discipline, often through a somewhat despotic regime of fear and punishment.

Lent Half[24] 1935 commenced on 24 January, and Henry would have arrived, along with fifty-four other new boys,[25] the previous day, coinciding with the return of established fifth- and sixth-formers. He would have been met by Streatfeild, who was to act *in loco parentis*, and shown to his study bedroom. Unlike other similar establishments where the younger boys slept in dormitories, Eton prided itself that most boys (unless they were brothers) had their own rooms from their time of entry. Each was sparsely, but adequately, furnished, with a bed – which was screwed to the floor at the top end, but hinged, allowing it to be folded up and held by a strap against the wall behind a curtain during the day – a sock (food) cupboard, table, Windsor chair and a 'burry', scarred with previous boys' names in pokerwork. The latter dominated the room and was a compendium of desk and bookshelf with fold-down top and drawers that could be used for shirts, collars, socks and underwear. Washing and sanitary arrangements were minimal. Many houses had a maximum of three or four baths and scarcely more lavatories. The boys' rooms had no piped water or wash basin, instead a wash box with a hinged top and a cupboard beneath for a water jug.

Boys were expected to provide any other furniture deemed necessary and would usually obtain an armchair, boot box, brush box and ottoman for sports gear, the latter's padded top serving as additional seating accommodation. Curtains and a mat for the bare wood floor were also left to the occupant's choice, as were any pictures or other embellishments. Prints by the Medici gallery, water-colours of Eton and Windsor, or Peter Scott's bird studies were popular choices. Older boys and those with different cultural tastes might adorn their rooms with photographs of current idols of stage and screen. Each room had an open fire-place, but coal supplies were strictly rationed, brought from the shed outside to each room by Ben, whose duties also included cleaning the boys' boots.

After the new boys' tea, when parents had left and unpacking had been com-pleted, the new arrivals found they had very little time to themselves. Tradition decreed that during the evening they would be summoned over to the Music Schools, where they would be given a singing test by the Precentor to assess their suitability for the Chapel choir. A fortunate few who were deemed acceptable would be given a surplice and entitled to time off from formal lessons to attend choir practice. Most were silenced after a few notes and allocated seats among the East Block of the Lower Chapel. The results of Henry's trial are not recorded. It was then back to the house for an early night in readiness for the start of the new Half.

For a new boy the first few weeks could be disorientating, confusing and often miserable. Eton was home to some 1,152 boys, and its physical dispersion through-out the town gave it more the character of a university than a school. In many respects it could be viewed as a town within a town and, like many closed societies, fostered numerous obscure customs and rules with which the newcomer needed to acquaint himself. Apart from learning the physical geography, including 'bounds' and the names of masters, there were the names of important senior boys and captains of sports teams, for both the House and the school, the numerous combinations of twenty-seven House and sporting colours and a glossary of jargon. This knowledge would be subject to examination by senior members of the House. A third failure to demonstrate the desired proficiency would usually result in a beating. Eton, although considered by outsiders to be totally 'upper class', had its own hierarchical structure, and with a family background in 'trade', Henry may have had to suffer the jibes of the sons of the titled and landed gentry, whose 'old money' was considered socially superior. If so, he was of strong enough character and ability to transcend any stigma.

Codes of conduct and dress had to be learned. Boys were permitted to walk only on the west side of Eton High Street, and any 'beak' (master) seen had to be 'capped' – a salutation requiring the raising of a finger in the direction of the boy's hat. Any boy found eating in the street would be fined 2/6d (12^{1}/$_{2}$p), which would be donated to the Eton Mission, a charitable institution run by the boys to provide aid to poor communities in Hackney. The collars of greatcoats were not to be turned down, nor umbrellas rolled – privileges normally permitted only to members of Pop, an elite body of older scholars. Some parents too required polite instruction. Letters were to be addressed 'Esquire', their sons were no longer 'Master'. Among themselves peers would use each other's Christian names, but those of differing ages would resort to surnames or titles.

There were books to be purchased. For those so desiring, new copies, bought at Spottiswoodes, would be gilt embossed with their owner's name and House; otherwise they could be purchased second, third or fourth hand for a few pence at the book pound.

After a fortnight new boys would be introduced to another traditional feature of school life: fagging. Younger boys could be called upon by their seniors to perform minor chores, including tidying rooms, running errands and making tea. The cry of 'Bo-o-o-y' shouted down from the Library would cause a flurry of activity as boys ran to meet the call, the last to arrive being 'rewarded' with the task required. Non-responders known to be within earshot would be sought out for punishment. The lucky ones were those with accommodation best placed to reach the rooms of older boys quickly. Upper boys not in the Library could not call for a fag, and would have to hunt down some poor unfortunate. It was a time of fool's errands and practical jokes to catch the unwary and uninitiated. The new boys would have to suffer this irksome duty for a year at least. Nevertheless it was seen as character forming, and, as they grew to become 'fag masters' themselves, they learned that man management is better achieved by encouragement or reproof rather than continual admonishment.

The school was divided into six blocks,[26] each approximating to a year, some subdivided into removes through which boys passed during each Half, these being further divided into divisions. Henry entered Eton in 'F' Block – the bottom of the school and the equivalent of the fourth form – Division XXX, his placing within this reflecting his performance in the Common Entrance Examination. Initial subjects included Latin (Mr Denys Wilkinson), Mathematics and Geometry (Mr William Hope-Jones), French (Mr Hubert Hartley) and Drawing (Mr Menzies-Jones), together with English, History, Science and Geography. Physical fitness was encouraged with a session of PT. Lessons were taught Monday through to Saturday, starting at 7.30 a.m. and ending about 6.00 p.m., except for Tuesdays, Thursdays and Saturdays, which were established as half-holidays. Intensive though this may appear, a considerable amount of this teaching time was spent on non-academic activities designed to broaden outlook and develop character.

Each schoolday morning Henry would have been awakened at about 6.45 a.m. by a knock on the door and the maid calling 'Time to get up Mr Maudslay.' Leaving a can of hot water for washing, she would move on to the neighbouring room. After a quick wash, it was time to dress. It was not conducive to linger. During the winter months the houses could be cold and damp, often with the stench of the Thames Valley fog that might persist until midday. Boys of the Lower School and less than 5 feet 5 inches tall did not wear the traditional tail-coat, wearing instead a short black Eton jacket (known as a 'bum freezer'). A large turned-down Eton collar was worn outside the jacket with a black tie, and the uniform was complete with a black waistcoat (always worn with the bottom button undone), striped trousers and the traditional top hat. An umbrella would soon be added to protect the top hat from inclement weather.

Early School commenced at 7.30 a.m. At about 7.25 there would be a mad dash as boys descended from their rooms, grabbing hot tea or cocoa and a biscuit (or one of the previous night's buns) before dashing out to the dull-painted school-rooms, where pupils and masters alike would assemble half awake for first lessons.

Lower School boys would return to their House at about 8.30 for a proper breakfast (usually porridge) in the Boys' Dining Room before Room Fagging, cleaning the grate, laying a new fire and generally tidying their fag master's room. The process was then repeated for their own accommodation, listening for the bell, which would allow them ten minutes to seat themselves among the 500 boys attending Lower Chapel at 9.20, presided over by the Lower Master. (Attendance was compulsory for all except 'members of other denominations', who remained in their Houses).

Chapel lasted about twenty minutes, with prayers, a short lesson, a psalm by the choir and the finale hymn sung by all. Then it was on to Second School. After a brief free break at 10.30 to snatch a quick cup of cocoa or lemonade and a bun, Third School would start at 10.55 a.m. for an hour. At the end of each morning during his first year Henry would attend 'Pupil Room' – an hour's work at prep exercises, where his tutor would be able to assist with any specific difficulties. Eton placed great emphasis on the Tutorial System. In addition to his House Tutor each boy had a Classical or Modern Tutor, whom he would share with four or five other boys. The tutor did not teach his tutees formally but was responsible for supervising the academic aspects of the boys' lives and developing a close interest in their studies. For his first two Halves, Henry Streatfeild would be both House Tutor and Classical Tutor to Henry.

Boys' Dinner, the only formal meal of the day, took place at about 1.30 p.m. and lasted for half an hour or so. It was the only meal presided over by the House Tutor. Boys would assemble in the dining room on the ground floor and stand, awaiting the arrival of the senior members of the House. The Captain of House and members of the Library would enter, positioning themselves at the head of the main table of polished oak. The door would then open to admit the Dame and Tutor. Streatfeild would say grace, after which the remainder of the boys would be seated, either at the main table set down the length of the room at right angles to the Tutor's or at another parallel long table with their backs to the three tall windows that formed the longer wall opposite the fireplace. The meal would then be served from the kitchen via a hatch in the wall at the opposite end to the Tutor's Table.

Afternoon School would commence at 2.30 p.m. on Monday, Wednesday and Friday, excepting half-holidays. The timetable varied according to the season of the year. In the winter months most afternoons were given over to sports (Michaelmas was the only Half when games were compulsory), followed by a forty-five-minute break for tea at about 4.15 p.m. Two Lower Boys would be allotted to fag for each member of the Library, the remainder being at the disposal of other senior members of the House. The boys would need to ascertain their fag master's requirements, go down to the town and purchase ingredients on account, then cook and serve. Dependent upon the degree of the fag master's compassion, severe penalties could be incurred for burnt toast or burst sausages. Their seniors served, the boys would then congregate in established Messes of two or three for the last twenty minutes of the break. Using a small sink and gas ring in the middle of their corridor, they would prepare their own meal under the supervision of the maid, who would lay tables in the boys' rooms, provide hot water for tea and clear up afterwards. Bread, butter and milk were provided by the House, although extra provisions could be bought from the School Stores or local shops such as Rowlands, the confectioners at 122 High Street, Eton, whose delivery boys would cycle up to the House, leaving purchases on 'the slab' just inside the entrance. Boiling was allowed on all days, and scrambled eggs became many a boy's speciality. Many considered this meal the best time of the day.

Last School commenced shortly after 5.00 p.m. before the boys returned to their Houses for Lock-up at 6.00 p.m., when they would spend study time in their own room doing 'extra work', as prep was known, before the supper bell rang shortly after 7.30 p.m. If work was completed early boys might indulge in passage football, kicking a ball along the corridors, each side trying to score at the opponent's end having negotiated a scrum in the middle. Boys were not allowed to leave their House between Lock-up and 7.15 a.m. without their Housemaster's permission or a special ticket.

After supper Lower Boys were subject to more Room Fagging: getting the fag master's bed down, collecting hot water and general tidying. The boys would then gather at 8.30 p.m. for formal prayers by Streatfeild, after which he would pay a visit to each boy in his room, an activity that enabled masters to gain greater insight into their charges and the boys to learn social ease. Lower Boys would be expected to have their lights out by 9.15, the Seniors by 10. Some Houses enforced compliance by throwing the mains switch.

Schoolwork continued on Saturday mornings, with the afternoon being free. In the evening boys might attend a concert in the Music School, or a film presentation in the School Hall. Sunday mornings provided the opportunity for a 'Long Lie', with the boys rising at about 8.45 a.m. in order to be in the Dining Room to answer M'Tutor when Absence was called. Two attendances were called for at shortened Chapel services at 10.30 a.m. and 5 p.m. Streatfeild would invite his new boys to visit his study for about forty minutes, where he would read aloud from a popular novel or preside over intelligence tests and observation games or ask his pupil to select and read a passage from a book of his choice. Streatfeild also kept track of his charges' academic progress by a system of monthly Order Cards and Tickets given to boys, which had to be completed and signed by the various subject masters. There were no games on Sunday, and, for those not seeing their tutors, Sunday afternoons were free. The river was out of bounds (except in the Summer Half, when bathing was permitted at Cuckoo Weir), but boys were allowed to walk into Windsor and visit the castle grounds to listen to the band, although the side streets were still strictly out of bounds. All shops were out of bounds on Sundays, although older boys could go into tea shops after 3.30 p.m., and younger boys meeting their parents or friends were permitted to enter, having obtained leave from their Housemasters.

Athletics began with the closure of the football season. This year events were moderated by a flu epidemic that swept through the school during the last week of March. During the Easter Half there was no strict organization of games, although every boy was expected to take part in some form of physical activity.

The most notable date in the school calendar was 4 June, King George III's birthday. Traditionally, from its foundation by Henry VI in 1440, Etonians had recognized the monarch's birthday with a holiday. That of George III's successor fell during the holidays, and hence 4 June was retained and became a fixed date celebrated by the entire school. Flower-sellers paraded in the streets around Eton, and it was the one day of the year when all members of the school, not only members of Pop, were permitted to wear a buttonhole. Parents were invited to visit the school and view a number of established events. Tickets were strictly controlled and issued through House Tutors, with instructions that they 'must not be given to chauffeurs and others'. After Early School and breakfast, followed by Chapel at 9.25 a.m., formal school activities ceased and the celebrations took over. At 10.45 members of the Upper School in court dress would perform speeches – enacting extracts from famous literary works. Cricket started during late morning. Lunch was a semi-formal affair hosted by the Housemasters. During the afternoon boys would invite their guests to their rooms, for a tea comprising strawberries and cream with chocolate or walnut cake from Fuller's and a pot of tea served by the boy's maid. At 6.00 p.m. the formal calling of Absence in School Yard and Weston's Yard signalled the start of the evening's activities, which centred on the Procession of Boats along the river, their crews dressed as sailors of George III's reign, finishing with a closing fireworks display at 10.00 p.m.

The final week of each Half was devoted to the school examinations: 'Trials'. Each boy would be given a number and go to his appointed Trials Room, where he would be invigilated by a master with whom he had had no contact during that Half. Each subject had a paper lasting a maximum of three hours. Results were made known on the last day of the Half at 'Reading Over'. Boys would crowd into Upper School and sit nervously on the benches lining one side, or on the floor waiting for their block to be called. Masters, still formally attired in their gowns and white bow ties, supervised them. Boys living at a greater distance and needing to leave quickly would already have changed into their ordinary clothes. The Lower Master would read out the block's results in order from the sheets he held: Distinctions, First Class, Second Class, Pass and Failure. The latter was very rare, but after two failures the pupil would usually be asked to leave the school. For most boys Trials merely decided the order of the Absence List and their seating positions in Chapel. Knowing the worst, the boys would then head off to see their Classical or Modern Tutor to discuss their detailed marks by subject, which would be written on a Trials Card for the boy to take to his House Tutor. After he had added his comments, it would be sent to the boy's parents to provide a termly report on their son's progress.[27]

Since 1919, when Eton was the first school to organize its own scout troop for

the younger boys, the activity had attracted a large following. There was no com-
pulsion, but, having earlier been a wolf cub, Henry soon joined the 1st Eton
College Troop as a member of the 2nd Kangaroo Patrol, under the leadership of
Patrol Leader Jameson. Run energetically by the Revd George Snow, assisted by
Mr Watkin Williams and Troop Leader F. M. Hepburne-Scott, the troop met in
their own time at 12.50 p.m. every Saturday. Once a fortnight, having given their
names to Patrol Leaders the previous day and with a signed Bill of Absence
secured by the Scout Master permitting their travel 'out of bounds', scouts would
assemble on Thursday afternoons outside the troop room at 'The Old Christopher',
a former coaching inn opposite College Chapel in Eton High Street, and then
cycle out into the country in pursuit of various tasks. (Only scouts and boys with
medical conditions preventing participation in sports were permitted to have
bicycles.)

One of Henry's first scout meetings was a field day on 2 February, when Patrol
Leader Jameson gave him tuition on how to light a safe fire. However, it was not
until Saturday, 30 March, that he and Roger Peek were admitted formally to the
troop when they were invested into the 2nd Kangaroo Patrol.[28] The next day found
them assisting their patrol producing model camp kitchens in a competition contributing to the Hoare Cup. Despite their relative lack of scouting experience,
they still succeeded in achieving second place. Perhaps spurred on by Henry's
enthusiasm, his close friends Peter Wake and Charles Pilkington also donned the
contemporary uniform of wide-brimmed hat, knee-length dark shorts and knee-
length socks[29] and were invested as members of the 1st Kangaroos. Unfortunately
the troop had to forsake what could have been a high point of the year when a
delayed start to the Summer Half meant that the boys were unable to contribute
to the 1,800 scout beacons lit across the country to salute the Royal Jubilee on
6 May. Nevertheless the following month provided a further opportunity to
reflect their allegiance to the monarch when the troop assembled at Burnham
Thorpe on 3 June to sing and celebrate George V's birthday.

Another major event was the annual summer camp, this year held between
30 July and 6 August, in a valley known as the Golden Bowl at Encombe, Dorset,
an area familiar to Henry from his Beaudesert nature trip. At 3 p.m. the main party
arrived. An advance party of boys and masters had already prepared the site. After
unpacking their kit, making beds and settling into their tents, the boys were given
a talk on camp rules, notices were read and a short camp fire held. The following
day parties were sent out to forage for suitable brushwood with which they would
create a range of useful gadgets. Meanwhile others prepared the kitchen and dining areas. In these respects many considered the scouts more self-reliant than the
older boys of the Eton College Officer Training Corps.

Ingenuity was soon displaying itself in creative form. On the morning of 1 August the camp awoke to find a Belisha crossing of beacons and studs had been constructed by Patrol Leader Lawrence to enable 'safe access' to the washing area. Not to be outdone, others were soon exhibiting their technical skills by the erection of a plank seated aerial runway.

Wood-gathering was the order of the following day; it was hard work pushing the trekking cart. Peter Wake succumbed to a bug and was forced to visit the doctor's tent. The next day, after a foot inspection by the doctor, the scouts made an expedition to Syre Head.

The camp was joined by another party of scouts from Sheffield, who pitched their tents in an adjacent field on 4 August. During the afternoon of the 5th there was a short walk towards Kimmeridge, where they found a secluded bathing place, before getting back to camp for high tea at 7 p.m. After the judging of each patrol's efforts at gadgets, the results of the inter-patrol competition were announced. Winners were the co-Lions with 162 points and 47 for their gadgets. The 2nd Kangaroos scored 122 points (plus an additional 33 for gadgets), placing them fourth out of five. A final camp fire, culminating in the singing of the round 'Frère Jacques' brought the week's activities to a close. The next morning the troop completed final packing and returned by train after a 'thoroughly good and memorable camp'. Henry then proceeded to Shinness. Visitors this year included Gordon and Sarah Lucas, Rustat Blake, the Pritchards, the family solicitor Eric Ellis and his wife Mary and Mrs Maudslay's cousin Charles Blount, with his eldest son, John, aged 15.[30]

The boarding houses were let to masters on a fifteen-year tenure, enabling most boys to retain the same House Tutor throughout their time at Eton. Henry, however, would be exceptional in eventually having three different House Tutors. His first change came at the end of the Summer Half 1935, when Henry Streatfeild moved to another house, Gulliver's, and the Hopgarden transferred to the authority of 40-year-old John David Hills, MA, recently promoted Senior History Master.[31] The son of a Welsh clergyman, Hills had been educated at the Merchant Taylors' School. Following distinguished war service with the 5th Battalion, Leicestershire Regiment, when he had been twice Mentioned in Despatches, awarded the MC and Bar and Croix de Guerre, he went up to Lincoln College, Oxford, as a Classical Exhibitioner. He had joined Eton as an Assistant Master in 1921. During 1930–32 he had been Officer Commanding ECOTC and now his military interests were maintained as a lieutenant colonel in the Territorial Army. In common with a number of the masters, he shared the Headmaster's keen interest in mountaineering and was a member of the Alpine Club.[32] The epitome of an Eton master, Hills was always dressed immaculately in his black tailcoat, pinstripe trousers, butterfly collar and white tie. Seen as an entertaining character and exemplary figure by those who liked him, he was also a figure of some controversy. In 1930 he had married Lady Rosemary Baring, daughter of the 2nd Earl of Cromer and fourteen years his junior, causing disquiet among some of his peers, who accused him of snobbery, identifying too closely with her aristocratic background. He was also an outstanding public speaker, although, because of this, he sometimes took insufficient trouble to prepare, 'talking the most appalling drivel at inordinate length'. Some considered him autocratic and self-opinionated, and were frustrated by his ability to be right in most cases when there was a difference of opinion. But no matter the opinions of some of his professional companions, John Hills had a natural empathy with those whose lives he would help mould in his role as Housemaster.

Far from being a cloistered academic Hills was also extremely worldly, encouraging contact with people and places outside the school. To his boys he adopted an open approach, encouraging discourse at all times. At Boys' Dinner (served by his butler and a maid) he would often discuss tactics, using salt cellar and pepper pot in the time-honoured manner to illustrate a point, earning him the boys' sobriquet of 'the man who won the War'. His enlightened attitude also introduced two jugs of beer on to Top Table, although the other boys were restricted to water. On occasion Lady Rosemary – 'Mrs M'Tutor' – would attend, seating herself on the table close to the window to provide an element of contact with the junior boys. An accessible, stimulating, often fascinating mentor, Hills developed relationships with his pupils that were were warm, reassuring and encouraging. One of his later pupils recalled:

> J. D. Hills was exceptionally kind to me and I was very fond of him. I remember thinking that he had three layers: a surface of great charm and assurance and panache . . . as a teacher . . . below that there was a certain flamboyance, vanity, snobbery and superficiality, then there was real kindness, sympathy, imagination and a conscientious loyalty in the school.[33]

As with many of his pupils, Hills's attitudes and inspiration were to make a significant impression on Henry, and a firm friendship was to develop that would last beyond schooldays.

The Michaelmas Half 1935 began on 18 September. Henry had now performed well in both Classical and General Totals and passed Maths, French and Latin prose as individual subjects, enabling him to go up to Remove E (Third Remove) Division XXVI. With regard to formal lessons, the one hour's compulsory drawing each week was dropped, to be replaced by Divinity, although many boys, including Henry, whose father and uncle were both accomplished artists, continued with the subject on a voluntary basis in their own time. Rather than compulsory still-life subjects, they were encouraged to draw whatever they found interesting and venture out to work au plein air when the weather permitted. Mr Hartley still took French, but Maths was now the responsibility of Mr Arthur Kerry. Science, traditionally not one of Eton's strong points, was now taught by specialist science masters, with Division Masters covering any shortfalls in this area. Although John Hills was now his House Tutor, Henry retained Henry Streatfeild as Modern Tutor, but the formal relationship of 'Pupil Room' was replaced by the more informal 'Private Business'. This took place three times a week (twice during the summer) under the Tutor's guidance in the relaxed sitting-room atmosphere of the Hopgarden and was intended to broaden pupils' outlooks and encourage them to form their own opinions and express them publicly to others.

Eton's proximity to Windsor invariably developed a close affinity to the royal family. During the summer the King and Queen had driven through Eton and visited the school as part of George V's Silver Jubilee celebrations. Now, during the opening weeks of Lent Half 1936, two more royal occasions dominated proceedings. After the death of King George V on 20 January, an address was read on Saturday, 25 January, publicly proclaiming the Accession of His Royal Highness King Edward VIII. Members of the ECOTC lined the street while the proclamation was read at 12.20 p.m. by the Town Clerk at the Eton end of Windsor Bridge. When he had finished, there was a fanfare of trumpets and a roll of drums, then the band played the National Anthem and the crowd, including many boys, gave three hearty cheers for the new monarch. Three days later the mood was more sombre as the school, by special command, were summoned to Windsor Castle to witness the late monarch's state funeral. At 11 a.m. masters and boys, including the two Lascelles boys and other sons of European monarchy, excepting the ECOTC who had paraded earlier, lined the route from the King George IV Gateway to the Lord Chamberlain's Office. The boys were divided into blocks, each under the charge of a master, and walked formally via the Home Park to the castle to take up position behind the ECOTC near the Norman Gateway. There they waited in cold conditions for the arrival of the Royal Train at 1 p.m., signalled by the breaking of the Royal Standard from the Round Tower. The muffled bell began to toll, the minute guns were fired and the crowds fell silent as the strains of Chopin's funeral march could be heard preceding the slow approach of the cortège. The oak coffin rested on a gun carriage drawn by naval ratings and followed by the King's three sons, including the former Prince of Wales, now King Edward VIII. Little could the boys or other spectators have imagined that by the end of the year they would become subjects of yet another new monarch.

By 5 February 1936 Henry had transferred to Remove E, Second Remove, Division XXIV. Not being one of the Classics set who would take both Greek and Latin, Henry instead appears to have concentrated on strengthening his English and Latin. The latter was now under the tuition of Mr Sheepshanks, with Mr Robert McNeile and Mr Evans for Maths and French respectively.

Henry was a keen scout, and the first scout troop meeting of the Half was held on Saturday, 1 February, at 12.50 p.m., followed at 6.00 p.m. that evening by the troop's annual campfire sing-song. On the afternoon of 13 February a number of boys went with the assistant scout master and Mr Francis Warre-Cornish on an expedition to Highstanding Hill, where they concentrated on tracking, firelighting and scout's pace. Henry and Richard Birchenough took advantage of the opportunity to complete their Second Class tests. Another field day on 18 February started at 1.00 p.m. in the Troop Room, where the scouts were briefed to track down a fictional gang of smash-and-grab criminals who had allegedly robbed a Windsor jeweller's shop. A further expedition to Highstanding Hill on the afternoon of 5 March saw Henry leading Sheill and Hewitt on a tracking expedition and assisting in firelighting.

The next field day started at 11.30 a.m. on Tuesday, 17 March, and adopted a contemporary political flavour. After a meeting at the Troop Room, where Mr Warre-Cornish was formally enrolled as assistant scout master, the scouts proceeded by bus and car to Caesar's Camp, where they cooked lunch before taking part in a Wide Game. Playing the roles of French and German explorers embarking on a secret mission, they set out at 2.45 p.m. Their objective was to avoid the opposing team, and plant their national flag (a French tricolour or German swastika) at the 'North Pole' before the other party reached it with their flag. Both teams wore numbers in their hats for identification, to be noted if seen by the enemy. En route both teams had to navigate to their respective 'Embassies' for final directions to 'The Pole'. On reaching the 'Embassy' the boys were to discover a further complication. The staff there were found to speak only their respective languages of French or German. Displaying stereotypical Teutonic thoroughness and efficiency, the 'Germans' were the winners. Four days later the troop assembled to present a gift of carpentry tools and tool case to the Revd Snow as he handed responsibility for the troop over to Mr Watkin Williams, a square-cut, solidly built man, well liked by the boys.

Summer Half 1936 commenced on 29 April. Henry had transferred to Remove E, First Remove, Division XXIV, with Mr Richard Young taking over his Maths tuition from Mr McNeile. During the first month of the new Half the scouts enjoyed a range of activities designed to further their practical and social skills. On 11 May they were given a demonstration on care and use of the hand axe and gathered for a talk on worldwide scouting, before being encouraged to correspond with other scouts overseas. The 24th saw the Slough District Empire Day Rally on College Field. Various members of the troop showed visiting scouts around the school and entertained them to tea on Fellows' Eyot. The next day saw a campfire sing-song practice, before they embarked the following day on a bus trip for a field day at Gilwell Park, the scouting movement's training camp near Loughton, Essex.

Every Monday for the first three weeks of June the scouts met at Fellows' Eyot at 9 a.m. to study camping skills, firelighting and fieldcraft in preparation for the forthcoming Slough District Weekend Camp. Among the party from No. 1 Troop, Henry and Hewitt were promoted from being Patrol Seconds to full Patrol Leaders during the camp. Setting out after Boys' Dinner on the afternoon of Saturday, 27 June, they arrived at the campsite in Lascelles Road, Slough, where they joined up with five other local troops. During a successful campfire that evening the Eton scouts performed a sketch from the previous year's camp, entitled *The Lunatic*, with R. J. Lubbock in the title role. Rising early on the Sunday, the scouts had breakfast and, after clearing up, were inspected before the flag was hoisted and the scouts held their own church parade. The remainder of the day saw combined games before they struck camp and returned to school. The following morning, back in their Troop Room, the boys were given a talk and film show describing scouting in Dar-es-Salaam by Mr J. W. T. Allen, Divisional Secretary for scouts in Tanganyika Territory.

On Sunday, 26 July, a short meeting was held to finalize details regarding the annual camp, which would be attended by some 100 boys. The following day the advanced party of Scout Master Watkin Williams, Peek and Troop Leader Peter Wake arrived to erect the tents, taking lunch afterwards in Corfe. The next arrival was the Revd Snow, to supervise the central cooks, bringing with him Mr Warre-Cornish, Henry and Montague Johnson. (Henry was by now Patrol Leader of Kangaroos with Roger Peek as his Second.) They were followed by the remainder of the troop, including a young Francis Pym, a member of Mr Lambart's House and in the 1st Beavers Patrol.[34]

On the 28th they rose early and were ferried to Swanage for breakfast, after which they returned to the site to lay out the store tent and erect washing gadgets. More wood was required for gadgets, and expeditions were despatched the following morning to gather suitable material. The weather began to deteriorate in the afternoon as efforts were made to assemble the aerial runway. In the midst of this activity Claude Elliott arrived with Mr Lambart, the Honorary Scout Master, to view the camp, demonstrating his mountaineering courage by accepting a ride on the aerial runway, which was met with great cheers of delight from the boys. Meanwhile, other boys, under the supervision of the Revd Snow, had prepared a boiled beef dinner.

The end of the Summer Half had been marred by the death of the Provost of Eton, Dr M. R. James, on 12 June 1936. Best remembered by most for his ghost stories, he was a friendly man well liked by the boys and beaks alike, and the block of new schoolrooms completed soon after would be named the Montague James Schools in his memory. The 30th dawned bright and sunny, with the promise of a fine day, and packed lunches were taken over to Swyre Head. After they had eaten, the Revd Snow entertained the boys to a reading of the late provost's story 'Wailing Well', an eerie tale of scouts at camp.[35] That evening the scouts gathered round for traditional campfire entertainment.

Despite persistent rain the following day, an expedition was made to Kimmeridge, with another campfire scheduled for the evening. Bathing was less popular than in previous years, but the few who did walked across to Chapman's Pool, meeting up with Lady Rosemary Hills and Mrs Allsopp, who were camping nearby with the Eton Girl Guides.[36]

The scouts held their own Sunday church parade and service under cover from the rain in a cart shed on 2 August. In the afternoon conditions had improved enough to prompt Henry, Peek and Birchenough to set off on a hiking expedition. There were not usually many hikers. Hiking was the final test for the First Class badge and regulations decreed that it could only be completed when at camp.

The following day an inter-patrol competition was staged to find Peter Wake who had (intentionally) 'gone missing' and who was finally traced sheltering with a troop of scouts from Northampton, who were camping nearby.

Under Henry's engineering eye this year the Kangaroos won the kitchen gadget competition, their *pièce de résistance* comprising a multi-purpose rack holding plates and inverted mugs on the top level and cooking utensils beneath, with pot lids and jugs supported on individual sticks.

The intrepid bathers again went down to Kimmeridge in the afternoon for a further dip, but a bitterly cold wind deterred all but the bravest, so they sat and practised an African porter's song (in Swahili) for a performance at that evening's campfire. Others went beachcombing, collecting stones and fossils, or fishing net floats. A small group threw stones in an effort to hit a floating tar barrel.

As might be expected, the sun shone again on 8 August, the day that camp was struck. After the main party had departed for the train, those who remained cleared the site and motored to the Corfe Castle Hotel for lunch, before return-ing with the masters to Eton. This was to be Henry's last camp with the scouts. He was now eligible to join the ECOTC and soon would relinquish command of his patrol to R. J. Lubbock. Leaving Swanage, Henry headed north to Shinness, to meet the remainder of the family, Colin Richardson would join them for the period 15–25 August, his departure coinciding with the arrival of the Pritchards from Higham, Suffolk, who were soon to be joined by other family friends, taking the social entertainment well into September.

Michaelmas Half 1936 commenced on 16 September. Financial pressures had forced an increase in fees to £245 p.a., an extra £15 with an additional £5 for games and extras. Although this increase was not mandatory for boys already in the school, most parents acceded to the request. (Financial expediency was working both ways; at the same time masters had been told that their salaries would be reduced by 3 per cent to aid the school's financial stability).

By now most of Henry's contemporaries were wearing the traditional Eton tailcoat, long pointed collar and white tie. The latter gave many a new boy problems. The tie was made of a paper-like material, and it was necessary to learn the art of tying it properly, and many were thankful for assistance from a friend or neighbour to teach them the intricacies. In theory a new tie should be used each day, but this was seen as being extravagant, and with care one could be made to last three days, on occasion even four. Many would now have acquired the peer-group totem of a 12-foot long woollen scarf, usually hand knitted by their mother, sister or doting aunt. Without the requirement to fag, the boys now had more free time and could afford to frequent the 'sock shops' of Rowlands, the Berkeley or Quaglino's in search of additional sustenance to supplement House catering. Boys would meet to indulge in such juvenile extravagances as large bacon and egg fry-ups or 'Banana Mess' – the so-called 'caviar of Eton' – comprising two bananas topped with a scoop of ice cream and two wafers. Over indulgence was prevented by permitting goods 'on account' only up to an allowance of a shilling (5p) a day, any excess requirements having to be paid for in cash. The 'sock shops' were important as social venues. As their education progressed, the boys' discussions would wander from natural history and stamp-collecting and begin to range across diverse topics to include gambling, alcohol and girls. On free Sundays such conversations would continue as Henry, in the company of Tim Vigors and John Harley, took their exercise along the Long Walk in Windsor Park.

The new Provost, Lord Hugh Cecil (youngest son of former Prime Minister Lord Salisbury), was installed on Sunday, 27 September 1936. Members of college assembled under the colonnade beneath Upper School, while Henry stood in fine drizzle with other Oppidans lining the pathways of the School Yard. A staunch supporter of freedom and justice for the individual, the new Provost nevertheless was to display a degree of eccentricity, particularly in religious matters, which would place him frequently at odds with Headmaster Claude Elliott.

The school list of 30 September 1936 records that Henry had moved up to Block D, Third Remove, Lower Division XX. In addition to English Literature, as a 'non-Greek', he attended Mr Edward Hedley for seven hours of Latin each week. Mr Hugh Haworth, a reserved man, but a kind and sensitive teacher with a fine tenor voice who had trained as a singer, took three hours of French, reading Jules Verne's *La Tour du Monde*. There were four hours with Mr Thomas Smyth for Maths, with a further six hours devoted to English and an hour of Divinity, studying St Matthew's Gospel. On scientific topics, Chemistry was split as a separate subject from Physics or Biology. Mr Peter Lawrence ('Baby' on account of his small stature) now concentrated on the fundamentals of Mechanics in four lessons, each of an hour.

The origins of the ECOTC date back to 1806, when the Eton Rifle Volunteers were formed to counter the perceived threat of a Napoleonic invasion. Membership was not compulsory, although most boys were members, resulting in a battalion some 600 strong comprising four companies. To qualify for acceptance, recruits were required to have attained their 15th birthday, be physically fit and over 5 feet 4 inches tall. On Thursday, 1 October 1936, while the rest of the corps were attending a field day at Chobham Common, Henry enlisted in the ECOTC, taking the regimental number 460. Initially Henry found himself in No. 11 Platoon of No. 3 Company, alongside twenty other members of his House and seventeen from Mr Roe's House. Also enlisting at the same time were Greville Gidley Kitchen, Richard Birchenough and Humphrey Lyttleton, son of one of Eton's Housemasters and later jazz musician. Excused all schools for a week, the new recruits were put through an intensive routine of drill training and square bashing.

During Michaelmas and Lent Halves, new recruits drilled three times a week in top hat and tailcoat on the parade ground behind the fives courts. Unlike the scouts, this activity took place during school time. Until they had mastered basic marching and rifle drill, their only military trappings comprised a 1914-pattern short model Lee Enfield magazine rifle and webbing belt to carry a bayonet. When considered by the adjutant to be proficient in these basic skills, recruits were permitted to wear the corps' distinctive uniform, comprising a mulberry-coloured tunic with pale blue facing, badges and piping around the peaked cap. Since uniform was worn only two or three times a week, most boys settled for acquiring theirs from a second-hand pool of caps and tunics. Some had them re-tailored to achieve a degree of smartness, although others seemed determined to try their officers' patience by relishing the most unmilitary appearance. Puttees were another source of frustration for those who wished to meet required

standards on parade, almost invariably unwinding at embarrassing moments. A
year or so later a young cadet by the name of Michael Bentine is reputed to have
displayed an application of lateral thinking for which he later would become
renowned, contriving to glue his platoon's puttees in place, only to find himself
spending the remainder of the day after parade extricating his fellows from the
tenaciously adhering fabric.[37]

Having qualified to wear the uniform, recruits then received a grounding in
military skills, including map-reading, compass work and maintenance of equipment, instructed by masters who had been commissioned as officers. Weapon-
training was undertaken, culminating in military-range and open-range shooting
using the standard issue .303 Lee-Enfield rifle. Once basic competence had been
achieved, cadets would be taken for field days to nearby military training grounds,
including Windsor Park, Chobham Common and Lower Star Post. These days
were intended for instruction in basic battle training, the boys forming up and
advancing over the heath before dropping on to their bellies and crawling until
stiff and tired, whereupon they would be ordered to stand up to run in a final
charge at 'the enemy', usually a battalion from another school. Exercises were
supervised by umpires, normally regular Army officers or officers of the corps on
horseback. Despite the competitive nature of these activities, they were often seen
by the boys as occasions for considerable hilarity, much to the chagrin of the
masters in charge, who attempted to re-establish their authority as officers by
ordering long marches with full kit, or other military-style admonishments. After
an assessment of the results and discussion of the lessons learned, corps members
were provided with a hearty meal. At the end of the day the cadets marched back
to the station and on to a train back to Eton. Conduct on the train was usually
not that becoming either of officers or gentlemen. Lavatory rolls would stream
from the windows, cigarettes would be handed round and a good deal of under-
age drinking took place. On arrival at Windsor Station, all would have regained
their composure, forming up behind the current regimental band, which would
play them back to Eton to be saluted by their commanding officer, Lieutenant
Colonel Leslie Jaques, MC. They would pass the ornate lamp standard known as
the Burning Bush, in the middle of the High Street at the junction with Common
Lane, before wheeling into New Schools Yard.

Mrs Maudslay had been considering a move from Sherbourne, and during the
summer her attention had been drawn to Fox Hill Manor, on the northern fringes
of Broadway in the Cotswolds.[38] The 35-acre estate focused on the main house
with three reception rooms, a billiards or games room,[39] five bedrooms and dressing rooms, plus three bathrooms. A servants' wing contained four rooms, bathroom and kitchen. Partway down the drive there was a separate stable block with

stalls for five horses and a detached coach house, converted into a large double garage, with two flats over. There were two estate workers' cottages and a model farm. Fox Hill Manor itself, originally known as 'Furze Hill', had been designed by J. L. Ball and built in 1909 on land formerly part of 'Top Farm', purchased from the 5th Earl of Harrowby the previous year for £1,300 by George Hookham, a Birmingham engineer. The property had been sold to Major Edric Wield Forester (Rtd) for £8,750 in April 1925 and in April 1933 was bought by William Walter Brough Scott, MFH, Master of the North Cotswold Hunt and nephew of C. T. 'Charlie' Scott, MFH, whose company had constructed the railway line from Cheltenham to Honeybourne in 1906 (part of the line intended to connect Cheltenham with Stratford-upon-Avon and Leamington Spa). The change of ownership had not been a straight sale: Fox Hill was exchanged for Scott's current home, Little Buckland House near Evesham, plus a balancing payment of £5,100.

Built on the west-facing slope of Willersey Hill, the house had been designed on sun-trap lines with a south-westerly aspect. As one approached it, the drive opened up into a gravelled area with a grass central island. The slope of Green Hill extending up to the left created the effect of an amphitheatre, with the house standing on stage to the right. Constructed of the local oolitic Guiting stone, it glowed honey gold in the sun, regaining its affinity with the landscape on duller days. The architecture was typically a simplified Gothic, Cotswold vernacular, with small leaded windows with mullions and marked drip mouldings over windows and doors, essential to protect the relatively porous stone. Among the detailed embellishments were two sundials, one above the main entrance, the other on the western wall. The year of construction was carved over the front door and cast into the rainwater heads of the downpipes. Entering through the double front door capped by semicircular arch and flanked by classical columns, visitors were struck by the unusual layout. A plain cross corridor presented a wall instead of an accommodating entrance hall and staircase. To the right were the service areas of the house; to the left the main hallway, staircase and large family rooms. Immediately behind the corridor, taking up the entire rear of the centre range, was the dining room. Across the hallway the lounge angled off to the south-west with windows on three sides and a large fireplace with apsidal wall niches either side. Mirroring this on the opposite aspect of the house was the moderate kitchen with Aga range, and pantry, linked to the dining room by a short passageway containing the back stairs. Upstairs the capacious bedrooms included fitted wardrobes and built-in bookcases. Most rooms were floored with oak.[40] Hot water for washing and heating was provided by a coke-fired boiler in the cellar.

To the rear of the house the west-facing slope had been levelled to provide two small grassed terraces with stone retaining walls and steps. That immediately next to the house contained a small rectangular pond with four neatly trimmed yew hedges placed symmetrically to relieve the expanse of stone, two either side of the projecting central bay window of the dining room. Below the second terrace a further area had been laid out as a tennis court before the hillside sloped down to Linch Meadow and an orchard.

The postal address was Broadway, although the main drive led out on to Campden Lane, running down Willersey Hill, at the foot of which lay the village of Willersey, with old barn houses grouped around the green and duckpond 'like casual knots of worthies delivering crop gossip or weather lore through the slow process of the years',[41] church and traditional village inn, The Bell. Situated some 600 feet above the Vale of Evesham, the location afforded panoramic views of a score of small villages and the island mount of Bredon Hill, to the long blue ridge of the Malvern Hills. Farther south the Forest of Dean gave way to the Black Mountains of Wales. Weather and lighting created constantly changing hues, as did the seasons, the vale becoming a sea of pink and white fruit blossom in spring. Mrs Maudslay's purchase of Fox Hill for the sum of £12,000 was completed on 18 November 1936, the Deed of Conveyance being signed by Mr Scott, witnessed by his Land Agent, R. F. Mayhew of Jervaulx, Ripon, Mrs Maudslay being witnessed by family friend Walter Howard of Barford, Warwickshire. Final attestation was applied by her London solicitors, Ellis, Peirs and Co., in the form of two small red seals, bearing their mark 'EP & Co.'. Evidence would suggest that Mrs Maudslay and Tita did not move into the house until the following spring, the interim probably being used to undertake redecoration. In keeping with the times, Mrs Maudslay was to employ and provide accommodation for a number of household staff. From Sherbourne came William Simmons and John Summers. Mr and Mrs Bond were to be enrolled as cook and butler/handyman. By 1938 they would be joined by C. W. Sutton and Thomas Thomason.

After preparation by his Housemaster and attendance at several special services held during the preceding weeks, Henry received Confirmation in Eton College Chapel on 5 December 1936. This spiritual event, however, was soon to be eclipsed by one of greater national importance. On the evening of 11 December a scene was enacted in most of the houses as boys in their pyjamas and dressing gowns crowded around M'Tutor's wireless set to hear the abdication speech of Edward VIII. For one of Henry's close friends in the Hopgarden, George Hardinge, the event had a direct family significance. His father, Alexander Hardinge, was Private Secretary to Edward VIII and had been involved intimately with the developing crisis.[42] Whether or not the other boys fully appreciated the situation, the impact of losing their monarch was not lost on many. There was a strange feeling of uncertainty in the air on 17 December as the boys left their Houses for Christmas at home with their parents.

Lent Half 1937 commenced on Wednesday, 20 January. The school list of
3 February 1937 records Henry as being in Block D, Second Remove, Division XIX.
Latin was still maintained with Mr Leslie Jaques and French with Mr Hugh
Haworth. Maths and Geometry were with Mr Arthur Kerry and, as a result of
restructuring to introduce a greater scientific element, Mr William 'Nick' Roe's
science lessons studied the topic of heat. Scouting had now given way to soldier-
ing and the new intake of ECTOC recruits began drilling on 27 January 1937.
Parades were held on the Parade Ground on Monday, Thursday and Saturday at
12 noon and Wednesday and Friday at 3.40 p.m.

A comparison conducted in 1937 of Eton boys and Durham boys of the same
age showed the Etonians on average 3.5 inches taller and 18 pounds heavier, largely
because of greater length of leg – but the Etonians did show signs of dental decay.
The difference was attributed to a better balanced diet, albeit sweeter, although
Etonians from some Houses would disagree.[43] All agreed, however, that it was not
due to a rigid regime of physical fitness. Unlike some of the public schools that
placed great emphasis on sport, there was no strict organization of games at Eton.
Many boys restricted themselves to the 'Field Game' – Eton's unique game based
loosely on football, but combining elements of rugby too. PT had only recently
become compulsory for Lower Boys, and all were expected to take up some activity, 'doing a time' as it was known, every day, either on the sports field or on the
river, becoming a 'Dry Bob' or 'Wet Bob' accordingly. New boys were given a
swimming test at Cuckoo Weir, a quiet Thames backwater, to ensure they would
be able to keep afloat in the event of an accident. Diving in from a grass bank, the
Acropolis, dressed in singlet, shorts and plimsolls, boys had to prove that they
could tread water for a minute with arms held above their heads. Those who
passed became 'Nants' in Eton parlance. Those who failed took cricket.

A hierarchy of vessels was available to suit a range of abilities, and a competitive spirit was fostered, encouraged by Claude Elliott, himself a keen sculler. In
addition, the Wet Bobs had an attractive clubhouse up river on Queen's Eyot, where
food and beer were available. It became a favourite destination for excursions.
For leisure and exercise boys could row a single-oared dodger or two-oared gig
while still wearing their Eton jacket. Then came the whiffs and canvas-stretched
riggers, with further racing designs for crews of two, four or the full eight, wearing singlet and padded shorts. Activities on the river usually took place along the
three miles of the Thames between Rafts and Boveney Lock and were organized
and run by the Captain of Boats,[44] who held one of the most influential appointments, short of Captain of the School or Captain of the Oppidans. A strict code
of conduct was laid down and enforced by the watermen stationed at various

points along the towpath: boys were not permitted to venture into the back-
waters, nor tie up except at approved landing places. Due consideration should
be given to members of the public, and, should a boat containing ladies come into
sight, any boys undressed for bathing but not in the water were to take cover behind
screens provided at the bathing-places. The boats themselves were stored in the
College Boathouse and maintained by Alf Claret, and his two assistants Charlie
and George. The latter, George Windsor, was one of the school's characters.
Ex-Navy and known to all as 'Froggie' because of his swimming style, he was a
portly man with a large walrus moustache and flat cap who seemed always to
move at a predetermined slow pace. Nevertheless he understood the boys and their
ebullient nature well; as a young man at the turn of the century he himself had
driven a horse and cart across the frozen Thames for a wager. Although cricket
was regarded as the premier Eton sport, rowing was still highly regarded, the
highlight of the season being the competition at Henley for the Ladies' Plate,
against older college and university crews.

Henry's interest in rowing appears to stem from this period, although he had
participated with some success in junior competitions already. He combined this
activity with running, which was very much a minority sport at Eton, being
permitted as an alternative to football, although one or two masters were keen
participants and acted as coaches to those who showed promise. In this respect
Henry may have been encouraged by Streatfeild, who had won the School Mile
in 1914. However, it appears that that the key instigators of Henry's running career
were fellow 'Beaudeserter' Tim Vigors and his friend John Harley, who sought
relief from the rigid regime of school life by going on cross-country runs two or
three times a week.

According to Vigors, Henry preferred initially to stay in his room, studying a
range of subjects, including the latest developments in aircraft manufacture. In
fact his aversion to games and other exercise seems to have manifested itself to
the extent of feigning sickness in order to be excused games. However 'having received permission to stay in his room on the grounds of a bad chest, he was much
more likely to be found inhaling nicotine than Friar's Balsam'.[45] Not surprisingly,
Vigors and Harley noted that he had grown thinner and paler. Determined that
Henry should accompany them on their runs, the two finally managed to persuade him to venture out for a gentle jog.

Rather nonplussed that Henry seemed to keep up with little effort, they finally
lengthened their stride to full stretch. To their complete dismay Henry was not
only keeping up, but he eventually outpaced them. Seeking to capitalize on their
discovery, Vigors suggested that they should place a bet with a local bookmaker
on Henry winning the Junior Mile in March. After some persuasion Henry even-

tually agreed, swayed perhaps by Vigors's offer of a five shilling bet for free and the assurance that, although he would have to go into training (supervised in the strictest secrecy by Vigors and Harley), he would not be expected to give up smoking.

And so it was that this year was the first in which Henry would make his mark and demonstrate the makings of a determined athlete. The School and Junior Steeplechases were held on Wednesday, 17 February. The former was a major event in the sporting calendar. The Steeplechases were run cross-country over fields, and ended with the notorious School Jump, a leap of about 15 feet across a stream known as Jordan, which meandered across the school playing fields. A considerable period of torrential rain had made the going extremely heavy and necessitated the positioning of two watermen with long poles at two of the swollen water jumps to assist non-swimmers who might get into difficulties. There were some 350 entrants for the Junior race over a distance of some $2^1/_2$ miles. However, Henry's training was already producing results. He took the lead from the start, with Tim Vigors following strongly until about half distance, when he started to fall back, relinquishing second place to J. Chaworth-Musters ma. with Ronnie MacAndrew and Gilliat coming up into third and fourth places. Henry managed to maintain his lead, despite having virtually to swim across the final water jump at the River Jordan, some 50 yards from the finish, winning in a time of 14 minutes 50 seconds, 15 yards ahead of Chaworth-Musters.

Shortly after a unique two-day holiday to commemorate the accession of His Majesty King George VI, Long Leave[46] commenced on Saturday, 27 February, and after their return Lower Boy entrants for the Junior Mile assembled on Kennels, the athletics field near the river to the east of the college, at 4 p.m. on Friday, 5 March. Despite heavy going, Henry took the lead from the gun, maintaining his position to win comfortably from Ponsonby, who had moved up into second place on the final lap, with Ronnie MacAndrew in third. Henry's time was 5 minutes $17^3/_5$ seconds.

Having negotiated odds of 50 to 1 for a £1 bet with a Windsor bookmaker, Vigors collected his winnings with satisfaction, flouting the rules again by calling in at a pub on the way back to collect half a dozen bottles of beer for a celebratory party in Henry's room.[47]

Mrs Maudslay and Tita had now moved into Fox Hill. His mother's presence in Sherbourne was to be greatly missed. In the minutes of their March meeting, the village's school managers noted: 'Regret was expressed at Mrs Maudslay's departure and the correspondent was asked to write her a letter expressing the Managers' thanks for her services and gifts.'[48]

Assisted by the Revd Gibb, his wife and daughter, the family had been invited to various lunches and soirées in the neighbouring villages. The ending of the Half on 31 March most probably gave Henry his first opportunity to visit the new family home and begin to meet the children in his mother's and sister's new social circle. Although not exclusively, many of these were girls, including Susan Ismay, daughter of Colonel and Mrs Hastings Ismay of Wormington Grange, and her near neighbour Rachel Studd, daughter of Captain Edward ('Eddie') Studd of Little Warren, Stanton. Four years younger than Henry, Rachel had recently returned home from a period in Guy's Hospital after contracting polio. Now able to walk unaided, she went on therapeutic walks with Henry, accompanied by her sheepdog Patrick, during which they discovered many common interests, including listening to popular gramophone records of the period. Other mutual friends would soon join the circle: Phoebe Cresswell and her brother from Charringworth Manor, Chipping Camden; Rosalind Forrester, whose mother was a lady-in-waiting to Queen Mary, and Colonel Guy Edwards's daughters Louise and Elizabeth, of Rockhill, Upper Slaughter, the latter known to many as 'Come along Elizabeth' owing to her inability to keep pace when riding, despite her father's urging. Many had connections through the North Cotswold Hunt, although Henry's lack of participation in equine pursuits seems to have placed him at no social disadvantage.[49]

At the commencement of Summer Half 1937 Henry was in Block D, First Remove, Division XVIII. Maths was now taken by the Lower Master and French still with Mr Haworth (who also coached rowing, cycling along the riverbank with megaphone). Scientific studies now saw an introduction to Chemistry with Mr Cyril Sladden, 'Teapot', a hawkish-looking Housemaster and an ex-serviceman, holder of both the MC and DSO. It was during this Half that Henry's only recorded visit to the College Library is noted, when on 19 June the Library list shows he took out Kinzett's *Chemical Encyclopaedia* for a day. Gradually Henry's activities settled down into a regular routine of academic studies, track and river events, combined with parades and training with the ECOTC.

On the athletics track Henry was already flourishing. He had developed a distinctive style, noted by a contemporary: 'He reminded me of a high stepping pacer when he ran and appeared to glide.'[50] In the school sports he won the Junior Steeplechase in 16 minutes 16 seconds, the Junior Mile in 5 minutes 17 and $^2/_5$ seconds, and Half Mile in 2 minutes 18 and $^3/_5$ seconds. This sporting success was reflected in the title of junior victor ludorum.

Henry's sporting promise was not so immediately evident on the river. The final of the Junior Novice Sculling was held on 12 June 1937. Henry was positioned on the second station on the Windsor bank. J. Brocklebank, on Eton first station, made a good start, but Henry was closing as he got to the wall. By Hesters he was only two lengths behind, but then lost ground as he hit the bank. Undeterred, he regained his composure and continued the pursuit, but, despite several attempts to pass the leader, Henry had to settle for second place, finishing five lengths behind J. Brocklebank, but five lengths ahead of G. Brocklebank in third place, leaving J. M. Wilson to bring up the rear.[51] It was a fast contest, Brocklebank's winning time of 10 minutes 10 seconds being only 2 seconds outside the course record. The *Eton Chronicle* recorded: 'All four scullers showed great promise, particularly J. Brocklebank…The standard of sculling in the heats was quite high and auguers well for the future.'

A fortnight later saw better fortune as Henry competed in the final of the Novice Pulling on 24 June. Findlay and Shaw minor (Eton I) took the lead from Sir H. Bruce and R. A. Roberts (Windsor I). Henry, partnered by Anstruther (Eton II), was in third place, leading J. Brocklebank and Gell (Windsor II). By Hesters Henry and Anstruther had taken Windsor I and were two lengths astern of Eton I. Despite gaining slightly on the Ryepeck (a pole placed in the river as a turning point), Henry and Anstruther lacked the ability to produce a closing push and gradually fell astern to finish six lengths behind Eton I. Nevertheless, they had retained second place, despite being heavily challenged by an advancing Windsor II. The winners were strong, completing the course in 10 minutes 47 seconds, and the main failing of the Eton II pair was their tendency to rush forward and lack consistency, 'but they are young and should go far', the *Chronicle* noted.

On 12 June the ECOTC had turned out at its smartest for a visit by HM King George VI and Queen Elizabeth, with their daughters the Princesses Elizabeth and Margaret Rose, as they made a state entrance to Windsor via Eton. Arriving in cars at Agar's Plough, the royal visitors were met by a guard of honour who presented arms and dipped colours in salute. After talking to senior members of staff, Their Majesties boarded a horse-drawn carriage and drove off to the echo of three cheers called by the Captain of the School.

The battalion was scheduled for a further major annual inspection on Thursday, 15 July, by HRH Duke of Gloucester, KG, KT, KP, CGMG, GCVO, ADC. In preparation they paraded and practised for inspection. On Monday, 5 July, and Tuesday, 13 July, and on the day of the parade, cadets were permitted to attend Chapel and Second School in uniform. This was to be the last major parade to be taken by the current commanding officer, Leutentent Colonel Jaques, who resigned his command on 17 July to be succeeded by Leutentent Colonel W. R. Colquhoun.

School ended on 26 July and that morning Henry marched across Barnes Pool Bridge as part of the corps contingent departing for the annual camp at Tidworth

Park on Salisbury Plain (where the Revd Gibb had been stationed at the start of the First World War). There, the College Corps would pitch their skills against Charterhouse. The camp over, Henry returned home. This year, breaking with tradition, the family would not be at Shinness, which had been rented out for the season to a Miss Wheatley, and it is believed that he spent most of his holiday at Fox Hill.[52]

On 20 September, two days before Henry returned to Eton, his mother completed a transaction to enlarge the Fox Hill Estate. From neighbour Mrs Marion Anderson Burges she concluded the purchase of an adjacent field for £200. Amounting to 7.842 acres, it was situated on Little Hill close to the south-eastern corner of the estate and a little way from Bibsworth Covert. The family was now well established in the locality. Tita, a keen horsewoman, had joined the North Cotswold Hunt (MFH: W.W.B Scott), almost invariably riding side-saddle, as she found it difficult to stay on riding astride. Many family friendships were formed among the hunt members, including that with Major Harold Lane, MC, and his wife, who were also relative newcomers, having moved into Rex House, Willersey, in 1935. The acquaintance was to be curtailed prematurely when the 46-year-old major died suddenly after contracting pneumonia, Mrs Maudslay and Tita being among the mourners attending his funeral at Willersey parish church on 28 October.

Returning to Eton for the start of Michaelmas Half 1937, Henry found himself in Middle Division C, Third Remove, Division XIV. Etonians took the School Certificate later than most other public schools. This lack of cramming for the certificate allowed them to experience a great many activities outside the standard syllabus before being forced to specialize. In this block boys could select between Classics, History, German and Science. Not surprisingly given his family's engineering background, Henry selected increased specialization in science. He saw Mr Donald Bousfield for Maths, Major Le Gendre George Horton-Fawkes for French and Mr Charles Kenneth Hillard for Chemistry.

On 1 October the year's influx of new recruits signed up for the ECOTC, among them Daniel Patrick Macnee[53] and Christopher Howard.[54] Having been in the corps for a year, Henry qualified to sit the Tactical Examination for Cert. A, Part 1, on 16 November. When the results were published in Battalion Orders on 11 December, every one of the 112 candidates had qualified. There were twelve distinctions, won mainly by those with sights set on a military career. In this instance Henry was not among them. The threat of international conflict was beginning to cast its shadow over the school. Masters and boys were being instructed on action to be taken in the event of a gas attack and each House was to prepare two gas-proof refuge rooms. Shortly before Christmas masters had visited the Gas Defence Section at RAF Uxbridge, where to their personal discomfort they had experienced first hand the effects of the lesser types of this weapon.

Christmas was spent at Fox Hill. Mary Gibb organized a short play performed in front of family and guests, the final scene of which required Henry to kiss Rachel Studd, much to the embarrassment of both parties. By now Henry and Rachel were conducting regular correspondence between each other during term time at their respective schools. The relationship was purely platonic, and with typical modesty Henry's letters rarely hinted anything of his sporting achievements, concentrating on general events and activities with friends. A heavy frost created the opportunity to skate with Susan Ismay and her friends on the frozen lake at Wormington Grange. Confidence gained, a fast and furious ice hockey match later ensued.

Lent Half 1938 commenced on 18 January. Henry was now in Middle Division C, Second Remove, Division XIII. Latin continued with Mr William Colquhoun, Maths with Mr Richard Young. French was still with Major Horton-Fawkes, Chemistry with Mr Hillard and Physics with Mr Roe. Maths now extended to incorporate Geometry and Trigonometry. Boys returned to find the captured Bulgarian gun that had stood on the Parade Ground for some twenty years was being dismantled and cut up for scrap as the nation's rearmament programme gained momentum.

A week later the boys were treated to a fine view of the aurora borealis, which first appeared as an arc and then seemed to merge into a round cloud. The whole of the western night sky was lit with a vivid red glow, becoming gradually intermingled with shafts of white light. The entire town and surrounding countryside were illuminated by an almost supernatural glow, brighter than moonlight, which lasted several hours. Police and fire brigades were harassed by callers ignorant of nature's phenomenon and convinced that one of Slough's factories must be ablaze.

Meanwhile, Henry continued his academic studies and athletic training. In the School Steeplechase, run on Wednesday, 9 February, he was to take the lead from the start, closely followed by Michael de Chair, Barclay and Mathieson. These positions were held until Butts, when Mathieson drew ahead to win easily. Henry had fallen progressively further back in the field and failed to be recorded among the first six finishers.

Perversely, success seemed to have transferred itself to the water. On 1 March 1938 J. B. D. Goldie, Captain of Boats, published the list of crews for Lower Boats, showing the crew of St George as:

A. C. Garton (Capt.)
J. C. Sladden
Spring-Rice
G. R. E. Napier
R. A. Roberts
T. A. Brocklebank
H. E. Maudslay
R. O. Scott
H. R. James (Cox)

Henry was on better form for the Mile, run for the first time on Timbralls on 4 March. He won in a time of 4 minutes 53 and $^3/_5$ seconds,[55] but even so the *Chronicle*'s reporter still found aspects to criticize:

> The middle distance runner must have three qualities: speed, stamina and track tactics. On Friday we saw much of the first and second but lamentably little of the last. Although Maudslay won a fine race he would have returned a better time by lapping slower than 66 seconds the first time and faster in the third lap. Blow ran the only well judged race; his rather 'stiff' and a slowish second lap cost him the victory. Although Parker finished strongly he wasted his energy in the second lap. Crichton and Ponsonby were too much influenced by the old fashioned method of reserving all for the last lap, but both gave ample evidence of good style. Barclay running second to Maudslay for the first two laps, but a recent illness had its effects. de Chair who had also been ill proved a tactician, if out of training. Maudslay's and Blow's finishing in under 5 minutes were good performances even if we remember the almost perfect conditions.

On 8 March, having successfully completed all his ECOTC tests, Henry was presented with Certificate 'A' confirming that he had fulfilled the necessary conditions to qualify in the infantry, thereby becoming eligible for a commission in the Supplementary Reserve, Territorial Army, Territorial Reserve of Officers or Active Militia of Canada. Should a national emergency occur requiring the mobilization of the Regular Army and the Territorials, he was required to notify the Under Secretary of State at the War Office 'with any offer of service he may wish to make'. In the school sports, held on 26 March, the last Saturday of the Half, Henry came third in the school Half Mile, beaten by Cunning (2 minutes 7$^1/_2$ seconds) and Earl Cathcart (the latter becoming senior victor ludorum).

The Half ended on 30 March. On Wednesday, 20 April, the family gathered at

2 p.m. in the parish church of St James's, Chipping Campden, along with friends and well-wishers, many from the hunting fraternity of the surrounding shires, for the marriage of Tita to 32-year-old Captain Gordon Barker of the 4/7th Royal Dragoon Guards, Garrison Adjutant at Colchester Barracks.[56] Awaiting the bride's entrance in a church decorated with lilies and cherry blossom, those assembled sat listening to Dr E. Armstrong, organist of Christ Church Cathedral, Oxford, perform Bach's setting of 'Jesu Joy of Man's Desiring' and Brahms's 'A Rose Breaks into Bloom'. They rose to sing 'Praise my Soul the King of Heaven' as Tita entered, escorted down the aisle by her godfather Rustat Blake. She wore a long close-fitting gown of white satin trimmed with gold embroidery and pearls, her net veil edged with old family lace held in place by a coronet of pearls and gold leaves. Gordon's brother Maurice was best man and Joanna Herbert one of her five young attendants.

Tita was given away by her mother, dressed for the occasion in a black silk dress, enlivened with pastel blue, with a black straw hat and veil. After Psalm 41, the congregation knelt and sang 'O Perfect Love', the first verse being sung solo by chorister Roland Dyer. This was followed by the address given by the Revd Gibb.[57] The organist played the 'Air and Minuet' from Handel's Water Music while the newly married couple signed the register, and they left the church to the triumphal 'Bridal March' from Parry's Birds of Aristophanes.

For Henry the event may have been memorable, but not in the intended manner. A week or so earlier he had contracted measles and was confined to quarantine in bed. With uncertainty as to whether he remained contagious, he was permitted to attend the wedding under strict instructions that as far as possible he should avoid mixing with the other guests and was allowed to view proceedings only from the very back of the church.

The wedding party returned to Fox Hill for the reception, along with over 200 guests. In addition to family members, including Noel and Mary Gibb and Captain and Mrs Arkwright with their daughter. Academia was represented by Mrs Hemmings, the Sherbourne schoolmistress, the Beaudesert 'dynasty' of Mrs Richardson, Austin, Barton and Colin Richardson with Enid Keyte, in addition to retired Eton master James Montague Ellis and his wife. Mr and Mrs Ted Hiatt and Major and Mrs Negus and their daughter were among several attending from Sherbourne. Also present was Canon Bernard McNulty, who had christened Henry, accompanied by his wife, together with a strong military presence comprising serving and retired family members together with representatives from Gordon's regiment and Colchester Barracks.

Among the wedding gifts for Tita were, from her mother, household linen, a fur coat, diamond ring and grandfather clock; a tea set and coffee set from John and his wife and a silver salver from the staff at Fox Hill House. Henry gave his sister a set of hors d'œuvres dishes and a watch, while his brother-in-law received a 'Revelation' suitcase. In keeping with tradition, the 4/7th RDG presented a silver salver engraved with the regimental badge and the signatures of current serving officers. A silver cigarette box similarly decorated was the gift of officers of the 5th Royal Inniskilling Dragoon Guards.

As the reception drew to a close, Tita, now attired in navy blue dress, coat and hat, with navy and white shoes, appeared with Gordon to acknowledge their guests' final farewell before departing for their honeymoon on Exmoor. On their return they would take up residence at Ball Farm, Colchester, with the promise of an early visit to Barford for a reception to be held by local residents who had been unable to make the journey to Campden to attend the wedding.

A week later the holidays were over, and Henry returned to Eton. The school list for Summer Half 1938, published on 11 May, records Henry in the Fifth Form, Middle Division C, First Remove, Division XIII. Once again his tutors had changed, reflecting his progress through the school – Latin: Richard Tindall, Maths: Mr Arthur Huson, French: Mr Adam van Oss, Physics: Mr Charles Mayes, Chemistry: Mr Robert Weatherall. The latter was a popular master, instilling enthusiasm among his pupils by exclaiming 'That's science!' whenever a notable fact or example came to light.

With war clouds gathering, Claude Elliott had begun to prepare a strategy should hostilities break out. Realizing that the Home Office's recommendation that the school should be disbanded in such an event was impracticable, he began to formulate Air Raid Precautions (ARP) for the school. Newly appointed ARP masters took their duties less than seriously at first, although one or two individuals who knew that Claude Elliott had refused to provide a place in 1935 for Ribbentrop's son, Rudolf, speculated whether the college might now be on Luftwaffe target lists, and perhaps mused on John Betjeman's poem written the previous year: 'Come friendly bombs and fall on Slough!' The town of Eton was divided into sectors, five of which covered the school itself and the boarding houses. Mr Reginald Marsden was in overall control, and each sector was supervised by a warden, aided by three assistants and two messengers. Meanwhile, Mrs Elliott organized Dames and Masters' wives into a team of VAD nurses, practising their skills on numerous schoolboy volunteers.

The first test of these provisions came on the night of Saturday, 7 May. A practice blackout was staged to cover south Buckinghamshire, commencing at 11 p.m. and remaining in force for three hours, during which period local emergency services dealt with a mock air raid on Eton. Commander J. Hassard-Short, the regional ARP Organizing Officer, flew over the area to observe the effectiveness of the blackout. There were still many lights showing, but:

> So successful was the blackout at Eton that it was Father Thames and
> Windsor's royal castle that reminded me I had overshot my mark. Turning
> back I searched Eton in vain for some sign of life. Peace reigned. The College
> slept – or so it seemed – and the Thames in sympathy looked dreamy too as,
> catching the moonlight, it wound its silvery way past ancient towers and
> famous fields towards London and the sea.[58]

As the observer suggested, appearances can be deceptive. On the ground all was
not going according to plan. As the appointed hour approached, spectators began
to gather around the Burning Bush, only a few hundred yards from the Hopgarden, admiring the spectacle of the school buildings bathed in the bright
moonlight. But there was no sign of the three RAF aircraft from Hendon that
were intended to represent the attackers.[59] Regardless, umpires tried to set off a
pyrotechnic to simulate a bomb in Queen's School Yard, near the Lower Chapel
in South Meadow Lane, only to find that its percussion mechanism would not
work and they had to resort to setting it alight. A second charge was set off a short
distance away at the junction of Keats Lane and Dorney Road, representing a gas
bomb and creating a 'contaminated area'. A first-aid post had been improvised in
the school gymnasium, where a number of the older boys acted as casualties,
receiving initial treatment before being taken on stretchers to lorries converted
for use as ambulances for transfer to casualty-receiving centres. This too posed
problems, as reported in the following week's *Slough and Windsor Express*:

> Unfortunately there was not enough room for all and one boy, reported as
> seriously hurt, was, after several unsuccessful attempts had been made to
> place him in an ambulance, requested to leave his stretcher. He did so without
> aid, and then vanished.

Despite these incidents, many of the provisions worked well, and a number of
valuable lessons were learned.

Meanwhile, more peaceful activities continued. In the second race on 2 June
against No. 2 on Windsor bank both crews went off at a fairly fast pace, but Henry
and the remainder of No. 1 had a cleaner start, giving them the edge after the first
few strokes. Utilizing the beneficial current, they were able to exploit this lead to
the Ryepeck above Athens, when No. 2 made a challenge and succeeded in taking
the lead and gaining a quarter length by Upper Hope corner. Instead of taking his
crew close into the Windsor bank, Crawshaw the cox kept well out, losing further

ground, allowing No. 2 to pull a full length clear. The distance closed again to a quarter length on rounding Sandbanks, but the heavier and stronger crew of No. 2 were able to reassert themselves and draw away again, to win in a time of 9 minutes 6 seconds.

Despite the grim spectre of impending conflict, the traditional celebrations to mark George III's birthday were still staged on 4 June 1938. Parents were able to see an exhibition of early English watercolours, with recent work by the boys in the Drawing Schools, together with aquaria and local wild flowers in the biology laboratory. There were the usual speeches and on the playing fields the Kneller Hall Band of the Royal Military School of Music provided a background to the traditional sound of leather on willow.

After 6.30 Absence in School Yard, the Procession of Boats took place at 7.15 p.m. Among the Lower Boats, Henry was rowing No. 2 in the scarlet-ribboned crew of St George, which included Derek Mond[60] and Christopher Howard.[61]

At 10 p.m. the day's events were brought to a close by the traditional fireworks display; fifteen set pieces comprising some ninety different types of pyrotechnic reflected in the shimmering water. The tableaux names suggest an exotic atmosphere: 'The circumfuse love wheels', 'Special prismatic illumination of the river bank' and 'King Tutankhamen's fan'. After a concluding display of 'Grand Pyrotechnic Portraits of Their Majesties the King and Queen', surmounted by the legend 'God Save the King' there was the final 'Good Night' to send the spectators homeward. With hindsight many of the fireworks' names seem prophetically inappropriate: 'Flight of International Bombs' , 'Grand aerial illumination with large and powerful floating lights' and 'Flight of powerful repeating shells'. Two demonstrated almost uncanny prescience: 'Wells's Water Skimmers' and 'Discharge of Powerful Water Mines'.

The Eton College *Chronicle* of 9 June 1938 confirmed Henry as a member of the crew of the Lower Eight (Eton 1): Bow – Hoare Nairne, 2. Napier, 3. Pember, 4. Maudslay, 5. Roberts, 6. Hepburne Scott, 7. Spring-Rice; Stroke: Merriam (replacing Ellis who was ill). Cox: Crawshaw.

The ante-finals of the Junior Pulling were held on 22 June. Henry participated in Heat III, on the Windsor station, partnered by Derek Mond. Brocklebank and Roberts took the Centre station and the two Howard brothers were on the Eton side. The former pulled away confidently until reaching Sandbanks, when it became apparent that Henry and Derek were closing. Rounding the Ryepeck together, the latter succeeded in stealing a march and maintained their lead to the finish, crossing the line in 14 minutes 25 seconds.

The following day, in the final, Henry and Derek Mond (Eton) were set against

Lumley Smith and Sweeting (Windsor) and Balfour and J. M. H. Wilson (Centre). After a good start, Maudslay and Mond had gained almost a length over Balfour and Wilson on reaching the railway bridge and two lengths over the others. A sudden spurt by the centre crew took Henry by surprise and allowed the former to gain the lead and pull across for the shorter course. It was not to last, however, and a determined effort by Henry and Derek saw them regain the lead at Lower Hope corner and extend their advantage up to the Ryepeck, where they were four lengths ahead. After this there was no contest, and they came in easy winners in a record time of 14 minutes 11 seconds.

> The winners were a very strong pair who owed their pace to their vigorous use of their legs and to the very powerful finish with which they drove their legs home. They swung well and kept their length through all the race. The second and third pairs were promising, but did not possess the winners' life or firmness and were unable to keep going very hard after the Ryepeck.

On 23 June 1938 the Eight had their last week of practice before Henley (held on 29 June). The unevenness of the School Pulling pairs and the massive size of the crewmen meant that Eton would have no quick and neat crew to show immediate promise.

During Heat 11 of the school's Junior Sculling ante-finals, Henry on the Windsor station beat both Thompson (Centre) and Lumley-Smith (Eton) in 16 minutes 18 seconds. On Thursday, 7 July, conditions on the river were reasonably good for the finals, with the crews benefiting from a slight downstream breeze. Godley made a good start and soon pulled slightly ahead, leaving Henry a quarter of a length in the rear. By the railway bridge, however, Wilson had found his rhythm and pulled two lengths ahead of Henry, who was now alongside a flagging Godley. Henry then made a misjudgement and went too far into the bay, costing him a length to Godley. Turning too late, he then went into the wall, losing a further six lengths and effectively putting him out of the contest. Nevertheless, his performance over the year had been of sufficient standing for the *Eton Chronicle* of 30 June to congratulate the Hon. D. J. Mond and H. E. Maudslay, the winners of the Junior Pulling, on receiving their Lower Boat Choices.

Academic studies were not to be ignored, for the School Certificate Examinations commenced on 12 July, a week before the remainder of the school started the end of Half trials. On 23 July, relaxing from the rigours of cerebral exertions, Henry attended a concert given by the Eton College Musical Society. During the performance he subconsciously demonstrated his artistic and mechanical interests, doodling a pencil sketch of a sports car on the back of his programme. The Half ended on 26 July. At Reading Over Henry learned that he had exceeded the minimum of three passes in School Certificate subjects and was therefore considered as passing the trials.

As usual, on 27 July 1938 the 438 members of ECOTC went off to summer camp. As they departed, marching across Barnes Pool Bridge and down Eton High Street to Windsor, they were accompanied by the fifes and drums of the Scots Guards, based at Victoria Barracks. This year's camp was held at Tweseldown Racecourse, Aldershot, where the Eton Corps would join with OTCs from twenty-nine other public schools. The camp was in reality a succession of field days, involving various manœuvres and practical experience with equipment. Smoking and drinking were acceptable, if not openly encouraged. This year, however, the new aspect of aeronautical instruction was introduced, open to all cadets over the age of 16 who had attained a high standard of training and gained Certificate 'A'. Some 160 boys went daily to RAF Odiham, from where they travelled by air to various airfields, where they were given instruction in aspects of aerial recon-naissance, photography and bombing. It is possible that Henry was one of this select party.

After the week-long camp the boys were left with six weeks' holiday. During this, on 10 August, one of Eton's science masters, Clarence Fletcher, married Isabel Chenevix-Trench at the Royal Military College Chapel, Sandhurst. Among their recorded wedding gifts was a silver jam spoon from Mrs Maudslay, who, back at Fox Hill, was continuing her charitable work. On 28 July, assisted by Miss Cusack and Miss Bloomer, she was running a stall selling Madeira embroidery and other fancy goods at a fete held by the Revd Gibb and his wife in the grounds of the Old Rectory, Saintbury, in aid of the Saintbury Church Restoration Fund. As Henry's ECOTC camp came to a close, the family journeyed back to Shinness for the summer. Among the guests this year was Gwen Maudslay's cousin, Air Commodore Charles Blount, now commander of No. 4 Bomber Group at Linton-on-Ouse, Yorkshire, accompanied by his wife Joan and sons John and Christopher. Other friends and relations came to stay for various periods, including, on 22 August for a ten-day visit, John Harley, a friend of Henry's from Eton, along with Aubrey and Hilda Pritchard. On 1 September Tita arrived from Colchester, regrettably without her new husband, staying for a most enjoyable fortnight.

After an enjoyable holiday, family and friends returned home to face the deteriorating international situation as the country prepared for conflict.

Chapter 3

Floreat Etona

Justam ludus vindicet
cum labore partem!
dulce foedus societ
cum Munerva Martem!
Sive Causa gloriae
pila, sive remus,
una laus victoriae –
Matrem exornemus!
Donec oras Angliae
Alma lux fovebit,
Floreat Etona!
Floreat! florebit!
(A. C. Ainger, Eton School song – 'Carmen Etonense')

Boys returned to Eton on Tuesday, 20 September 1938, to find advanced ARP activity. Many of the Houses were now visibly protected by sandbags and shutters, and lectures were given in action to be taken to extinguish incendiary bombs. The government was now issuing gas masks to the civilian population. A consignment of face pieces, filter containers, valves and headbands arrived at the school, and masters effected final assembly of some 3,000 masks in School Hall under the watchful eye of Mr MacKinnon. Discovering, however, that the entire allocation for Eton was insufficient for the civil and academic population, Claude Elliott issued instructions that permitted over half of the school's boys to return to their homes and donated their allocation of gas masks to the town. Ordinary school was to be suspended, and any boy whose parents so wished could go home. Conversely, during this period officialdom reversed its views on Eton's vulnerability and began preparations to evacuate London children to the district. Henry did not return home; presumably after due consultation with his mother (and probably his Housemaster too) it was decided that he should remain at Eton. Along with those who stayed on, in lieu of formal lessons he was instructed in how to prepare shelter rooms and lay sandbags.[62] In each House small groups crowded around wireless sets to hear the news, and a party of 120 boys was permitted to journey to Heston airport to see Prime Minister Neville Chamberlain's return from Munich on the evening of Friday, 30 September, lining the road from the airport buildings. One member of the Hopgarden, the Hon. Richard Wood, was son of the Foreign Secretary, Lord Halifax. He subscribed to his father's view that Britain needed time to rearm and gather its allies if it were to have any hope of surviving a war against Germany. These views were the antithesis of those held by John Hills, who was deeply affected by the settlement with Hitler, believing it to be submission to blackmail, although as a historian and military man the Housemaster accepted that there could be more than one perspective.

The school list for Michaelmas 1938 recorded that Henry had been classed in the last trials and was now in the Fifth Form, Upper Division B, Second Remove, Division IX. His tutors remained John Hills and Henry Streatfeild, and his sporting successes continued: with his partner Derek Mond, the pair put up a better performance and won the Junior Pulling. His supremacy on the track was asserted by winning the School Mile comfortably in 4 minutes 53 3/5 seconds. There was a large field, and, although challenged by J. O. Blow at the beginning of the last lap, he managed to hold him off, beating him by 15 yards. Bill Parker came in third.

In order to overcome the problems of a waterlogged course, it had been decided that the Steeplechase should now be run during the Michaelmas Half rather than in February. Already predictions were being made as to the outcome. The *Eton Chronicle* of 6 October maintained: 'We suspect that Maudslay will lead the field, unless he makes a major tactical error.' The event took place on Thursday, 20 October, and Henry did not make a tactical error. It was the usual fast pace from the start and Henry was not able really to establish himself in the lead from A. Drewe until crossing Bell Farm. Approaching Butts, Drewe slowed, enabling M. B. de Chair and C. W. Parker to take up the challenge against Henry, who by now was 10–15 yards in front. Coming across the corner of Prince of Wales Plough, de Chair seemed to close on Henry, but then the grass was reached and Henry was able to pull ahead, increasing his lead of the 150-plus field to some 40 yards. He completed the 3-mile course in a record time of 15 minutes 4 seconds, with de Chair coming in second place and Bill Parker in third. It had been hoped that some of the seniors might be able to clear the Jordan for the first time in forty years, but even the best were defeated by the slope of the far bank, landing with insufficient momentum to keep going and falling back into the water.[63]

This year Henry was sitting seven subjects for the School Certificate of the

Oxford and Cambridge Schools Examination Board: Scripture Knowledge, English, Latin, French, Elementary Mathematics, Physics and Chemistry. The examinations were held shortly before Christmas. When the results became known, he would be away skiing in Switzerland.

Henry had arranged to travel via Lucerne to Arosa, with Peter Wake and Christopher Snell. At nearly 6,000 feet in the northern Rhaetian Alps, the resort is situated on a broad terrace at the upper end of the Plesur Valley, at the end of a route that climbs and winds its way following the mountain stream up from Chur, through 19 miles of spectacular pine-forested scenery dotted with steepled churches presiding over crouching villages. From the resort's position in a sheltered mountain bowl, there are extensive views to the south, and a variety of pistes made it ideal for skiers of all abilities, with nursery slopes at the doors of the main hotels. Near the settlement's centre, two small lakes, the Untersee and the Obersee, used respectively for bathing and boating during the warmer months, provided facilities for skating and curling. Other Alpine activities available included cross-country skiing and horse-drawn sleigh rides.

His mother had agreed to relay his examination results, and accordingly on 5 January 1939 a greetings telegram arrived addressed to 'Maudsley [sic] Alexander Hotel, Arosa': 'Passed with seven credits congratulations and love Mummy and Tita.'

Returning to school for the Lent Half 1939, Henry was placed in the Fifth Form, Block B, Upper Division VIII, First Remove. His tutors were J. D. Hills and J. L. Hinton. He now had moved up one remove, and this is the first entry in the school calendar with a 'c' after his name, denoting attainment of his School Certificate. As a specialist in Science, Mr Hillard taught him for Chemistry and Mr Jack Hinton for Physics. Science was not Eton's strongest faculty; an inspection in 1936 had criticized the lack of time devoted to the subject and failure to structure the course effectively. Even for those who had passed the School Certificate, Eton's curriculum ensured that pupils continued to receive a rounded education. Those like Henry taking Modern Languages, Maths and Science were given compulsory extra studies of either History or English.

Older boys in particular had long hours out of school, and numerous extra-curricular societies were organized to encourage interests and help occupy their time profitably. Two of the most active were the Scientific and Natural History Societies, and Henry became a member of both. Often boys were encouraged to take part themselves in the presentations, rather than relying solely on visiting speakers, and on 27 February 1939 Henry gave a talk to members of the Scientific Society on the subject of 'Aeronautical Design', no doubt drawing information from his subscription to *Aeronautics* magazine. Visits were arranged to processing and production plants such as United Dairies, Huntley and Palmers' biscuit factory at Reading and Morris Motors at Cowley. The Natural History Society, with over 300 members, had its own museum and bird sanctuary on the Thames. Musical interests were also encouraged, in terms of both performance and appreciation. Otherwise spare time was spent in their own pursuits, including the frequenting of the several 'sock' shops. These included that at the Five's Courts, run by Jack and his wife, part of Rowlands, where members of 'Pop' and the Eight could go behind the counter to obtain a degree of privacy apart from the other boys. In 'Tap' one could obtain a lobster cutlet and 'Tap Savory' – a delicacy of mashed sardines and tomato sauce on toast, cut into slices and sold for 3*d* each. The latter establishment again enjoyed the privilege of selling beer to senior pupils, a tradition for some time banished but restored by Claude Elliott in 1938 following strong lobbying from the boys. 'Tap' was solely the boys' domain and came under the authority of Captain of Boats; nevertheless Henry's visits to this and other establishments appear to have been relatively moderate in comparison to those of his rowing companion Derek Mond.

The beginning of the year had seen another milestone. Henry became an uncle on 28 January, when Tita gave birth to Gwen Maudslay's first grandchild, Annette, at Fox Hill.

On Friday, 10 March, the new cinder running track at Kennels was inaugurated with a Mile event. Charles Garton, Captain of Boats (and also Captain of Athletics), fired the gun, and twenty-five runners set out on the School Mile. Birchenough took the lead, setting a fast pace and completing the first furlong in $27^{1}/_{2}$ seconds. The first quarter was set at 61 seconds, with Henry pressing Birchenough, being himself chased by Parker, Ponsonby and Hope-Jones. Coming down the back straight on the second lap, Henry managed to take Birchenough, as Hope-Jones powered his way through to third place. At 2 minutes, 18 seconds, the half-mile was reached, but halfway round the third lap Henry showed signs of faltering, and Hope-Jones took the lead as the former touched the wood on the inside of the track and stumbled, losing ground. As the bell rang at 3 minutes 32 seconds, the order was Hope-Jones, running strongly, Maudslay, Godley, Parker and Ponsonby. Gaining new strength, Henry made a challenge for the lead, catching up and overhauling the leader just before the final back straight. Hope-Jones made a determined bid to hang on, but Henry had timed his run to perfection, taking a marginal lead of 3 yards to breast the tape in a time of 4 minutes 38 seconds, 6 seconds outside the Eton record of 4 minutes 32.25 seconds, set by J. M. Fremantle in 1893.

The ante-finals of the School Half Mile were run on Friday, 17 March 1939. Entered in Heat I, Henry came a comfortable first ahead of Poe and Barton. The finals were run during the following fortnight. On the appointed day there was a cold wind blowing down the back straight, and, unusually, Henry found himself continually challenged over the first quarter mile. Under normal circumstances Henry's finishing time of 2 minutes 2 seconds should have made him an easy winner, but this time he was no match for Hope-Jones, who began to pull away from him to finish comfortably ahead, establishing a new school record.

Henry also had been representing the school in the annual triangular athletics competition, where Eton's finest pitted themselves against their opposite numbers from Stowe and Lancing. Contestants assembled on Kennels on Saturday, 25 March, where the new running track (which had already been in use for a fortnight) was officially declared open by Lord Desborough. This year the contest was to be a hard-fought battle, with Eton performing well in track events, although outclassed in field sports. Henry brought victory to Eton in the Mile, finishing in 4 minutes 49.3 seconds, outpacing J. B. Dwight of Stowe, with Etonian A. C. Ponsonby taking third place. The overall result of the competition remained in the balance until the very final event, the relay. Eton required only second place in this to retain the premier position that they had held since the first race. Whether overconfidence caused complacency or not is hard to discern, but Stowe managed to gain six points, thus beating Eton by a single point in the final reckoning.

Trials began on 30 March, Henry achieving a distinction. In the midst of them he still found time for competitive running. On the afternoon of Saturday, 1 April, Eton hosted an athletics event against the Achilles Club on Kennels. The visitors included a number of Olympic runners and winners of the inter-varsity sports. Despite being handicapped in all events and running on the outside of the track, they displayed a superiority that still prevailed, beating their hosts by 52 points to 37. Nevertheless it was the general consensus that the best performance of the day was that shown by Henry. Putting up his best time of 4 minutes 35.8 seconds, he displayed strong tactical skill, pulling well away in the last lap to beat his two Achilles opponents B. F. Brearley and S. L. Dorman by a margin far greater than the handicap of 29 yards.

Henry travelled to White City Stadium with du Putron and Drewe for the Public Schools Challenge Cup Meeting on 14 April, where he ran the Mile, beating R. W. Taylor of Bedford in 4 minutes 42 seconds, the fastest time of the five qualifying heats. In the following day's *Daily Mail*, J. P. Jordan described Henry as 'a powerfully built boy with a beautifully smooth action'. The final was on the Saturday, but Henry was off-form. Despite being the favourite after the previous performance, his race lacked the timing and judgement that characterized his runs. Letting the competition gain too great a lead on the third lap, he was unable to regain ground only managing third place, 30 yards back in a time of 4 minutes 37 seconds.

Commenting on the athletes' performance, the *Eton Chronicle* recorded:

> The season has produced some remarkable athletes, of whom most have
> reached their present level by hard practice as well as natural ability. They
> would agree that with the improved facilities for training this hard work has
> not been a drudgery and that practising for races . . . is a far more interesting
> occupation than it looks to the onlooker.

Henry returned to Eton for the Summer Half 1939 after a holiday at Fox Hill
punctuated by the distribution of gas masks by the local Evesham authorities.
Now in Block B, Upper Division VII, First Remove, he was marked with a distinction in the trials and was now labelled as a specialist in Mathematics, having
changed from Science. His Housemaster remained John Hills, who was soon to
become a father, resulting in Henry's Modern Tutorship being taken over by
Mathematician John Herbert.[64] Mr Robert Parr took Maths for Specialists
(Dynamics) in Room 19. As a Maths Specialist, Henry would also have had to take
History and English. He also took extra studies in German for four days a week,
under Mr Arthur Marsden in New Schools, adjacent to the Hopgarden.

   In 1939, 4 June fell on a Sunday, and as a consequence the annual celebration
of George III's birthday was held on Saturday, 3 June. After Chapel the boys went
back to their Houses to ensure that they were correctly dressed, purchasing a
carnation for their buttonholes from the flower-sellers near Barnes Pool Bridge
and wearing a coloured waistcoat if they so wished (privileges at all other times
accorded only to members of Pop). Their hats were ironed, or 'lushed', a service
provided free of charge on this day by the three main Eton outfitters, New and
Lingwood, W. V. Brown, or E. C. Devereux. The weather was perfect with brilliant
sunshine. Parents and guests began to arrive by mid-morning, including several
from Middle Eastern countries, resplendent in native dress and with servants
carrying heavily tasselled sun shades. After enjoying a picnic lunch, they would
watch the cricket or walk around the school grounds and listen to the Band of the
Welsh Guards playing at various times on the Brocas, Upper Club or Fellows'
Eyot, before being entertained by their sons for tea in the Houses. As afternoon
turned to evening, those who were in the Procession of Boats went to change out
of tailcoats into their Georgian naval uniforms. Each boat carried its own colours,
the coxes of the Lower Boats being dressed as midshipmen, those of the Upper
Boats as admirals. Rowing Number 2 in *Prince of Wales*, Henry donned a crimson
striped shirt, dark blue monkey jacket and white trousers, with a straw hat with
crimson ribbon, gold crossed oars and a few flowers.

   Thus attired, the crews attended Absence in School Yard before taking the boats downstream through Windsor Lock to Windsor Home Park, below Black Potts, where supper was taken in a marquee. For those who wished, beer or cider was served, although most oarsmen, aware of the high level of coordination required for the evening's activities, abstained.

At the onset of dusk small groups of guests made their way down to Fellows' Eyot, below Windsor Lock, and sat on the grass awaiting the procession. (Shooting sticks and campstools were not permitted, and, in an exception to regulations, boys were not to wear their top hats: 'They are a nuisance to themselves and everyone else.') At a quarter past seven, with the light almost gone, floodlights illuminated the river and the band began to play. The first boat, the dark blue ten-oared *Monarch*, crewed by senior members of the school including such celebrities as the Captains of School and Oppidans, Captain of the Eleven and Master of the Beagles, entered the pool of light, followed by two other Upper Boats, including *Prince of Wales*. The boat's crew comprised:

D. Graham (Captain)
H. E. Maudslay
Hon J. R. Godley
K. A. H. Mason
J. A. Fielden
R. Hill
R. A. Roberts
J. E. D. Lakin
D. A. Hoy (Cox)

As each boat passed, the oarsmen stood up two by two, doffing their hats to salute those watching. They were followed by the Lower Boats, their crews having not only to stand, but also to hoist their oars to a vertical position, a feat requiring perfect timing and coordination if the crew were to avoid a ducking.[65]

The procession was normally one of good humour and jollity, but this year current events cast a solemn shadow. During the previous week the Navy's latest submarine, HMS *Thetis*, had sunk during trials in Liverpool Bay, with the loss of all but 4 of her company of 103 naval personnel and Cammel Laird artificers. The sixth boat in this year's procession was the submarine's namesake. As *Thetis* entered the spotlight, spectators could see that there were no festive flowers, nor ribbon. Instead her crew wore only a stark black crepe band. Those assembled on the riverbank fell quiet and stood in silent tribute until the boat had disappeared into the darkness again.

The traditional fireworks display brought the day to a close. A penultimate tableau with the faces of Their Majesties surmounted by 'God Save the King' was followed by a final setpiece of the Eton College Arms and motto 'Floreat Etona'. As the spectators dispersed and returned to the college buildings for final farewells, the boat crews had linked arms and were making their own way back, passing through Weston's Yard and into the street. Jostling their way good-naturedly through the throng, they struck up William Cory's traditional song at the tops of their voices:

> Rugby may be more clever
> Harrow may make more row;
> But we'll row forever,
> Steady from stroke to bow;
> And nothing in life shall sever
> The chain that is round us now.

Half an hour later peace had descended again on the town as guests departed and boys returned to their Houses for Lock-up.

Ten days later the Second VIII[66] were to row against the local Jesuit school, Beaumont College, Old Windsor, on the latter's water on the fringes of Windsor Great Park. After a moderate start that might have given Beaumont the advantage, Eton were soon into their stride and began to pull away. At the halfway mark Eton's lead had stretched to two lengths, with the final bend in their favour, enabling a further length to be gained.

Rowing throughout the Half had been dogged by misfortune. Charles Garton, Captain of Boats, had been ill for most of the time and unable to row. His deputy, R. W. A. P. Lewis, had been forced reluctantly to stand down, his large stature being incompatible with the remainder of a light crew. The Eight still found it difficult to pull away smoothly and with force from the start: 'There must be a quicker spring of legs and hips and a fiercer thrust in the bow four', commented the *Chronicle*. Considerable shuffling of the crew took place, and it was only two weeks before the annual competition against other public schools and varsity crews in the centenary Henley Royal Regatta that the final order was settled. Rowing Number 2, Henry was the lightest of the crew:

J. M. H. Wilson	11st 2lb (Bow)[67]
H. E. Maudslay	10st 1lb
A. P. Sandford	11st 2lb
John Skinner	11st 2lb
Hon. J. R. Godley	11st 3lb

A. C. Garton	12st 6lb
D. Graham Campbell	11st 10lb
Hon. D. J. Mond	11st 5lb (Stroke)
R. K. Kindersley, KS	7st 1lb (Cox)

He was very nearly prevented from taking part. The crew departed for Henley, but soon had to send a spare man, for Henry had recently been confined to bed without food, in an attempt to starve a fever of 100 degrees. It says much for his constitution that he was declared fit in time to row. Eton's first event, Heat 12 of the Ladies' Challenge Plate, was held at noon the following Wednesday, when the Eight beat St Edward's School, Oxford, by three lengths in 8 minutes 16 seconds, despite a strong headwind. Shortly before 6.00 p.m. they competed in Heat 19 against Bryanston School, who had beaten a crew from St Paul's School. Again Eton was triumphant, winning by a length in 7 minutes 40 seconds. The following day the crew challenged Lady Margaret College in Heat 23, again winning by a length in the slightly longer time of 7 minutes 55 seconds, despite a good start and early lead by their opponents. On Friday, 7 July, they went into the semi-final Heat 26, but their good fortune was not to remain, and Clare College beat them in a time of 7 minutes 46 seconds. Eton made a good start, but Clare took advantage of smooth water and drew steadily ahead. In the final, Clare beat Corpus Christi, Cambridge, the Eton crew drawing a degree of consolation knowing that they had lost only to the overall victors.[68] While magnanimous in its general comments, the *Chronicle* was ready to give advice:

> Of this year's Eight it can be said that though they were never really quick with their legs or blades, they improved markedly in the racing and they raced in the right way. They went off hard, being smoother and crisper each time, and they settled out to row with a stride that would give them something in hand for the finish.

Academic studies could not be neglected, for that July Henry sat a supplementary School Certificate paper in Additional Mathematics. His sporting activities had no adverse effect on the result and he passed with a Credit.

The annual inspection of the ECOTC took place on Tuesday, 11 July 1939, when 534 boys were reviewed by Major General A. Thorne, Commanding London District, accompanied by Brigadier Major W. Goschen and Captain C. Tryon. In his address after the march past, Major General Thorne remarked that he had been deeply impressed by the boys' bearing and efficiency on parade, despite heavy rain, which forced the cancellation of exercises. The corps now embodied

an Air Section under the command of Science Master Christopher Hartley (who
held the acting rank of pilot officer), comprising those boys, including Henry,
who intended to apply for admission into the Royal Air Force. Instead of corps
parades on Monday mornings, members would attend lectures on the theory of
flight given by RAF officers, and muddy field days were replaced by trips to
Northolt aerodrome for practical instruction and air experience flights in an
Avro Tutor trainer. The station was also home to No. 111 Squadron, the first to be
equipped with the eight-gun Hurricane, providing the boys with the opportunity to view the RAF's latest monoplane fighter at close quarters.[69]

   To celebrate the sporting achievements of Mr Hills's House during 1938-39, a
memorable 'Sock Supper' was held on 31 July. Senior members in attendance
included Captain of the House, the Hon. Richard Wood,[70] Peter Wake, Captain of
Football; Michael Chinnery,[71] Captain of Cricket and Henry, Senior Wet Bob. The
House had enjoyed more than moderate success during the year, Henry and Derek
contributing greatly to a House whose talents lay mainly among the 'Dry Bobs':

   Aquatic Cup: H. E. Maudslay, D. J. H. Mond, G. E. C. Hardinge, J. E. A. Mond
   and T. D. M Shaw.
   School Mile: H. E. Maudslay
   School Steeplechase: H. E. Maudslay
   School Pulling and School Sculling: D. J. H. Mond
   Lower Boy Sculling: J. E. A. Mond
   School Racquets (Singles and Doubles): D. C. Quilter
   School Tennis (Singles and Doubles): D. C. Quilter
   OTC Team Race: H. E. Maudslay, P.Wake, D. F. Gilliat, R. Peek and C. R. Muir
   School Chess Cup: M. J. A. Spears
   Junior Fives: R. H. Montgomerie

The supper fare was relatively modest, with grapefruit followed by salmon may-
onnaise and raspberry ice dessert. There were the inevitable speeches, with toasts
to 'The King', 'This House', 'Our Guests' and 'Floreat Etona'. Although the evening
was not extravagant (the school took steps to prevent prolific spending), Henry
was finding that his social and sporting commitments were beginning to have an
adverse effect on his finances. On return to Fox Hill, and after a frank discussion
with his mother regarding the overdraft he had run up on his allowance, he
vowed that he would become more financially cautious during his final year.

   The growing international tension was probably the cause of the summer visit
to Shinness being briefer than usual with fewer guests[72] It was to be a good season
for the guns. Between 15 and 23 August Henry and Walter claimed 23 grouse,

3 black-game, 1 wildfowl and 32 rabbits. Also 36 trout were taken from the loch. For all, however, family and social events were eclipsed portentously by the declaration of war on 3 September.

In the absence of the feared mass onslaught by the Luftwaffe, school reassembled for the Michaelmas Half on Wednesday, 20 September, with the Sixth Form returning the following day. Most of those who had gone home at the time of the Munich crisis were now back. Teaching had been deemed a 'reserved occupation', and the majority of the masters were able to continue with tuition. The air-raid precautions were complete, and each House now had its own air-raid shelter, with additional masters being allocated to Houses as wardens. There was a plethora of instructions detailing action in the event of an air raid: 'If in your House, go to the shelter by the exit nearest to your room as quickly as possible. At night hang your trousers and dressing gown on your door knob.'

Other instructions would follow: no doubt to the delight of some of the younger boys, baths would be rationed to three per week, a maximum of 6 inches deep in order to conserve both water and fuel. They could be taken between noon and 8.30 p.m., but boys would be allotted precise times and were urged to be punctual both in arriving at the bathroom and leaving so as not to inconvenience their fellow bathers.

On Sunday, 29 October, the King and Queen, accompanied by the Princess Royal, inspected the first aid post established in the School Gymnasium and paid a visit to the shelter in Housemaster Mr Charles Rowlatt's garden at Angelo's, adjacent to the Hopgarden. The carrying of gas masks was now compulsory. As a result the wearing of top hats in Eton itself was discontinued – a custom that would not be reinstated after the war, although they were still to be worn beyond inner Eton, past Barnes Pool Bridge or Fifteen Arch Bridge. *The Times* of Thursday 5 October remarked:

The boys of Eton College are to lay aside their top hats 'for the duration'. The reason is that either top hats or gas masks may be worn, but not the two together – and the gas masks, so to speak, have won by a head. The universal badge of the citizen of today has been preferred to an increasingly distinctive headdress. And so Etonians have joined the hatless brigade.

At present [a representative of *The Times* was assured] they are wearing nothing on their heads, and are quite happy about it, though headgear will probably be necessary when the colder weather comes. But a coloured House Cap would not go well with a tail coat.

It soon became apparent that respirators would become useless if boys had to carry them every day (in any case, spot checks revealed that the containers carried by some boys held sweets rather than masks), and the rules were relaxed. The masks were now to be kept in convenient locations in boys' Houses and need only be carried when boys went out of inner Eton.

Henry was placed 13th in Fifth Form, First Hundred, Block A, Division IV. (For admission to Block A boys had to have obtained the School Certificate.) His tutors remained J. D. Hills and Modern Tutor J. S. Herbert. Maths for Specialists was taken by Mr Philip MacKinnon (Calculus) and Dr Laurence Lefevre. Extra studies (German) continued with Mr Marsden. One of the privileges of being a Specialist was to attend Friday afternoon lectures, when guest speakers would be invited to make a presentation.

As usual the new school appointments were announced. Sir Anthony Meyer would be Captain of the Oppidans,[73] but the next senior position, that of Captain of Boats, was bestowed upon Henry, who replaced Charles Garton, who had gone up to Magdalen College, Oxford. The Captain of Boats was responsible for almost everything that occurred on the river, including the organization of all of the school's internal racing and, in theory at least, had the potential to fire the master coaching the Eight. The post holder also took on the mantle of Captain of Athletics during Lent Half, when there was a limited amount of rowing. Henry was also successful in being elected a member of the exclusive Eton Society, under the presidency of the Hon. Richard Wood.

The Eton Society was a self-elected body of some two dozen senior boys – the elite of Eton. It had been established in 1811 as a debating club, initially meeting in a room above Mrs Hatton's lollipop shop, thereby gaining its more familiar name of 'Pop'.[74] Debates had ceased during the 1920s, and by the late 1930s it had become the effective boy authority, serving to monitor the dress and behaviour of pupils in public. Candidates had to be nominated by existing members, although others could also blackball them to keep them out. The final selection was made by secret ballots held after morning Chapel and before Boys' Dinner on the first and last Sundays of each Half. Election to Pop has been likened to a politician getting into the Cabinet. Members of Pop had no official powers, but they exerted considerable influence and enjoyed a range of unique privileges. They were permitted to sit on the Long Wall, the low wall running along Eton High Street outside the entrance to School Yard. Members could walk in the street arm in arm, use a reserved room in the School Stores and stop any member of Lower School for fagging duties.

Membership of Pop was apparent to all through a distinctive dress code. Successful candidates would pay an immediate visit to their tailor to be fitted out with the appropriate indicators of rank. Light grey spongebag trousers and a coloured or patterned waistcoat (in Henry's case set off by a watch chain to which were attached small medallions indicative of his sporting achievements), high winged collars or 'stick ups', and black braid sewn on to trim their tailcoat. Collars of greatcoats and changecoats (worn in public over sports kit when not actually playing) could be turned down.

In more peaceful times stamped sealing wax would be applied to the back of a newlyly 'lushed' silk top hat. A fresh bloom in the buttonhole and a cane or rolled umbrella added the final touch.

> Walking down the street in Eton you just felt as though you could do any-
> thing. You had total control over people. People used to look at you as you
> came down the street. The costume set you apart and made you aloof, you
> just shut yourself off from everybody. These were lesser mortals. You wore
> chequered trousers, a waistcoat of your choice – whatever colour, whatever
> design – braided tailcoat, stick ups, a handkerchief if you wanted, you looked
> very different from everybody else. It really did set you apart.[75]

For sports, members of Pop could wear buff shorts rather than grey. Membership of Pop would also be proclaimed by a large sheet, bound in Eton blue with crossed Pop canes, hung on the wall of a member's room alongside the rules of the other school societies to which the boy belonged.

Henry set an example by winning the annual Steeplechase on Thursday, 12 October. This year the course had been revised, and was of a shorter length of $2.\frac{1}{2}$ miles, reputedly to keep all the entrants within a seven-minute run of their gas masks! The redesign had the advantage of allowing spectators to see both the start and the finish. As usual no one succeeded in clearing the jump across the Jordan. Henry was again first, having led the field of 100 competitors all the way, improving by 8 seconds his previous year's time. Nevertheless, not everything in his life was running so smoothly.

In common with his peers, Henry was now permitted an allowance from his bank and also a cheque book. Financial management often had to be learned the hard way. On Wednesday, 13 December, the day after Trials began, Henry wrote his mother a letter about a matter that had been causing him some concern. Unconsciously proclaiming his social status, which was contributing to some of his problems, the letter was written on white notepaper headed with the Eton Society scroll and enclosed in an Eton Society envelope:[76]

> This is a very sad letter for me to write because I have failed badly to keep
> expenses down and must say that things have worked out nearly as badly as

last Half. I want you to let me straighten things out with my own money. I got an income tax demand [sic] which I sent on to Eric[77] the other day and although I suppose that that shouldn't be touched I don't want you to have to pay for everything.

I expect that you think that Henry should have managed things better and that it will be a good thing for me to feel the pinch a little bit. That's absolutely right, I'd like to feel that I was doing something by way of reparation. Another thing I know you must feel is that I ought to worry more about my finances, and not just hope that things will be OK. I'm assuming these things, but think that I'm probably right in suggesting them.

As far as worry is concerned I've had enough of it this Half to last for several years. I have not bothered you with the sticky side of some of the problems I get, but they are not much fun for anyone who feels his responsibility. As for feeling the pinch, I'll be in the ranks of the RAF soon enough, that will be quite frugal and tough enough to do me a good deal of good.

Henry went on to explain the circumstances that had caused this financial situation and to detail the present position:

I knew that I'd have to spend a good deal this Half – and I'm afraid that I treated myself to a wireless set as well.

I have tried to do my various jobs well and the money just goes when you are concentrating everything on something else. I'll show you all the accounts in detail next holidays and can account for everything. I may be a bad financier but I am honest.

| Assets (current account) | £3.0.0. |
| Liabilities | £35.0.0. |

£40 would put things straight until next Half, but I insist that it should come from my own money. I have landed myself in a very expensive position in life and don't want you to have to bear it all. You helped tremendously through the last holidays but even so I had to pay for a good deal and half of this Half's allowance has gone on these:

Linguaphone Morse Course[78]	£1.0.0.
Morse Key and Apparatus	£1.0.0.
Pop subscription	£3.0.0.
Wireless[79]	£8.8.0.

Wells' bill[80] for fixing up my room,
Rails, blackout &c.   £15.13.0.

These are all extras which one doesn't calculate for.

I suppose I shouldn't have got the wireless but in my position now I have to be fairly sophisticated and the wireless is the quickest way when you have practically no time.

The Morse apparatus is for learning the Morse Code, essential when I join the RAF and the sooner I get good at it the better.

In conclusion he added:

I seem to have taken a lot of space to explain that I have spent a good deal more than you or I expected. You seemed alarmed over the telephone and with all the justification in the world. But there is something I would like to say. Tap is where most people get rid of their money on eat and drink. I've only been in there three times this Half. Still there is no excuse for anything. I gathered from your voice that you were rather sick with me.

I'm sorry to have to write you this sort of letter – I hope my tutor may write you a letter that may bring you some consolation. I think the sooner I get called up the better.

Best love from
Henry.

Long leave had been cancelled owing to the difficulties of transport, and as a result the Michaelmas Half ended on 18 December, two days earlier than planned. It was to be a significant day for those in the Hopgarden, as the House said fare-well to John Hills, who was leaving to take over a new appointment as Head-master of Bradfield College, a school of 280 pupils near Pangbourne.[81]

With a slight reduction in the number of boys in the school, the boarders in each House were reduced to a maximum of 36. Next Half the Hopgarden was trans-ferred to Henry's Modern Tutor, Assistant Master John Stewart Herbert, a former Cambridge rowing blue and a gifted mathematician who held the rank of captain in the ECOTC.[82] Since the Munich crisis he also had been officer in charge of the Report Centre for the Southern Division, Slough ARP. Herbert was considered more remote than Hills and known to enjoy his drink. To some the rapport nec-essary to create a surrogate father figure for the younger boys was totally absent. This deficit was less apparent to the older boys, notably those in the Library, including Henry.[83] Nevertheless, Herbert was fully aware of all aspects of activity in the House, and little went unseen. In keeping with tradition, his wife accompanied him to the formal lunch, although the more astute detected a degree of resentment that her husband was so heavily preoccupied with his duties, which resulted in a growing tension. As a result, the atmosphere was never quite the same as in Hills's day.

At the commencement of Lent Half 1940 on 24 January, Henry was listed fifty-second in First Hundred, Block A, Division III. Mr Herbert by now fulfilled both roles of House and Modern Tutor. Mr MacKinnon and Dr Lefevre continued their teaching of Maths for Specialists, and a broader curriculum was maintained with extra German. The Captain of the Oppidans and President of Pop had both left the school to join up and had been replaced by Glyn Rhys Williams and Ronnie MacAndrew respectively.[84]

The nation's reversion to GMT between November and February meant that conditions were too bitter for early school, and it was discontinued for the first three weeks of the Half, part of the time lost being made up by another school on Tuesday and Thursday afternoons. Wartime measures were becoming more stringent. During the first week of February the college authorities circulated a letter to parents suggesting ways of reducing incidental expenses. Boys' pocket money could be reduced to no more than 50s (£2.50) per Half; the practice of presenting leaving presents to masters was to be discouraged and dark blue over-coats (more practical during the holidays than the prescribed black or dark grey) could be worn. One suggestion, namely that school dress could be purchased either tailor made, or ready made in London, was to create great consternation and opposition from Eton traders.[85]

The Eton College Economy Committee had also decided that there should be no further expenditure on House colour shirts and scarves. The implications of this were that boys playing for their Houses would be unable to turn out in uni-form colours. On 17 February, after a suggestion from Eton languages master Mr Peter Spanoghe, Henry made an appeal to Old Etonians who had received House colours for football to return their shirts in order that the current Houses might use them. It was hoped to acquire twelve shirts and scarves for each team and intended that these should become the Houses' permanent property for issue to team members only for House games. The appeal appeared in the following day's press, quoting Henry: 'I know Old Etonians will find it hard to part with their shirts, but the cause is a very worthy one and every present Etonian will appreci-ate their generosity. We hope the war will be over before the shirts are worn out.'

The subject stirred strong emotions, House colours were highly prized and not to be relinquished easily. *The Times* of Saturday, 24 February, published half a column on their emotional significance under the title 'The Song of the Shirt'. This made the suggestion that a shirt's history may become more illustrious if worn by a succession of notable players rather than having merely one owner and subsequently being kept as a souvenir in a drawer. The appeal was to be echoed by 'Peterborough' in the *Daily Telegraph*. The same day as his letter appeared in *The Times*, Henry was representing his school in a cross-country event staged against Wellington School. Each side fielded seven runners over a course of some 6 miles, the first six home scoring points for their team. Always the strong distance runner, Henry was triumphant, leading home two Wellington opponents, his premier placing enabling the school to win by a total of two points. There was little time for celebration or reflection: the following day, Sunday, 25 February, saw 400 boys taking part in a more serious game, participating as casualties for an ARP practice in Slough.

As Captain of Athletics, Henry had cause to become involved in a wide variety of sports issues, as demonstrated by a letter by 'Discontented Pugilist' published in the *Eton Chronicle* of 22 February requesting an explanation as to why the School Hall should not be used for the finals of the School Boxing. The following week's edition contained Henry's diplomatic reply that preparation for the event would require greater manpower than available and that there was no desire to establish a precedent.

The athletics season opened during the first week of March. Running in the School Mile on the cinder track at Kennels on Tuesday 12 March Henry made a slow start for the first lap, but battled more successfully than Philips the leader against a strong headwind on the back straight to take the lead for the second lap. Despite being pursued closely by Arbuthnot, he was able to maintain his position and finish in 4 minutes 49.7 seconds. It was his third successive win, equalling the record set by G. K. Dunning in 1911, 1912 and 1913.[86] As a result the Mile Cup became his own permanent possession.

Some two weeks later, during the afternoon of Easter Saturday (23 March), a triangular contest against Stowe and Lancing College, held at Eton, saw Henry again successful, completing the Mile in 4 minutes 49.4 seconds. He paced himself just ahead of Arbuthnot, and the two runners gave Eton the first two places and a badly needed seven points, placing them overall leaders in the competition with only one event to run. This, the relay, again went to Eton, giving the school a grand total of 50 points to cement the afternoon's victory. Unable to be at home for Easter, Henry sent his family a GPO greetings telegram: 'Best Wishes to you all for Easter. Love Henry.'

A week later, on 30 March, Henry added to his double of the Steeplechase and the Mile by taking the tape in the School Half Mile, easily beating John Somers

Cocks and H. Arbuthnot in 2 minutes 5 seconds.

Trial Eights were to be decided on the Thames regatta course at Henley on Saturday, 9 March, after a period of bitterly cold weather, which curtailed much practice afloat, because of both the conditions on the river and a coincident bout of influenza. In the first month of the Half, when it was impossible to train on the water, the crews were put through rigorous physical exercises by Jerred, their coach, continuing a practice from the previous year developed by Captain Ames. In the decisive event, the Dark Blues beat the Light Blues by a length and a quarter.

During Easter leave Henry had stayed with friends holding a house party at 4 Ennismore Gardens, Kensington.[87] Much to Henry's annoyance, James[88] had not packed his new green coat, and he had to make do with his old brown check one until his mother was able to send him the required garment. Nevertheless he was enjoying himself, even if some conditions were as basic as those at school: 'Camping in a large house where the water is only hot in one bathroom – (quite the House atmosphere!) – don't take that seriously – I only had one cold bath in the green room.'[89]

A school concert was held during the evening of Monday, 1 April. As a demonstration of affinity with the country's French allies, the performance opened with the assembled audience standing to sing 'La Marseillaise', the words of which were printed in the programme. After a dozen pieces, the evening concluded with the school song: 'Carmen Etonense'.

The following day saw an athletics match Eton vs Gordonstoun. In the Mile Henry and John Somers-Cocks were pitted against P. Dolan and J. Mercer of Gordonstoun. Henry came home the triumphant victor in a time of 4 minutes 57 seconds, pursued by Somers-Cocks. His success helped ensure that the home team beat the visitors by 30 points to 27.

Despite his uncle's connections with the Army, Henry had already decided that he would enlist in the Royal Air Force. Having commanded Nos 2 and 4 (Bomber) Groups during 1937–8, his mother's cousin, Air Vice-Marshal Charles Blount, OBE, MC, had been appointed Air Officer Commanding No. 22 (Army Co-operation) Group at Farnborough on 17 July 1939 and was now Chief Air Adviser to General Lord Gort. In this role he was based at Maroeuil, near Arras, as commander of the Air Component of the British Expeditionary Force in France, Westland Lysanders and Bristol Blenheims supported by a handful of Hawker Hurricanes providing tactical support for British troops.[90] Henry already had discussed an aviation career with his son, John Blount,[91] and AVM Blount had been instrumental in arranging an interview for him with Air Commdore Albert Fletcher, CMG, CBE, MC, Deputy Director of Personal Services at the Air Ministry, to discuss his future.[92]

The examination for entry into RAF College Cranwell, which was usually held in November, was cancelled from Michaelmas Half 1939. Instead boys were permitted to submit their application direct to the Service of their choice. Wednesday, 3 April 1940, found Henry attending No. 2 Recruit Centre, RAF Cardington, where he formally enlisted in the Royal Air Force as an aircrafthand, pending pilot training. The following day he was placed on the Reserve and returned to Eton. His actual call-up would not be for another two months.

Henry's final period at Eton began with the commencement of Summer Half on Wednesday, 1 May 1940. He was now in Fifth Form, First Hundred, Block A, Division III. Mr Herbert continued to fulfil roles of both House and Modern Tutor. Maths for Specialists continued under Mr MacKinnon (Calculus) and Dr Lefevre. Physics was taken by Mr Edward Davies, FCS. Extra studies now concentrated on Maths with Mr MacKinnon, essential if he were to ensure progress in the RAF. A number of other boys, although not Henry himself, took Extra studies in military subjects (including Hygiene, Geography, Map Reading and PT). He continued as a member of Pop, now under the presidency of J. A. Lyttleton (brother of later jazz musician Humphrey Lyttleton and son of Eton Master Hon. G. Lyttleton).

The inter-House Athletic Cup results were published in early May, Mr Assheton's House gaining the trophy with 77 points. Despite Henry's influence, Mr Herbert's House could manage only third place with 33. Nevertheless Henry was spending an increasing amount of his time pursuing sporting and Pop activities. Fortunately, perhaps, the wartime situation and shortage of paper led to the abandonment of Trials during the Lent Half of 1940.

Privileged senior boys were permitted access to Luxmoore's garden, which had been created from an island of waste ground in the river by H. E. Luxmoore, a former master. Past a gate bearing the motto 'Et Amicorum' and crossing a hump-backed wooden bridge, one entered a tranquil world of walks, lawns and cherry trees, with a vista of the grey college Chapel belfries rising above the red brick and stone of Eton's secular buildings. Relaxing here on 5 May, Henry wrote to his mother: 'Thank you again for a lovely holiday – there's no place like home and if I can just come home for the summer it will be perfect.'

He had just come from a meeting with Claude Elliott after Chapel to discuss arrangements for the Procession of Boats on 4 June. With no fireworks, this would be the final event of the day, starting at 6.00 p.m. A degree of austerity was to be observed. The procession would be confined to a short course below Romney Lock and crews would not be in celebratory dress. Henry and Derek Mond had decided that it would be inappropriate to have the traditional Home Park party for the boat crews. Instead, Henry would have tea in his room, with a buffet for those who attended. Overall it would be a very contracted event.

> Please don't ask anyone but Mary [Gibb] from home outside the family as
> she's a friend of longest standing. . . . Leave invitations and organisation to
> me and it will be OK! I'll ask you to bring some 'eats' I expect; will let you
> know well beforehand. . . . Do hope Jo [cousin Joanna Herbert] will be able
> to come.

With Henry having been awarded the Mile Cup, Mr Dunning was considering
presenting a replacement trophy. Henry and his mother had thought of offering
to provide this, but tentative enquiries suggested that Mr Dunning would not
entertain the thought. Mrs Maudslay had considered offering to contribute to the
cost of the replacement, much to Henry's horror. On 15 May he was to write to her:

> Mr Dunning is not a retailing silversmith. If you suggested giving him £100
> because he has re-presented the cup to the school I don't know what he would
> say but can guess what he would feel. I think my tutor may have suggested to
> you what he has suggested to me, namely that we should present a cup to be
> called the Dunning Cup for some event that has no trophy.[93]

Henry had just received the cup, which was given pride of place on the wash box
in the corner of his room before being sent to the school office to be kept securely in the safe until his mother could take it home when she visited on 4 June.

On Tuesday, 14 May, Holland fell to the German forces. That evening Anthony
Eden, Secretary of State for War, an Old Etonian and previous boarder in the
Hopgarden, broadcast an appeal for all men between the ages of 17 and 65 to enrol
at their local police station to form the Local Defence Volunteers (later to become
the Home Guard). The local force would defend the north bank of the Thames in
the Windsor area under the command of Lieutentant Colonel Colquhoun.[94] The
ECOTC (known now as the Junior Training Corps) had already been active in
this capacity, forming the Eton College Anti-Parachutist Observer Corps. Four
patrols operated at dusk and dawn in an effort to locate any enemy who might
have landed. If found, the enemy was to be destroyed by a 'Task Force'. Other
patrols mounted vigils to defend railway lines, bridges, waterworks and Slough
factories. Whole holidays and half-holidays became duty days, with the occasional night patrol. Now any member of the corps over the age of 17 would be
eligible to become a member of the LDV. With the corps' rifles and a single early
Bren gun, the Eton College LDVs were probably among the best equipped in the

country at a time when other local LDV units were advertising in the *Windsor and Slough Express* for donations of any weapons held by members of the public. An acute shortage of equipment meant that many of the newly formed squads learned arms drill using broom handles and proceeded on patrol with garden implements and other improvised weapons.[95]

Henry was one of the first to volunteer for the new organization: 'I have volunteered for the parachute Local Defence Volunteers – in fact I was the first to put my name down at the police station – many other boys have done so and the whole of us are being taken over by the officers of the OTC.'[96]

Parental consent was required before any boy could be formally accepted as a member of this new force. 'Please send your written permission for me to join to my Tutor – I don't believe we shall have any parachute raids here until the Germans think they have finished with France – that will take a goodish time in spite of the mess we're in now!'[97]

The Eton boating season began with the preliminary heats of the School Pulling on Wednesday, 15 May, and Henry's responsibilities as Captain of Boats kept him fully occupied until after they were completed on Friday. Although he could do no better than third place, Henry considered that he had done as well as could be expected, those who beat him having been rowing together for two years. There was little time for reflection, as the Eight was starting its training for the schools races at Henley, scheduled for the first week of July. Henry thought they were 'quite hopeful' and 'wouldn't be surprised to see us win with the first eight and the second should go quite fast', although with the deteriorating situation he was doubtful whether the races would be held. In the event his fears proved to be correct.

Besides which, the Eight had other priorities. Under the auspices of Mr George Tait, the rowing master and coach, they were making their contribution to the national salvage drive to collect waste paper and old scrap from houses in the town and college. In their spare time members could often be seen in their shirt sleeves hauling heavily laden carts to the collection points. One enterprising group 'double-harnessed' two bicycles together with a wooden bar to pull their cart.[98]

Mrs Maudslay wrote to John Herbert, giving her permission for Henry to join the Local Defence Volunteers.[99] Acknowledging her cooperation on Monday, 27 May, Henry wrote: 'Thank you . . . for your permission to join the volunteers. I think my brown corderoy [sic] trousers would be very useful on duty as we don't wear full uniform, could you send them please?'[100]

With his 18th birthday approaching in two months' time, he was already giving consideration to a practical gift: 'Can I ask for a birthday present in advance? – a licence to use and posses a revolver or automatic? I'm afraid it's what I would like more than anything else at present.'

Outlining how the boys were putting their military skills to use defending the
nation, he told her:

> We are really getting well mobilised here and we [the OTC] patrol the land
> between Eton and Slough an hour before dawn and an hour after sunset –
> only a few on duty at a time of course. It's an obvious landing ground for
> saboteurs of Slough factories, some of which are very important. We know
> the ground perfectly, and should be able to cope with them very well. I'm
> afraid this sounds all very morbid – but it's very encouraging to see people
> getting a move on about things and we all feel much better for it.[101]

News was now filtering back of Etonians who were already on active service:

> I saw John Harley[102] on Sunday – he is commissioned in the Coldstreams and
> stationed not out of range of Eton. He says Tim[103] is in the East of England
> flying a Spitfire. Also saw Rex (Whitworth) and Compton – Rex looks well
> and as if he's enjoying life in the Army.[104]

A contemporary of Henry's brother, John, Michael Crossley from Halford in
Warwickshire, some 8 miles from Sherbourne, was now a flight commander with
No. 32 Squadron, operating from French forward bases. Within a month he
would be commanding the squadron at Biggin Hill throughout the critical stages
of the Battle of Britain.[105]

   With the German assault on France, AVM Blount had been one of the many
voices pressing for greater fighter support, essential if the RAF were to hold its
own against the Luftwaffe. As a result, thirty-two more Hurricanes were deployed
to bases across the Channel on 13 May, but in doing so Air Chief Marshal Sir
Hugh Dowding, Commander-in-Chief of Fighter Command, appealed to the
War Cabinet to retain his Command's remaining fighters at home for the defence
of the British Isles. Denied these extra aircraft, AVM Blount and the other military leaders acceded that the RAF's operations would have to be conducted from
southern England, and the Air Force's evacuation began on 19 May under the
codename Operation *Back Violet*. Charles Blount was among the last to leave, on
22 May, flying out of a wrecked Merville airfield in the last serviceable aircraft, a
Tiger Moth with virtually no navigation aids and seated on his briefcase wrapped
in his greatcoat in lieu of a parachute. He soon re-established his 'Back Component HQ' at RAF Hawkinge in Kent, from where he intended to command aircraft operating from advanced landing grounds in the Lower Seine area, Operation *South Violet*. The rapid German advance precluded this plan, releasing AVM

Blount to perform a vital role collating intelligence information gathered by Army cooperation flights and the embryonic 'Y' Service (monitoring German wireless traffic) to aid the seaborne evacuation of the British Expeditionary Force.

Down on the beaches of Dunkirk, other relatives of the Maudslay family were engaged in critical operations. Captain William (Bill) Tennant, brother-in-law of AVM Blount, had landed at the port on 27 May as Senior Naval Officer ashore, Dunkirk, having volunteered to take front-line charge of the naval aspects of Operation *Dynamo*.[106] Improvisation was the keynote; assisted by 12 naval officers and 160 ratings and identified by the letters 'SNO' cut from silver cigarette paper and stuck to his steel helmet with sardine oil, he supervised the evacuation of 338,226 French and British troops before being brought back to Dover in the company of General Alexander aboard MTB 102 on the night of 3/4 June.[107] Among those who would be grateful for Tennant's organizational skills was Gwen Maudslay's brother, Major General William Norman Herbert, CB, CMG, DSO.[108] With the 50th Northumberland Division, he was part of a force tasked to block the roads south of Arras, thereby cutting off the advancing German Panzers from supplies and communication. After a battle near the First World War site of Vimy Ridge, the British troops were forced to pull back and retreat to Bray Dunes to await evacuation.

The fate of the Army in France prompted a number of boys to reconsider their selection for the armed forces:

> Charles Pilkington and some of my friends think they would like to join the RAF! They used to be going into the Army and were very sniffy about the RAF but I think that recent events have put some hard sense into their heads as to which is the more pleasant! – not the happiest of motives but decidedly true at present.[109]

Confirming his friends' lack of aviation knowledge, Henry was shortly to write to his mother:

> Charles Pilkington and Robin Muir are joining the RAF, both in the Library here[110] and two of the very best – but they know NOTHING about flying so will you send me my PICTORIAL FLYING COURSE which Tita gave me many years ago – it's on the shelf in my bedroom I think – I'd like it as soon as possible as they want to cram as much as possible before their first interview on Thursday.[111]

Mrs Maudslay at least agreed to consider the prospect of Henry obtaining a firearm certificate: 'Thank you so much for saying that you'll find out about the possibility of a revolver – I noticed one on the Headmaster's desk when I went to see him the other morning.'

Despite the seriousness of the situation there were still lighter moments:

(The Headmaster) had been sleeping in the armoury all night on watch ready to issue rifles to the striking force of the OTC (who sleep in the gymnasium and are different boys each night), they are roused if the patrols spot parachutists. Anyway, he had got out of the armoury with Brocklebank who was sleeping there too – the door shut behind them and the dawn patrol had come home and found the two of them trying to get in by the skylight in their pyjamas! Mrs Elliott had been on VAD duty that night and came in and asked him about his exploits – the war is not without its complications.

The increasingly serious nature of the international situation was now to make a more marked impact on the domestic population. It had been announced that many of the usual activities for the 4 June would be curtailed. There were more important issues at stake: 'I'm afraid things are still pretty hectic with me. The Procession of Boats is cancelled for the 4th which comes as a relief to me in many ways .... I'm going on the dawn patrol at 3 am on the 4th so won't be at my brightest!'

There would be no lunches for parents in the Houses (to the relief of Masters and Dames), no music nor evening fireworks, which would contravene the blackout. Henry recommended that his mother seriously should reconsider her attendance. 'It will simply spoil your memories of previous occasions.' When Mrs Maudslay announced that she still had every intention of coming down, he suggested that she should travel up to London on the 3rd and stay overnight with Tita,[112] and they then could travel down together, arriving at Eton in time for tea. Tuning his wireless to broadcasts by members of the new coalition government, Henry was beginning to develop his opinion of politicians and form his own philosophy about the situation:

It seems that Gamelin[113] wasn't quite the bright boy he was made out to be – I'm sure we will pull through alright – near to London one can feel the fighting spirit of Winston's government. Morrison spoke on the wireless tonight – very well and Beaverbrook in the capacity he now has is magnificent.

If anyone at home gets pessimistic remember – if we win everything will be OK so cheer up – if we lose we'll all be dead, so why worry? (N.B. the latter is absurd but has an excellent effect on people who are really worrying as it makes them realise the futility of doing so).[114]

With a month or so to go until the end of the Half, those about to leave Eton made their final preparations. Just as there had been initiation rituals on entering the school, other traditions were to be observed on departure. For those of families who had been educated at Eton for generations there was the duty of carving one's name in Upper School, although by 1940 shortage of space had restricted this practice only to those who could claim a 'family corner'. The names of more recent families were inscribed on an overflow area on the stairs, the carving being administered by the School Office for a fee of 10s (50p). Membership of the Old Etonians' Association was solicited for a fee of 50s (£2.50), with additional subscription for membership of the 'Vikings' – the Old Etonians' rowing club. There was the traditional leaving portrait photograph taken by Hills and Saunders at 109 High Street, Eton. This was not only for self and family, as tradition decreed that copies (often signed, first name only) should be exchanged with others and given to the House Tutor. Auctions of effects were held, selling items to other members of the House, often at token prices. There would be a tip for the maid and farewells to M'Tutor and M'Dame, no doubt with promises to remain in touch and return at a later date – promises that many of Henry's contemporaries would be unable to keep. At a final interview, Claude Elliott presented each boy with his 'Leaving Book', a selection of poems by Thomas Gray (himself an Old Etonian), the traditional parting gift.

The exact date of Henry's departure is unrecorded, but he is believed to have left Eton at the beginning of June,[115] thereby avoiding many of the final rituals, although he did not neglect farewell gestures to those with whom he had built a firm bond. On 16 June Eleanor Herbert wrote to Henry 'to tell you how much we miss you and to try to thank you for the exquisite tumblers which both your tutor and I think are such beautiful ones . . . and will always be one of our most treasured possessions'. Apologizing for not having written earlier, she explained: 'But what with the Senior Eden getting scarlet fever and one thing and another I haven't had a moment.'

Having Henry in the Hopgarden for the few months since they had taken it over had made a great difference to both her and her husband. She had tried to tell him something of their feelings the night before he left, but felt she had 'failed horribly' and looked forward to seeing him again as soon as possible: 'Take care of yourself – and all the luck in the world.'

An undated letter (presumably written at this period) from Henry's tutor to Gwen Maudslay echoed the sense of loss: 'Saying goodbye is inevitably a hopelessly inadequate process. I just wanted you to know that during the 14 years I have been a beak Henry has been the best I have yet met.'

On 18 June, the day after the French had appealed for an armistice, the Eight had decided that they would not row at Henley, thereby breaking a tradition dating back to 1861. Henry was quoted as saying that he was 'anxious that the Eight's decision should do as little harm as possible to the school's rowing'.[116] Their decision was possibly influenced by Henry's departure combined with the fact that training was becoming increasingly difficult, with the crew losing one day a week to war agricultural work. Despite this evidence, in the records of the ECOTC Henry is not officially listed as leaving until the formal end of the school year on 27 July. His corps' record shows that after four years he had attained the rank of sergeant,[117] gaining three 'Efficients' in 1937, 1938 and 1939, Certificate 'A', Part I in December 1937 and Part II in March 1938. In the comments column regarding his future the entry states 'Not known – left during the holidays'. Nevertheless it was general knowledge that he had joined the RAF, as evidenced by entries in the *Observer* and the *Sunday Times* of 30 June, the latter under the headline 'Rowing Fixtures cancelled':

> H. E. Maudslay the Captain of Boats and Captain of Athletics has left Eton College to join the Royal Air Force and the duties of Captain of Boats have been taken over by the Hon. D. J. Mond, son of Lord Melchett.[118] The suggested races for the eights and fours between the leading rowing schools intended to take the place of Henley have been cancelled as so many schools are now engaged on national service. At Eton some of the boys are working in local factories every half-holiday and even on Sundays.[119] In the circumstances a school Eight cannot be trained properly for serious races.

Meanwhile, Henry had already commenced training for a far more earnest task.[120]

Part II

Arms and the Man

Chapter 4

Per Ardua . . .

Life's duties call us; whate'er befall us,
High lot or lowly, weal or woe,
Brother with brother, thou our Mother,
In thee united we will go!
For home and kinsfolk, for old comrades,
For king and country and for thee!
(A. C. Ainger, Eton School song – 'Vale')

Henry arrived at No. 1 RAF Depot, Uxbridge, for mobilization alongside other 18-year-old members of the new intake on Thursday, 20 June 1940. With suitcases in their hands and overcoats over their arms, the latest recruits viewed their future with a mixture of excitement and apprehension, feeling very self-conscious in their 'civvies' among the smartly turned-out uniforms.

Their surroundings exuded military atmosphere, notably the main square, a parade ground bordered by red-brick three-storey barrack blocks, which were home to the recruits. There to greet them in usual sardonic manner would have been the corporal, who was to become their mentor in the intricacies of foot drill, brass and boot polishing and the whole initiation into the world of uniformed men. Here Henry would become 920288 Aircraftman Second Class Maudslay, H. E.

The first few days were to be a confusion of parades, learning to march in step and turn to the right, left and about, saluting on the spot and to the right and left, to a variety of imaginary notables: 'Field Marshal approaching from the left. Ey-es left.' 'Squadron Leader approaching from the right. Ey-es right.' Occasionally, just to keep recruits on their toes, the unexpected: 'Army Private approaching from the left. Ey-es left. As you were. You do not salute Army Privates.'

Kit was issued. Two pairs of heavy, metal-studded boots, one pair of plimsolls, two pairs of non-stretch braces, three pairs of thick woollen socks, two sets of long john-underwear, three head-first blue shirts, two loose collars, two back and front studs, black tie, forage cap, peaked cap, two cap badges, webbing, backpacks and belts, tee shirts and belts. Toiletry and housekeeping requirements were catered for with a safety razor, shaving brush, canvas 'housewife' to hold sewing requisites, mug and plate, eating utensils and cleaning brushes. Finally, a kitbag, into which everything was crammed. All was very new, very stiff or hard and with buttons of dullness that seemingly defied any amount of polishing. Evenings would be spent pressing uniforms, rubbing soap down the inside of trouser creases to produce a razor-sharp edge, polishing buttons with a 'button stick', an ingeniously shaped piece of metal designed to keep the 'Brasso' off clothing, and striving for ever to achieve a polish on boots to rival those of the corporal's.

A more military appearance resulted from a visit to the tailor, adjusting the stock-sized jackets and trousers into a better fit for each individual. Nothing, however, seemed to alleviate the coarseness of the underwear, which itched and scratched, despite extensive laundering. A visit to the barber's for a 'straight over the top with the clippers' haircut was arranged. Even those who had the foresight, or so they thought, to have a short back and sides from a civilian barber before-hand were to be subjected to the ritual shearing, leaving an overall one-inch hair length. The torment continued: on to the medical officer for an FFI (Free From Infection) inspection, together with vaccination against smallpox and inocula-tions against paratyphoid and typhoid to bring entrants up to the minimum medical requirement. Having been inoculated at school previously, Henry re-quired only one inoculation and one vaccination, both in the same arm. However, many would spend the next day in bed, excused duties, with post-inoculation fever.

Back in the barrack room they learned the ritual of bed making, for sleep by night and show by day. The beds were far from comfortable, the mattress com-prising three hard, unyielding square 'biscuits', stuffed with horse hair, on a steel bed with three steel slats in each half. Some might have been lucky enough to have a newer type, with diamond wires held by steel springs at the sides and ends, but these offered little more comfort, the steel bars across the middle where the two halves met proving spine-jarringly uncomfortable. Three coarse blankets and a pillow, two sheets and a pillowcase made of what seemed like canvas, com-pleted the bedding materials.

Reveille was sounded at six o'clock each morning, recruits getting washed, shaved and dressed as quickly as possible. Beds were made by sliding the foot under the head, piling two of the biscuits on top, folding the blankets in half lengthways, and two of them in half and half again and placing them on the two biscuits. The third biscuit was leant against the bedhead across the blankets and the third blanket laid across the biscuits and tucked in at the foot and the head of the bed and under the sloping biscuit to form a chair on which one could sit after lunch and in the evenings when not polishing equipment or performing other duties.

Beds made, recruits fell in outside to be marched to breakfast. The usual format was two ranks: 'Tallest on the right, shortest on the left, in two ranks, size. Front rank to the right, rear rank to the left, TURN. Quick march.' The right-hand marker stood firm, the next man stepped behind him, the next stepped beside him, the next behind him, and so on, until there were two ranks, with the tallest men at each end and the smallest in the middle. After numbering off, fours were formed, the even numbers taking a step to the rear and another to the right, before marching off to the dining hall.

Having eaten, recruits made their own way back to their barrack block, ready to parade on the square, where the RAF ensign was hoisted for the day prior to attending lectures on aspects of service life, including Air Force Law and King's Regulations, Administration and Leadership.

Training was given in the care and use of the Service respirator, more robust than the civilian version and supplied to every new entrant. Practical experience was given in the efficiency of this equipment, with airmen entering a building into which tear gas had been released. After noting that they could breathe without any discomfort while wearing the respirator, they were told to remove the mask and made to run round in a circle twice before being allowed outside with streaming eyes.

The main meal was taken at midday, with a high tea at about five o'clock. Evenings were free, although equipment had to be cleaned and beds made up for sleeping before 'Lights out' at 10.15 p.m. On occasion the curfew would be extended until 1 a.m., allowing those who so wanted time to sample a taste of London's night life.

On 21 June 1940, 920288 AC2 Henry Maudslay wrote to his mother from No. 5 Room, STRUMA, No. 1 Recruitment Centre, RAF Uxbridge, Middlesex. It was a very simple postcard:

What an address! Very well at the moment and will be moved on in a day or two, so it isn't worth you writing here.

Conditions better than last time![121] Best love to all those at Fox Hill from Henry.

Written up the left-hand margin was the reassuring comment: 'P.S. Have been given sheets and a pillowcase!'

Henry was correct, for within the week he and his fellow recruits were deemed ready for posting to No. 4 Initial Training Wing (ITW), Bexhill on Sea. A passing-out parade was held, in full kit, clearance chits signed and railway warrants issued. The following day the squad marched down Uxbridge High Street to the station for the next stage in their training.

On arrival at the ITW, cadets were given another physical examination and a meal. During the medical inspection Henry experienced one of the less pleasant aspects of Service life. Stripped to the waist he had to leave his wallet for a short period with the remainder of his clothes, since it was too big to fit in his trouser pockets. Returning, he found it had been stolen. The loss was a blow, because it contained not only money, but also his driving licence, civilian identity card and Service identity document – Form 1250. The latter was soon replaced, and a new, smaller, wallet obtained. His sister loaned him 30s (£1.50), and with that and his recent pay he was set up again until he could arrange to have his account transferred. The original wallet would subsequently be found and handed in to the police, who returned it to Henry's mother at the end of June.

No. 4 ITW at Bexhill occupied a varied collection of hotels, boarding houses and other buildings commandeered throughout the seaside town: the Sackville Hotel, Metropole Hotel (the upper storeys of which had been destroyed by fire on 21 May, fortunately without loss of life), the eastern half of the de la Warr Pavilion, Egerton Park Pavilion and part of the Sackville Garage. Recruits were housed in billets that varied widely in decor, furnishing and catering. Henry found himself attached to No. 4 Squadron, 'B' Flight and billeted in Roberts Marine Mansions, a large brick-built Gothic block on the eastern stretch of the Marina overlooking the sea, some 200 yards east of the de la Warr Pavilion. Built originally in 1895 as the Marine Hotel, in August 1903 it had been converted by Sir John Reynolds Roberts, JP, into a residential convalescent home cum private hotel 'for members of both sexes, whether employers or employed of the drapery and allied trades'.[122]

The day following arrival, after a first parade at 07.25 and an inspection, lectures began. Those who had already demonstrated mathematical ability by obtaining a minimum 60 per cent in examination were allowed to start on navigation immediately. As well as formal testing, recruits were continually assessed by their instructors, records being kept of performance, bearing, speech, intelligence and so on.

Except for fifteen minutes at 10.00., fifty-five minutes' break at 12.30 and a further fifteen minutes at 15.45, the whole of the day from 07.25 until 18.00 was spent attending lectures, drill and PT. Coursework was hard, necessitating study in 'free time' during the evenings. Once a week there would be a full squadron parade, and an inspection of billets was conducted at Roberts Marine Mansions every Friday at 11.00 hours.

The purpose of the ITW was to build up the raw recruits in terms of both physical and mental fitness, seeking to retain a degree of independence and enthusiasm while generating a sense of comradeship and team spirit. Tuition comprised lectures, usually of forty-five minutes' duration, on mathematics, physics, navigation, meteorology, theory of flight and principles of engines, armament and weapons training, anti-gas measures and RAF law. Not surprisingly, great emphasis was placed on the former, and any recruit failing the preliminary examination in mathematics would be barred from pilot training. Each instructor was a specialist in his own particular field, and generally lectures were interesting to those who realized the necessity of the tuition. Signalling in the form of Morse code and aircraft recognition was practised daily in fifteen-to twenty-minute sessions, although recruits were expected to undertake further study in their own time to build proficiency.[123] Moving as a single body of men, recruits marched between billets and classrooms, the timetable requiring a fast pace that made telling demands on the legs of those less fit.

Classroom studies were punctuated by daily half-hour periods of strenuous physical exercise and drill, with and without rifles. Regardless of weather, the seafront became the parade ground for drill and physical training. The latter was also carried out on the pebble beach and comprised various activities, including push-ups and leapfrog. The regime was intensified with route marches and cross-country runs up and down the steepest hills. Additional instruction was given in swimming, allied to lectures about the Air-Sea Rescue Service, culminating in practical dinghy drill in full flying kit. In the early days many were to feel the exhaustion caused by such physical exertion, but they gradually felt less so as the course progressed, and they were able to take advantage of the evenings to seek refreshment in local pubs. Henry seems to have enjoyed most of this physical activity, revelling in the degree of fitness to which he was no stranger. 'Lights out' was at 21.00, but usually most of the cadets were so tired by the end of the day that no one objected to early bed.

One afternoon per week was given over to organized games, cadets being allowed, within reason, to select their preferred sport. There were strict regulations regarding the dress and conduct of cadets during this activity:

Dress: Cadets and Airmen. Sports and Organised Games.
The dress to be worn when proceeding to or returning from each type of sport is as follows.
CRICKET: Flannels, Service dress jacket and cap.
GOLF: Service dress whilst proceeding to and returning from the
                  Links, changing into golfing kit or slacks and cardigan at the

Clubhouse. Shorts and singlet are not to be worn on the golf course.

HOCKEY, PASS BALL, ROWING, RUGGER, SOCCER and SQUASH:	Shorts, service dress jacket and cap.
RIDING:	Riding mufti.
SWIMMING:	When the barrack rooms are close to the beach, cadets and airmen are to undress in their quarters and progress direct to the shore with greatcoat over their bathing costumes. Respirators are to be taken onto the beach on these occasions and laid carefully on the greatcoats, not on the sand. Cadets and airmen proceeding to the local baths are to wear Service dress and change at the bath.
TENNIS:	Flannels or shorts, Service dress jacket and cap.

Respirators are always to be carried except when actually taking part in games. Respirators will not be taken out in boats. Cadets and airmen taking part in organised games unless conveyed by mechanical transport are to be marched to and from the sports grounds, fields, courts etc. If the party is too small to be formed up conveniently, individuals forming it are to proceed in an airman-like manner. Cadets and airmen are to take the most direct route between their billets and the sports ground. Under no circumstances are they to walk about the town or enter shops, cafes etc. unless they are properly dressed in Service dress.

Sundays were their one free day, but many spent their time in private study and writing up notes from the previous week's lectures.

It would appear that Henry had either been able to obtain leave, possibly travelling from Uxbridge to Bexhill via Fox Hill, or more likely been able to meet his mother and sister en route in London. On the evening of Monday, 24 June, he sent another postcard, addressed from his new billet: 'All very well and happy. Am going out to get some fresh air. Lovely seeing Tita and you. Thank you so much for letter. May be going to the West Country, but I'm afraid not near you. Best love Henry.'

The first few days at Bexhill saw Henry fully occupied in learning the new routine. The transition was not helped by the fact that every night since arriving had been interrupted by air-raid alerts, disrupting sleep and taking him down to the billet shelter. On 27 June he took the opportunity of a lunchtime break to sit in the ground-floor café of Erich Mendelsohn's de la Warr Pavilion and write to his mother while eating a dubious meal of poached eggs and buns, washed down with cold Horlicks. 'Tonight, or rather last night, was the first night since Uxbridge when we have not spent the hours between about 1 a.m. and 4 a.m. in the air raid shelter. I'm so tired I sleep like a log lying on the floor. We are packed there like sardines.'

Despite his physical fitness, the prolonged periods of drill and marching were already having an adverse effect on his feet: 'We are allowed socks of Air Force blue, and I could do with several pairs of medium thickness if you could send me some, rather on the big side, if possible.'

Commenting on his compatriots, he noted that they were rather a mixed bunch, those who had already been through OTC training seemingly being the least efficient. He hoped that he was not like them and had made a resolution to 'try like hell at everything'. Already he felt that he was becoming indoctrinated into the Service mentality of doing as he was ordered and not having to think for himself: 'My brain will go soft from disuse! I never get a chance to use it.'

Already a degree of frustration was beginning to set in. Henry had once considered joining a civil airline in order to learn to fly and be one step ahead if hostilities developed. His cousin John Blount, already serving in the RAF, had advised his mother against it, probably saying that the Service did not take civil flying into account. Now Henry began to regret listening to that advice:

> Those with any flying experience solo are going straight into cadet units and being pushed in every way. All I do is stamp the parade ground and polish buttons. I wouldn't mind that, but I know that those who have flying experience but know very little of discipline etc. don't have this drill to do so much.

Henry completed the letter on the return to his billet, where he found another letter from his mother had been delivered, telling him about recent air raids (possibly the night of 24/25 June, when most of the country south of a line Hull to Blackpool, excluding Wales, Devon and Cornwall, were placed under alert between 2335 hours and 0240 hours; damage was done to Bristol and other bombs fell in rural areas). She also confirmed that she had found his pen, mislaid after his last leave, and suggested that, if he had time, Henry might be able to meet up with her brother, Major General Norman Herbert, who would shortly be visiting the area and staying at Lydford, which she believed to be near Paignton. Concerned that either his peers, or authority, might take a 'dim view' of such a meeting with a senior officer, Henry wrote back:

It would be grand to see Uncle Norman, but he could not possibly look me
up and I'd have to be very careful about how I visited him. We would have to
arrange a meeting place where I would not be likely to be seen by any of my
colleagues – for obvious reasons.[124]

On 26 June a Movement Order was issued detailing the transfer of No. 4 ITW to
Paignton on 30 June and 1 July. The unit would travel in three trains.

The first freight train was to leave Bexhill West Station at 1940 hours on Sunday,
30 June 1940, and would arrive at Paignton 0737 hours on Monday, 1 July. OC
No. 3 Squadron would detail 11 airmen, OC No. 4 Squadron 34 airmen, and OC HQ
Squadron 3 airmen, including 2 medical orderlies to travel aboard this train.

The second freight train, under Flying Officer John Beard, was to leave Bexhill
West Station at 2020 hours, 30 June, arriving Paignton 0847 hours the following
day. Three trucks on this train were to be reserved for equipment and stores of
No. 54 Group. OC HQ Squadron would detail 8 airmen, OC 3 Squadron 20 cadets,
and HQ 54 Group 20 airmen to travel with this train.

Finally, the passenger train under Flight Lieutenant William Jordan, the Adjutant, carrying 211 airmen of Nos 1 and 2 Squadrons, 67 airmen of No. 3 Squadron
and 46 airmen of HQ Squadron, was to leave Bexhill Central Station at 0950 hours
on 1 July.

Squadron Leader Joshua Westmoreland would supervise the entrainment,
with the equipment officer, Flight Lieutenant Robert Cross, assisting transport and
loading arrangements. Officers in charge of each of the squadrons were to arrange
for all personnel to be at their respective entraining stations thirty minutes before
trains were timed to leave. Unexpended portions of the day's rations would be given
to the airmen for consumption on the journey.

On Sunday evening the first party of the airmen paraded, comprising forty-
eight cadets of No. 4 ITW under the command of Pilot Officer John Straton-
Ferrier. Each carried a rifle, bayonet and complete kit, including a filled water
bottle and one blanket. When they arrived at Bexhill West Station, kitbags were
loaded into a luggage van and the airmen assembled in groups of six at forming-
up places on the platform allotted by Squadron Leader Westmoreland. Markers
then went on to the platform to mark off positions of carriage for each unit. The
airmen then marched on to the markers in threes and turned inwards to the train,
with the second groups following, assembling them in sixes opposite each carriage. Any airman requiring to relieve himself would not be allowed to do so
while lined up outside the station and would have to wait to use the lavatory
accommodation available in the carriages once on the move. With a blast on a
whistle, all boarded simultaneously and precisely on time, and with military

precision the train pulled away at 1940 hours. Following a route: Redhill–
Woking–Salisbury–Exeter, it arrived at Paignton on schedule at 0737 hours after
an uneventful overnight journey.

The second train, carrying 28 cadets from No. 4 ITW and 20 other ranks from
No. 54 Group HQ, departed some forty minutes later, following the same route,
arriving Paignton at 0847 hours. The final detachment, under Flight Lieutenant
W. H. Jordan, left Bexhill Central Station shortly before 1000 hours on Monday
morning, arriving at 1705 hours that evening.[125]

On arrival at Paignton, Henry was billeted initially in the Palace Hotel in
Esplanade Road, a spacious three-storey Victorian building set in its own land-
scaped gardens commanding splendid views across the bay. Built in 1870, for the
founder of the Singer sewing machine company, the white stucco house had been
requisitioned for military use shortly after the outbreak of war.[126]

Bearing in mind the nightly events following his arrival at Bexhill, Henry turned
his attention to the ARP orders:

1. On the air raid alarm being sounded by short blasts on whistles all personnel
   will proceed to the lower dining hall in the Palace Hotel.
2. The top floor will go down first and the ensuing in charge giving the order
   'Top Floor all clear', the First Floor will then follow on.
3. Should the alarm be sounded during the night, every airman will take with
   him to the shelter, respirator and one blanket.
4. The senior NCO in the building will also take charge until the arrival of the
   Squadron Duty Officer.
5. The Senior man in each bedroom will ascertain that the windows of each
   bedroom are closed before proceeding to the shelter.
6. The NCO i/c of each floor will enter all rooms to see that they are cleared of
   personnel.
7. No smoking will be permitted in the air raid shelter.

His room contained a wash basin with hot and cold water, and was again shared
with two colleagues, whom he described as being 'quite pleasant chaps'.

On 3 July, along with the other members of his course, Henry was summoned
to an interview with Pilot Officer Straton-Ferrier, a middle-aged reservist officer
with an eyeglass who had been posted in from Loughborough on 15 June. It was
a routine affair, lasting only a few minutes, ostensibly to ascertain the recruits' well-
being, but also to assess their suitability for a future commissioned rank. Henry
found him exceedingly pleasant and seems to have been not in the least put out

when, having mentioned that he had seven credits from Eton, Straton-Ferrier replied that he had two sons at Harrow, both of whom had eight! Conversation then turned to the Cotswolds and Broadway, making Henry feel very much at home. As Henry was to write later to his mother: 'Wonderful what a good man can do.'

Following the interview Henry went on drill practice. 'Standing too smartly to attention' resulted in an 'extremely painful' bruised left heel, placing him on twenty-four hours' 'light duties' and causing him to miss first parade and the initial maths exam. He was unperturbed, being confident that he knew more maths than most of his fellow cadets. A number of lectures were held in the Torbay Country Club, a large country house 'in the style which I think is a sort of Georgian with a bit of classical influence and an Italian staircase in brown marble'. It seems to have been a recent requisition, for Henry commented that their initial sessions concentrated on moving furniture. Nevertheless, training would soon adopt a more serious tone.

Henry's request for new socks was heeded, and, with a mother's concern, Mrs Maudslay asked how he was coping with his laundry. Writing on 4 July to thank her, Henry replied that he had decided to do his own collars, socks and handkerchiefs and that he could get the rest of his requirements done locally. He did not dismiss his mother's offer of assistance totally, however, asking if he might send future mending home to her?

He was cheered by news of family friends. Mary Gibb, daughter of Revd Gibb, was returning to her home near Broadway. 'You can't work if you have to spend all your nights in an air raid shelter,' he told his mother.[127] Anne and her friend Cecily were joining the Transport Corps. 'Magnificent work . . . they are just the right type, and should make a great success of it.'

He also expressed concern that his mother was taking on too much work, with the husband and wife team of the cook and handyman away. 'Don't overwork yourself – it's criminal of you to let yourself clean two cars single handed.'[128]

Commenting on how pleasant his new surroundings were and the absence of air raids, he thought that he would be there for about seven weeks. Leave to visit Fox Hill would be unlikely. Perhaps she might like to visit him?

Henry finished his letter with a further request that his yellow wireless set should be sent, either by Carter Paterson (the ubiquitous pre-war haulage company) or possibly via one of the local wireless distributors. Turning it on at full volume would help him to get up at six o'clock every morning.

Although he had only been in Paignton for three days, he had already discovered that he could hire a Standard 12 (naturally) for 4d (2p) a mile, and hoped to be able to get out into the country, possibly making contact with two friends from

Eton who were due to be posted soon to nearby Torquay. Petrol rationing, although introduced three weeks after the war had started, had not precluded such leisure motoring yet. Another discovery was a comfortable restaurant in the town with an orchestra where he could obtain a fine four-course lunch, including coffee, for 3s (15p). It was a luxury to be savoured and not devalued by familiarity. Henry felt that he would go there only occasionally when feeling tired and in need of a break. After all, they were allowed only an hour for lunch, which usually turned out to be rather a battle, 'noisy, but good and clean'.

He regretted that it seemed unlikely he would be able to see Uncle Norman during his visit to the West Country. He had consulted an atlas, and the only Lydford that he could find was in Somerset, not Devon, and too far away.

Those on the course had already formed their opinions of the staff and instructors. Some were permanent, such as Flying Officer George Bruce Pearson, soon to become officer in charge of instruction on recognition and ships; others such as Squadron Leader Moray Ridgeway, who gave a talk on 'navigation and signals in operational flying', were injured officers from the Palace convalescent home in neighbouring Torquay. Henry found most of the officers 'absolutely charming', but unfortunately 'we hardly see anything of them'. There was one exception – the squadron officer, Pilot Officer Charles Gass, whom Henry disliked by instinct, soon finding that his feelings were shared by the rest of the course.

NCOs who had control of their day-to-day existence were 'a good lot', especially the older ones who carried out administrative duties. The, mainly young, sergeant PT instructors were considered keen but 'absolutely fantastically brainless . . . more out-witted bundles of muscle I have never seen'.

The pressure of work was mounting as the course progressed. Already the effects were apparent; those who on the outset had been unable to march in step or co-ordinate commands with action had made progress, and the squad was now earning gradual praise and encouragement from its superiors.

After dealing with his mother's minor rebuke about the legibility of his writing, which Henry put down to the reduced-size writing paper and unfamiliar pen, he wrote: 'It will be better when I've finished this rather cramped block of paper – could you send my other pen please?'[129]

He told her that they were now working hard, starting each day at six o'clock, including Sundays. In addition there were also secondary duties to attend to – such as Fire Picquet, which had occupied him for the previous twenty-four hours. It seemed to him a remarkable coincidence that, having just completed this task, he was down for a further twelve hours of guard duty, spending the night in the guardroom fully booted and dressed with rifle and bayonet, getting what sleep he could around a two-hour spell of sentry duty.

Nevertheless, there must have been some time for relaxation, as evidenced by a request for two pairs of bathing shorts. Two sets of summer underclothes would be appreciated and could she send a shirt or two and collars? Unfortunately he was unable to send any samples of the shirt and collar required and so had to wait some time until his request could be met. Things might ease up in a few weeks. 'It would be HEAVENLY if you could come for a few days here. The weekend after the 19th would be best, as I am still finding my feet, and there is a very great deal to learn.'

The unit had now settled into its new accommodation and working routines.

Mon–Sat:

Reveille	0545 hours
Guard dismounting	0600
Clean Barrack Rooms	0600
Breakfast	0645
1st Working period	0800
Sick parade	0830
1st Working period (Permanent Staff Stn HQ)	0845
Wing Commander's Orderly room	1030
Cease work (cadets)	1230
Cease work (staff HQ)	1245
Dinner	1245
2nd Working parade (Staff HQ)	1400
2nd Working period (cadets)	1430
Cease work (cadets)	1730
Cease work (permanent staff)	1745
Tea	1745
Supper	1930
Guard mounting	2000
Fire party parade	2000
Roll Call	2215
Lights out	2230

Sundays:

Guard mounting	0600
Reveille	0630
Clean Barrack Rooms	0630
Breakfast	0730

Sick parade	0830
Church Parade	
(as detailed in Daily Routine Orders)	
Dinner	1200
Tea	1600
Supper	1900
Guard mounting	2000
Fire party parade	2000
Staff Parade	2215
Lights out	2230

The following week saw a minor upheaval in routine. No. 4 Squadron was at only 50 per cent strength, and it was decided that this contingent should be merged with No. 3 Squadron. It was a blow to the cadets, who had now become used to the peculiarities of their officers and NCOs. Henry now found himself in 'C' Flight of No. 3 Squadron. He had moved from the Palace Hotel to the Ramleh Hotel, 'a ramshackle affair' but relatively clean, commandeered from William Adams, its peacetime proprietor, and was now billeted in a basement room, which was painted a sickly pink. 'Not too pleasant to wake up to,' he noted. The room was shared with nine other occupants, and he was less than impressed by the lack of washing facilities. The nearest basin at the top of the stairs had to be shared with another room, while the hotel seemed to have only two lavatories. 'My company in this room is physically clean – they seem OK that way and not too noisy, but of course their ideas on all subjects are very elementary.'[130]

Within a week, the introduction of tin basins would improve the situation, but, with only 2 baths to serve 175 hot and sticky airmen, conditions remained far from ideal. At least there was one compensation for being stationed in Paignton: Henry was able to send 1-lb pots of Devon cream to members of the family to enliven their otherwise rationed menus.

On Saturday, 13 July, Henry was given two more inoculations and watched as the syringes with large-bore needles were charged with what he estimated was about 1.5 cc of a very viscous liquid. That evening he went to see the 5.45 p.m. performance of *Ninotchka* (supported by *Think First*, from the *Crime Doesn't Pay* series) on its last day at the Regent Cinema. Greta Garbo and Melvyn Douglas starred in a story about a girl raised in the strict code of Soviet Russia who is sent to Paris on a government mission. There she falls in love with a French count and fails in her negotiations to sell the confiscated jewels of a Russian grand duchess. He thought it good, but not brilliant, and rounded off the evening drinking coffee with a fellow Etonian he had met as he left the cinema.

Spare time was in greater abundance now. Writing to his mother the following day, his arm still slightly stiff from the inoculation, he commented: 'I went for a long walk after church parade this morning and got out of the suburbs just in time to have about half a hour in what you could call country with a little imagination, providing you didn't look too closely through the hedges.'[131]

He had intended to hire a car to drive out further and eat a sandwich lunch, but found that all cars were booked, so had to return to town for lunch, contenting himself by spending the afternoon propped up on his bed writing home. His golf clubs would be useful, since he would be able to play on Saturday afternoons, as would his running shoes, 'without spikes . . . rubber soles with a deep tread pattern', just in case he should get the opportunity to run. It amused him greatly that, should anyone slacken during drill, the entire squad would be sent off to run around the parade ground. Now that his boots were broken in, such activity provided a welcome respite from the tension of drill!

Replying to his mother's request as to what he would like for his forthcoming birthday, Henry had no hesitation:

I should still like a small automatic pistol or revolver, as I have no rifle or even bayonet of my own. (I was issued with one but we have had to hand them in again – it was an awful old crock of a rifle anyway – not even a Lee Enfield pattern.) If the Germans arrive I couldn't do anything but throw stones at them. I know that getting a licence would not be easy, but I haven't got exactly a criminal record and feel that it might be done somehow. I expect I would be able to get the C.O.'s permission to keep one.

Sensing that this request might be viewed with some concern, he added: 'Please don't worry over this if you don't think it's practicable.'

In the event, although Norman Herbert offered his revolver, Henry decided that, since no one else had one, it would be best to decline. Thinking of a more suitable alternative, he suggested a cigarette case to go with his lighter.

Keeping up to date with events was not always easy. Newspapers were in short supply, as was the time to read them. Managing to obtain a copy recording the King's Birthday Honours List, Henry was pleased to see that his mother's cousin Charles (Air Vice-Marshal Charles Blount) had been made a CBE and her near neighbour, General Ismay of Wormington Grange, Broadway, a KCB.[132] His morale also had been boosted when he chanced upon a copy of the *Daily Telegraph* and discovered that 'Peterborough' had reprinted his appeal for House shirts.

News of friends and relatives was highly welcome, despite the risk of arousing nostalgia. His sister and brother-in-law were leaving their flat and moving nearer

to Gordon's new posting at Camberley. 'I'll be very sorry to feel that Tita and
G[ordon] are leaving their very comfortable flat – I'm afraid we'll all be sorry
from our own point of view as well as theirs – we had some very happy days there
together.'

Also valued were the copies of the *Eton Chronicle* sent by his mother, retaining his links with the college and occasionally updating him on the progress of
his contemporaries. 'Please write all the news, even the most unimportant things,
as it helps terrifically if I can keep a picture of everything that's going on at home
in my mind.'

In closing his letter of 14 July, he again reiterated his suggestion to his mother
that she should visit for his birthday at the end of the month:

> It would be grand if you could come here for the weekend of the 28th. There
> are some very good hotels in Torquay, which is only ten miles by bus, with a
> service every six minutes, and some (hotels) here which are quite good, and
> I'll investigate during the week and write. Can I take it that you'll be coming
> unless I hear to the contrary? There's quite a good service direct from
> Paddington and you could stay the Friday night with Tita if she isn't too busy
> preparing to move. I'll get Saturday late afternoon and evening off and most
> of Sunday.

One might imagine not only that Henry was eager to see his mother and catch up
on the latest news, but perhaps also that he felt that her seeing the hitherto unex-
perienced world of Service life might help her understand his future letters more
easily. Despite his obvious desire to encourage the visit, Henry's strong sense of
concern still came to the fore:

> If you do decide on the weekend of the 28th, be prepared for a line putting
> you off at the last minute as I may get wind of any attack in rather good time.
> Don't come if there is any indication of invasion – I don't know that you should
> really come at all – do consult Uncle Reg and Uncle Norman if he's available.

Henry's fears were unfounded, and his hopes realized. Until now his main contact with home had been by letter, but on Saturday, 20 July, he telephoned his
mother and discussed arrangements for her visit. Finding far less trouble in placing the call than he had imagined, he vowed to call her more regularly. The next
day he booked her a room in a neighbouring private hotel, the Balholm, in
Esplanade Road. Run by two elderly sisters, the Misses Slater, it had a traditional
pre-war, if not Edwardian, atmosphere.

Sitting on his bed that evening, with writing pad propped on upraised knees, Henry confirmed the arrangements in a letter to his mother, warning her of what to expect: 'It has the distinctive flavour of aspidistras, is run by an oldish lady who I didn't take to much, but it's absolutely next door and there isn't anything better by a long way in Paignton.'[133]

Outlining his plans for her visit, he suggested she might take the Saturday train arriving at 4.30 p.m. or, if she liked to arrive in the morning, they could lunch together from 12.30 until 2.00. He had engineered to swap duties and would be free from 5.30 p.m. until midnight and then they could have most of Sunday together from 10.15 a.m. until 10.00 p.m. A late Devonshire tea was suggested, hiring a car to drive out to Torquay to look up their relatives the Lucases. The evening might be spent at a show, rounded off with a late chat back at the Balholm.

Sunday could start with a shared eight o'clock breakfast (perhaps he was anticipating something a little better than the standard porridge and baked beans on toast given to the cadets?), and she would be able to attend the Wing Church Parade at nine, 'which I think you'd enjoy. We have it in a tent.' They would then have twelve hours together and could escape into the countryside, away from the seaside atmosphere, which was becoming rather too familiar for Henry. There were lovely little villages, though 'not a patch on any of ours of course at home'. Ever practical, he asked her to bring the RAC guide from his room at Fox Hill and a Michelin guide. These would be essential, since the removal of signposts to confuse invading Germans also effectively disoriented all but the locals.

The remainder of the letter concentrated on domestic and family matters. After a month in the RAF, he confided that he was really 'shaking down' with his companions and did not feel in the least bit lonely. The sense of companionship was heightened by the discovery of a considerable number of Old Etonians, not all contemporaries, but nevertheless a link with that which was secure and familiar. George Hardinge, ex-Hopgarden, was now in the RNVR and only 12 miles away at the Royal Naval College at Dartmouth, although getting leave to visit him might prove difficult.[134] Mrs Barker, his brother-in-law's mother, had promised to let her friends know of Henry's whereabouts and ask them to make contact. To facilitate all the writing he expected to do, Kelly, his childhood governess, had sent him a bottle of scarce Parker ink.

His mother had been busy actioning his requests for running shoes and golf clubs, although Henry felt that, with the little free time he had, he might send the latter back and concentrate on running, since it was better for training and keeping fit, and took less time. The wireless set had arrived, but was in need of a new battery.

He commiserated with his mother about having to hand in her saucepans, kept so brilliantly polished by Mrs Bond the housekeeper, as a contribution to Lord Beaverbrook's aluminium appeal. 'We will turn your pots and pans into Spitfires and Hurricanes', he had proclaimed, and Lady Reading, chief of the WVS, had broadcast to the nation's housewives earlier in the month: 'We can all have the thrill of thinking, as we hear the news of an epic battle in the air, perhaps it was MY saucepan that made part of that Hurricane.' Thousands of tons of material poured in – the WVS in the Torbay area collected 3 tons 15 cwt of metal. In reality, apart from boosting morale and contributing to national unity, the appeal was unnecessary. The aircraft and munitions factories had plenty of scrap aluminium, much unwittingly imported by the Germans in the form of Luftwaffe machines that failed to return. Henry seems to have sensed the futility of it all: 'I feel that appeal has been very badly managed.'

He ended: 'I'm longing for Saturday.' Then, as an urgent PS, he added a request for her to bring the flat black box and white leather case that contained his geometry instruments, together with his Morse key and buzzer.

As the end of the course neared, it brought with it the inevitable examinations. Henry's maths exam came on Tuesday, 23 July. All spare time was spent in revision, since any cadet failing to achieve the required standard would be suspended from the course, and this was known to be a not infrequent occurrence. Henry had no cause for concern. The following day saw an official visit by a group of senior officers from Nos 50 and 51 Groups, with a visit on the 26th from HRH Duke of Kent, in his capacity as Chief Welfare Officer for the RAF, after which Henry was free to look forward to his mother's arrival.

Her visit appears to have gone as planned. With a mother's reserve (and perhaps a little concern), Mrs Maudslay had decided against Henry's request for a firearm as a birthday gift and had settled for the cigarette case, purchased from Fortnum and Mason, with his name engraved inside in her own hand. Henry found it 'absolutely grand' and 'a joy to use'. A greetings telegram arrived from his sister – a bright design of a wicker basket of flowers, with ribbon and roses entwining round the handle, which framed the handwritten message:

920288 Aircraftsman [sic] Maudslay. Palace [sic] Hotel Paignton
Many Happy Returns today. Tita Gordon Annette.

His mother's presence had a practical side too. Henry took advantage of her needlework skills to have his coat altered. Invariably the weekend passed quickly, but she stayed on for a few days, providing her with an opportunity to see some aspects of her son's training. Writing home on 2 August, he confirmed: 'I was one of those drilling outside your hotel and could see you looking out of the window – how I longed to wave! The ones on the ground were receiving Morse signals from an Aldis signalling lamp.'

The course was progressing faster than Henry had anticipated and he believed that it would be over in about three weeks' time, after which he hoped to be with an operational squadron by November. Above all, an appointment to a commission would result in a new issue of clothing: 'What really matters is that if they give me what I want I'll have some comfortable clothes for the winter.' As with most airmen, the standard issue clothing never seemed to fit, despite modification by local tailors. His mother's needlecraft skills had had the desired results, and his coat now felt '100 times better'.

After a final inspection of the cadets by the AOC and an address by Mr (later Sir) Beverley Baxter, Conservative MP for Wood Green, on 15 August, Henry was promoted to leading aircraftman and officially completed his course the following day. The hoped-for commission and new uniform would have to wait, but at least it meant an increase in pay, and he was able to take forty-eight hours' leave and visit Fox Hill en route to the next stage of his training. So far he had not been near an aircraft, but things were about to change.

As the Battle of Britain reached its most critical stage in the skies over southeastern England, Henry was reclassified as being suitable for aircrew, remustered as 'Group 1' (single-engined training) and transferred for administrative purposes to No. 51 Group Pool, prior to being posted to the seemingly relatively peaceful skies of southern Yorkshire to commence flying training.

Chapter 5

. . . Ad Astra

Oh! I have slipped the surly bonds of earth
and danced the skies on laughter silvered wings;
Sunward I've climbed, and joined the tumbling mirth
Of sun-split clouds – and done a hundred things
You have not dreamed of – wheeled and soared and swung
High in the sunlit silence.
(Pilot Officer John Gillespie Magee, 'High Flight'[135])

Brough aerodrome lies south of the A63 Hull to Leeds road, to the west of Kingston upon Hull, sandwiched between the railway line and the northern shore of the Humber Estuary.[136] It was the home of the Blackburn Aircraft Company, which had established its factory on the site in 1916 to build both seaplanes and landplanes. During the interwar period the company had produced a range of types for both the RAF and Fleet Air Arm, and by 1940 it was producing the Skua fighter dive-bomber for the FAA and the Botha twin-engined general purpose bomber and reconnaissance aircraft.

Sharing the grass airfield was No. 4 Elementary Flying Training School (EFTS). Pre-war a number of civilian-operated flying schools had been employed to provide reserve RAF officer pilots with their initial training. Established in 1935 as No. 4 Elementary & Reserve Flying Training School, this had been operated at Brough by the North Sea Aerial & General Transport Company Ltd until April 1936, when the contract had transferred to Blackburn. The civilian instructors were carefully screened, and only those who were fully qualified were employed, and themselves subjected to periodic examination. The Central Flying School was responsible for passing recruits by means of travelling examination boards, which ensured the maintenance of high standards. With the outbreak of war, 'Reserve' was dropped from the title, and the civilian instructors were gradually replaced by RAF personnel. Originally under the control of No. 50 (Training) Group, in July 1940 it had transferred to become part of No. 51 Group.

Henry arrived on Monday, 19 August 1940, after a reasonable journey from Broadway via Birmingham. He was one of sixty airmen reporting for duty from No. 4 ITW who comprised the unit's Course No. 9. In keeping with wartime austerity, accommodation was spartan. There was nowhere to unpack his kitbag, no shelf, nor even hooks for his clothes, although there were promises that things might improve in about four weeks' time, when the preceding course moved on. Almost immediately any impressions that he had moved away from the war zone were quickly dispelled. That night the Luftwaffe mounted an attack on the Hull area. Although the only significant damage caused was well away in Bridlington, the enemy activity forced him to spend between 10.30 p.m. and 3.15 a.m. of his first night in an air-raid shelter.

The course had been structured originally to last ten weeks, but heavy losses incurred since May 1940 meant that the most able pilots were now being posted from EFTS to Operational Training Units (OTUs) after only fifty hours of flying. The tuition timetable was arranged to provide practical flight experience during the morning, followed by classroom tuition in the afternoon continuing the study of subjects from ITW in such matters as navigation, meteorology and mechanical aspects. There would be instructional films, a hangar tutorial to explain the aircraft's fuel system or a practical demonstration of compass swinging to evaluate and record compass deviation and an introduction to the Link Trainer.[137] The next morning would commence with more classroom studies, switching to flying in the afternoon, weather permitting. Physical fitness continued to be emphasized, with weekly organized games, daily PT, and drill practice twice a week. Flying was assessed continuously, with formal tests at each stage of the syllabus. Mid-term saw a written examination in ground subjects, failure in which could mean removal from the course.

On the second day, 20 August, Henry assembled with the other pupils of 'B' Flight to be issued with his flying kit and introduced to the instructors and the aircraft on which he was to be taught. The school was equipped with the RAF's standard *ab initio* trainer, the Tiger Moth, together with a number of Blackburn B.2 trainers, produced by the local company. The latter was a two-seat, single-engined biplane, powered by either a de Havilland Gipsy or the more powerful Cirrus engine, cruising at about 80 knots and stalling at half that speed. With a metal, stressed skin fuselage, metal-framed, fabric-covered wings and strong, forward-swept wide track undercarriage, it had docile flying characteristics and was well able to withstand the frequent punishment of heavy landings inflicted by novice pupils. Its most unconventional feature was the cockpit layout. Other RAF trainers had tandem seating, where the instructor sat behind the trainee, but the

B.2 had side-by-side accommodation. This made the aircraft rather wide in the beam, but produced a roomy and more intimate cockpit. Less attractive perhaps than the Tiger Moth, B.2s were rugged, forgiving machines, well liked by those who flew them.

Henry must have hoped that his instruction would have commenced with the Tiger Moth, for he expressed slight dismay when his instructor, Pilot Officer Frederick Hillman, took him for his initial air experience flight in Gypsy-engined B.2 G-ADFR. (The aircraft were camouflaged and carried RAF roundels, but retained their civil registrations, which reflected the school's origins.) This twenty-five-minute flight was designed to give the pupil his first taste of being airborne, familiarizing himself with the cockpit layout while the instructor did all the flying. The following day, in B.2 G-ACEM, Pilot Officer Hillman gave him his first taste of handling an aircraft.

After taking off and climbing to a safe height, Hillman demonstrated the basic controls, giving explanations through the Gosport tube intercom to Henry, who watched his instructor's actions and the effect they had on the aircraft's attitude. Henry was then allowed to hold the stick and effect slight climbs and dives, returning to straight and level flight using the ailerons to keep the wings level. A second session in B.2 L6892 (one of three purchased by the Air Ministry and fitted with the more powerful 135 hp Cirrus Major I engine, which noticeably improved performance) demonstrated the way speed picked up in the dive, and decreased in the climb, culminating in a stall if allowed to get too slow.

Three days later, Saturday, the 24th, with Sergeant Mansfield as instructor, Henry made two flights in G-ADFV to introduce him to the technique of taxiing the aircraft on the ground, which required particular skill and judgement, since the B.2 was not fitted with brakes. Sergeant Mansfield then took off, and they practised medium turns, experiencing the necessity to coordinate ailerons, rudder and elevators.

Now it was the weekend, and during the fine evening Henry was able to venture beyond the airfield boundaries, exploring on foot for three hours. He had spoken to his mother earlier in the week by phone, and she had sent him a bunch of white heather, possibly 'for luck'. On Sunday he wrote to keep her informed of his progress: 'The flying is quite satisfactory so far and I'm not worrying myself over that, although we are rather behind having been kept on the ground by bad weather quite a lot, nor should the navigation give much trouble but I'm not just a natural adept at Morse code.'[138] (His mother had recently sent him his Morse key and buzzer, together with the set of Linguaphone records, to enable off-duty practice.)

He was not particularly impressed by the standard of ground tuition: 'The instructor on all ground subjects is rather dim, and the instructors are ridiculously overworked, taking huge classes.'

Referring to his flights on the 24th:

> Flying is very tiring and I had one flight of 65 minutes yesterday doing
> various sorts of turns. The timekeeper had to enter it as two flights of 30 and
> 35 minutes as we are not supposed to train for more than half an hour at a
> time since one has to concentrate so hard. We do not fly cross country at this
> stage of training, so all my flying is confined to messing about in the vicinity
> of the aerodrome.

Stating that he was not going to mention any military subjects, he immediately
continued:

> We have two types of elementary trainer here, the Tiger Moth and the
> Blackburn B.2. The Moth is the best small biplane of its kind, Peter Pritchard
> trained on it. The B.2 is a local product, obsolete, slow and sluggish, with side
> by side seating (which is its only redeeming feature). It is far too easy to fly to
> be of any real use in my mind. Anyhow, for my sins I'm on the B.2. It's not
> very difficult and I don't get much satisfaction from flying it since I know
> that it's very easy.

To allay further any fears his mother may have about the dangers of flying, he
added: 'Still, if it's any consolation to you, the B.2 is so slow that the last two people
who spun into the ground in B.2s climbed out with nothing more than a few
bruises.'

While this was broadly true, Henry was relating a relatively minor event. On
21 August Pilot Officer Hillman, demonstrating forced landing procedure to
another student, had stalled during approach in rough weather. On 3 September
LAC J. Simmonds and his instructor Sergeant Gresser would overshoot on landing and run into the boundary hedge, again without injury. Meanwhile, enemy
activity was still causing disrupted nights.

> I didn't get my head on the pillow until 5 am this morning. . . . The war here
> is just an infernal nuisance, and that and the weather waste a lot of time. For
> myself I'm too tired to work much in off-duty time. I just sleep or go for a
> walk, which is the only exercise that I get since we only get our early morning
> P.T. if there has not been an air raid of more than one hour during the
> previous night. So far I have done P.T. once![139]

Henry saw little chance of getting home or seeing his mother again until the end of term, after the exams. The rail timetable to Birmingham did not correspond with the thirty hours' break he was allowed either Friday–Saturday, or Saturday–Sunday. At the best he would be able to reach Birmingham at 2 a.m., but would have to leave to return again at midday. He had investigated the possibility of making the journey by motorbike, but found that increasingly strict rationing limited him to an allowance of petrol for only 200 miles a month. Local air raids deterred him from inviting her to Brough, although it might be possible to meet at a hotel somewhere along the Great North Road. He recalled his father's remarks about the Ye Old Bell at Barnby Moor north-west of Newark – an old coaching inn with oak panelling, open fireplaces and diamond-pane windows. It seemed a good place, although Henry admitted that he had never been there himself.

Training continued on Monday, 26 August, once again with Pilot Officer Hillman in B.2 G-ACZH. The week's tuition concentrated on take-off and landing procedures. Perhaps as a measure to remind pupils that flying could have its dangerous moments, the syllabus now introduced 'Action in the Event of a Fire' and 'Abandoning Aircraft' – both subjects underlined in red in Henry's logbook. Pilot Officer Hillman was an experienced pilot and a good psychologist, and Henry was already expressing confidence in his tuition.

On Thursday they were up again, practising take-offs, turns and approaches in G-ACEO. Gliding approaches had been the previous order of the day, coming in with the throttle back and merely being content to return the aircraft to earth. Today saw powered approaches, using the throttle to pull the aircraft in, maintaining speed just above the stall. Practice continued the following day, and by the end of the month Henry had completed 5 hours 10 minutes dual instruction.

The weather improved at the beginning of September, allowing flying every day, including Sundays. Henry spent 1 September in G-ACEP continuing turns, take-offs and powered landings. After a disturbed night with an attack on Hull, 2 September started likewise, with the addition of instruction in spin recovery in G-ACEO. With its inherent stability and docile nature spinning, the B.2 required great determination. An earlier trainee at Brough wrote:

> the nose would rise to hover uncertainly above the horizon as the throttle was closed. Then with a kick on the rudder and the stick hard back the aircraft would swoon gently like a Victorian maiden, gyrating reluctantly. Recovery required no effort, even the thought of action, stick forward, opposite rudder, seemed sufficient and, left to its own devices, the B.2 could and would quite rapidly regain level flight and its normal prissy progress.[140]

Henry was unwise enough to comment that he thought spins were fun, prompt-ing Hillman to produce a particularly vicious example, but his pupil remained unperturbed.

Halfway through Monday, 2 September, his instructor was replaced by 'B' Flight commander, Flight Lieutenant Leonard Snelling, for an assessment test to ascer-tain whether he was ready to go solo. The test comprised just three circuits and landings, so there can have been very little that needed adjustment. After another couple of circuits with Pilot Officer Hillman, Henry was ready to go. Hillman taxied out into wind and, while Henry was engrossed in his pre-take-off cockpit checks, got out of the aircraft, leaving Henry alone in the wide cockpit with a strange, unfamiliar vacant right-hand seat. 'Go up and do a circuit, don't make a mess of it, and I'll be waiting for you here.' Taking off, Henry flew over the now familiar Blackburn factory buildings and the cement works with its 200-foot high chimneys. Ten minutes later, he brought G-ACEO in for his first solo landing.

That evening Henry sent his mother the good news. 'I went solo today for the first time after about 7 hours dual, which isn't too bad. Landings gave some trouble at first, but that is not unusual! . . . You'll be glad to know that my instruc-tor told me that the landing. . . was a "peach".'[141]

As if to emphasize the speed at which progress was being made, the same day that Henry was writing to tell of his initial solo flight, the next consignment of sixty airmen were arriving at Brough to commence Course No. 10.

The anticipated change of billet had occurred. As a result of the number of night raids being mounted, and a desire to disperse accommodation, on 28 August the authorities had obtained local billets for thirty-eight airmen. Henry found him-self residing with Mrs Len Johnson of Elloughton and her sister. Fearing showers of incendiary bombs, both ladies slept downstairs, donating their two double beds upstairs to their billetees. Henry noted that neither his hosts, nor the RAF, were ones for squandering opportunities:

> As they are paid per man. . . yes. . . 4 men to 2 beds. Selected alphabetically. The beds are colossal in depth and by no means too wide and things would be easier if my companion was not one of those who think pyjamas unnecessary – after all, they do stop the smell! Don't worry about my billeting – you must take it as a joke, which is the only possible way for me to take it.[142]

As if to emphasize his light-hearted attitude to his present situation, he added a PS in the left-hand margin: 'I eat my peas with honey. I've done it all my life. It makes the peas taste funny, but it keeps them on the knife.'[143]

Now that he had flown solo, Henry's training now took on a new tempo. On

3 September he took off with Pilot Officer Hillman and practised take-offs, turns and glide approaches and landings in G-ACEO. The instructor then got out and Henry went solo again to repeat the exercise. Satisfied, Hillman took him up again to demonstrate steep turns and climbing turns requiring the simultaneous use of rudder, aileron and elevator, and side slipping – losing height rapidly in a short distance, using opposite aileron and rudder. Nearly an hour was spent demonstrating these more complex manoeuvres. After lunch, it was back into the air again to repeat the morning's first two flights, bringing the day's total flying time to two and a half hours.

The next day Henry experienced his first exercise in the Link Trainer, a twenty-five-minute familiarization 'flight'. That afternoon, as Hillman led Henry out to the aircraft, they headed not for the B.2 but towards Tiger Moth N7115. With Henry in the rear seat, the previous day's exercises were repeated, Hillman's initial demonstration including the less sedate spin characteristics of this aircraft. After each dual session, Henry would take off solo to practise recent advice. On the 5th they moved on to steep and climbing turns and side-slips in N9321, reiterating the procedures learned on the B.2 and sensing the differences between the two aircraft. For the first time Henry was instructed to include spin recovery in his solo routine. A half-hour exercise on the Link Trainer consolidating straight and level flying at various speeds and on various courses completed the day's activity.

It was usual for pupils to retain the same instructor for the entire course, but on 6 September Pilot Officer Hillman transferred to the other flight. He was replaced for the remainder of training by Pilot Officer Jackson, a middle-aged, quietly spoken man to whom Henry took an immediate liking. After dual and solo flights to enable the new instructor to assess his pupil, they flew Moth R4972 to the allotted area to practise the rudiments of low flying. The next day introduced Henry to holding a compass course and instrument flying, with the canvas hood pulled over N6527's rear cockpit, blacking out any visual reference to the outside world and putting into practice experience gained on the Link Trainer during ground instruction. It was not easy; neither the aircraft nor the Link Trainers were equipped with a gyro horizon, and orientation was only by means of the turn and slip indicator, rev counter and airspeed indicator.

The country was now in a heightened state of readiness for the anticipated German invasion. On Saturday, 7 September, it was reported that Luftwaffe bombers were converging on airfields in the Pas-de-Calais, from which they took off to mount large incendiary attacks on the London Docks. Barges and other small vessels were congregating in French ports. At 8 p.m. that evening Home Forces Headquarters issued the codeword 'CROMWELL'. Its purpose was to signify that conditions were suitable for a German invasion and place the Home

Guard on the alert, at action stations. However, in many places it was misinter-
preted as meaning that the invasion had actually begun. Church bells were rung
in several localities and road blocks appeared, making travel even more difficult.
Home Guards crept about the hedgerows with armed rifles and the Tiger Moths
of Training Command were fitted with light bomb racks hastily improvised for
such an occasion. When the Germans landed, instructors, including presumably
those at Brough, should they be within range of the enemy beachheads, were to
take off and execute Operation *Banquet Light*, attacking the invader with anti-
personnel bombs. Regardless of the situation, training continued, with another
half-hour of Link Trainer instruction concentrating on climbing and gliding at
various speeds. In the evening Henry and a friend ventured into Hull with the
intention of seeing a performance by the local New Theatre Repertory Company
of Frank Vosper's thriller *Love from a Stranger*. Arriving too late, they settled for
supper, during which Henry was surprised to hear a call for a Lieutenant Martell,
whom he assumed to be the son of his Uncle Norman's commanding officer,
General Martell.[144]

   Notwithstanding the confusion of the previous night and taking advantage of
a day off, Henry breakfasted late on the following Sunday, spending most of the
morning in the bath and going for a walk in the afternoon. In a spare moment
before lunch he took the opportunity to update his mother on progress:

> The flying is great, and I'm enjoying it tremendously – at last I have been
> getting enough time in the air to make real progress and the mid-term exam,
> which I'm in the middle of now seems to be going as well as I can hope . . .
> I have now done about 10 hours dual and 3 hours solo. In answer to your
> questions, from now on I fly both dual and solo, but when solo, I am under
> my instructor's direct orders.
>
>   I have changed from B.2s to Tiger Moths, much lighter and more sensitive
> machines and a real joy to fly. They are reputed to be difficult to land, but
> I have not found any difficulty and enjoy flying them tremendously.
>
>   I can now do spins, sideslips, steep turns and steep gliding turns also
> climbing turns, so that apart from fine aerobatics the situation is pretty well
> in hand. I have also done some low flying between 100 and 200 feet with my
> new instructor. This is not allowed solo so you need not worry! Whenever
> possible I always fly at about 4,000 to 4,500 feet for my ordinary solo practices,
> which is a very safe height and one can get a very reliable cloud 'horizon' to
> practise on.[145]

The next few days were spent consolidating his flying experience and adding precautionary and forced landings to his repertoire. He was now allowed to fly limited cross-country circular tours planned by his instructor. The increased work-load had reduced time off to one day a week, just enough to do the laundry and catch up on outstanding correspondence. A letter from J. S. Herbert, his old tutor, had informed about contemporaries, including his ex-Captain of House, Geoffrey Jameson, now serving with the King's Own Yorkshire Light Infantry and possibly stationed near to Brough. Peter Wake, currently working in a logging camp in Canada, had written to say that he would shortly be returning to the UK to enlist in the Army. Henry was also making contacts locally, accepting an invitation from Mrs Byrom of Everthorpe Hall to take tea with her on 8 September.[146]

On Tuesday, 10 September, routine was disrupted by an official visit by the Inspector General of the RAF, Air Marshal Sir William-Mitchell, who saw an anti-gas parade and reviewed the school. Training both in the air and synthetic was now concentrating on various configurations of turn. The following day, as if to emphasize the importance of this, LAC Harry Taylor, a member of Henry's course, was seriously injured in an accident to B.2 G-ACER. During a gliding approach, the pilot had allowed the speed to drop and attempted a turn without opening the throttle. The aircraft stalled and spun in. Taylor died a day later in Hull Royal Infirmary. The superstitious might have noted that he had completed a total of thirteen hours' flying. Not wishing to cause his mother undue concern, Henry did not report the incident in letters to Fox Hill. On the 13th a further inspection was the order of the day, as the school received a visit from members of the Central Flying School.

Shortly after starting a letter to his mother on the 14th, the sirens sounded, compelling Henry to take shelter and complete his writing the next day. This time Humberside escaped the attentions of the Luftwaffe, who flew on to attack Bootle and Preston. Meanwhile even the local press was offering advice as to how best to deal with the disruption created by the nightly air-raid alerts:

> a good idea is to plug the ears with cotton wool and try to forget that there is any such thing as air raids. . . . If there is any great activity overhead [you] will still be able to hear it and take cover. . . . This will save [you] many hours of sleeplessness and enable [you] to face each day's raids without feeling tired and fatigued.[147]

Recent letters from his mother had focused his thoughts on family matters. A letter from his grandmother, living with his mother at Fox Hill, had hinted that Mrs Maudslay was still working hard to maintain their home. In earlier letters she had discussed moving to a smaller property. A likely house had been seen in Broadway, but it was unlikely that Fox Hill would sell. The chances of effecting a move seemed to become more remote with the effects of the war intensifying each week. 'It looks as though we are booked for a very uncomfortable autumn. I only hope to get trained to be some use.'

His recommendation to his mother was that their home should become a permanent family hotel but he urged her not to overwork. 'Whoever can should take every opportunity to relax and keep mentally calm and quiet.'[148]

News of Kelly, the family governess and nanny, also gave him cause for concern. She was now suffering intermittent discomfort from a gall bladder condition and living in retirement alone in a London flat at 127 Gordon Court, Du Cane Road, Shepherd's Bush. The Luftwaffe was now beginning to switch its attention to the civilian population, and for nearly a month had been mounting small-scale attacks against the capital:

It's not much of my business but I must say that with her physical condition I believe that one should try to get her into the country – some sort of Red Cross or canteen work would have to be the excuse, which one would have to put very tactfully as Kelly is the last person to run away from anything, but if she could help in Willersey in evacuation and Red Cross dressings and so forth, so much the better.[149]

His sister and her husband were now out of London and establishing themselves in Camberley, having enjoyed six days' leave spent shooting at Shinness, accompanied by Sutherland, the Keeper, and Donald, the Labrador. Meanwhile, their young daughter, Annette, now some eighteen months old, was staying with Mrs Maudslay, who had recruited a nanny to help look after her.

Already the weather was beginning to become distinctly autumnal at Brough.

I shall wear my RAF winter underclothes soon to save my own! However the pants are about the same size as the ones you and Mrs Arkwright made for the Finns, so I may have to send for my own pants. . . . The RAF supply me with a 'comforter' which is very good in its way, but very short – so if anyone has any time a scarf in RAF blue would make a big difference to life. Also, if this would be possible, a polo neck sweater. I've only found one polo neck that ever fitted me, that's the green one you will find in my room, the ordinary patterns don't seem to fit me. Both of these would really be business, but don't dream of doing anything about them if you are busy as I won't be flying at high altitudes till I get onto the next course.

By now Henry had moved to a new billet. His various experiences prompted him to advise his mother on the required approach should she find herself required to house wartime guests.[150] He had never found them all together yet:

1. Comfortable bed with plenty of spare blankets. (Terrible when one's opportunity of a comfortable night is spoilt by cold.)
2. Ample facilities for washing – hot water, and if you can provide, soap, towels too it makes things much easier.
3. Mirror with a good light for shaving.
4. Somewhere to store clothes, and a few coat hangers of the sort that take trousers as well.
5. Cocoa and a light supper at night, and tea and digestive biscuits in the morning. (By tea and cocoa I mean a good big mug and more in the pot.)

In his view, making billetees comfortable and welcome would encourage them to return at reasonable and convenient times, rather than staying out until all hours. His current billet also required that he should enter and leave by the back door. 'Not that it bothers me or anyone else, but it's the wrong attitude.'

While he was continuing to practise the basics, now extended to restarting the engine in flight and taking off and landing out of wind, Pilot Officer Jackson gave Henry his first taste of aerobatics (or acrobatics as Henry recorded in his logbook) in N9175 on 16 September. On Tuesday, the 24th, after further practice, both solo and dual, there was a twenty-five-minute general progress test in N9175, with Flight Lieutenant Welsh as the examiner, checking Henry's adherence to procedures and confidence in handling the aircraft. Again, there was no cause for concern, and he was cleared to continue. That afternoon he and Jackson took N9175 on a forty-minute cross-country. Remarkably, this appears to have been the only major flight away from the confines of the aerodrome. The remainder of the month was spent refining technique in the air and completing test assessments on the Link Trainer. On 27 September, after a mere five weeks' instruction, the course was over. Of the original sixty pupils, forty-seven had made the grade. S. J. Woolley, Link Trainer Instructor at No. 4 EFTS, confirmed that after five hours of instruction Henry had satisfactorily completed the Elementary Link Trainer Syllabus with a rating of 'Average'. With actual flying hours totalling 21.05 dual (3.15 under the hood on instruments) and 20.15 solo, Flight Lieutenant Snelling appended his signature to the large rubber stamp in Henry's logbook. As a pilot, Henry was assessed as 'Above average', with no special faults requiring attention. It was a glowing report and yet another example of Henry's determination to try his hardest in everything he undertook.

There was little time for celebration. The next day he was posted to Tern Hill in Shropshire, to continue his training on twin-engined aircraft along with twelve others from the course. He had always hoped that there would be the opportunity of leave between postings, but it was not to be. Anxious to notify the family, he sent his mother the brief telegram: 'Posted today Saturday. Wiring address on arrival. Many thanks socks. No leave at present. Love Henry.'

Whether Henry volunteered for bombers, or the choice was dictated, is not known. With a background that clearly demonstrated his ability as a team leader, it would not have been a difficult decision.

Chapter 6

Legion of the Lost

There's chaps from the town and the field and the till and the cart,
And many to count are the stalwart, and many the brave,
And many the handsome of face and the handsome of heart,
And few that will carry their looks or their truth to the grave.
(A. E. Housman, 'A Shropshire Lad', XXIII)

Situated on the A41, approximately 1 mile south of its junction with the A53, some 2 miles west-south-west of the town of Market Drayton, RAF Tern Hill is an attractive station. It had been an airfield during the First World War and was redeveloped in 1936, with permanent, neo-Georgian administration buildings ranged on a wooded hillside overlooking the main flying field. Three hangars on the main site were supplemented by three more on the south side of the airfield. As if these were not enough, three dispersal sites had two smaller hangars apiece. By late summer 1940 it was home to No. 24 Maintenance Unit, and every day a detachment of Spitfires would arrive from No. 611 Squadron to assist in the defence of the industrial north-west, replaced at night by a detachment of two Blenheims from No. 29 Squadron. Also in residence was No. 10 Service Flying Training School, equipped with twin-engined Avro Anson trainers. It was to this latter unit that Henry was posted, as part of No. 26 Course, arriving on Saturday, 28 September 1940.[151]

Accommodation for trainees in 4 Room, A Block, was very spartan: 'A barrack room which is one huge refrigerator.' Some things had improved: he now had a locker for his possessions, and the food was rather better. Clothing was still a problem. His uniform, tight at the best of times, was now almost impossible with thick underclothes and a sweater underneath.[152] The latter were obviously essential, since within two days he had written to ask his mother to send further thick underwear and a big blue sweater from home. If someone could knit a thin, sleeveless V-neck sweater, this also would be appreciated. He had ordered a new uniform from a local tailor in Market Drayton (cost £5) together with four new Viyella shirts.

Life was made more tolerable by his fellow pupils, some of whom had been with him at Brough, others joining from other Elementary Flying Training Schools: 'The most congenial set of companions I have met.' Senior cadet and the cadre's leader was Michael Foulis,[153] assisted by Lucian Ercolani, son of the founder of the Ercol Furniture Company, who had joined the intake from No. 10 EFTS Weston-super-Mare. Henry soon established a rapport with the latter, finding him to be a keen oarsman who had captained his House at Oundle. Another with whom Henry was to strike up a friendship was Ralph Allsebrook, son of a leading north of England county court circuit judge, who had recently completed a degree in Modern History from Trinity College, Oxford, forfeiting a fourth year at university to read Law in order to join the RAF.

Henry's initial impressions of the instructors were good too, as they took him through the initial tasks so that he could familiarize himself with the larger and more powerful aircraft he would now be flying as a Group II trainee, destined for twin-engined aircraft. The Avro Anson was a low-wing monoplane. Powered by two Armstrong Siddeley Cheetah engines, it cruised at about 185 mph and could carry a crew of six, being used for a range of aircrew training purposes, as well as coastal reconnaissance and ferrying. It was another forgiving aircraft, with easy flying characteristics, but at 42 feet long and with a wingspan of 56 feet, weighing in at 5,375lb, it was considerably larger and more demanding than the Tiger Moth.

The British and Commonwealth Air Training Plan was now beginning to be implemented, whereby aircrew under training, and indeed complete training units, would be sent to the Dominions for initial instruction well away from the crowded and dangerous skies of the British Isles. Within a day or so of arrival, the course learned that members of No. 10 Service Flying Training School would soon be sent to continue their training in Canada. Henry may have told his mother when he phoned her shortly after his arrival. Conscious of the security implications, his letter of 30 September cautioned her: 'You must not say when or where I am going and never mention it in conjunction with the name of this station. (You may just say that I am likely to go overseas, but don't if you can avoid it.)'

The thought of going overseas to continue his training aroused the old sense of frustration: 'I loathe the idea of leaving this country now and it seems such a waste of time, the double journey.' His impatience may not have been helped by the knowledge that his old school friend Tim Vigors had now destroyed six enemy aircraft and possibly four more, and had been awarded the Distinguished Flying Cross.

The day started early at 0800. There was an hour for lunch at 1230, then work resumed until 1630, when an hour was allowed for an evening meal, before the day's final session, finishing at 1930. Flying was limited to no more than five hours in every twenty-four, and time in the air was accompanied by yet more ground instruction, with lectures lasting forty minutes, followed by ten minutes for questions. There were fifteen minutes of PT and aircraft recognition each day and two half-hour periods of drill per week, with an afternoon of organized games.

Flying training commenced on 1 October, and at 1145 that morning Sergeant Gilbert took Henry up in Anson N5330 for a forty-five-minute familiarization flight to cover both ground handling and flying characteristics, together with safety procedures. Among the new features to remember were a retractable undercarriage and hydraulic flaps. The undercarriage was manually operated by a chain-driven screw gear requiring 140 turns cranked by a reluctant passenger. Two days later the lesson was repeated, this time including action to be taken in the event of fire. Single-engined flying was demonstrated on Saturday, 5 October, the Anson maintaining height at 85 mph with a light load and full throttle on the live engine. After the engine had been restarted, a demonstration of low flying was given.

Flights were made on 7, 8 and 10 October with Sergeant Reid, and, after 6 hours 35 minutes dual instruction, a 25-minute test was taken in N9911, with Flying Officer David Fearon as examiner, confirming Henry's ability to fly the Anson solo. This was followed after lunch by solo circuits and landings for three-quarters of an hour, during which he gained essential experience and confidence. The Anson was a very manoeuvrable and yet stable aircraft, but rather heavy on the controls in a climb or dive, requiring frequent use of the trimming handle.

Next came instrument flying, under the guidance of Sergeant Gilbert, combined with routine circuits, until the month's activity was curtailed on the 13th after a map-reading exercise with Sergeant Gilbert, bringing Henry's total time for flying the Anson to 10 hours 25 minutes. Although he was unaware of it at the time, this would be the last occasion that he was to fly in the UK for over five months. Now, for the time being, course members were to be granted leave, a wise move in the eyes of many. Saturday, 12 October, had been disrupted with an 'Alert' and at 0720 four days later a lone Junkers 88 dropped four high-explosive and six incendiary bombs on the airfield, causing a fire in one hangar and injuring six.[154] Two of No. 29 Squadron's Blenheims and twenty training aircraft were destroyed or badly damaged.

There was to be a further 'Alert' on the 19th, not that this concerned Henry. He was at Fox Hill for the weekend, paying a visit to his dentist, Mr Shovelton in Evesham,[155] on the Saturday morning for a routine check-up. Arriving home, he found a new bicycle waiting for him, a present from his mother. During this time he sought opportunities to try out his camera, taking various photographs of the countryside around Fox Hill and others of the family, including some indoor ones of Annette, despite his reservations about the light being too poor. There was an added bonus. His old governess Kelly had travelled to Fox Hill. He had intended to travel down to London by train on the 21st, to see family friend and solicitor Eric Ellis, and his wife, Mary, before journeying to Camberley to see Tita and Gordon, then on to Eton for the Steeplechase on the 22nd, looking up John Hills at Pangbourne, near Reading. Unfortunately the break was all too short and he was unable to fulfil his plans.

Leaving the film with his mother to arrange processing, he was back at Tern Hill by 22 October. After a lift to Worcester from his mother and Uncle Norman, he caught the train to Kidderminster. Waiting for the train to Shropshire he had a chance to purchase a fitment for his camera case, and then travelled the remainder of the journey with Sergeant Laurance 'Lance' Forty, who had been spending leave with his parents in Kidderminster. Six years older than Henry, Forty was a keen sportsman who had played several seasons with Kidderminster Rugby Football Team and whose father was managing director of a local engineering company.[156]

Arriving back at camp, they found that the first echelon had departed for their port of embarkation the previous day, but their own departure had been delayed, and the main body of the course was forced to wait, kicking its heels until the situation was resolved. Henry wrote to suggest that his mother might like to come up and visit him: '[It] will be very lovely up here if you could come for the weekend. I don't expect I'll have much opportunity to find a place for you to put up, but if you could find a place within bicycle range of the station and could come up with the two bikes it would be perfect.'

It was probably during this period of anticipation that Henry learned of the death of his mother's cousin. Air Vice-Marshal Charles Blount had been killed on Wednesday, 23 October 1940, aged 46, when the aircraft in which he was travelling as a passenger crashed shortly after take-off.[157] His early and untimely death was felt deeply and gave Henry cause to reflect on the fact that the elder of Charles's two sons, John, himself serving in the RAF, had been a strong influence on his own decision to join the Service.

Henry grew more despairing of the time he was wasting while the authorities and slow-moving organization decided what was to become of them. He wrote home on Wednesday, 30 October, his letter commencing 'Address as usual!':

There is no change in any situation at the moment, and I have the awful prospect of wasting about twice as much time again as I have already been forced to waste before I can get on with the job.

    The whole thing is disgusting and disheartening. I could do more work as an ordinary civilian to help the war effort and by the time the Air Ministry have finished with our particular legion of the lost I'll have grey hair and senile decay. . .

Pausing for a little self-analysis and reassessment he added:

This sounds too much like self pity I'm afraid which is a bad thing and demoralising, but how can anyone be expected to fight for a country which treats volunteers of under military age like this, God knows.

    . . . Don't think I'm miserable about the RAF – it hasn't got me down but it has continuously got on the wrong side of my temper, for the first time in my life I've acquired a permanent hate! It ought to be directed against Adolf but it is misfired by RAF administration.

Eton had instilled the qualities of independence, team spirit and leadership. Perhaps with a degree of tongue in cheek, or youthful confidence: 'I can quite see that I shall be compelled at a later date to organise the whole show myself.'

    Nevertheless, optimism remained, and Henry must still have thought his posting might be imminent, as he told his mother that she might not hear from him again for a long time. Already his mind had moved forward and he had begun to give consideration to the situation he might find overseas. He knew that a large number of children had been evacuated to Canada and had heard that conditions for them were not always easy, despite considerable hospitality from Canadian families. His thoughts were coloured by memories of the Eton Mission and the Anglo-Canadian links of his tutor, whose wife and children were now in Canada.[158] Perhaps there might be a way of helping her while he was over there?

It's difficult for British evacuees to exist in Canada as they are allowed no money at all. The forces can however always arrange to draw from accounts in this country. I hope to help Lady Rosemary Hills in this way for my Tutor and so may need some extra money in my Eton account.

Lest his mother should think he was being overambitious and idealistic, he added: 'I will be very careful with this, as I hope you will be!'

    Time hung heavily. The following day he wrote again, apologizing for letting off steam in his previous communication. The letter was headed 'Still waiting'. There was little news, and much of Henry's time was spent reading books, a habit he was cultivating to alleviate periods of inactivity, and the various letters from family and friends forwarded by his mother via Fox Hill: 'I managed to get about 8 Penguins including *Pekon Picnic, The Miracle of Peille,* some tripe by Stephen Leacock and others which should not be too bad. . .'

With his forthcoming overseas posting in mind he instructed:

All letters to me in the future MUST have your name and address on the back of the envelope and if you can bear the expense of the extra stamps it would be safer to forward stuff on under fresh cover, with the address written on very carefully and correctly. Please don't send anything that can't be repeated until I give you a definite address.

In the meantime his letters should be addressed to

920288 LAC H. E. Maudslay
10 S.F.T.S. RAF
c/o RCAF Headquarters
OTTAWA
CANADA.

Broaching the subject for the first time, he revealed that he had been giving thought to the dangers of the Atlantic crossing: 'I don't like being morbid but it's as well to face facts so I'm enclosing some suggestions for what to do with some of my things if we get torpedoed or otherwise dealt with.'

There was also thinly veiled concern at the remoteness of his likely destination:

I wonder if you could send on your old copies of Punch . . . also the Weekly Times if it could be managed and an occasional Field or Sporting & Dramatic. One feels badly enough isolated as it is and those particular papers are probably the most comprehensive in supplying the things one misses.

He went on to regret that Eton had ceased to forward his subscription to *Aeronautics,* suggesting that his mother should seek to obtain the back numbers required to bring up to date those that he had already collected. 'They are well worth binding as a history of the war in the air.'

For the first time his letter had drawn the active attention of the censor. After a comment that he expected the journey to be very uncomfortable, Examiner 4980's scissors had been at work to remove one and a half lines from a paragraph that possibly let slip his likely port of embarkation or length of journey. In doing so the censor also removed the title of a 'superior news letter' circulated by the Imperial Policy Group and recommended to his mother by Henry that was written on the reverse of the sheet.

Chapter 7

Chronicles of Wasted Time

There is a tide in the affairs of men,
Which, taken at the flood, leads onto fortune;
Omitted, all the voyage of their life
Is bound in the shallows and in miseries.
On such a sea we are now afloat
And we must take the current when it serves.
Or lose our ventures.
(William Shakespeare, *Julius Caesar*, Act 4, Scene 3, 218–224)

Henry and his companions left Tern Hill at the end of October 1940[159] to begin the next stage of their Air Force career. Those selected to transfer to Canada for training were initially despatched to an Embarkation Unit for a brief period prior to being transported to their port of departure. Embarkation Units, or more correctly Personnel Despatch Centres (PDCs), such as that at Wilmslow, were renowned for their sparseness, mediocre food and lack of cleanliness. Mercifully most found their time spent there was short.

After a week or so the detachment was transferred to Liverpool for embarkation. Despite the wartime austerity, conditions were not as bad as anticipated. Henry had half expected that they would make the crossing in a cattle ship. Instead the contingent were embarked aboard a large twin-funnelled liner, her dull camouflage indicative of her change of circumstances. The 20,022 grt (gross registered tons) HMT *Duchess of Richmond* was one of the vessels belonging to Canadian Pacific Steamships Ltd, which in early 1940 had been pressed into war service.[160] Only a few days earlier, during 26/27 October, Canadian Pacific's flagship, the 42,348-ton *Empress of Britain*, had been lost. On her final approach to Liverpool from Suez, she had been bombed and set on fire. Subsequently taken under tow, she was then torpedoed and sunk, with the loss of 45 of her complement of 643. This was a time of considerable U-boat activity, and during the months of October and November losses amounted to 136 vessels, totalling some 605,000 grt.

Recently, in three days alone (18–20 October) thirty-two vessels had been lost when two eastbound convoys, SC7 and HX79, had been intercepted by nine U-boats.

Two months earlier the *Duchess of Richmond* had completed a transatlantic crossing carrying Professors Tizard and Cockroft, the government's foremost scientific advisers, together with a number of military scientific developments, including the highly secret cavity magnetron that was to revolutionize the development of radar. Compared to later troopships, the *Duchess* took on board only a moderate number of personnel. Her seven decks had been configured originally to accommodate some 1,566 passengers in three classes, but now the average load for a wartime westbound passage was only half that number, the extra space being given over to cargo.[161] Once aboard, Henry was surprised at the relative comfort of his quarters, a converted state cabin that he shared with three others, making the journey 'absurdly comfortable'. Indeed, the *Duchess* still retained a degree of her peacetime ambience. His initial reaction was that circumstances would soon change. Writing on a Canadian Pacific letter card, dated Sunday, 3 November 1940, (inspected by Examiner 422), he confided to his mother: 'Very little to say except that the quarters are better than I had expected – whether or not things will get less comfortable later on I do not know – but expect that we, the untouchables, will soon be segregated from the main body of passengers!'

The vessel slipped her moorings at 4 p.m. on Friday, 1 November, escorted by the destroyers *Harvester* and *Hurricane*, to join other vessels proceeding from Avonmouth as part of Convoy WS4.[162] The passage was smooth, with beautiful, clear mornings and evenings: 'Several days might have been May.' He was fortunate. To their crews the Canadian Pacific's Duchess Class were known as 'Drunkards', owing to their propensity for rolling in rough weather. A routine was soon established, with emphatic instructions over the loudspeakers: 'Always carry lifejackets'; 'Always carry a full waterbottle'; 'Always lock portholes when the blackout signal sounds'; 'No smoking on deck at night'; 'Never shut cabin doors in case they jam in an explosion'. After tea only the minimum essential lights were permitted. All had to be in bed by 2145, but some, including Lucian Ercolani, preferred to sleep on deck, in contravention of regulations. After rising at 0600 and taking porridge for breakfast at 0715, routine cleaning was followed by a daily parade and general inspection at 1000. A snap inspection held on 4 November had revealed a lowering of standards: beard stubble, dirty boots and buttons, lack of ties and other misdemeanours prejudicial to military efficiency.

On 2 November, as the *Duchess* sailed north, those on deck could see the Scottish hills to starboard and Ireland to port as they met up with other vessels from the Clyde, joining the convoy off Orsay. During the afternoon the sea conditions deteriorated and a number of cadets suffered from severe seasickness, though Henry seems to have been unaffected. The *Duchess* was making about 12 knots, sailing in the starboard rear position (44) of the convoy of seventeen vessels and Royal Naval escort, paid an occasional visit by a patrolling Short Sunderland flying boat. However, on 5 November, the *Duchess* separated from the convoy, now sailing faster as an independent, taking a northern course as she zigzagged her way to avoid lurking U-boats. Towards late afternoon she was some 1,000 miles east of Newfoundland when star shells and shell bursts accompanied by smoke were seen over the horizon. About 20 miles to the north the German pocket battleship *Admiral Scheer* was attacking Convoy HX84, eastbound from Halifax. Although the *Duchess* picked up an SOS from the stricken Canadian Pacific merchantman *Beaverford* as she fought a gallant but losing engagement with the enemy, the lone liner was in no position to offer assistance. The *Duchess* master, Captain William Brown, had little option but to rely on her superior speed, in excess of 15 knots, to take her away from the scene of the battle. That night, still fearing the German raider's presence, all were advised to remain dressed.[163]

Regular meals were taken in a salon deep in the innards of the ship. There were frequent boat drills and parades with lifebelts, PT for an hour every alternate day and other forms of exercise. Despite this activity, a degree of boredom was inevitable, broken by letter writing, card games and reading. A Polish officer practised classical pieces on a grand piano in one of the first-class saloons. Airmen, crew and the few other passengers put on a variety show on 6 November; a young Scottish girl, resplendent in kilt, played a piano repertoire of Scottish melodies and sang traditional songs, with the airmen soon joining in with gusto. The following day found the *Duchess* proceeding cautiously through poor visibility, while down in the ballroom, against a background of the ship's foghorn, Joseph T. Thorson, the Canadian Minister of War Services, gave a talk on the geography and history of Canada. Another concert followed that evening. Henry was delighted to discover that the vessel had a well-stocked library, which enabled him to get through some fifteen slim Penguin volumes in the ten days before they reached their destination.

The distant coast of Newfoundland was sighted on 8 November as they approached the Gulf of St Lawrence. The following day they entered the St Lawrence Seaway and navigated inland, providing an impressive sight for those along the waterway. With a length of 600 feet and 75 feet beam, the *Duchess* was one of the largest liners to travel the full route to Montreal. The journey now held more interest for the observer, with wonderful views of the countryside stretching along each bank, the lakes and the wildlife, the trees in their late autumn colours with the darker greens of the spruce and the mountains beyond – inspiring thoughts of earlier family holidays in Scotland and making Henry regret that he did not have his brother's cine camera to capture the scene in colour.

Henry penned his first Canadian observations home. Realizing that the letter would not reach his mother in time for her birthday on 14 November, he intended to send another cable with appropriate greetings, while a birthday present and other souvenirs would be posted as soon as possible. Security prevented him from giving any details about the trip (and had prohibited the use of his camera so far), except to say that they were progressing to Quebec – that 'is only just half way to our final destination'. His most striking impression of Canada so far was the temperature. Comparing it to his pre-war skiing holiday, he commented: 'I'm very well, but will be confronted by the most frightful cold – Switzerland is said to be nothing to this place.'[164]

The trip was still something of an adventure, retaining much of the feel of a continental holiday to visit old friends. Henry had thought of cabling Peter Wake, currently out in Quebec Province, inviting him to drive down to visit the boat for a few hours. A glance at the map brought home the vastness of the new country. 'Distances certainly mean something here', he wrote on discovering that Peter's address was over 400 miles away.[165] Regretting that he did not have the address of Alec 'Oaty' Gibb, Mary's younger brother who was at school in Montreal, he decided that he might still seek out Lady Rosemary Hills.

Communication with home was difficult, and he had heard nothing from England nor news of the war's progress since his departure. The deficit stirred an emotional homesickness and fuelled a desire to return quickly to England. 'I'll apply for a transfer to two engined training as soon as I get the opportunity, but if it means wasting time I shall train on singles and transfer if poss when at an OTU.'

Quite what his mother made of this first letter when it arrived at Fox Hill is not known, but the joy of hearing from her son must have been tempered with amazement at the envelope. Shortage of high denomination-postage stamps necessitated the application of no fewer than thirty 1d stamps – twenty-four covering the entire back of the envelope, requiring eight cancellation stamps. A further six stamps on the front, plus an airmail label and a rubber stamp 'Deposee en Mer/Mailed on the high seas' left scant room for the address. As if this were not enough, adding to the montage was a white label stating 'Opened by Examiner 1229' – evidence of the censor's cursory interest.

The vessel docked at Quebec, perched magnificently on the Heights of Abraham, in the early evening of 9 November. As darkness fell, those aboard were fascinated to see once again the lights of a city. The following day Henry cabled his mother via Western Union and Cable and Wireless, reassuring her of his safe arrival after the Atlantic crossing: 'ARRIVED WELL LOVE — HENRY MAUDSLAY'.

The *Duchess* slipped her moorings during the night to complete her journey to Montreal. A surprise pay parade was held at 10 a.m., with each airman being given $25 to supplement the month's pay given to them before leaving England. Docking at Montreal at noon, the airmen paraded in front of the Customs Shed and were allocated their railway carriages for the last leg of the journey to their final destination. This was the newly constructed air training camp at Moose Jaw, some 45 miles west of Regina, Saskatchewan, which was to become the new home to No. 10 Flying Training School, henceforth renumbered as No. 32 Service Flying Training School and part of No. 4 Training Command. The journey was to take two days and two nights in old and dirty rolling stock, pulled by two great CPR locomotives.

After a brief stop on the outskirts of Montreal, at about 7.30 the train reached Smithfalls, and the airmen were permitted to stretch their legs, some venturing into the town and finding a bar, delaying their return to the train, much to the consternation of the officers in charge. The weary travellers slept in their seats, or on the luggage racks, waking next morning to find themselves amidst a snow-covered landscape. After stopping briefly at Port Arthur, the train pulled into Fort William for a quarter of an hour, during which airmen stretching their legs in the falling snow began to discover the true nature of Canadian winter temperatures.

Arriving at Moose Jaw at nine o'clock on the evening of 12 November, they were taken to a vast, recently expanded airfield some 4 miles out of the town, previously home to the Moose Jaw Flying Club – much of the recent development so new that many of the buildings and facilities were still under construction. Each major air station within the BCATP in Canada was designed to accommodate 1,200 men, with a hospital, recreation hall, gymnasium, drill hall, messes, etc. There were five wooden hangars (later increased to seven), almost cathedral-like in their construction, massive multiple timber cross beams supporting the roof and sliding doors occupying the whole of one side. Each was capable of holding 20 Ansons (the establishment of each SFTS was to be an incredible 110 aircraft).

The buildings were of wooden construction, typical of North America. To many they resembled the wooden huts in use at the more basic airfields in the UK, except that they were green in colour rather than brown. Once they were inside, however, it was discovered that they were asbestos lined and maintained at a not uncomfortable temperature, above 60 degrees, by efficient oil-fired steam central heating systems and externally fitted double glazing. Both were essential in a country where winter temperatures could drop to 50 degrees Fahrenheit below zero (82 degrees of frost). It was usual to stop outside work at 30 degrees below zero, except in windy conditions, when it ceased at 20 degrees below (62 degrees of frost) on account of the wind chill factor. Fortunately, during Henry's stay the weather remained relatively mild, perhaps justifying the location's native Indian name 'places of warm breezes'. Even so, when outside, the new trainees soon grew accustomed to hearing a faint cracking noise as their nostril hairs alternately froze, and then thawed with each inhalation and exhalation.

Designated as No. 26 Course, the airmen were split into flights and shown to their accommodation, each of their huts holding eighty-six men. The course was scheduled to last ten weeks and would be a combination of ground school and advanced flying exercises, including night flying and instrument flying. Henry was allocated to 'X' Flight, under the command of Flight Lieutenant W. Cooper. Writing to his mother on her birthday, from his new billet, Block 20 B, 14 November (adding 'Many happy returns' beneath the date), Henry described his surroundings:

Apart from the fact that we have no lockers and sleep on tiered bunks of two storys [sic] the accommodation is not bad, warm and too new to have got dirty yet. The room sleeps about 80 when full!

Temperatures get low here, it was well below freezing when we arrived after the first snowfall of the winter, but cleared up today to a lovely sunny day – just like Switzerland – this won't last long and we will have to put up with temperatures of from 20 to sometimes 40 below.[166]

Cadets had been issued with extra clothing to combat the cold – hats with ear flaps, balaclavas, thick gloves, underwear and mukluks (overboots which, though clumsy, were much warmer than the standard RAF flying boot). These were supplemented by personal items from home. 'Your socks are gorgeous,' he told his mother, adding heavily: 'Some more would be welcome.' He was also appreciative of the uniform he had had made in Market Drayton. 'Comfortable, well-made clothes make all the difference in the world in this weather.'

But already a degree of disillusionment was setting in. Many trainees, including Henry, had been told that they would be operational by November. The uncompleted facilities and lack of organizational urgency served to emphasize it was unlikely. It was a situation Henry did not intend to tolerate for any longer than he had to:

Don't write anything important to me here, as I hope to get moved on to somewhere where I'll get trained. The building for ground instruction is not yet ready, nor are the facilities for flying. There is a landing ground and some hangars and a few aircraft, but much of the equipment is not ready. What hell this is for anyone who wants to get trained – who joined the air force [sic] to fly – is a thing most people don't understand. Most of my colleagues seem completely apathetic – yet here we are, doing nothing, getting nowhere – up against the ghastly prospect of continuing this into a deeper and deeper winter – no one seems to care a damn! I do. . .

   I shall apply for a transfer as soon as possible and hope to get it as staying here will mean an awful waste of time. I joined the RAF to fly and of the 5 months I've been with the RAF I've done about seven weeks flying. The rest of it I learnt in the Boy Scouts years ago – so that about 3^1/$_2$ months can be counted as utterly wasted. I could have been doing useful work at Cambridge – in a Munition factory or on the land – it's perfectly damnable. If I'd wanted a cushy job on the land I could have opted for it.

Henry's despair at the poor order, discipline and organization had been compounded that day with the news that members of ground staff had been picked up 'dead drunk' in the snow in the early hours of the morning. As a result, visits to the town were now restricted to the hours of 4.30–10.00 p.m., and then only if the appropriate pass had been granted.

   With a population of 20,000, Moose Jaw had been founded in 1882 as a strategic railway depot and farm supply centre. During the 1920s it had gained a certain notoriety as a staging post on the liquor smuggling run to Prohibition-regulated Chicago. Despite being hit hard by the 1929 recession, its regional prosperity and pioneering confidence survived, reflected in wide treeless avenues flanked by solid brick warehouses, hotels and porticoed banks. At night the bright lights beckoned invitingly to those who had grown used to a year of British blackout, and the town became a welcome respite from the tedium of camp life and the institutional meals prepared by imported RAF cooks who 'wreck the food before we get it'.

   Moose Jaw is delightful and very up to date, though not big. The people are charming and although the cost of living is otherwise high, food is good and cheap. I dined last night with some friends at the best hotel in town for 66 cents – under 3/- [15p] – asparagus soup, salmon, half a colossal chicken EACH(!) with all accessories and finished up on vanilla ice and coffee because we couldn't eat any more.

Down in the centre of town, on the corner of Main and Fairford Streets, the Moose Jaw War Services Auxiliaries had established a War Services Club in a converted flat in the Bank of Montreal building, a magnificent structure with a façade in the style of a Greek temple, with fluted columns, Corinthian capitals and lotus flower decoration. All members of the armed forces were welcomed as honorary members and plied with traditional Canadian hospitality. It was a haven of comfort and civilization, well furnished, with a reading room with the latest copies of both English and American magazines including *Punch* and *Life*, a canteen for light meals and other areas for letter writing and cards.[167]

During the following week Henry requested an interview with the Chief Ground Instructor (CGI), citing 'personal reasons'. Henry marched in to be met by a very serious-looking officer, no doubt expecting to hear a tale of homesickness or 'woman trouble'. He relaxed noticeably when he heard Henry's request was for a transfer in order to speed up his training and offered the intentionally reassuring information that training should start in about a month and they would be flying Ansons – the twin-engined aircraft for which Henry had been hoping. The news seemed a mixed blessing – the desired result, yet more time wasted.

Having updated her briefly on these facts, Henry's next letter to his mother, written on Wednesday, 27 November, concentrated on the more social aspects of his new life. There was a strong camaraderie among the recruits, and Henry admitted, perhaps surprisingly, that the long journey and shared adventure had 'opened up' the course members, and he found that he liked a good many more than he had believed initially he would. His own popularity had been enhanced by his photographic prowess. The first roll of film, taken during the rail journey from Montreal, had been processed, prompting a spate of orders for prints from his colleagues. Most requests were for a splendid shot of a CPR locomotive taken at Champlain, resulting in a demand for fifteen enlargements.

He was reading avidly 'in an effort to stay sane' and had begun to attend the local Church of England church. To help pass the time and maintain fitness, he purchased a season ticket to the local swimming baths at the Temple Gardens Mineral Spa, on the corner of Fairford Street E and Langdon Crescent, not far from the War Services Club. Here was an excellent pool maintained at a constant 40 degrees Centigrade by a natural hot spring, where Henry went every evening for exercise and to improve his technique. Ice skating was another popular pastime. Perhaps recalling the spring term in 1933 when the lake at Beaudesert froze over, enabling the boys to learn how to skate, he purchased boots and a pair of ice hockey skates for 25s (£1.25), but the ice rink, open only in the evenings, was crowded with experienced locals, making his attempts as a novice seem more than inadequate:

> The standard of skating is staggering. . . everyone from the smallest child of say 11 or 12 skates really well, and all very fast. . . My ankles are so infernally

supple naturally – and weak from wearing RAF boots. [Speed skates] are said to be less tiring when you are used to them.

Despite the CGI's reassurances, by 27 November the training situation showed no signs of improving. Even round-the-clock efforts by teams of Canadian workmen had not completed facilities to the extent that ground instruction could start. (Formal handover from the contractors would not be until 19 February 1941.) There were administrative and political rivalries at work too, stemming from the fact that, when the BCATP had been drawn up, it was decreed that the RAF schools in Canada would be kept completely apart from the RCAF and responsible to London, although working under the RCAF for day-to-day control – a disruptive state of affairs that was to continue until 1942.

Henry's frustration had almost reached boiling point. In a letter received by his mother on Christmas Day, he risked the scissors of the censor and the wrath of his commanding officer: 'Our station is by no means ready for use yet and there is not even any hope of getting on with the lectures. . . Our own administration is. . . quite dreadful . . . there is no DRIVE behind the organisation.'[168]

Suggesting that his mother might find someone to print his grievance, he added on reflection: 'Better not though, I suppose.' He then recounted:

A certain SFTS knew that it would move to a station in Canada which would not be ready for use for some months, nor did it know whether it would be equipped even then. After accepting a first course of 50 pupils who were given a fortnight's rather half-hearted introductory training on 'twins' the school grounded these pupils and occupied a few hours of their time daily in lectures even more half-hearted than before. These soon ceased – well over a month ago . . . no hope of anything for weeks, more probably months – weather getting worse, depressed, frustrated, stagnant – had we been allowed to continue in our training in England even with the difficulties there are, we would have our wings by now and be well on the way to operations. . . .

It's MAD to keep us waiting here, but those who failed to transfer us earlier are now afraid to admit their mistake, so we must suffer for it – officially we are 'having a good time' – not much work – just the usual fatigues – and we can enjoy the amenities of Moose Jaw – delightful, but we didn't join the RAF to go on holiday to Canada!

Can you imagine anything so as [sic] going to a film – seeing London bombed and the RAF in action in the 'March of Time'– and then just going back to a row of wooden huts where we eat and sleep – sleep and eat – sit and think?

Perhaps believing that the letter *might* be intercepted and stopped by the censor, Henry wrote out a condensed copy to be sent by sea. The sentiment was the same, even though the words were slightly different:

> the situation is more utterly rotten than I could ever have believed in my wildest dreams. I knew this course should never have come here – a despicably inefficient waste of time. . .
>
> Nothing we can say or do will help us towards the only thing we want – the work for which we volunteered; instead we go to the cinema to see London bombed, our capital with our friends – then to return to a row of huts where we eat and sleep and sit and think and voraciously read dull books in a desperate effort to stay sane. At Eton I learnt that the basis of a successful organisation is to have everywhere the right man in the right place. Is this it?[169]

Adding to the sense that they had been forgotten was the continued absence of any news from home: 'Longing for a letter from you, but have heard nothing yet.' Back at Fox Hill, Mrs Maudslay would be puzzled by her son's comment, for she had sent several letters. It later transpired that he had forgotten to cable his Moose Jaw address. As a result for a long time she was addressing letters via the temporary Ottawa address that he had given her before departing, thereby further increasing the time taken for them to reach him. Meanwhile, her time was busily occupied running the estate and assisting local benevolent organizations. Earlier in the year her neighbours the Arkwrights had established the Willersey House War Comforts' Fund and in March helped instigate the Willersey and Saintbury Social Centre in the refurbished Willersey Village Hall, where, on 21 November, Mrs Maudslay assisted in the organization and running of a Bring and Buy tea in aid of the Infant Welfare Fund. During the proceedings she won a box of chocolates, which she kindly donated for sale to swell the proceeds to £6.

After further delay in Moose Jaw Henry was relieved to hear that training would recommence: 'This is the best letter I have been able to write for months. We have started training – haphazard and incompetent training, but we have at least started – it's absolutely grand – though I haven't even felt the controls of an aeroplane yet.'[170]

He apologized for the depressing nature of his previous letters, wondering how much had been censored despite it all being true. With Christmas approaching, he had been shopping for suitable gifts, but was unimpressed by most of what he saw. All the Christmas cards were 'too hearty for words' and he finally settled on a gift of some crystallized fruits for the family: 'I don't expect there'll be any from

France this Xmas . . . if they arrive they will have to "go round" as far as presents are concerned. I couldn't even find moccasins here which surprised me, all the clothes and so forth are just like home.'

Nevertheless there were some items that he knew his mother and sister would appreciate: 'I'd like to know what size you take in silk stockings.'

After nearly two months on the ground, flying recommenced on Saturday, 7 December, and Henry was taken up as a passenger by Flying Officer Bould[171] for a one-hour familiarization flight in Anson R9832, before being allowed twenty-five minutes of solo circuits in R9821. Circuits were invariably flown with the wheels lowered, to avoid expending energy cranking them up and down.

The Avro Anson was not the most suitable of aircraft for the Canadian winter climate. The aircraft were Mark Is, powered by Armstrong Siddeley Cheetah engines, which had been designed for temperate latitudes, and there was great difficulty in getting them started. Engines would be stopped only when refuelling was necessary, each pupil sitting in the pilot's seat until relieved by the next, or the ground crew. (Later Canadian-built Ansons were powered by Jacobs or Wright radial engines better suited to the freezing conditions.) Nor was it the warmest of aeroplanes, fabric covered and with large Perspex side windows, which were draughty and on occasion known to crack, sometimes even to explode, under the severe temperature variations experienced.[172] For the crew, the rudimentary heating was as good as to be non-existent, and there was no improvement on the standard RAF Sidcot flying suit, a waterproof, windproof outer with fur collar and pseudo fur liner, which, although satisfactory for temperate Europe, was barely adequate for the extreme conditions of the Canadian winter.

The next three days saw further flights both solo and with Flight Lieutenant Cooper. Surprisingly, on 10 December, Henry was permitted to take up R9739 solo without any preliminary dual and practice flying on one engine, an exercise he had not undertaken for over two months. The weather closed in, and there was no further flying until the 16th, the same day that administration caught up with Henry, when his logbook entries for Tern Hill were finally signed off, showing that on posting to Canada he had flown for a grand total of 51 hours 45 minutes. He had yet to complete any night flying. Then it was back to intensive training with Flight Lieutenant Cooper, with almost two flights every day, the flying being generally concentrated entirely before, or entirely after lunch, leaving half the day free for ground instruction. On 19 December he made five flights before lunch! Gradually the syllabus expanded to include stalling, climbing and gliding, precautionary landings (with engine power available) and forced landings (without power), occasionally using the Relief Landing Grounds at Buttress and Bishopton. He switched instructors to Flying Officer Burton on the 20th, and on the 22nd was taken on his first Canadian cross-country flight in R9739, experiencing for the first time the vastness of the country, although in his own words 'it's just not England and it's very grim never to see a green field'.

It was something to which he would soon adapt. On good days with sunshine the visibility could be excellent, and practice brought familiarity with the new landscape. With the Canadian countryside laid out in sections, orientation was easy, assisted by the sun, and from 10,000 feet one could even make out the curvature of the earth. Railway tracks were the greatest aid to navigation, being kept clear of snow and standing out against the white wastes. One favourite ploy of those lost was to descend low over a railway station to read the platform name – a practice strictly disapproved of by the authorities. Alternately one could circle one of the numerous brightly painted grain elevators also thus marked, although some carried only the grain company's name, a trap for the unwary. Night flying, however, could be quite hazardous. Frequent snow showers could hamper visibility, making it difficult to observe and identify ground features, blacking out the lights of airfields that were often used as turning points on navigational cross countries. But that was still to come; with the exception of three demonstration night landings with Flight Sergeant Patterson before completing his first solo-night flight on 23 December, Henry's flying was confined at present to daylight hours.

On Sunday, 22 December, he sent a simple six-word cable to Fox Hill: 'BEST WISHES XMAS LOVE. HENRY MAUDSLAY'.

He had received a letter from Tita and a card from Kelly. His mother had sent a Christmas box of food and cigarettes, together with a card and calendar, which he pinned over his bed.[173] She also continued to forward a considerable number of letters from his various friends. Christmas itself was spent pleasantly enough. There were typical camp festivities and several local families, sensing the loneliness that the occasion would bring, opened up their homes and extended family hospitality to the young men from England. According to Henry, apart from the inevitable desire to be with his family and friends, everything was fine until the evening of Christmas Day:

> One of the pupils who is superficially quite a g———-n from Oxford . . . took rather more whisky than he could stand. I had to take the situation in hand single handed and collected a black eye in the process, rather a nasty one, and have had to use make up in the form of grease paint and powder as I find that people here jump to remarkably nasty conclusions.[174]

With a day off for Boxing Day, flying recommenced on the 27th. But already rumours were circulating that the course would soon be over. By 2 January they were firm enough for Henry to cable: 'HOPE TO RETURN TWO MONTHS STOP WRITING HERE LOVE — HENRY MAUDSLAY'.

The Wings exam was looming, and there was less time for leisure. The two sections that made up the course were flying in seven-hour shifts day and night except 5–8 a.m. Daily routine commenced with an early breakfast, usually no more than a ham sandwich. After a parade at 7.30, it was straight to lectures or flying until lunchtime. The midday break was a spartan affair, comprising a couple of hot dogs in the canteen, then back to work through to 4.30 or 5.00 p.m. Whenever possible the evening meal would be taken out of camp, since it was the only certain means of eating well. Evenings would be spent brushing up on navigational theory, night flying or practising instrument flying on the Link Trainer.[175]

As the pupils became more proficient, they were tasked to fly with each other, acting either as pilot or as navigator, taking turns to map read in half-hour stints, landing between sessions to change seats, which helped to keep the circulation going and create some illusion of warmth. Henry's first such flight was with LAC Ernest Peacock, a mixture of single-engined flying, steep turns and climbing turns in R9820 on 28 December, although most of the remainder of his 'twinned' flights were with Lucian Ercolani, interspersed with more personal tuition by Sergeant Gilbert. Henry's first real test of proficiency came immediately after lunch on Sunday, 5 January, when he piloted R9275 on a 2 hour 20 minute solo navigation test. All went well, and he continued with the next stage of his training, some ten days of intensive daylight instrument flying, despite suffering from a minor cold that must have made getting airborne rather miserable. In addition, between 7 and 17 January there were twelve daily Link Trainer sessions. Each lasting between half an hour and an hour and a half duration, they amounted to a further 8 hours 45 minutes' practice and examination under the attentive eye of Pilot Officer R. D. Boyd.

Mail from home had become more regular by now, if via circuitous routes – a letter from Derek Mond posted in Eton arriving via Brough *and* Tern Hill! There was still no response from his mother to the request about stockings, and Henry sent a cable on 11 January expanding the question to include shades of lipstick and powder. There may have been an additional incentive, for he also requested Lady Rosemary Hills's address and that £10 should be transferred from his Eton account to the Montreal Bank, Moose Jaw. A similar request, sent on 29 January for another £20, suggests that, with the end of his course imminent, Henry was either thinking of purchasing gifts to bring home, or anticipating the need to settle outstanding Mess bills.[176]

After a final navigation test on the 17th, in R9739 with Lucian Ercolani, the next three nights were given over to further practice of solo night circuits and landings, but the emphasis was still on instrument flying and navigation. This was examined on the 28th, when he had to fly a triangular cross-country course lasting an hour 'under the hood'. Accidents at this stage were rare and minor, usually resulting in the ignominious sight of an Anson standing on its nose at the end of its landing run. Henry was fortunate and escaped such a fate. On 29 and 31 January there was extensive formation flying practice, and then, with an alacrity that had been distinctly lacking at the commencement of the course, Henry's training was over.

Squadron Leader Byram, the chief flying instructor, signed the typed slip confirming that, after a total of 113 hours 15 minutes, training, with only 11 hours 50 minutes at night, Henry was entitled to wear the coveted 'Wings' of his flying badge. The station commander, Group Captain C. E. H. James, MC, added his signature to a rubber stamp in Henry's logbook, along with an assessment of 'Above Average', and no special faults to be watched. The crowning moment came shortly after noon on Saturday, 1 February 1941, when the successful pupils of No. 26 Course assembled in the Station Drill Hall to be presented with their wings by Group Captain James. For many, including Henry, success also brought with it a commission, transferring them from the rank of LAC to that of pilot officer.[177]

There was little time for the newly qualified pilots to celebrate; within forty-eight hours they would be on their way back to the UK. At 0715 hours on 3 February, and in buoyant mood, the fifty graduate pupils of No. 26 Course left by rail for Ottawa on the first stage of their return to England. Even as they left, the ghosts of their occupation were still being laid to rest at Moose Jaw. Shortly before lunch the station commander saw fit to address all RAF officers on the station regarding grievances still occurring in correspondence to England. He stressed the need for bringing all genuine complaints to light for investigation and the importance of scotching immediately all frivolous and unjust accusations. The subject would be raised with senior NCOs the following day.

(The teething problems experienced by Henry were resolved and by the end of the war the BCATP had become a highly efficient system, training a total of 136,849 aircrew at an average of 2,230 a month.)

Freezing conditions hampered navigation of the St Lawrence at this time of year, necessitating a longer rail journey to ice-free waters, a number of the contingent ensuring warmth by riding part of the journey on the locomotive footplate. The airmen staged through Debert Camp near Truro, Nova Scotia,[178] before being packed aboard a 19,429 grt Dutch East Indian vessel, the *Johan van Oldenbarn-evelt*.[179] The ship had recently been impressed and converted by Harland and Wolff, Belfast, as Troopship No. 32 and was now waiting to join her first trooping convoy outbound from Halifax through the North Atlantic waters. Normally sailing between the Middle East and the East Indies, the vessel was equipped for tropical conditions, and there were numerous problems as items of equipment froze in the sub-zero Canadian temperatures. After what seemed a lengthy wait, during which Lucian Ercolani recalls alcohol was readily available (and essential) to combat the bitter cold, the vessel and her human cargo of 199 troops departed from Halifax on 17 February 1941 as part of Convoy TC009. It must have been an anxious voyage for those in the know. The German heavy cruiser *Admiral Hipper* and battle cruisers *Scharnhorst* and *Gneisenau* were to sink eleven British Merchant ships during February 1941. As the convoy departed from Canadian coastal waters, Allied Intelligence confirmed that the two battlecruisers were in the North Atlantic. Nevertheless, despite this threat, the U-boats and long-range Fw 200 Condor aircraft, Henry's convoy, escorted by H-Class destroyers HMS *Havelock* and HMCS *Assiniboine*, returned safely to the Clyde on 24 February. After due processing through No. 3 Personnel Reception Centre, Bournemouth, where they were informed of their next posting, the new aircrew were to enjoy a brief period of leave before continuing with the next stage of training.

Henry went home, no doubt to expand upon his earlier correspondence, learning at the same time recent domestic news and seeing for himself some of the effects of the war upon his mother's own rural community. In addition to rationing and the blackout, there had been several instances of enemy action. Despite being relatively remote from major targets, the Cotswolds lay beneath the Luftwaffe's routes to the industrial Midlands, Bristol and the South Wales ports. It was not unusual for enemy aircraft, perhaps lost or damaged, to lighten their load as they passed overhead. During the winter of 1940–41 a number of villages in the Vale of Evesham had received incendiary bombs and the occasional high explosive. In nearby Broadway, outbuildings to the rear of the celebrated Lygon Arms hotel had been destroyed by incendiaries. As if this were not enough for concern, there had been several other unexplained fires causing damage to property and giving rise to suspicions of an arsonist in the locality. Fox Hill fortunately had remained unscathed.

Chapter 8

Preparation for Battle

No easy hope or lies
Shall bring us to our goal,
But iron sacrifice
Of body, will and soul.
There is but one task for all –
One life for each to give.
What stands if Freedom fall?
Who dies if England live?
(Rudyard Kipling. 'For All We Have and Are')

After spending a week or so with his mother, Henry arrived at his new unit, No. 25 Operational Training Unit (OTU) at RAF Finningley, on Monday, 17 March 1941.[180] Here he was to continue the final part of his training before being sent to an operational squadron. Training in Canada, while providing a solid grounding and safe practice, was unrepresentative of the conditions to be found in Britain and Europe. The latter's overcast skies and poor weather reduced visibility and the ability to pinpoint one's position. In Britain, unlike the flat prairies, it was all too easy to get lost in the maze of winding railway lines, rivers, woods and roads, with masses of small towns all looking alike, not to mention the hills projecting dangerously up into the cloud base during the hazy March days. At night the blackout caused confusion and potential disorientation on all but moonlit nights, both in the air and on the ground. The OTU was intended to provide experience of European navigational, weather and night-flying problems together with familiarization of UK radio and airfield procedures.

RAF Finningley lies south-east of Doncaster, between the main A638 and A614 roads, and is another of the pre-war expansion airfields constructed during the mid-1930s with substantial brick-built accommodation in neo-Georgian style, mainly in the north-west corner of the site behind an arc of five type 'C' hangars, which, in 1941, fronted on to a grass flying field.

No. 25 OTU was a new formation, having been formed officially on 1 March 1941 from 'C' Flight of No. 106 Squadron, the remainder of that unit, an operational squadron, having moved to Coningsby in early February. The unit comprised three Flights:

'A' Flight	Equipped with the familiar Anson, this flight provided navigation training and further dual and solo experience on twin-engined aircraft.
'B' Flight:	This conversion flight enabled pilots to switch pilots from Ansons to Hampdens. The latter's narrow fuselage prevented dual control; at best instruction could be given with an experienced crewman standing behind the pilot. As an interim stage, 'B' Flight was equipped with a mix of Wellington and Hampden aircraft. Pilots were to be given an hour's dual by day on the former, giving them the opportunity to familiarize themselves with a larger, heavier machine before being sent off solo in the Hampden. Many of the Wellingtons had seen decidedly better days, were well flown and decidedly tired.
'C' Flight	Once converted, pilots were given full operational training on this flight's Hampdens.

Henry found himself one of forty-four pupils comprising the first course to train crews for both the Hampden and the new twin-engined Avro Manchester. Unfortunately, because of a range of technical and production problems, the Manchesters for training were not forthcoming (every Manchester produced was required by the operational squadrons to combat their appalling serviceability), and it was decreed that Finningley should instead turn out twenty-four Hampden crews per month. (Each crew comprised one pilot, one air observer and two W/T air gunners). The following month the number of Hampden crews was reduced to twelve, plus twelve Manchester crews.

Life at Finningley was most pleasant. Although accommodation was at a premium and the Officers' Mess unable to cope with wartime numbers, the situation had been eased by the conversion of married quarters into officers' rooms. Henry's room was in the last house on the right after the main gate. As at school, heating was a problem through shortage of fuel, despite night-time sorties to appropriate coal from other sources: 'This is an infernally cold part of the world . . . I'm more than ever thankful for Uncle Norman's leather waistcoat.'[181]

To facilitate his travel around the station, Mrs Maudslay had sent the new bicycle up by rail, and the ever practical Henry had a carrier fitted locally. Writing to thank his mother on 17 March, he insisted that she should rest after the exertions of the previous week. Having learned that Harold Gibb was unwell too, he sent his regards for a speedy recovery, adding a PS requesting that his mother send on the two large lipsticks and rouge that he had bought from Canada for the reverend's daughter Mary. A further PS was written on the back of the envelope: 'Can you please send my golf clubs and coat hangers which got left behind!'

Training commenced on Wednesday, 19 March 1941. As usual, the course was a mixture of ground and air instruction. Flying began for Henry on 22 March with a series of DR(Dead Reckoning) navigation exercises flown in the Ansons, which continued on almost a daily basis until the end of the month. After the maps of Canada with their vast open tracts of countryside, the detail of the standard RAF 1:500,000 topographical maps was overwhelming, and the trainee pilots flew initially as navigators in order to readjust. During his first flight, a two-and-a-half-hour trip with Sergeant Hubbard at the controls of N5079, Henry suffered a severe bout of air sickness. Two days later, as they flew over the Humber, near to Brough, in R3310, Henry regretted not being near enough to visit the Byrons, who had been so kind to him while he was training there. On his next trip, flying as second navigator, he was able to take the controls of N5079 for a short period, while Flying Officer Elmer Coton,[182] the pilot, went back to assist the navigator, Pilot Officer Walton, 'unofficial, but very pleasant after such a long time'.

News came from his mother, the family's second car, known familiarly as 'the Beetle' (most probably a black Standard Flying Eight or Ten), was to be overhauled by his brother for Henry's use. It would certainly make travel easier, petrol permitting. Mindful of this fact, Henry wrote back: 'Could you ask John [Maudslay] to fit an extra petrol tank? – it needn't be very big, but if I ever get an extra ration for leave etc. it might be useful.'[183]

Thanking her for his golf clubs, which had arrived safely, Henry told her he had heard from Peter Wake, who had returned from Canada and was now with 168th OCTU at Droitwich, Worcestershire, some 20 miles from Fox Hill.[184] Peter's uncle, Captain Pollen, lived at Mickleton, a short distance down the Fosseway from Broadway, and Henry suggested that his mother should meet him. He had lost touch with other friends and asked her to contact Peter Pritchard's mother to obtain his new address. Henry thought it possible he was near Finningley and hoped that he might end up posted to the same Bomber Group when he had finished training.

Meanwhile, Mrs Maudslay had been exchanging correspondence with Eton's headmaster. On 4 December 1940 a lone German aircraft, probably either lost or being targeted by the anti-aircraft batteries defending Windsor Castle, had released two bombs, which fell on the college. One demolished a master's residence, the other failed to explode immediately, doing so two days later, destroying part of the Upper School and Headmaster's Schoolroom and blowing out the east and north windows of the Chapel. There were no casualties, but considerable damage was inflicted upon the fabric of School Yard. In recognition of her gratitude to the school, Henry's mother had sent Claude Elliott a cheque for £100 as a contribution towards the restoration of the Upper School. Expressing his thanks, he responded on 28 March commenting that a more immediate requirement for funds lay with the Remissions of Fees Fund. This complemented bursaries made possible through the generosity of Lord Camrose and enabled grants to be offered to subsidize students whose parents, suffering financial losses because of the war, could no longer afford the school fees. This £100 would probably support two boys, enabling them to remain at Eton for their final year. Would she consider her donation being used in this manner?

Commenting on the news that Henry had now returned safely to England: 'He is one of the best boys we have had in the School since I have been Head Master and Eton as a whole owes a great deal to him, while I am particularly grateful to him for the help he gave me in Pop and as Captain of the Boats at a specially difficult time.' In his own hand he added: 'Again, thank you for your most generous cheque which increases the debt we already owe you for Henry's career at Eton.'[185]

Mrs Maudslay tried to phone Henry on 1 April to discuss the matter, but her son was out, celebrating fellow Tern Hill and Canada companion Peter Dixon-Spain's birthday with well-hung roast pheasant, but the next day he received a note from her sounding out his views. Henry was in full agreement with the headmaster's suggestion and replied on 2 April: 'Remissions of Fees Fund sounds just the thing. I hope you like the idea.'

Approval was duly communicated to Mr Elliott, who was away on a short holiday, and he registered his pleasure at the decision a week or so later: 'It might enable some boy who would otherwise be taken away to complete his time at Eton and we know by experience the value of the last year here.' Commiserating with her about the strains imposed by the war, he added: 'Yes, I am afraid that these are terribly anxious times for you. Everyone here who knew Henry is so fond of him that they have been thinking of him and of you.'[186]

Now that he was well established at Finningley and training was going well, Henry thought it would be a good idea if his mother came to visit him. He could book her into a hotel in Doncaster. Writing to her on Sunday, 30 March, he suggested she could drive up in the Beetle. A weekend would be best. Although he would have to work on Saturday morning, he could still get Saturday evening and Sunday afternoon and evening free. He was expecting a possible visit from Uncle

Norman, who might be in the area on 4 April, but did not recommend that his mother attempt to rendezvous. It would be too rushed and, being the middle of the week, he would have little free time to spend with them.

Henry had taken up running again, spurred on by Matthews, a member of the admin staff, who, he thought, had taught at Stowe, played rugger for Glamorgan and also played cricket for England.[187] More clothes were needed from home: 'Can you send my 2nd best grey flannel trousers – not the lightest colour pair but the most serviceable of the others? Also the sleeved sweater with the two broad blue bands on it, and a couple of shirts, the check Airtex ones would do well.'[188]

Breaking off from his letter to take a run with Peter Dixon-Spain, he returned, exhausted, to recount: 'We thought we'd go out by the front and go on turning left until we came in at the back – it turned out to be about 6 miles, a good deal more than we had expected, however we got in in time to get a cup of tea.'[189]

Somewhat strangely, in view of Service protocol, Henry requested: 'Could you address me as plain H. E. Maudslay Esq. on letters – it seems to be OK and I prefer it to the other rigmarole!'

There had been a navigation test at the end of March, and training on the Anson had continued through into a wet April with the objective of revising their piloting skills. On the 3rd he flew a forty-five-minute dual in N5318 with Squadron Leader Burnett before being allowed to go solo with three crew. After two more solo flights, there were two local night-flying exercises (basically circuits), and on the 8th, accompanied by Peter Dixon-Spain, he went up in Wellington T2970 of 'B' Flight with Flying Officer Harris at the controls for a familiarization flight. Two days later, after two flights in a Hampden, standing and watching over Flying Officer Coton's shoulder, Henry was airborne solo for the first time in the type he was to fly on operations when he took P1234 up for a half-hour of circuits.

With an internal bomb capacity of 3,000lb and a 500-pounder under each wing, the Hampden, along with the Vickers Wellington and Armstrong Whitworth Whitley, was one of the twin-engined medium-heavy bombers providing the mainstay of Bomber Command during the first half of the war. Powered by two reliable Bristol Pegasus radial engines, the aircraft carried a crew of four in a narrow but deep slab-sided fuselage that tapered markedly into a slender tail boom carrying a twin-finned tailplane. Its unusual appearance gave rise to the sobriquet of the 'Flying Suitcase' or 'Flying Tadpole'. From a pilot's perspective, the narrow, fighter-style cockpit was cramped and cluttered, with several features not found on other aircraft.[190] Visibility was excellent, from wing tip to wing tip. It could perform tight turns like a fighter, with the illusion being enhanced by sliding back the pilot's canopy, exposing the occupant to the noise and buffet of the slipstream. The aircraft had few nasty habits, the most severe being the 'stabilized yaw', a condition attributed to poor flying, whereby the aircraft skidded sideways and the rudders locked full over before it flipped onto its back, often with fatal results. There was a marked tendency to swing to starboard on take-off, and landings required care with the hold-off if multiple bounces were to be avoided.

The next week was spent gaining this experience with daylight local flying. After two solo flights on 10 and 12 April, Henry was taken up for a test the following day in P1234 with Pilot Officer John Ruck-Keene, an experienced pilot with some 350 hours to his credit, 70 of them on Hampdens. On the 16th he practised asymmetric flying in the Hampden[191] for the first time, confirming that the design's small tail area necessitated large displacement of the rudder pedals in order to counteract the drag of the 'dead' engine, which was increased by the non-feathering propeller. Three subsequent flights extended the training to instrument flying, with Pilot Officer Ralph Allsebrook as check pilot. One incident served to show that training in Yorkshire was more hazardous than Canada. On the night of the 16th, at 2200 hours, a Hampden and an Anson carrying out local flying at about 800 feet were fired upon by an enemy aircraft, believed to be an Me 110. No damage was done, and the enemy left the area when three of the airfield defence Hispano cannons opened fire.

Three days later the dangers of home defences were brought home strikingly to Henry. Saturday, 19 April, was a day of low cloud when he took Hampden P1248 up on a local instrument flying practice with Pilot Officer Ralph Allsebrook and Pilot Officer Jeffrey Ransom as crew. Returning to base, Allsebrook and Ransom took the aircraft up again, piloted by the former, but without Henry. Shortly before half past four, at 2,800 feet over Sheffield, the Hampden hit a barrage balloon cable, which severed part of the port wing. The aircraft became uncontrollable, and Allsebrook was forced to bale out. Unfortunately Pilot Officer Ransom was unable to exit in time and was killed when the aircraft came down in Concord Park, Rotherham Road. In theory the accident should never have happened. Apart from the fact that such areas were clearly notified to airmen, the balloons themselves carried a 'squeaker', a transponder that could be heard on the aircraft radio, increasing in volume as the danger approached. The incident served to highlight yet again that the hazards of wartime flying were not confined to the night skies over Germany.

Henry's mother and sister arrived the same day in the Beetle, recently fitted with the additional petrol tank behind the rear seat. Pulling up at the guard room, they asked the corporal to put a call through to the Mess and were met by Henry on his bike. He had arranged accommodation at Punch's Hotel, south of Doncaster town centre on Bawtry Road, Bessacar. No doubt one of the topics of conversation must have been Ralph Allsebrook's recent narrow escape. In his letter thanking his mother for visiting, he commented reassuringly: 'Ralph Allsebrook (with an odd looking face) is back in the Mess already in good form – but won't fly for a few days probably.'

After an enjoyable time, they caught a train for home on the evening of the 20th, Mrs Maudslay travelling via London with Tita. The Beetle remained at Finningley, where Henry had rented a lock-up garage. Although some work had been carried out, the car still required a good service and inspection of the fuses.

To date, Henry's training had concentrated on the essentials of flying and navigation. In order to qualify as an operational pilot he had to learn the skills of his trade – bombing. Transferring to 'C' Flight, on 22 April he flew P1236 with Flying Officer Mills to see how it was done, followed by a flight with his own crew, Pilot Officer Wood, Sergeant Brown and Sergeant Leggett. The next three flights focused on flarepath approaches, the first by day so that he could feel the rate of turn and descent while still having a number of visual references, the next two 'for real' at night, his first experience of the Hampden in the medium of darkness. Another bombing practice, a flarepath approach and a cross-country lasting a record (for Henry) of 3 hours 40 minutes completed the month's flying.

About 23 April Mrs Maudslay was involved in an unfortunate accident. As she was cycling down Willersey Hill near Fox Hill, a hen ran across her path and struck her front wheel, pitching her off her bike. Striking her head as she fell, she suffered concussion plus the inevitable cuts, grazes and bruises. Subsequent medical examination proved she had suffered a slight fracture of her skull, with damage around the cheekbone and eye socket. Expressing his concern, Henry wrote on Saturday, 26th:

My dear Mummy,
I am so sorry you have had such a beastly accident. Do take it as easy as you can, just concentrate on resting and giving things time to heal up, and you'll be OK.

I'll get some leave in a few weeks now, at the end of this course, and hope to find you comfortably convalescent and taking a well earned rest. It takes something like this to make you take a rest!

All well here and I'm taking great care of your car. The important thing is not to worry about anything.

Very best love, Henry.

To cheer her and wish her well he also sent a gift of a small china animal.
May was devoted entirely to bombing, air gunnery and cross-country flying,

first by day and then by night. Excitement was caused at 0315 hours on 7 May when an enemy aircraft dropped three bombs on the aerodrome, damaging a hangar, the airmen's married quarters and an Anson. This may account for Henry being unable to call his mother that evening. The next morning, anxious to hear progress of her recovery, he rang Fox Hill from the crewroom and spoke to Uncle Norman. His mother was progressing well at home with a nurse in attendance, but shortly would be undergoing a minor operation to attend to her antrium (eye socket) and cheekbone.

As training intensified the number of flying accidents began to mount. At 0500 hours on 8 May Sergeant Lesley Robertson, coming into land too fast after a moonlight cross-country, overshot the runway and ran into the boundary fence. The following day another cross-country homecomer, Sergeant E. S. Clarke, mis-judging his height when landing in mist, stalled at a height of 15 feet and damaged his undercarriage, and three days later Pilot Officer Ruck-Keene, piloting a Hampden on target-towing duty for air firing practice, force landed at Kealby Bridge with engine failure. There were only minor injuries with these incidents, but fate was not to stay her hand for much longer. In the early hours of Saturday, 17 May, a Hampden on floodlit landing practice fell out of control at 200 feet and dived vertically into the ground between Doncaster and Bawtry, killing Sergeant Richard Hickmott and his two crew after sixteen hours of Hampden experience. Then on the night of 18/19 May came a personal blow for Henry. Peter Dixon-Spain and his crew of three set off on a night navigation exercise from which they did not return. The Court of Inquiry speculated on three reasons for their loss: shot down by an enemy aircraft, engine failure or loss of control while flying on instruments. It was noted that Pilot Officer Dixon-Spain had less experience than was desirable on the Link Trainer, attributable to a lack of facilities at Finningley.[192] No trace was ever found of the aircraft or crew, and it is assumed that they crashed in the North Sea. It was a hard loss to accept – only ten brief days earlier Henry had enjoyed dinner with Peter and met his new wife, Margaret, for the first time. She was now a widow after little more than a month of marriage. The tragedy of his loss was made even greater with the knowledge that the course was almost at an end.[193]

On Thursday, 22 May, after a total of 59 hours 50 minutes' pilot training with No. 25 OTU, Henry was assessed as an 'Above average' medium bomber pilot, an 'Average' pilot-navigator and 'Average' in bombing. Having completed a grand total of some 172 hours of controlling an aircraft (only 30 of which had been at night, his anticipated fighting medium), he was now cleared to join his first oper-ational unit. An acute shortage of bomber crews at this period meant no time was to be wasted. That afternoon he was to report to No. 44 Squadron, based at RAF

Waddington, along with three other members of his course: Sergeant Lesley Robertson, Sergeant Stanley Saunders and Pilot Officer Tristan 'Sally' Salazar.[194]

It must have been a charged time for Henry. His course flying had been completed on the 18th and he had managed to obtain forty-eight hours' leave to visit his mother, stopping off for half an hour en route back to Waddington to see his brother John, and again for a quick meal at Ye Old Bell at Barnaby Moor. It is not known when he learned of his friend's disappearance; it may have been just before he set out for home, or perhaps on his return. Understandably, there is certainly no hint of anything untoward in his letter sending his mother his new address, yet surely emotions were strained: 'It was grand seeing you looking so well (considering everything) and I loved every minute of my time at home. Officers' Mess Waddington, nr Lincoln will find me this afternoon – and I'm *very* glad, as it's the station I want to go to.'[195]

Chapter 9

Metamorphosis

The pale wild roses star the banks of green
and poignant poppies startle their fields with red,
while peace like sunlight rests on the summer scene,
though lilac that flashed in hedges is dull and dead:
in the faint sky the singing birds go over,
the sheep are quiet where the quiet grasses are.
I go to the plane among the peaceful clover,
but climbing in the Hampden, shut myself in war.
(Herbert Corby, 'Poem')

Situated on the Lincolnshire heights 5 miles south of Lincoln, in a triangle of land between the A15 and A607 roads, Waddington was a pre-war station like Finningley, offering superior brick-built accommodation, although the airfield itself remained a grass field without surfaced runways. The locality had recently suffered the attentions of the enemy. A fortnight earlier, on the night of 8/9 May, six high-explosive bombs had been dropped on the airfield and neighbouring village. On the main camp, bombs had hit the NAAFI and a nearby slit trench, killing eleven, including seven ladies of the NAAFI staff. In the village, a landmine had destroyed the church, while another had landed in the vicarage garden, causing a large crater. There were 19 houses that had been destroyed, 71 seriously damaged and 160 slightly damaged. Moreover, 1 person had been killed, 6 seriously injured and 43 slightly injured. In all 400 people had been affected – a heavy toll for a minor attack on this small Lincolnshire community.

The airfield was home to two Hampden squadrons, Nos 44 and 50, and also to No. 207 Squadron – the latter struggling to remain operational with the more recently introduced Avro Manchester, whose two Rolls-Royce Vulture engines were proving to be notoriously unreliable.

Commanded by Wing Commander Sidney Misselbrook, No. 44 Squadron was one of the principal squadrons of No. 5 Group Bomber Command. By mid-1941 their twin-engined Hampdens, although solid and reliable, were becoming out-dated by developments in design and concept, as a new generation of four-engined heavy bombers, represented by the Short Stirling and the Handley Page Halifax, came into service. Eventually No. 44 Squadron would have the honour of introducing the newest of the four-engined 'heavies', the Avro Lancaster – a development of the Manchester – but in May 1941 the prototypes were still being assessed and service trials would take another six months. Meanwhile No. 44 soldiered on with its Hampdens.

Henry was officially posted to the squadron with effect from Thursday, 22 May 1941. The first few days were spent with the formalities of arriving, accustoming himself to his new surroundings, meeting his flight commander, Squadron Leader John 'Joe' Collier, and getting to know the other members of 'A' Flight.[196] Many of the squadron personnel, both air and ground crew, were volunteers from southern Rhodesia, a number of the latter being professional men, doctors, lawyers and architects, awaiting pilot training. Recognized by their 'Rhodesia' shoulder flash and distinctive accents, they had outlandishly flamboyant (offi-cialdom would claim 'scruffy') dress sense. History had bred them with a strong sense of independence, a few filing the crown off their metal cap badges to demonstrate their resentment of Britain's refusal to grant Dominion status to their country. Easy-going and informal, they had a manner that was warm and welcoming.

On arrival Henry had tried to phone Fox Hill, but, on asking the operator for 'Broadway 189', he discovered there was an eight-hour delay on calls. Instead he contented himself with a brief note to his mother confirming his arrival, telling her 'This seems to be quite a nice place' and that for the moment he had a room to himself in a hut, although he would be moving shortly to a new billet off the camp. 'The adjutant says it's rather a good billet, but I am not sure that I trust him, as he strikes me as a tough guy who probably has odd ideas.'[197]

The following day he moved to his new billet, Manor Farm, a long, low two-storey house, built at right angles to the scarp, nestling on the slope just below the ridge in Boothby Graffoe village, with a wide panoramic view of the flat expanse of the Vale of Trent, situated on the edge of the Lincolnshire scarp. The area's mel-low yellow limestone architecture was not unlike that of his home in the Cotswolds, although thatched roofs were replaced by stone or pantiles. Advising his mother that there was still some six hours' delay in obtaining a phone connection and that she should still write to him at the Officers' Mess, he outlined his first impres-sions of his new home. Contrary to his previous belief, the adjutant had been perfectly correct.

Manor Farm (or the Old Rectory as it was sometimes known) was the home of

'Gino' and Frankie (Frances) Henson with their two sons, Richard and William, aged 9 and 8 respectively, and 4-year-old daughter Gillian.[198] The Hensons made him feel welcome right from the start. When he returned from having his hair cut in Lincoln the previous evening, they had invited him to join them for after-dinner drinks. Henry thought them 'very pleasant people. . . Very jolly people I think; they run a farm.' Mrs Henson spent most of her time working for the County War Agricultural Committee. His billet was intended only as sleeping accommodation, although Mrs Henson frequently provided Horlicks and biscuits in the evenings; meals were provided in the Officers' Mess, and flying kit was kept on the airfield in a room near the Mess that he shared with two companions from Finningley. No petrol ration was issued; to get to the airfield, an RAF bus collected them, although Henry kept the Beetle at the house in case he missed it. Cryptically he stated: 'I have not done any work yet, but hope to get going soon.'[199]

But first there was to be a short respite. After twelve Hampdens had mined the approaches to Brest on 26 May, to reduce the chances of the damaged *Bismarck* reaching the port, the squadron was notified that it would not operate again for the remainder of the month.

Henry had assumed that leave would not be forthcoming for some time now that he was on an operational unit, but took full advantage of the lull in activity to pay a surprise visit to Broadway for five days at the end of May. His mother was recovering well from her accident, although her nurse was still in residence. Rationing was becoming an increasing problem, and Henry was concerned that he had no ration book and his provisions were coming from the rations of others at Fox Hill.[200] In keeping with many other households, Mrs Maudslay sought to improve the family's self-sufficiency, already well catered for with Jersey cows to provide dairy products, and had recently obtained two hives of bees, cared for by her brother Reginald, resplendent in his apiarist's clothing. Henry may also have come across some of the evacuees billeted with Captain Richard Arkwright, their neighbour at nearby Willersey House, one of whom once fell into the goldfish pond on the Fox Hill terrace.[201] The war news was not good. The Germans were consolidating their foothold in Crete, and there was fierce fighting in Greece. In the Atlantic HMS *Hood* had been sunk by the *Bismarck*. Then came the morale-boosting report that the German battleship itself had been pursued and de-spatched by naval forces. Combining with these mixed fortunes partway through his leave, on Wednesday, 28 May, came the sad news from Saintbury Close that the Revd Gibb had died at the age of 62. A redoubtable man, he had been a close friend of the family, and his passing was mourned by many.[202]

Henry returned to Waddington on Whit Sunday, 1 June, and his customary letter home thanking his mother was full of family news: a letter had arrived from

Uncle Norman, containing a photograph of his daughter Joanna,[203] which Henry had placed in his room; chocolates ordered from Fortnum and Mason should arrive at Fox Hill soon, the bag given to him would be most useful. It was fortunate that on their visit to Finningley his mother and sister had been able to purchase two rolls of material from Vickers in Doncaster, for it had been announced suddenly that clothes rationing would take effect immediately. This was to ease the demand for raw materials and release factories and machines for the war effort. Oliver Lyttleton, Minister of Production, had broadcast to say: 'The British people will not grumble if they are assured that any sacrifices they make are necessary and are being utilised to further the vigorous prosecution of the war.' Not one to grumble, Henry raised his old concern about service issue clothing:

> Rather a jolt I imagine – thank goodness corduroy trousers don't take many coupons – they last for ever and are all I'll need at a rate of about 1 pair per 2 years! I don't have any coupons so rather wonder what happens and if I can get anything – not that much is needed, but I don't relish RAF underwear.[204]

Bad weather combined with a cold kept Henry on the ground, 'doing nothing except fill in the charts on the Flight Office wall', listening to the radiogram in the crewroom – 'which of course I adore' – and witnessing pay parades. By 4 June he had recovered sufficiently to be able to make his first flight with No. 44 Squadron: a trip in P4414 ferrying aircrew to Lindholme, repeated the following day in AD747, which had now been allotted as his aircraft, carrying the squadron code letters KM and individual identification 'O'. On the 8th and 9th he carried out half-hour air tests ensuring the serviceability of this aircraft, possibly in preparation for operations that were subsequently cancelled. On 6 June he wrote: 'I'm doing a bit of flying now but not operational yet. The cold is going and I'm getting settled in here and I like it VERY much.'[205]

His mother had phoned on 7 June, shortly before he was due on duty, allowing only a brief conversation. Writing to her later that day, he reassured her that he had recovered from his cold and that he was now fully settled in and enjoying life:

> I like everyone in my squadron a lot, which is fortunate. Lincoln is a nice old town – I visited the Cathedral for the first time yesterday (but) only had time for a brief look round. Decided to go over for the service on Sunday morning, but I'm on duty all tonight so will be asleep then.[206]

The trip to Lincoln had been occasioned by the arrival of a visiting aircraft for an overnight stay. Discovering that the navigator was a travelling companion from his return trip from Canada, Henry ran him in the Beetle to Lincoln, where they adjourned to the Saracen's Head, a notorious drinking haunt of the 'Bomber Boys' known locally as 'The Snake Pit'.[207] While there and celebrating 'in the manner custom dictates' he ran into J. Baxendale, an Old Etonian now in the Coldstream Guards, who brought him up to date on news of fellow Etonians Tim Vigors and John Harley.

Old acquaintance was also renewed on the evening of Monday the 9th, when he met Peter Pritchard, a flying officer with No. 61 Squadron flying Hampdens from Hemswell a few miles to the north of Lincoln.[208] They spent the evening at the Savoy cinema, seeing *The Marx Brothers Go West*, the Pathe Gazette and *East of Piccadilly* starring Judy Campbell and Sebastian Shaw. Although Henry's letter makes no reference, they may well have discussed Peter's narrow escape while making an attack on Kiel on 23/24 March. His aircraft had been hit by flak, and the port engine seized. After jettisoning guns, ammunition, bomb sight and all other expendable equipment, they eventually crossed the English coast but were forced to abandon their aircraft over Driffield, all landing safely by parachute. Despite this ordeal, Peter was 'in very good form' and now a deputy flight commander. He had been forced to cancel his most recent operation a week earlier when he became ill shortly before take-off, but was now fully recovered. Henry reported that he had 'grown a lot and is at least as tall as me, looks extremely fit [and] says all his family are very well'.[209]

On 10 June No. 44 Squadron was expanded with the creation of 'C' Flight, under the command of Flight Lieutenant Peter Burton-Gyles, DFC,[210] who was promoted to the rank of squadron leader. As if to underline the squadron's increased offensive capability, operations were ordered for the coming night, and Henry found himself on the Battle Order for the first time, crewed up with three men with whom he had never flown before.

During this period it was usual for new crews to be sent on mining operations for their baptism of fire, presumably on the basis that they might see something of the enemy defences without being exposed directly to them (although this did not always hold true, some mined areas being extremely close to strongly defended ports). The operations were known as 'gardening', the mines were 'vegetables' and, to complete the horticultural analogy, the areas in which they were sown were given the names of vegetables and flowers. Henry's first operation was to be no exception. While the majority of the squadron's aircraft were to take part in an attack on the *Scharnhorst*, *Gneisenau* and *Prinz Eugen* at Brest, Henry was to be one of four Hampdens briefed to carry out gardening in the 'Gorse' area, off Quiberon, mining the approaches to the U-boat base of Lorient.

A letter to his mother written and posted that day gave no hint of the impending operation. Whether because of security or out of concern for his mother's feelings cannot be known. Instead it was again full of recreational comment and requests for various items from home. The previous day he had been out in the early morning to shoot rabbits. He had seen plenty but managed to bag only one, which he was able to 'deal' with, prompting a request for his mother to find his large knife in a leather sheath (if he had not given it away) and send it on to him. It would facilitate future hunting expeditions. Could she also send four of the buttons off his blue Captain of Boats blazer? They would be ideal for the thick black cotton overall flying suit that he would be getting for the summer; besides, he did not think he would have occasion to wear the blazer very often.[211]

After another brief air test during the afternoon, Henry took off from Waddington at 2340 hours in AD747, carrying a single 1,500lb mine. To be effective, mine-laying required a precise technique. The weapon was released at a relatively low altitude and fell, retarded by a parachute, to lie on the sea bed until triggered by a passing vessel. Since the primary objective of mining operations was to 'replant' the enemy's swept channels, narrow stretches of water varying between a quarter of a mile and a mile wide, accurate navigation was paramount. Any mine falling outside the swept channels was regarded as worthless. To assist accuracy and to lessen the force of impact, it was usual to release the weapon from heights between 400 and 1,000 feet – not the healthiest of altitudes when flying close to a defended shoreline. It also left little room for manœuvre if one lost height during a turn. Speed was also critical, as the parachute could be pulled off if the mine was released too fast.

By all counts the operation was uneventful and completed successfully. The mine was released at 0128 hours from 500 feet; the parachute was seen to open and the weapon strike the water. AD747 returned unchallenged to Waddington, touching down at 0550 hours. Two of the other Hampdens had planted their vegetables successfully, but Pilot Officer Tristan Salazar was unable to establish his position accurately and returned to base with his mine. Of those aircraft despatched to Brest, all returned safely, reporting hits in the dock area but none on the ships.

The squadron did not operate on 11 June, but the following night it was detailed to attack the marshalling yards at Soest. Although Henry took AD747 up for an air test, the crew were not included on the night's Battle Order. Out of a total of ninety-one aircraft despatched by No. 5 Group squadrons, only forty-two aircraft claimed to have bombed the target. Two aircraft failed to return, both from No. 44 Squadron: Flight Sergeant Colwyn Mercer and his crew were all killed when their aircraft fell north of the Ruhr, and Flight Lieutenant Patrick Shaughnessy's plane came down in the sea; his observer drowned, but the remainder of the crew were rescued and taken prisoner.

These recent losses, combined with news of his cousin, Flying Officer John Blount,[212] recently posted missing and now safe as a prisoner, may well have given Henry cause to consider the future and strengthened the realization that he might not return from operations. He had seen the way that the Committee of Adjustment moved in swiftly to clear the rooms and lockers of missing aircrew, parcelling up possessions to prevent unauthorized 'acquisition' by others and felt prompted to raise the issue with his mother, albeit couched in relatively optimistic terms. As a footnote to his letter of 12 June he added: 'Don't take this too seriously! but do mark and read – If I make a landing on the wrong side of the sea, see that you get ALL my personal stuff back from the adjutant here – If I'm a prisoner I'll want it again and people aren't too good that way!'

On Friday, 13 June, Waddington received a visit from Marshal of the Royal Air Force, Viscount Trenchard, GCB, GCVO, DSO, DCL, LLD, accompanied by Air Vice Marshal John Slessor, DSO, MC, AOC No. 5 Group. After lunch in the Officers' Mess, Trenchard gave an informal talk to officers in the anteroom. At 1730 hours the teleprinters were chattering, printing out No. 5 Group Operation Order, Form B, No. 454, confirming another attack against the German cruisers *Scharnhorst* and *Gneisenau* at Brest. The attacking force comprised 110 aircraft, including 37 Hampdens from No. 5 Group, 13 of the latter from No. 44 Squadron (one being flown by Group Captain Boothman, AFC, Waddington's station commander and a previous commander of the squadron). Inspecting the Battle Order, Henry was pleased to find on this occasion that he had been allocated Mancunian Sergeant Leonard Leggett, a gunner from his Finningley crew. They were away at 2310 hours, again in AD747, with a load of four 500lb SAP[213] bombs in the bomb bay and a 250lb SAP on each of the wing racks (the more experienced crews carried a single 2,000lb armour-piercing bomb). Over the target there was practically no low cloud and only thin layers between 14,000 and 16,000 feet. Identifying a river and pinpointing his position relative to the target, Henry made his run in from south to north. Even at 12,000 feet, below the cloud, observation was made difficult by ground haze combined with the enemy's smokescreen, which obscured the bomb flashes and prevented photography. Henry reached base at 0440 and found that all the squadron had landed safely, Flying Officer Roberts being compelled to return early owing to engine trouble. Other crews reported that the target had not been completely obscured, and, although no direct hits were claimed, most bursts were assessed as being within the target area.

In addition the squadron had despatched three new crews to lay mines in the 'Nectarine' area. They were not so fortunate. On return, Sergeant Stanley Saunders, one of Henry's training companions, crashed at Southrey, near Horncastle, killing all the crew. While the crews had been out, the enemy had paid another visit to Waddington. The local 'Q' site[214] had been attacked, the decoy attracting a number of bombs, including three long delays that went off some three hours later, injuring a police constable and airman who were nearby.

On the 15th the squadron sent nine Hampdens to Cologne and twelve to Düsseldorf. Henry was detailed for the former. He had yet to find an established crew, although this operation would see him flying with another of his crew from Finningley days, his navigator Pilot Officer Wood. As they approached the target area, little could be discerned, although the general target area could be estimated from the concentration of flak and searchlights. With no sign of a break in the cloud, the bombs were released blind. No results were seen, although some later crews reported the large red glow of fire after bombing. Disappointed, Henry wrote up his logbook entering the single word 'Bombing' in the duty column, with no mention of a target.

On the night of 17/18 June, after a day's rest, the squadron was back to pay a consecutive visit to Cologne, with three aircraft minelaying in the vicinity of the Frisian Islands. At last Henry had been able to arrange that Pilot Officer Wood and Sergeant Leggett should team up with himself and Sergeant Wayland, another gunner who had flown on all of Henry's trips, and they now formed an established crew. Taking off at 2318 hours in AD904, they reached the target area shortly after 0200. The target was Aiming Point B in the rail yards, but thick haze made target identification extremely difficult, despite the fact that earlier aircraft should have started fires with their incendiary loads. After a period of search, Henry made a run in from south-east and released a stick of one 1,000lb and two 500lb bombs from 13,000 feet at 0220. Bomb flashes were seen in the target area, but no results were observed. Later crews reported seeing a number of fires, one of which was visible 10 miles away on the return route. All aircraft returned safely, Henry landing at 0535.

There were no operations for the next two days, and no doubt Henry spent his free time developing his new hobby of painting using watercolours.[215] Despite the break in the offensive, the spectre of death still cast its shadow over the squadron. On the 19th two crews had flown to Tern Hill. Taking off to return shortly after midday, Sergeant Charles Grieg was first away in AD904 and circled the airfield waiting for the other Hampden. Pilot Officer Victor Lauderdale in AD747 accelerated across the airfield but suffered an engine failure shortly after becoming airborne and began to lose height, crash landing at Audley's Cross, 2 miles east of Market Drayton injuring all on board. Witnessing the accident, Sergeant Grieg circled the burning wreckage. Suddenly his aircraft stalled and dived into the ground, killing all the crew. The tragedy was compounded by the knowledge that three of the aircrew involved had already survived crashes on return from earlier operations. It is not known whether Henry realized that the aircraft involved were the two in which he had flown his operations to date, and if he did, did he reflect upon his own chances of survival?

Waddington hosted another official visit on 20 June, when the station was toured by the Hon. Vincent Massey, High Commissioner for Canada, accompanied by his wife Alice. The target that night was the battleship *Tirpitz*, now at Kiel after sea trials in the Baltic. Twenty Hampdens of No. 5 Group were detailed, half of them from No. 44 Squadron. Henry departed from Waddington at 2325, piloting AD930, KM-L. The aircraft found 10/10 cloud over Kiel. Despite the intense danger from the defences of this heavily defended port, and undaunted by thoughts of Peter Pritchard's narrow escape over the same target three months earlier, Henry descended as low as 1,500 feet in an attempt to identify *Tirpitz*, but the cloud was too dense. Climbing back to 6,000 feet, he released his load of four 500lb and two 250lb GP[216] bombs at 0150 hours through total cloud on to the estimated position of Aiming Point A in the town. Looking down, they could not even see the bombs burst. As a final gesture of defiance, a few bundles of leaflets were released before they set course for home. The poor weather continued to dog them all the way back to Lincolnshire. All aircraft returned safely, but Waddington was cloaked in cloud, compelling Henry to divert to Little Rissington, where he landed at 0455.

The weather clamped down and they were forced to remain in the Cotswolds until the 22nd, when he returned to Waddington, piloting AD152, KM-J. Little Rissington was only 15 miles from Broadway, and it must have been tempting to attempt a brief visit home, although there is no evidence to suggest that Henry did so.

In a brief note following the Kiel trip, he wrote to his mother: 'I've been given a very interesting job in addition to my flying duties which will keep me very busy. I've done five trips now and are [*sic*] very happy in my work. I've got my navigator and one gunner back with me from my old Finningley crew which is very nice.'[217]

Henry's additional duty was that of organizing the Intelligence Library. This provided aircrews with a quiet area where they could relax and study a range of information concerning the general war situation (Germany had just declared war on Russia), together with tactical material on aircraft identification, enemy defences, naval intelligence and escape and evasion. There were reports of recent operations, with reconnaissance photographs showing the damage to targets, plus the inevitable copies of official publications including *Tee Em* (training and flight safety presented in a humorous vein) and *Evidence in Camera* (photographic intelligence commentary). It was a demanding task, requiring attention to detail and an enthusiastic approach, updating the material and maintaining the aircrews' interest through creative displays.

His charm and easy-going manner were already being noted by his contemporaries, and not only his flying companions. A member of ground crew recalls: 'I remember him as a most charming man, an officer and a gentleman in the truest sense of the word. He was unassuming, considerate and extremely good looking; hence our name for him of Tyrone Power.'[218]

Düsseldorf was the target for thirty Hampdens and eight Manchesters on the night of Monday, 23 June, and the squadron put up thirteen Hampdens. The operation was observed from briefing to interrogation by Brigadier General MacNeady and Lieutenant Colonel Cummings of the US Army Air Corps and by Air Commodore Johnstone, RCAF, and Air Commodore Baker, MC, DFC, of the Air Ministry. It was unfortunate, because, far from being a set piece, things went badly right from the start. Pilot Officer Denzil Biggane did not take off, owing to engine trouble, Sergeant Peter Gammon was forced to return to base due to sickness of his wireless operator and Sergeant Hall returned because of falling oil pressure and overheating. Of those who actually crossed the enemy coast, Sergeant Tyler suffered engine trouble and bombed the docks at Ostend, starting a fire; owing to an electrical failure, Sergeant Robertson could reach only Gilze Rijn airfield in Holland, which he attacked, only to find that part of his bomb load would not release, and Squadron Leader Burton-Gyles was unable to locate Düsseldorf, eventually bombing Cologne, which was under attack by a separate force of aircraft.

Taking off at 2300 in AD930, Henry was one of the five crews who actually reached the designated target, only to find that thick cloud and haze prevented accurate pinpointing. At 0120 hours Pilot Officer Wood released two 500lb and two 250lb GP bombs as well as 120 4lb incendiaries from 12,000 feet. Bomb flashes were seen, but no results observed.

Two other aircraft had been detailed to carry out Operation *Boom* against enemy airfields. Pilot Officer Baker set out for Bremen, but his engines began to overheat as he crossed the North Sea and to lighten his load he dropped his 250lb GP wing bombs on another aerodrome, which appeared on track. Shortly afterwards he was attacked by an Me 110, which he succeeded in evading, only to be coned by searchlights, which drew the attentions of two more Me 110s. Again he managed to evade these, but was forced to jettison his bombs safely and head for home. Sergeant Dart attacked Langenhagen airfield, near Hanover, encountering scant opposition.

The following day saw Henry practising formation flying in his newly allotted aircraft, AD975, but he had a night off on 25/26th, when the squadron sent seven aircraft to attack the shipyards at Kiel. The following night he was operating again against Düsseldorf. Once more the weather intervened to confound the planners with thick cloud, thunder, lightning, icing and snow. Of the nine aircraft despatched, one returned early with engine failure and only Sergeants Anderson and Jessop succeeded in reaching the target area. The remaining six found the weather conditions too daunting and attacked searchlights, flak positions and airfields en route. Reaching the vicinity of Brussels, Henry decided that their chances of finding the target were slim, and AD975 attacked an aerodrome at Haren from 8,000 feet. Their load of one 1,000lb and two 500lb GP bombs burst near the flarepath, but no results were observed. Despite the disappointing results of recent operations, the squadron could count itself fortunate that it had suffered no losses.

There were no operations for the next two nights, but the daylight hours saw further extensive formation flying practice in AD975 and a visit by the Inspector General of the RAF, Sir Edgar Ludlow-Hewitt on the 28th.

Letters brought news of home, providing a reassuring sense of normality. Mrs Maudslay was recovering well from her injuries, and there was no visual impairment. She was now able to get up and would be going soon for a final consultation with a specialist in Birmingham. The nurse had left, but Tita and Gordon would be coming to stay for a short while. His grandmother's electric wheelchair had broken down, and Mrs Maudslay was having great difficulty in finding anyone capable of repairing it. The buttons from his blazer and sheath knife had been found and sent on. But among the domestic detail came depressing news from Uncle Norman: Peter Pritchard was missing. Writing home on 28 June, Henry expressed his concern: 'I do hope he will have been as lucky as John Blount. Have just heard that he was on a job over the water – but shouldn't abandon hope by any means. I'm very sorry for Mrs Pritchard and indeed for all who know Peter who really is one of the best.'

Sadly Henry's hopes were not to be realized. On the night of 11 June, only two days after Henry's meeting with him in Lincoln, Flying Officer Pritchard had taken off on an operation to lay mines in Kiel Bay. His aircraft was hit by flak at low level and came down in the sea, with the loss of all the crew. Peter's body was washed ashore in the area of Maglehoj Strand, Lolland Island, Denmark, and buried in Kappel Cemetery; that of his gunner was also recovered and buried in Kiel Cemetery. No trace was found of the other two crewmen, and they are commemorated on the Air Forces Memorial at Runnymede.[219]

Henry was still billeted with the Hensons, who had recently returned from a few days' holiday in Derbyshire, where their son was at school. Ever sensitive to the needs of aircrew for as much relaxation as possible on non-flying days, Mrs Henson indulged Henry: 'I had breakfast in bed at 9.15 today out there [i.e. Manor

Farm], came in here at 10.30 – will probably work through until 5.30 am tomorrow so feel justified.'

On 29/30th the squadron carried out its final operation of the month, sending 12 Hampdens as part of a 106 aircraft force to attack the Beschimag Shipyards at Bremen. On reaching the target, Henry, in AD975, was met by concentrated flak and searchlight activity, which made it impossible to pick out any significant ground detail. Unsure of his exact position, he decided to seek an alternative target. Using the river junction to identify the docks at Emden, he released a stick of four 500lb and two 250lb bombs, which were seen to burst. Pilot Officer Biggane bombed the docks at Hamburg, and even the squadron commander, Wing Commander Misselbrook, encountered difficulties and bombed Bremen town. The remaining nine Hampdens bombed the primary target, all returning safely.

The station stood down for the final night of June. It had been a busy month for the squadron. Henry had operated almost every third day and already had seven trips to his credit, totalling over $47^1/_2$ hours' operational flying. At this stage Bomber Command was still debating the length of a tour and whether it should be measured in the number of trips or operational hours flown. To the crews it was 30 operations; to the civil servants it should be no more than 200 hours. At this rate, no matter who won the debate, Henry was a quarter of the way through his first tour.

Chapter 10

Learning the Ropes

The scar has healed where late last summer died
the glittering Hampden, and tore the building down.
Only the garden did not suffer: wide
now are all the healing blossoms of the town,
and where she crashed and burned, and where they fell
tenacious grasses move in ebb and flow,
and none would look, for nothing there will tell
how men were killed there a year ago.
(Herbert Corby, 'No Trace')

July heralded in the second half of 1941 with fine weather and exceptionally warm days. There were no operations on the first day of the new month, but there was a one and a half hour formation practice flight in AE152, KM-J, landing at Coleby Grange, with a short fifteen-minute hop back to Waddington later in the day. An air test scheduled for AD975 early on the Wednesday signified that the squadron would be active again on the night of 2/3 and eleven Hampdens were detailed as part of a forty-aircraft force to destroy the railway marshalling yards at Duisburg, Henry taking Hampden AD930, KM-L. After a briefing witnessed by Major General Beith, take-offs commenced at 2255, Henry getting away at 2300. Over the target, cloud and haze made identification of the target extremely difficult, and in the event only eighteen aircraft, including two of No. 44 Squadron's aircraft flown by Pilot Officer Bell and Sergeant A. Wilson, were successful in attacking the target, without seeing results. The remaining nine aircraft attacked alternative targets at Essen, Düsseldorf and Cologne. Henry thought he had found the latter target and bombed an estimated aiming point determined by ETA at 0205 from 12,000 feet. The target had been detailed to a separate force of thirty-three Whitleys and nine Wellingtons, and fires had been started already when Henry's stick of one 1,000lb and two 500lb GP bombs fell to add to the conflagration, although no results were seen. It is possible, however, that he had been deceived by a decoy fire. According to the records of Cologne's Civil Defence forces, only twenty incendiary bombs fell on the city. AD930 landed safely at Waddington at 0525. Otherwise it had been an uneventful trip, and all the squadron's aircraft returned safely.

After a day without flying and a night off, another air test of AD975 on 4 July signified that Henry would be operational again, as ten Hampdens were detailed to attack the submarine base at Lorient in support of the Battle of the Atlantic. This time the weather was more favourable and conditions over the target were ideal, allowing all ten aircraft to reach and identify their target, dropping forty 500lb and twenty 250lb bombs. Henry was detailed to attack any submarines that were identified. In the event none was seen, and Henry released his four 500lb and two 250lb SAP bombs in a stick from north-east to south-west, straddling the naval barracks and the naval fusilier school, although to the crew's disgust only one bomb was seen to burst. Other crews reported hits on the oiling jetty and a frigate. A large fire was started in a timber yard near Point de Gaurdan, and another was seen in the power station. Three other aircraft were successful in mining operations off the Frisian Islands. All in all it had been a good night's work, with every aircraft returning safely.

The next day brought a pleasant surprise for Mrs Maudslay as Henry arrived at Fox Hill for forty-eight hours' leave, during which he missed an operation by fourteen of the squadron's crews against the *Scharnhorst* and *Gniesenau* at Brest on the night of the 6th. Meanwhile, he learned of the wartime hardships being faced by the locals. During the previous month, Broadway had been in the news for having 'pubs with no beer', and licensees by mutual consent were now restricting their opening times in order to conserve limited stocks for their regulars. The basic petrol ration was to be reduced, and there was another hardship for Henry: during his leave the Beetle had broken down, leaving him stranded and having to be rescued by Uncle Reg. The following Monday, his leave over, Mrs Maudslay loaned Henry her car (registration FGT 918) for the return journey to Lincoln and for use at Waddington until his was repaired. She and her brother travelled back with him. They had arranged accommodation in the White Hart, Bailgate, Lincoln, close by the cathedral, a Georgian coaching inn with origins dating back to the fourteenth century. Its mellow panelled atmosphere would prove admirably conducive for two days' relaxation before his mother and uncle returned by train to the Cotswolds via London, where they took the opportunity to visit Tita, Gordon and daughter Annette.[220]

For Henry it was an immediate return to operations. Bomber Command's strategy had again turned to attacks against the German homeland, and the target for 7/8 July was the main railway station at München-Gladbach. Forty-two aircraft had been detailed, nine of them being supplied by No. 44 Squadron. Because of the persistent problems with the Manchester, which had resulted in an order being issued on 30 June grounding the aircraft, five of these Hampdens were to be flown by crews from No. 207 Squadron, the remainder being crewed by members of No. 44 Squadron, including Henry and his crew.

After the prerequisite air test, Henry lifted AD975 off at 2205 carrying a single 2,000lb HC blast bomb. Reaching the target at 0105, they released a flare, which illuminated the target immediately. Unfortunately the flare went out before Henry was able to get into a position to make a bombing run and the target was lost, with the result that the bomb was believed to have fallen in the centre of the town, very near to the main target. A large explosion was seen, followed by several blue flashes as electricity cables shorted, but no definite claim could be made. Two other crews reported that they had bombed the target, but the fourth, Pilot Officer Biggane, found his engines overheating and was forced to attack the nearest target, a railway crossing at Grevenbroich, between München-Gladbach and Cologne.[221] All the squadron's aircraft returned safely, Henry landing at 0415, although two aircraft from the remainder of the force failed to return.

(Elsewhere over the border between Germany and Holland this night, during an attack by forty-nine Wellingtons against Munster, Sergeant James Ward of No. 75 (New Zealand) Squadron climbed out on to the blazing wing of his aircraft in an attempt to extinguish a fire. His aircraft returned safely, and he was subsequently awarded the Victoria Cross.)

The following night saw the squadron contributing to an attack by forty-five Hampdens and twenty-eight Whitleys against the marshalling yards at Hamm. Having operated the previous night, Henry was exempt from this operation, which was to prove costly to No. 44 Squadron. Sergeant Alfred Wilson was shot down north of the Ruhr, and Flight Sergeant Eric Tyler went down over the sea, with the entire loss of both of their crews.

There was no flying and no operations for the next two nights, and Henry took advantage of the lull to write home on Thursday, 10 July. Thanking his mother for an enjoyable time at home, he thought that he might be able to obtain further leave very soon and asked her to send the registration book for her car in order to obtain petrol. Cryptically he stated that 'various things have happened which have changed the situation a lot. I may be able to go any day, and will want to draw petrol for all the way AND my special allowance of an extra 300 miles which I hope to get.'[222] He was also hoping that the generous allowance of petrol ration would allow him to reimburse Uncle Reg for his recent 'rescue mission'.

The change of circumstances had arisen with the news that No. 44 Squadron was to become the first squadron to be equipped with the new Avro Lancaster. As

part of the process to introduce the type into service, the squadron was to supply
a number of crews to carry out service trials at the Aircraft and Armament
Experimental Establishment at Boscombe Down, thereby gaining first-hand
experience of the new aircraft. It is most likely that Henry had been told he would
be one of the captains to be selected for these flights, which were scheduled to
commence around the middle of the month.

In the meantime the squadron's offensive had to continue with their aged
Hampdens. On the night of 11/12 July, eight aircraft were detailed to attack
Wilhelmshaven, two being flown by No. 207 Squadron crews whose Manchesters
were still grounded pending engine modifications.

Conditions were favourable, and all aircraft reached the target area, making
successful attacks, although haze made the observation of results difficult. Sergeant Anderson reported a moderate fire. The defences were active, but all the
squadron's aircraft returned, although one aircraft received a direct hit from
shrapnel, which bruised the wireless operator, and another suffered a punctured
tyre. Henry's target was the main railway station, and AD975's mixed load of high
explosive and incendiaries was released at 0127. Bomb flashes were observed, and
a photograph was attempted, but results remained elusive. Again German records
suggest that most of the bombs fell in open ground and only one fishing vessel
was damaged and a barrack hut burnt down with the loss of two lives.

Henry was given a week's leave and returned to Fox Hill in his mother's car on
the evening of the 12th. During the week he made a visit to London, where, on
17 July, eleven days before his twentieth birthday, in the presence of John
Sambrook and Elizabeth Howell, Clerks of Messrs Ellis, Peirs & Co., Solicitors of
Albemarle Street, Henry signed his will, ensuring that his affairs would be administered according to his wishes should he fail to return from operations. The night
before he came back to Waddington, a party was held at Fox Hill, when he was
able briefly to meet Peter Arkright, Ann Gibb and Dick and Joanne. He had also
been forced to listen to William Simmons (a Fox Hill estate worker) delivering a
long harangue about his relationship with a female acquaintance. At Waddington
Henry reported back to his mother:

> He also asked if he could borrow my 20 bore shot gun, I said he could, it's in
> the green case – it had better be kept in the flower room so that he returns it
> there every time after using. I think he'll keep it clean but it wouldn't be a bad
> thing if you reminded him that I'm very particular about guns being clean.
> He'll look after it OK.[223]

The Beetle had been repaired by Uncle Reg and was ready for the return trip.

Leaving at twenty-five past nine on the morning of 20 July, Henry took three hours and ten minutes to reach Waddington, 'including stops to give lifts and for the two gallons of petrol and pint of oil'. Henry seems to have been anxious to return. In his haste to depart, he forgot to pack his tennis racquet, golf clubs and shotguns. Despite his mother's provision of a packed lunch for the journey, he had not stopped to eat. '[I] felt so hungry on arriving that I ate the sandwiches as well as the Mess lunch. Will eat the cakes for tea.'[224]

Catching up on the latest news, he discovered that the squadron had operated on three nights while he had been away – against Hanover on the 14th, Cologne on the 17th and minelaying off Hamburg on the 19th. There had been a visit by Air Chief Marshal Sir Charles Portal, the Chief of Air Staff, on the 16th, with its attendant 'bull', but of greater significance, Squadron Leader Burton-Gyles and crew had been sent to Boscombe Down on the 17th, the first to familiarize themselves with the Lancaster. As if to emphasize this crew's prestige, on 19 July it had been announced that Burton-Gyles had been awarded a bar to his DFC.

Monday, 21 July, was spent reorganizing the Intelligence Library, which had got into an 'awful mess' while he had been away, before preparations for operations that evening. The target was the main post office and telephone exchange at Frankfurt. By contemporary standards this was to be the first large raid on this target – thirty-seven Wellingtons and thirty-four Hampdens. Twelve Hampdens were detailed by No. 44 Squadron, three again being taken by No. 207 Squadron crews. Henry took off for the operation at 2251 in AD930, with Sergeant Austin replacing Sergeant Wayland as gunner. It was Henry's first flight for ten days, without even the benefit of an air test. All crews reached the target and attacked, Henry dropping his load just south of the river opposite the centre of the town. Many bursts were observed around the post office, and large fires were seen around the inner town and the railway station. In the western part of the town a large fire was started in the marshalling yards. As they gained hold, some crews reported that the fires could be seen a quarter of an hour after leaving the target. Again German records are at variance with the crew reports, suggesting that the majority of aircraft attacked Darmstadt, some 15 miles away.

Despite the apparent success of this attack, the night's activities were tarnished by subsidiary operations. Two of the squadron's aircraft had been despatched to carry out mining off the Frisian Islands. On return, one of these, captained by Sergeant Donald Bruce, crashed on Greenstones, the staff residence for Lindum Hill High School for Girls, in the centre of Lincoln, killing all four crew and the school's senior French mistress.[225]

Meanwhile, the offensive against the three German warships *Gneisenau, Prinz*

Eugen and *Scharnhorst* continued as anxiety grew that they would soon be ready to venture out again to join the Battle of the Atlantic. On 23 July Henry flew AE152 to Coningsby in the company of five other Hampdens to be briefed for an attack the following day. The targets were to be the *Gneisenau* and *Prinz Eugen* at Brest and the *Scharnhorst*, which had been moved stealthily to La Pallice – an operation that would cost the squadron one aircraft, although Pilot Officer John Clayton and two of his crew would survive as prisoners of war. Henry may have been detailed as reserve, or there may have been a problem with his aircraft, but he did not operate against these ships. Instead he returned to Waddington on the 24th to be briefed with seven more of the remaining crews at Waddington and four from No. 207 Squadron (still flying No. 44's Hampdens) for an attack on the Krupp Germatia shipbuilding yards (Target GR3589) at Kiel. Again Sergeant Wayland was absent, and Sergeant Leggett moved into the upper gun position, while Sergeant Hayes joined the crew in the lower gun 'scuttle'.

After a take-off at 2245, AE218 arrived over Kiel at 0200, Henry making a run from south-east to north-west and releasing his load of one 1,000-pounder and two 500-pounders from 16,000 feet. Despite clear weather conditions and generally good visibility, no results were observed, owing to ground haze. A number of crews reported seeing fires throughout the target area and one huge red explosion was noted. Reports from Kiel archives again question the attack's accuracy, recording only a few bombs on the main target, with others on the nearby village of Wellsee, which killed five people.

The 25th saw a typically hot summer's day, and Henry relaxed by going into Lincoln to swim in the municipal baths – 'very clean and pleasant' – followed by tea in a Weiner café. The exercise had given him a tremendous appetite, and they 'nobly produced sausages and tomatoes on toast' to satisfy his hunger pangs.[226]

There was no flying the following day. Henry's thoughts again turned to domestic matters. A letter had arrived from his mother confirming that Mr and Mrs Bond, the general handyman and cook at Fox Hill, had left. Writing in reply, Henry hoped that this would not pose too much of a strain. Alluding to the two operations completed in the past week, he wrote: 'It seems an awfully long time since last Saturday and that unforgettable week, one does so much and covers so much ground here that the time simply flies.'[227]

He recalled that Richard Henson had been sent home from his first term at school with a bad cough. The Hensons had thought that Henry and Pilot Officer Wood would be away for the night that Richard returned and had given him a bed in Henry's room. In the event, Wood *was* away but Henry returned home to find the other bed in his room occupied by a strange boy – not that he minded, but 'it must have given the unfortunate boy rather a jolt to wake up on his first morning at home and find me shaving in the same room'. Reassuring his mother he added: 'I have not caught the cough!'

The Beetle was still giving problems, but after a considerable search Henry had found a reliable garage in Lincoln where they would undertake a major service. Such facilities were scarce in wartime Britain, most experienced mechanics either having been called up into the forces or being engaged on vital war work. The servicing of private cars, themselves considered a luxury, was deemed non-essential to the war effort.

> They traced a leaking washer in the carburettor very quickly and replaced it and so forth v. efficiently – also very pleasant people to deal with which is more than one can say for all the garages in Lincoln. One left me waiting for ten minutes only to say (looking) in the other direction without meeting my eyes that if I left the car for a fortnight they might have a look at it. Short-handed they are of course, but its strange how some people are very much nicer than others.[228]

During his leave Henry had met up again with the 16-year-old Rachel Studd from Stanway, a friend of some years with whom he had exchanged letters during his later years at Eton and participated in local amateur dramatics and games of tennis during Long Leave. He had intended to give her two gramophone records that she said she liked – an HMV recording of 'Blow, Blow thou Winter Wind' and 'It was a Lover and his Lass' and another of 'Yes my Darling Daughter' and 'Down Argentine Way' on the Bluebird label. If his mother was going into Broadway, might she find out if any of the Studds would be there and hand the records over?[229]

A major mining effort was detailed for the following night. Fifteen Hampdens were to 'garden' the Lorient area and then carry on to release their wing bombs on secondary targets in the area, mainly aerodrome flarepaths and the submarine boom in Lorient docks.

Henry took off at 2250. The crew had still no permanent replacement for Sergeant Wayland, and Sergeant Atkinson took AD966's undergun position. Henry's logbook erroneously lists Sergeant Hayes, gunner on the Kiel operation, as a crew member for this operation.

At 0240 hours Pilot Officer Wood located their position and planted their mine in the 'ARTICHOKE' area from 400 feet. Twenty minutes later he was over his secondary target, the U-boat base at Lorient, which he bombed with two 250-pounders from 8,000 feet. Mission completed, he returned home at 0540.

It had been a clear night, and Henry was obviously enjoying himself, as midnight signalled the start of his 20th birthday. Writing to his mother two days later:

'The first two hours of July 28th were great fun and I must tell you about them some day.'[230]

His optimism may also have been related to the fact that, having now completed thirteen operations, the crew were more likely to survive their full tour. This was nothing to do with superstition, merely the dubious evidence of statistics that suggested that the combination of experience and efficiency improved a crew's chances after twelve operations.

Henry's was one of seven crews who reported successfully attacking a secondary target. Six were unable to locate any suitable target and returned with their bombs, and Pilot Officer Salazar had been forced to return early with intercom trouble that prevented him from releasing his mine. The fifteenth aircraft, piloted by Sergeant Peter Gammon, a South African from Capetown, was hit by flak while searching for his mining area and crashed in the sea with the loss of all the crew. Much of the remainder of Henry's birthday was spent in bed. Finally rising at 4.30 in the afternoon, he considered going into Lincoln to see a film, but decided against it. There were birthday telegrams from his mother and brother John. Writing to his mother a week earlier, he had suggested that she should send him a professional studio portrait photograph of herself as a present, but it would appear that she had been unable to do so in time, for on the 30th Henry wrote to her thanking her for 'the washing and the chocolates'. Other letters had arrived from his sister, Kelly and Mrs Barker, the latter also sending a box of sweets and chocolate. His grandmother had sent a carton of cigarettes.

Cologne marshalling yards were the target for thirteen of the squadron's Hampdens on the night of the 30th. By all accounts it was not a successful night. The weather was extremely bad, with severe icing conditions and electrical storms on the outward route. Only three aircraft claimed to have attacked what they believed to be Cologne. The cloud was almost solid down to 4,000 feet, making positive identification impossible. Seven of the remainder bombed Aachen. Of the remainder, Pilot Officer Jean Sauvage[231] did not even manage to take off, damaging his aircraft as he taxied to the runway, and Wing Commander Misselbrook, the squadron commander, ran into appalling conditions at the Belgian coast and, after making two attempts, was forced to return early, jettisoning his bombs in the North Sea. Sergeant John Armstrong was even less fortunate. Experiencing engine trouble in addition to the adverse weather, he turned early for home, but was forced to crash-land at Carlton-le-Moorland, 9 miles from base, fortunately without injury to the crew, when both engines failed completely after an attempted overshoot. Adding to the confusion of the night, the No. 44 Squadron ORB contains no record of Henry participating in this attack, although his logbook states that he took part, flying AD975 and recording that he reached Cologne but experienced a hang-up over the target and had to bring his bombs back. To complete the confusion, the weather had clamped down over No. 5 Group bases, and he was diverted to Bircham Newton in Norfolk. While there he had a happy meeting with Pilot Officer John Stewart-Robinson, his old friend from Beaudesert days, now also a pilot. Catching up on news of old friends and family, he discovered that John was also friends with Pilot Officer Timothy Prescott Decie, who had recently arrived in Henry's flight.[232]

Henry and his crew flew back to Waddington later on Friday, 1 August. The month was starting badly for No. 44 Squadron. In addition to the previous night's failures, a Hampden up on an engine test during the early evening, piloted by Sergeant Godfrey LeBlanc Smith, dived into the ground near South Park, Lincoln, killing all on board and also members of the ground crew.

Saturday, 2 August, was a quiet day, enabling Henry to catch up on correspondence. In his previous letter to his mother he had promised to return the registration book for FGT 918, which presumably he had forgotten to take back with him when he returned the car and collected the Beetle on his previous leave. Much to his consternation he could not find the document. Perhaps he *had* returned it to her? Concerned that she might be unable to obtain petrol, he sent her some petrol coupons valid for her car with a brief covering note: 'Cannot find your registration book though I don't think I've sent it back to you yet, so enclose 5 galls in case you are short. You must be. Will send registration book soon. Letter soon.'[233]

Although no Battle Orders were posted, the squadron was kept on readiness for the next two days, each seeing Henry fly a routine air test to ensure maximum serviceability should operations be detailed. Operations were ordered on 5 August, with a major effort by Bomber Command of 263 aircraft against three targets. The squadron's contribution was split between two targets, the railway workshops at Karlsruhe and the main railway station at Mannheim.

The fifty-strong force of Hampdens detailed for the former included Henry among eleven crews from No. 44 Squadron. Seven of them found the target and bombed successfully. Piloting AD920, Henry ran into cloud, failed to identify the workshops and overshot the city. Continuing 40 miles to the south-east, he located Heilbronn, where he dropped his bombs in the centre of the town. Immediately after the bombing, the target was obscured by cloud, which prevented the assessment of results. Returning to Waddington, the crew dropped two tins of 'DECKERS' en route over wooded country near Mannheim. (These were small incendiary devices comprising a sandwich of celluloid strips and latex rubber surrounding phosphorous pellets. Carried in tins containing alcohol and water, they were released over suitable areas to dry out and ignite, theoretically setting fire to crops and woodland. They were not very effective.) Despite his inability to locate the primary target, Henry fared better than two of the others. Pilot Officer Cyril Anekstein and Pilot Officer Edward Thompson picked up what they thought was a recall signal and returned to base with their bombs, only to discover that the signal had been intended for an aircraft from Scampton. The entry in the squadron records states that Henry attacked Heilbronn *in mistake* for Karlsruhe. Whether or not he was embarrassed by his failure to find the target, or simply made an incomplete entry in his logbook, cannot be known, but the entry for this night simply reads 'Bombing', only the duration of the flight providing an indication that this was an operation.

It cannot have been a happy time for Henry. On 5 August he wrote to his mother:

> This is a wretched letter for me because I've lost your registration book. I'm almost certain that I left it in a drawer in the wooden hut and that drawer has been cleared out by someone else (my navigator) of the various odds and ends of his that were there and it may have gone in the waste paper basket. Otherwise I have searched every drawer, suitcase in the place down to the largest of my hats and underneath the linings of the drawers and simply cannot find it anywhere.[234]

He cannot have been consoled by the fact that during his search he found a long-lost registration book for his flight commander's car. The latter volunteered the information that a replacement document could be obtained for 5*s* (25p), and Henry suggested that his mother should make an application – although he promised to maintain the search for the original.

Aircraft operated for the next two nights, against the docks at Calais (losing Sergeant Gordon Bradbury and his crew on their first operational flight, all killed after their aircraft[235] began to break up in bad weather and hit trees near Barton Bendish, while trying to land at Marham, Norfolk) and the Krupp works at Essen. Henry's crew were not included in the Battle Orders, and he was able to go into Lincoln and collect the Beetle from its service. The cost of the entire service came to just over £1, including overhaul of the brakes, cable operated on Standards and notorious for getting out of balance if not adjusted regularly.

Rumours of a daylight operation gained credibility when Wing Commander Misselbrook, Squadron Leader Burton-Gyles, Squadron Leader Nettleton, Pilot Officer Tew, Pilot Officer Salazar and Henry (with Flight Lieutenant Marshal as reserve) were selected to practise daylight formation on 8 August. Henry's log-book makes no record of any flight on this date, so perhaps it was just as well that weather prevented the operation from taking place as planned the following day.

Instead, the crews, including Henry in AD975, continued their formation practice. On 10 August Henry learned that he was to attend a Beam Approach Course.

An increasing number of RAF stations were being equipped with the Lorenz Standard Beam Approach system to assist landings in poor conditions. It was not a blind landing system, but a means of enabling the pilot to line up on the runway and make a final visual landing. It comprised a radio beam transmitted by a ground station along the runway approach path. The signal was split, and, when tuned into the frequency, the approaching aircraft could obtain both visual and aural indications of any deviation from the runway centre line. Correctly positioned, the pilot received a continuous tone; if he was off to the right he heard dashes, to the left he heard dots, matched by a visual indicator. Two low-powered beacons, one on the runway threshold and another about 2 miles out, provided an assessment of range from touchdown. It was an effective system for its time, but required considerable concentration on the part of the pilot. A number of Beam Approach Training Flights were located at stations around the country, No. 6 BAT Flight, commanded by Squadron Leader C. W. Bromley, being based at Waddington, where an additional refinement had been instigated. A double row of electric lights across the grass defined the runway, as opposed to the more usual line of dim 'Glim' lamps and flickering paraffin flares.

No. 22 Course of No. 6 BAT Flight commenced on Monday, 11 August, with pupils being taken up for an initial familiarization flight in one of the flight's Airspeed Oxfords, by now the RAF's standard twin-engined trainer. The aircraft were conspicuous in the Waddington circuit with their yellow undersurfaces and unique yellow triangle markings, a warning to others that their pilots would be concentrating on their instruments rather than looking out of the cockpit.

In addition to flying experience and ground tuition, pupils had to complete five hours of Link Trainer instruction, comprising twice-daily half-hour sessions with Sergeant Brouard. By the end of the course Henry had completed 5 hours 20 minutes on the Link Trainer, together with ten flights totalling 11 hours 22 minutes, exceeding the course's average time of 10 hours 42 minutes per pupil.

The course finished on the 17th, and Henry found himself with a free weekend, visiting Lincoln on the Sunday to attend a service in the cathedral. Afterwards he stayed for a short while to see a little of an exhibition and parade staged by the Army and Home Guard. It was part of a weekend event in support of the 'Speed the Tanks' fund, particularly significant to Lincoln, since local engineering works had built the world's first tanks in 1915. The previous day a Matilda and two Valentine tanks had been given a ceremonial escort into the city along the Newark road to be met by the mayor, Councillor Tuck, in the LNER station yard. Today they were holding an exercise with the local battalion of the Home Guard. The watching crowds immediately took sides, cheering encouragement to their favoured team as if the event were a football match. The local consensus saw the Home Guard as victors, a view strongly disputed by the officer in charge of the tank crews when he spoke at the subsequent Rotarian lunch held in their honour.

Returning to his billet, Henry also took the opportunity to update his mother on the latest developments. She had received the registration book for her car (whether this was an official replacement, or whether Henry had discovered the original is not made clear). The Hensons were now suffering from their son's ailments. Mrs Henson and both boys were confined to bed with a nurse in attendance, prompting Henry to comment scathingly: 'The Henson family is not very fit.' On the subject of billets, Henry gave his mother advice should she find herself pressurized to open up Fox Hill:

> Ask for aircrew officers. They will be delivered and collected by RAF transport and if you give them a key to one of the doors as the Hensons have for us there will be never be any trouble about getting in and out in the early morning when they are flying.[236]

He was longing to get home again but did not envisage being able to take any leave for about a month. Perhaps his mother might like to come to Lincoln for a night or two at the White Hart before then? The squadron would be holding a cocktail party and dance the following Thursday: 'It might amuse you to drop in on the cocktail party. I haven't really met anyone here who would be any good to ask to make up a party for the dance and I can't say I relish the idea of just "attending" it.' RAF uniform in wartime Lincolnshire was 'not exactly the same sort of passport as the Guards, and I haven't the energy to go haggling for an introduction.' A day or so later, at a party at Scampton, it looked as though the issue might be resolved when Ralph Allsebrook said he might be able to attend and would try to arrange a partner.

Airborne with the squadron again on 19 August Henry found himself continuing where he left off, with a fifty-five-minute daylight formation practice in AD975, followed by operations that night against rail junctions at Kiel as part of a forty-two Hampden force despatched by No. 5 Group. No. 44 Squadron contributed sixteen Hampdens. Despite icing conditions and thick cloud in the Bremen area, fourteen reached the target, and all but three bombed their objectives. Henry was still without a permanent replacement for Sergeant Wayland, and Sergeant Cursett Sutherland occupied the under gun position.[237] Luck was not with the crew this night. When AD975 reached the estimated position of the target area at 8,000 feet, Henry found the target covered by 9/10–10/10 cloud and brought his bombs back to base. The other two aircraft, flown by Flight Lieutenant Redpath and Squadron Leader Collier, found the target but were unable to open their bomb doors, presumably because of icing. On return to base, the crews faced an additional hazard – an enemy intruder was in the area. Air-raid warning 'Red' was sounded and the flarepath doused. A stick of bombs fell across the airfield, leaving a crater between No. 3 hangar and the Watch Office, causing minimal damage but forcing the returning aircraft to circle in the darkness without navigation lights until the danger was over, a hazardous exercise at the best of times, its dangers compounded by the fatigue of a long flight.

Mr Stacey May, Secretary to the American Ministry of Aircraft Production, paid a visit to the station on 20 August, staying overnight as the guest of Wing Commander Lewis, the acting station commander. Making a thorough inspection of the station, he had an informal talk with officers from No. 44 and No. 207 Squadrons.

A night-flying test on the 22nd heralded operations that night. Fifteen Hampdens were laid on by No. 44 Squadron as part of a force of forty-one aircraft from No. 5 Group briefed to attack the main railway station at Mannheim. Fourteen of the squadron's aircraft reached the target, the fifteenth returning early to Manston with engine problems. Releasing a total of 33,050lb of bombs on the city, the crews reported a large number of fires, attributable to the high proportion of incendiaries carried by the force. The Mannheim records, however, state that the city received only six high-explosive bombs, damaging houses. Henry's own report confirms the degree of uncertainty, stating that his load of one 1,000 lb and two 500 lb bombs was estimated to have fallen south-east of the town on the east bank of the river. One burst was seen, and there were two large fires from previous sorties south of the town on the east bank. After a lull of four nights without operating, the squadron would return again to Mannheim, but this time without the Maudslay crew.

It appears that Mrs Maudslay was unable to attend the cocktail party on Sunday, 24 August. Ralph Allsebrook had been away on a course and Henry was unable to contact him to confirm arrangements. As a result Henry may have had to endure the evening alone.

The likelihood of a daylight operation was again revived on the 26th and 27th when yet more daylight formation flying was practised, but nothing materialized before the end of the month, and Henry was able to take a week's leave starting on the 28th. Leaving on the 9.24 a.m. from Lincoln, he avoided that afternoon's official visit by the General High Commissioner of southern Rhodesia, part of the Air Ministry's scheme to strengthen the links between the colonies and units with which their men served – by now a quarter of the squadron's strength was Rhodesian.

Arriving at the country station of Ashchurch at 1.20 p.m., Henry reached the haven of Fox Hill by late afternoon. Among the news would have been discussion of an incident at nearby Badsey two weeks earlier, when a No. 83 Squadron Hampden had crashed while the pilot was carrying out unauthorized low flying over his girlfriend's house. Leave was spent with the inevitable visits to friends and with a picnic party in honour of cousin Joanna, who was shortly to leave Fox Hill to return to school. Parties with Joanna and 2-year-old Annette were always good fun at Fox Hill. On birthdays Mrs Maudslay would continue the tradition she had followed for her own children and make an arch of greenery and flowers over the 'Birthday Girl's' chair. There would be games in the garden, with hunts for pennies hidden in not too difficult places – when twelve had been collected, they could be taken to 'Grandmother's Stall' (in reality a trestle table spread with a cloth) to select a suitable item from an assortment of gifts.

Returning back to his billet on Friday, 5 September, Henry discovered that the Henson boys were still unwell, but that Mrs Henson would soon be up and about again. But he must have been shocked to hear the news at Waddington. Throughout the previous month Bomber Command had been watching with concern as losses mounted. Recent events showed that No. 44 Squadron would enjoy no immunity. On 29 August the docks at Frankfurt were the target for a successful attack without loss, but on the 31st Pilot Officer Patrick Owen and his crew had been killed on an air test when their Hampden collided near Waddington with a Spitfire belonging to No. 412 Squadron. That night ten crews went to Cologne. Sergeant Stafford Harvey failed to return, and Flying Officer Sauvage was held in searchlights and extremely lucky to escape the mauling of a nightfighter that left his aircraft heavily damaged. Morale was boosted on 2 September when it was announced that thirteen Hampdens were going to Berlin and Frankfurt, but confidence had turned to shocked disillusionment the following morning when it was learned that Pilot Officer Edward Thompson, Sergeant Lesley Robertson, Sergeant Dennis de Brath and Sergeant E. Knight were missing, although it transpired that the latter crew had lost an engine over the target and were forced to abandon their aircraft over Dorking, all surviving with the exception of a gunner. Of the remaining dozen missing airmen, only two would survive to be taken prisoner. Fog on return resulted in diversions. Three of the squadron's returning aircraft were badly damaged and two crew wounded. Another Hampden was written off after being hit by a No. 50 Squadron aircraft while parked at dispersal. Life on the squadron was certainly less secure these days, and the loss of Sergeant Robertson would have struck closer to home for Henry, for he had been a fellow pupil on the course at Tern Hill. Perhaps as an escape, or possibly just as a means of spending a free evening, Henry went to the Savoy cinema in Lincoln to see *Wings of the Morning*, 'a tale of gypsy romance with an exciting racing element', starring 'Annabella', Henry Fonda and Leslie Banks, screened with *Married but Single*, a domestic comedy with Rosalind Russell and Melvyn Douglas, about a couple who believe that there should be a trial period at the start of their marriage.

Orders came through on the 6th for ten aircraft to be detached to an advanced base at Lossiemouth in preparations for operations mining Oslo fjord to hinder the German pocket battleship *Admiral Scheer*. Take-off was not until 1530, and before he left Henry was able to pen his customary 'back from leave' letter to his mother.

It was to be a frustrating visit. Arriving at Lossiemouth after a long flight, they found that operations had been planned for the following day. As time went on it became clear that, being a training station, Lossiemouth had limited refuelling facilities, which would not be able to meet demand. By the appointed hour, only six aircraft were ready to depart. AE298 was not one of them, leaving Henry and fellow pilot officers Tew, Anekstein and Nicholson disconsolately on the ground. Their aircraft was eventually refuelled and returned to Waddington. There they discovered that five of the remaining squadron had been briefed for attacks in the Frisian Islands/Kiel area, while four of No. 207's Manchesters were detailed for Berlin. As these crews took off shortly after nine o'clock that evening, Sergeant Archibald Watt, a southern Rhodesian from Bulawayo, failed to gain height. His Hampden staggered on for a mile beyond the north-east runway to crash at Branston Hall Farm, the mine detonating and killing all on board. After a slight delay, because of uncertainty as to whether all the Hampden's bomb load had exploded, the remaining aircraft took off, passing low over their compatriot's blazing funeral pyre.

Henry was again on the Battle Order for an attack against Kassel on 8 September, the first large-scale raid on this target. Nos 3 and 5 Groups were sending ninety-five aircraft split between the aiming points of the Kassel Land Armament Works and the Robert Henschel locomotive workshops. No. 44 Squadron's ten Hampdens were briefed for the latter target. The day was occupied with the usual preparations, air test and briefing. It was a clear night with good weather and very little cloud. Slight industrial haze hampered identification of specific aiming points, but the majority of the force claimed to have attacked their designated target, some crews descending as low as 400 feet to bomb. Arriving over the target at five minutes after midnight, Henry claimed to have identified his aiming point on target GN3819 and released AD930's load to straddle the target, causing a burst of white steam as a boiler house was hit. He could see numerous fires started by other attacks, accompanied by occasional blue flashes. There was a particularly large fire at the railway station west of his target, and smoke was starting to rise rapidly, soon to reach 4,000–6,000 feet. The crew released a bundle of leaflets before leaving the burning city, the rear gunner reporting that its glow could still be seen 80 miles along the homeward route. All crews returned safely except for Pilot Officer Anekstein, whose aircraft hit trees near New York when trying to make a forced landing at Coningsby with engine failure, injuring two of his crew. Unfavourable weather prevented operations for the next two nights, although two night flying tests were flown in AD975.

Gwen Maudslay phoned to talk to Henry on the evening of the 10 September, followed by a surprise call from Peter Wake, now at an Army camp near Barnsley, who suggested meeting in Doncaster for dinner when they could both get away. They had not seen each other for two years. Following the call from his mother, Henry started a letter telling her of his recent trip to Lossiemouth, although security prevented him from giving her any details. Nevertheless it gave him an opportunity to tell her news of his old friends and hint again at likely developments:

> I spent a night at Lossiemouth near Inverness recently – it's an OTU and I'd heard vaguely that Charles Pilkington had trained there, but wasn't sure – I thought he would be at a fighter OTU since he was starting off on fighters – but it isn't and now he's on Stirlings – I must say I rather envy that, but of course one can't be captain of one's aircraft so soon on the very big machines. However, it's a fine show to get on Stirlings. We don't stand any chance of that at all – but I have hopes of getting on to the other best 4 engine type which we have some day.[238]

The offensive continued with an attack by seven aircraft on Rostock on the 11th, costing the squadron another aircraft when Sergeant A. Dedman lost an engine over the target, forcing him to ditch 20 miles off Cromer. There was a happy ending to the story when it became known that all the crew had been rescued by HMS *Garth* after only thirty-five minutes in the water. Henry flew an air test of AD975 during the day but he did not operate that night.

The next day saw a fifty-five-minute air test as a precursor to the night's operations against Frankfurt. Most air tests were only half an hour or so, and the length of this suggests that Henry's non-participation in the previous night's attack may have been due to a technical problem. Alternatively he may have been one of several aircraft flown for the benefit of an official photographer visiting Waddington. In the event, only six of the scheduled force of nine aircraft were able to take off for Frankfurt. As the last three were preparing to take off, an enemy aircraft was reported in the area, and their take-offs had to be cancelled as the flarepath was extinguished.

It was an intensely dark night, and conditions were deteriorating as Henry approached the target area. Although he claimed to have attacked the main target, no results could be seen owing to 8–10/10 cloud, which ruined his attempt to obtain an aiming point photograph. Despite this, Frankfurt records state that some 75 high-explosive bombs and 650 incendiaries fell on the city and its neighbour Offenbach, causing 35 fires, mainly in residential districts.

That day the reason for the southern Rhodesia General High Commissioner's visit on 28 August become fully apparent. Information was received from No. 5 Group Headquarters that henceforth the squadron was to be known officially as No. 44 (Rhodesia) Squadron in recognition of the country's contribution to the air war against the enemy. Two months later there would be further acknowledgement of the squadron's record when King George VI graciously approved the squadron's crest.[239]

After two days of limited flying, on the night of 15/16 September 9 aircraft were sent to Hamburg as part of a 169-aircraft force, attacking railway stations and shipyards. Weather conditions over the city were good, but intense searchlight activity dazzled pilots and bomb aimers. Arriving over the target at 2200 hours, Henry made his run in at 10,000 feet, in the face of fierce flak. His individual report gives no indication that they had any trouble, but the general narrative records that, of the squadron's aircraft, 'Flying Officer Sandford, Pilot Officers Anekstein, Maudslay, and Budd, Sergeant Musgrave bombed either the docks or the town'. Identification in the glare of the searchlights was far from easy, and bombs were released over the entire city. Numerous fires were reported, some of which, as with the previous raid, 'could be seen for 80 miles after leaving'. Perhaps one crew had a gunner with very good eyesight? There is no doubt that, despite their efforts to prevent the bombers getting through, the population of Hamburg had suffered, 82 being killed, 229 injured and 1,441 bombed out, although their ordeal was nothing to that which they would experience nearly two years later in July 1943 as a result of joint efforts by both Bomber Command and the US 8th Air Force.

Operations of this nature demanded tremendous stamina and fortitude. Sitting for some eight hours in the cramped confines of the Hampden's cold, draughty and narrow cockpit, bombarded by engine noise as well as the enemy defences, placed great strain on the returning crews. On this night, fatigue was combined with bad visibility because of ground mist and the lack of a flarepath owing to the possibility of enemy aircraft in the area. As a result, Sergeant Cecil Musgrave ran out of fuel. His engines cut, and he was forced down into trees near Harmston,

5 miles south of Lincoln, killing two of his crew.

(Henry's logbook entry for this and the previous operation provides strong evidence that he filled in his entries at the end of the month, prior to submitting it for his flight commander's scrutiny and signature. The targets for the nights of 12 and 15 September are transposed.)

The moment that everybody had secretly been waiting for came on 15 September, when the prototype Lancaster arrived on a flight from Boscombe Down. Other than the select few who had been privileged to see it at A&AEE, this was the squadron's first view of the aircraft that was to replace their aged Hampdens and revitalize the RAF's night offensive against the Third Reich. So similar was it to its predecessor, the Manchester, that the uninitiated dismissed it as yet another of No. 207 Squadron's machines, as the new aircraft made its final approach to Waddington. Word soon got round that this was something different, and the station came out to inspect the latest arrival.

The Lancaster had been sent to Waddington not only to raise morale among the squadrons that it was shortly to re-equip, but also to ensure that there would be no problems operating this, the largest of the new 'heavies', from the airfield's grass runways. (The Lancaster weighed in operationally at 65,000lb, against the Manchester's 45,000lb and the Hampden's mere 18,756lb.) Already for several months parties of construction workers had been descending on Waddington to provide additional hutted accommodation (the Lancaster required a crew of seven against the Hampden's four) and extend technical areas such as the bomb dump and armament section. It was obvious that the conversion to operating the larger and technically more sophisticated machine would take time and that the squadron would have to continue with its Hampdens until sufficiently equipped and experienced with Lancasters. Nevertheless the squadron found itself operating with new vigour at the thought of things to come.

Chapter 11

Seasoned Tourist

Flame, smoke and noise surround us for a while;
A shuddering jerk – the load goes screaming down;
Cold hands and feet move levers for escape;
A chain of fire bespatters through the town.
Back to the darkness, friendly now, we speed
To count our wounds and set a course for home,
Speaking to Base, attentive to our need,
Watching for that far friendly line of foam.
(P. Heath, 'We, the Bombers')

Bad weather hampered operations for the next fortnight. Operations were laid on for nine aircraft on 17 September 1941, but cancelled, and those on the following day were restricted to three freshmen making an attack on the docks at Le Havre. Rostock was the target for the next night. In an attempt to economize on station working, some crews were detailed to operate from Swinderby. Henry flew AD975 there and carried out an air test in preparation before operations were scrubbed. Conditions seemed to be improving by the 20th, when ten Hampdens were briefed and took off as part of a seventy-four-aircraft force against Berlin – the 'Big City'. Taking off at 2000 hours, they began to pick their way through the German defences to the target. Conditions then began to deteriorate rapidly, and an urgent recall was transmitted to the force in an attempt to get them home before the weather clamped down over their bases. Ten aircraft, including four of the squadron's Hampdens flown by Squadron Leader Burton-Gyles, Squadron Leader Nettleton, Flying Officer Sauvage and Sergeant Knight, pressed on to alternative targets. The remaining six turned for home, hoping to find a suitable target en route. Four did so, including Henry, who bombed the aerodrome on the German island of Sylt before receiving his final diversion instructions to land at Linton-on-Ouse.

After flying AD975 back from Linton the following day, Henry heard that all aircraft had returned safely, although Pilot Officer Salazar's tailwheel had broken on touchdown at Middleton St George, leaving his aircraft stranded on the runway, where it was hit by Pilot Officer Cyril Anekstein, who was landing behind him. There were no casualties, but both Hampdens were badly damaged. Sergeant Knight, short on fuel, had been forced to put down on his first attempt at Pocklington and overshot, again causing damage but no injury.

Poor weather over Europe continued to prevent operations for the next week. Henry wrote to his mother shortly before lunch on 24 September, in a rare revelation of his flying activity. 'We fly less frequently, but the trips are getting more difficult. We took another rather satisfactory photograph the other day.'

Thanking his mother for all her letters, which 'make all the difference to life', he admitted he had not written for some time and felt obliged to apologize for the notepaper – pale blue sheets with a dark blue RAF crest and 'Officers' Mess, Royal Air Force, Waddington, Lincolnshire' printed in the top right corner: 'I don't like this crested notepaper, but if it's the price one must pay for a Mess Secretary who is efficient in other directions I suppose it's worth it.'[240]

It was some time since she had been up to Lincoln. Would she like a weekend at the White Hart? He had been able to draw ten gallons of 'operational' petrol that would make travelling around easier. In the meantime his social circle was widening courtesy of his old school. He had sent a postcard to renew contact with Old Etonian Sir Charles Wiggin, JP, at Honington Hall, Shipston on Stour, father of contemporary Etonian friend John, now serving as a lieutenant in the Grenadier Guards,[241] and also had a standing invitation from Lady Sylvia Fox, wife of Old Etonian, Major Sir John Fox, JP, to her home at Girsby Manor, near Burgh on Bain.

With more time to spare, Henry kept himself occupied seeking out the local rabbits or their synthetic alternative: 'Walked over Mr Henson's potatoes with a gun the other evening – saw nothing but had a lovely walk. Spent yesterday afternoon shooting clay pigeons – the air gunners have a trap for practice – it's great fun.'[242]

A daytime formation practice was accomplished on Thursday, the 25th. A night-flying test on the 26th suggests that operations were mooted, but subsequently cancelled on the advice of the Met man. Conditions seemed to have improved sufficiently to allow nine aircraft to be scheduled for operations on the 28th, but in the event only four took off, the remainder being cancelled because of the weather. Henry was one of those who managed to get off, but found most of the route covered by 10/10 cloud. The target was the main railway station at Frankfurt, and, although the weather cleared a little over the target area, pinpointing was still far from easy because of thick industrial haze. Flying Officer

Sandford, Pilot Officer Budd and Pilot Officer Salazar reached what they thought to be the target and saw their incendiaries burst. Henry was not so sure about his position and searched for a short while until he saw lights on the water's edge at a bend in the Rhine some 20 miles south-west of Frankfurt. In the absence of any other sign of enemy activity, these received the Hampden's load of 2 250-pounders and 360 incendiaries. Two tins of 'DECKERS' were unloaded in an attempt to set fire to woods in the Frankfurt area as they returned. Reaching the Lincolnshire coast, they found that the weather over base was not much better, and AD975 was diverted to Coningsby, to return to Waddington later in the day when the weather had improved. Others were not so fortunate. Three Wellingtons of No. 99 Squadron came down over East Anglia searching for the base at Waterbeach, with the loss of two crews.

Resting after the previous night's activity – the Frankfurt operation had taken eight and a half hours' intense concentration in the most appalling conditions – Henry was spared the next operation against Hamburg on the night of 29 September. Instead he found himself selected to join a force taking part in a low-level bombing exercise on the last night of the month, in preparation for a forthcoming operation. No. 44 Squadron contributed eight aircraft – including Wing Commander Misselbrook, Squadron Leader Nettleton, Flying Officer Sandford, Pilot Officer Budd, Sergeant Moss and Henry – operating in conjunction with eight more from Scampton and eight from Coningsby. Each squadron was to carry out a cross-country via Northallerton before being allotted a half-hour slot over the 'target' at Ferrybridge power station.

October started very much as September had ended. Adverse weather threatening to cloak bases in fog caused the recall of a small force sent to Karlsruhe on the 1st. The exercise against Ferrybridge power station was reordered for the night of the 2nd, but cancelled at 1755 hours. Henry was able to manage a fifty-minute night-flying test on the 3rd, this possibly being an attempt to mount the low-level exercise that had resulted in the aircraft being recalled after take-off. Further attempts were made to mount the exercise over the next four nights, but inclement conditions continued to restrict activity until the 10th. Even the BAT Flight, supposedly equipped for such circumstances, found the situation too severe, and on the 7th the crews of two Oxfords airborne in rapidly deteriorating conditions were instructed to abandon them by parachute rather than try to land.

There was one consolation, however. His mother had taken up the suggestion made in his last letter and came up to Lincoln with Tita on the 3rd, staying for three nights over the weekend. With the weather restricting flying, Henry was able to see more of them than usual, and contrived to stay each night at the White Hart. The benefit of the petrol he had been able to obtain was very nearly negated when the Beetle refused to start. Henry suspected battery problems and his mother loaned him £2 as a deposit in order to hire a spare battery. Mrs Maudslay and Tita left on Monday the 6th, his mother travelling to stay with Aubrey and Hilda Pritchard at Hill House, Higham, near Colchester, while Tita changed trains en route to travel back home. There was some confusion at Retford, and Tita found herself on a train to Sheffield! All was resolved, and, despite wartime schedules, Tita was able to reach home by eight o'clock that evening.

While Tita was arriving home that evening, Henry and John Sauvage were accompanying the Very Revd Robert Andrew Mitchell, MA, Dean of Lincoln, his wife and daughter to a party and dance that were being held at the local hall in Boothby Graffoe. The Dean had ministered to the townsfolk of Eton early in his career and to his delight Henry found they had another common link: 'The Dean and his wife were being extra charming – and related to our Bill Parker[243] at Eton, a year my senior and a long time in Pop. Ran with and against me many times.'[244]

Perhaps as a result of a deal allowing him to stay in Lincoln over the weekend, Henry found himself kept away from his billet and up all night on the airfield for the next few nights attending to various jobs. As if he needed further exercise, during the afternoon of 7 October a treasure hunt was organized across the airfield: 'Too hot to run, but it was a pleasant walk.'[245]

The weather improved on 10 October, allowing the squadron to operate for the first time for over a week, sending ten aircraft against the Krupps works at Essen and seven less experienced crews to attack Dunkirk. Intense searchlight and flak activity was encountered by some aircraft en route to Essen, and on reaching the target they found conditions were far from ideal. Crews were able to pinpoint the target area only by glimpsing the River Ruhr and canals in the neighbourhood, no other landmarks being visible. Of the force of seventy-eight aircraft despatched, thirteen claimed to have located their target, seven of them from No. 44 Squadron, including Henry, releasing high-explosive loads, which started a number of fires, a large blaze being observed by Henry. For good measure the crews also released the inevitable packs of leaflets extolling the Germans as to the futility of war. All aircraft returned successfully from Essen, but Sergeant Joseph Bonett, another of the squadron's Rhodesians, was lost over Dunkirk. News was later received that he and his crew were safe as prisoners of war.

Despite the threat of adverse weather, the night of 12 October saw Bomber Command mount its heaviest operational effort of the war, despatching 373 sorties. The majority of these, 152 aircraft, went to Nuremberg; 99 aircraft were detailed for Bremen and 90 more, including 8 of the squadron's Hampdens, were sent to a chemical factory at Huls, on the northern edge of the Ruhr. On this occasion Henry would be flying AE130. Overall the results were to be disappointing for the squadron. Rhodesian Sergeant Edgar Owen (flying Henry's usual AD975) was shot down over Belgium and only five of the squadron's crews located Huls beneath dense cloud. Bombing was scattered. Unable to identify the target area, Henry turned for home. Probably more by accident than by design, his route took him over the heart of the Ruhr, where, despite the cloud, the defences were active over Essen. Flak found his range, and the Hampden was peppered with shrapnel, although no vital damage was done. As they approached the French coast, they released their load of three bombs on a military encampment one mile south of Ambleteuese, south of Cap Gris Nez. Bursts were seen among the buildings and three medium fires were started.

The weather clamped down again, permitting only air tests on the 14th and 15th to ensure the serviceability of AE377 and AD930.

On the 16th new orders were issued by No. 5 Group in an attempt to facilitate operational planning. In future the squadron was to operate only on every third night during the non-moon period, the intervening periods to be devoted to operational training. Waddington was notified that it would not be required to operate until the night of the 18th/19th, and No. 44 Squadron continued its training programme with another daylight formation practice in preparation for the impending low-level operation. Weather prevented operations on the night of the 18th and training continued. On the 19th Henry flew another formation practice in AE399, completing the exercise with a Lorenz test, brushing up on the Beam Approach skills he had been taught by the BAT Flight. The following day the squadron carried out an impressive formation practice with eighteen Hampdens in three boxes of six, led by the squadron commander.

Meanwhile, Pilot Officer John Ruck-Keene, one of Henry's instructors from No. 25 OTU, had been posted to join No. 207 Squadron at Waddington, making his first operation with them as captain on 13 October. A week later he was dead, yet another victim of the Manchester's notorious reputation.[246]

The new schedule of operations enabled squadrons to improve serviceability and commit more aircraft to each operation. On 21 October sixteen aircraft were despatched to attack the shipbuilding yards and port area of Bremen as part of a force of 153 aircraft. Of these only 8 of the squadron actually reached the target area, finding that patches of thick cumulus cloud combined with ground haze to restrict identification of the aiming point. Only three were able to make a positive identification and attack the primary target. As Henry approached the target area, AE399's intercom system failed, leaving him unable to receive directions from his navigator, and he had to rely on his own observation to try to locate the target. It was no good. Although visibility was fine between the clouds and stretches of river could be seen, the shipyards remained elusive. By now the enemy defences were in full spate and it was obvious that the night sky over Bremen was not a particularly healthy environment. Admitting that there was nothing to be gained by remaining in the area, he released his bombs over the town. Violent evasive action precluded any observation of results, although he did note a fire west of the river near the target area.

Arriving safely back at base, Henry discovered that most of the squadron had encountered difficulties. Three had bombed the town, having failed to locate the shipyards, two had become totally disoriented in cloud and returned to base with their bombs. Sergeant B. Johnson, unable to identify his target, had bombed the estimated position of Wilhelmshaven, and another pilot had attacked what he took to be Wesermunde. Two pilots had been unable to persuade their Hampdens to climb through the turbulent cumulus en route and attacked concentrations of flak batteries near Cuxhaven and Borkem. Pilot Officer William Budd was missing and believed to have come down in the North Sea.[247] Once again the weather, the difficulties of navigation and ageing aircraft had played as great a part in the night's lack of success as had the enemy defences.

Operational orders were further modified on the 23rd in an attempt to improve results and lessen the losses of inexperienced crews owing to bad weather, while at the same time providing them with the experience necessary to bring them up to the standard when they could be sent out in adverse conditions. Henceforth the newer crews would operate on any night of good weather conditions, rather than every third night. On nights when the forecast was poor, all aircraft would be manned by experienced crews, who would have been rested during the 'good' nights. That night nine Hampdens attacked the docks at Le Havre, with the loss of Sergeant Peter Bell and his crew.

Poor weather dictated that eleven of the experienced crews were out again on the 24th, when a small force of seventy aircraft were sent against marshalling yards at Frankfurt. Conditions were worse than anticipated, and only Sergeant Nicholson was able to identify the briefed objective with any degree of certainty and bomb. Four more managed to grope their way to the general area of the city and bomb through 7–10/10 cloud, reporting glimpses of a few small fires through the murk. Conditions continued to deteriorate and the remaining six saw nothing of Frankfurt. Four returned home with their bombs. Squadron Leader Burton-Gyles spotted an airfield 32 miles south-south-west of Cologne, which he attacked. Henry seized the opportunity presented by a rail junction glimpsed through a brief gap in the clouds near Babenhausen, 10 miles south-east of Frankfurt. Making a quick decision, he released the bombs a few seconds before swirling cloud again obscured the ground.

As AD868's wheels touched Waddington's grass, Henry must have been physically exhausted. It had been a long flight in poor conditions, and he had already flown a three-hour aircraft test earlier in the day. On top of this, the operation had marked the end of Pilot Officer Wood's tour. He had already completed a number of trips before joining Henry's crew and was due to be rested, posted to an OTU as an instructor. The crew would be assigned a new navigator.[248] Given the prevailing circumstances and the certainty that the weather would not improve until the spring, how would the new man fare? Would he be able to keep track of their progress across the dark and hostile skies and bring them safely home, or would they end up suffering the fate of so many who had gone before them?

Mrs Maudslay had written frequently over the last few weeks, but had received no replies since Henry's letter of 8 October. Concern growing, she sent a cable enquiring about his health and asking why he had not written. Suitably chastened, Henry replied, apologizing for his lack of correspondence. He had hoped for forty-eight hours' leave, which would have given him the chance to get back to Fox Hill this weekend, but it was not to be. The weather and the strain of flying had taken their toll:

> At the moment I've got a cold which isn't getting any better so I suppose it will have to run its course. Fortunately it's not the stuffy sort and doesn't affect me for altitude flying.
>
> More uncomfortable is a very sore bottom – as you know there's only one pilot in a Hampden and once in one can't move. On Friday I did a three hour test in very bumpy weather and flew for $8^1/_2$ hours that night and haven't recovered underneath yet![249]

Seeking to reassure his mother that he was being well looked after: 'Mrs Henson was very kind about the cold and sent me to bed with a hot whiskey [sic] and honey last night – breakfast in bed this morning and so on – really too good for words.'

In his penultimate paragraph Henry told his mother: 'You may have seen in the papers that our CO has gone to America to be attached to the US Army Air Corps.' (This was a reference not to his squadron commander, but presumably to the Group commander, Air Vice-Marshal John Slessor, who earlier had embarked on a special mission with selected officers of the other two services to meet their American counterparts. The talks were to result in the strategic agreement that, if America and Japan were to enter the war, the Allies would concentrate on achieving a European settlement, while seeking to contain Japan until Hitler was defeated.)

Inclement weather precluded operations for the crew during the remainder of the month, the hiatus providing an opportunity for their new navigator, Flying

Officer McClure, to gain experience with his recently acquired crew. Henry's first flight with him on the 27th in AE377 is recorded in his logbook with the comment 'nearly operational!' The significance of this is obscure. The flight only lasted a quarter of an hour but could not have been an aborted operation, since records confirm that none was detailed this day.

An air test and undercarriage test on 9 October ensured that AE399 was ready for the night's training exercise, another practice low-level formation attack by seven Hampdens against the Ferrybridge power station. This time the crews faced an additional element of realism in the shape of the local searchlight batteries. A further night-flying test for AE399 the following day completed what had been a gruelling month's flying for Henry.

November arrived with a minor gardening operation by three Hampdens off the Frisians, followed by a ten-aircraft attack against Kiel the next night. The weather was reasonable, and newer crews were despatched, giving Henry a couple of nights' respite. At 1045 on the morning of Monday, 3 November, No. 5 Group issued an order for the day for a concentrated effort against enemy shipping: three Hampdens gardening, two freshmen Hampdens bombing together with six Hampdens, including two from No. 44 Squadron, for a 'special assignment'. The two captains chosen were Henry and his flight commander, Squadron Leader Collier.

In the event the bombing and gardening details were cancelled, leaving only the two Hampdens, which were briefed to carry out a roving commission to locate and attack any enemy shipping they could off the Frisian Islands and North Dutch coast. The weather was bad and visibility extremely poor. Squadron Leader Collier was unable to locate any suitable targets and returned to base with his bombs. Henry was more fortunate. Taking off at 1800 in AE399 and with what appears to have been a scratch crew navigated by Sergeant Rickard, he reached the allotted area and came across two stationary trawlers. These were attacked from about 400 feet with four 500-pounders and two 250-pounders, scoring two near misses, one 250-pounder falling some two lengths astern of one vessel, the second about 30 feet from the bow, although without any conclusive result.

A short while later Henry chanced upon four more vessels of 400–600 tons off Norderney, steaming west at an estimated 10 knots. The gunners of this group were awake and began to put up a strong barrage of light flak, necessitating a higher-level attack. With a vessel squarely in the bomb sight, the remaining 500-pounder was released from 1,000 feet, Henry's wireless operator and rear gunner using their guns to good effect strafing and silencing some of the ships' gunners. Evasive action and the heat of battle prevented any results being seen.

After another longer than usual delay, which must have caused his mother not

a little concern, Henry wrote to her again on 5 November, claiming that he had
only just received her letter, since his place in the letter rack had been changed –
a not wholly convincing story! Reflecting on the fact that he was coming to the
end of his tour, he told her: 'I shall probably be posted away from here quite soon
for a course, then a while at OTU and then back here sometime next year, but it's
all rather vague.'

Leave was still hard to get, although he hoped that he might be able to get some
in about a week's time, when he would return to Fox Hill and seek to improve his
fitness: 'Flying is a cold business nowadays, or else my circulation is not as good
as it ought to be. If that's the case, it's my fault for not taking enough exercise, so
there'll be some sawing of logs for me on leave.'

His grandmother's wheelchair was still out of commission: 'It must be very
trying for Granny not to have her electric bath chair. One ought to be able to get
at the trouble by checking over all the wiring.' Then, recalling his problems at
getting the Beetle serviced, he added: 'but I don't expect that any electrician has
time to do that nowadays.'[250]

Updating his mother on news of his friends, he related how John Sauvage had
been able to take a trip on a destroyer – presumably as part of a scheme to encourage inter-Service cooperation; it had been great fun, and Henry expressed a desire
to try the same for himself, should he be able to get the opportunity.

Early the following day he had to take Anson N9835 over to Swinderby, returning by lorry. He enjoyed his reacquaintance with the 'Annie', recalling his training
sessions with a degree of affection, despite the aircraft's uncomfortable draughts.
Henry had now completed twenty-nine operations since joining the squadron in
June and one more would be officially recognized as the completion of his first
tour, resulting in him being 'screened' and posted as an instructor to an OTU or
CU for six months before returning for a second tour.

The opportunity to complete his tour came on Friday, 7 November, when an
order came through for the squadron to operate. Originally there had been
rumours that the squadron was going to be sent to the German capital. Air Marshal
Sir Richard Peirse, C-in-C Bomber Command, frustrated by the enforced hiatus
in his offensive owing to poor weather, had decided to order a major attack by 169
aircraft against Berlin. A subsequent adverse weather forecast caused Air Vice-
Marshal John Slessor, AOC of No. 5 Group, to object to the plan, and agreement
was reached that the squadron's Hampdens would attack targets in and near
Cologne, including the power station at Knapsack, housing Europe's largest steam
generators capable of an output of 600,000 kilowatts and the target represented
in the dummy runs against Ferrybridge. As fortune would have it, Henry's crew
were ill, and he was forced to remain on the ground.

Writing to his mother, Henry displayed his disgust and disappointment:

Today has been extraordinary – and I got nearer to throwing myself off a
bridge than I have before. It's difficult to explain without giving things away –
but I put in a lot of hard practice for a certain 'job' and was even consulted
by the CO and others to an extent that was extremely encouraging on it.

Then my crew went sick, or off flying for one reason or another and I
couldn't go. Words fail me. I'd been looking forward to it for weeks.[251]

The results may have provided slight consolation. The Berlin operation was dogged
by the weather, causing heavy losses as aircraft iced up or ran out of fuel. The
Cologne force fared better, all returning safely, but causing minimal damage to
the target.

To make matters worse for Henry – while he mulled over the injustice of life,
he received a phone call from Hermione Slessor, the AOC's wife, inviting him to a
dance the next evening to renew his acquaintance with her 17-year-old daughter,
Juliet, whom he had met at a dance in Oxford two years earlier.[252]

Under normal circumstances the invitation would have been welcome. It was
not an everyday event in the life of a young pilot officer. However, in his depressed
state, the last thing Henry wanted was to meet his AOC at a social gathering. An
excuse was required, but the usual one, that he was flying, was completely out of
the question; 'one can't do that with the AOC'.

Events overtook themselves, though, and Henry's tour was brought to a close
without him completing his thirtieth operation. An entry in Henry's official
Service Record (Form 1406) indicates that he should have been posted to No. 24
Blind Approach Training Flight[253] at Bottesford on completion of his first tour, but,
with growing demand for experienced pilots to introduce the Lancaster, it was
confirmed that this posting was to be cancelled, and, instead of instructional
duties, Henry would soon be sent on detachment to Boscombe Down to begin
familiarization with the new bomber.

On 8 November Wing Commander Misselbrook signed the assessment form
to be glued into Henry's logbook, rating him as an 'Exceptional' heavy bomber
pilot, with no apparent weaknesses to be addressed. Since joining the squadron
he had flown a total of 66.30 hours day and 194.00 hours at night, bringing his
grand total of all flying to 450.15 hours.[254] It is interesting to note that, even had
the earlier criterion of a tour lasting 200 hours been continued, Henry would still
have had another $8^1/_2$ hours, roughly one more operation, remaining. At least in
Henry's case, both the Air Ministry and civil servants had been correct in their
assessment.

The longed-for leave came through, and Henry was able to return to Fox Hill on 9 November, a raw, cold Remembrance Sunday. Arriving home, he found his grandmother and Uncle Reg were both ill, seemingly suffering from a recent meal of oysters. His mother had bought him a magnificent cupboard, which she had placed in the spacious drawing room. Henry was delighted with the gift, although he commented that the room now seemed rather crowded and suggested that his mother should move the corner cupboard from over her writing table.

On Friday, 14 November, the family celebrated Mrs Maudslay's 60th birthday. In theory Henry should have been able to remain at home for a fortnight's well-earned rest, but after only a week he was recalled to Waddington for duty. Still officially on the strength of No. 44 Squadron, he was ordered to proceed to Boscombe Down, 2 miles south-east of Amesbury, for his course on the Lancaster. On 17 November he drove down to Wiltshire in the Beetle, via Fox Hill. Stopping for a break in Swindon, he set off again at 6.30 p.m., and arrived safely at his destination some two hours later, notwithstanding the difficulties of navigating in the blackout and the lack of signposts. He admitted to losing his way only once; when unsure of his whereabouts, telling his mother, 'I just stopped and asked the yokels in the nearest pub – they are always available after 6 p.m. and very reliable!'

Chapter 12

To Forge a New Weapon

> The impression has got around that the Avro Lancaster heavy bomber is merely a four-engined version of the twin-engined Avro Manchester. This is very far from the case and the Lancaster should be regarded as a completely new type. (*Flight*, 13 August 1942)

Arriving at his quarters at Boscombe Down, Henry found himself sharing a room with an engineering officer who was 'pleasant enough, but the type who goes to bed late, which is trying'. Admitting to being a bore, Henry resolved to continue his habit of going to bed early regardless. The food was acceptable, but, mindful of his relatives' recent misfortune, he was rather wary of the apple charlotte presented to him, 'made from apples that were almost cyder [sic]'. It appears to have done him no harm. With the cold nights of autumn, his billet heating was somewhat lacking, for he was soon to write and ask his mother to send his school eiderdown for added warmth.[255] There was little to occupy him for the first few days, and he spent time familiarizing himself with his new surroundings, and getting to grips with daily routine. There was time to venture into Salisbury and explore its narrow back streets in search for a gift for his mother: 'A lovely old city – I have been to the best antique shops – but they don't go in for vases, and have put me onto a man who does, and he will try to get one of the right size and shape.'[256]

The Intensive Flying Development Unit at Boscombe Down had been established on 15 November 1941 to fly three early production aircraft for 150 hours each in order to determine their engineering reliability and maintenance requirements. Air and ground crews were detailed from operational units, and the detachment comprised a cross section of No. 5 Group's operational pilots. Most were already there when Henry arrived, headed by Squadron Leader Burton-Gyles, DFC: Flight Lieutenant (A/Squadron Leader) John Nettleton, the South African 'A' Flight Commander and A/Flight Lieutenant Reginald 'Nick' Sandford, a small man, keen on music, who bought all the records for the Officers' Mess and who always wore his pyjamas underneath his flying kit 'for luck'. Both men would fly with distinction on the Augsburg raid later the following spring. Flying Officer Wilfred Herring, DSO, DFM, known to all as 'Kipper', recently posted to No. 44 Squadron and famed for bringing back a No. 207 Squadron Manchester from Berlin on one engine a month or so earlier was another notable. Others may have had less publicity or experience, but were all rated as highly efficient captains: Flight Lieutenant George Weston,[257] A/Flight Lieutenant George Wilkins, Pilot Officer E. Stringer, T/Flight Sergeant Jones, T/Flight Sergeant Stott, Sergeant Beeston and T/Sergeant Hackney. They had been posted in with skeleton crews, totalling another thirty-six aircrew.

Henry's first experience of the new aircraft came on Wednesday, 19 November, when he made a thirty-five-minute flight in L7529 (the third production aircraft) with Squadron Leader Nettleton at the controls on a local handling flight.

Being at Boscombe might make travelling home easier, but, checking the railway timetable, he was disappointed to discover that the service via Oxford was poor, although there might be a better service via Cheltenham. Driving home might be easier; he was allowed a petrol ration for driving from his billet to the flight's dispersal hut a mile and a half away and might be able to save some of that. It was just as well, since during his visit to Fox Hill he had inadvertently unpacked the Beetle's registration book, which could make getting petrol coupons difficult until his mother found it and sent it on.

On the positive side, trains from Salisbury to Waterloo ran frequently and visits to Tita would be easy. He was able to get away for the afternoon of Saturday, 22 November, and drove down to Salisbury in time to catch the 12.48 p.m. for London. It was about four o'clock when he surprised his sister with a knock on the door of her Hammersmith flat. Quite unperturbed, she readily agreed to accompany him for the evening to see a West End show. It was a spontaneous decision and no tickets had been booked, so they took off immediately to Leicester Square to explore the current scene. There wasn't much time to make a choice, the wartime shows started shortly after five o'clock. They considered Esther McCraken's *Quiet Weekend*, sequel to *Quiet Wedding*, playing at Wyndham's Theatre, or the musical *Get a Load of This* with Vic Oliver at the Hippodrome, Charing Cross Road, but both were very popular and there were no available seats. A copy of the *Evening Standard* reminded them of Walt Disney's animated Technicolor epic *Fantasia* showing at the New Gallery in Regent Street, which they both wanted to see, and there would be no need to book. The programme commenced at 7.10 p.m. and they spent an enjoyable evening.

It's simply super [he wrote to his mother the following day], marvellous music – perfectly reproduced and all sorts of scenes and dances working in rythm [*sic*] with it. You ought to see it – in fact everyone ought to see it, and it won't come to the provinces because of the special equipment needed.[258] If I get 24 hours I'll wire you to come and join me at it if that would suit you.[259]

With permission to be absent the following morning, Henry did not have to rush back and escorted his sister home, where she insisted on preparing a quick meal for him. Leaving shortly after 11.30 he took one of the last tube trains to Waterloo and caught the 1.25 a.m. to Salisbury. It was a fast train and with only one other person in the compartment he was able to stretch out and sleep for the entire journey. Driving to Boscombe, he arrived back in time to grab another few hours' rest before breakfast.

According to his logbook, Henry did to fly again until 8 December, although in a letter, believed to have been written on Sunday, 23 November, following his return from Tita's, he states that he had just flown back to Waddington, ostensibly to collect spares, and had lunch with the remainder of the squadron. Certainly his early arrival from London would have allowed him to be available for this flight.[260]

The next day allowed another forty-eight-hour pass to spend two days at home, probably travelling by train on 24 November to Cheltenham and being collected by his mother. Henry had commissioned a brooch for her from the Goldsmiths and Silversmiths Company Limited of 112 Regent Street, and she had received a photograph of the finished work for approval before it was despatched to her. Henry and his mother viewed the finished design and discussed a possible alteration, agreeing that it seemed best she should see the actual brooch before making any firm decision.[261]

Henry had expressed a desire to seek membership of the RAF Club, but was having difficulty finding an existing member to support his application. In desperation he turned to his mother, persuading her to have a word with his Uncle Godfrey (Herbert), who was believed to have friends who might be able to assist. As is often the case in life, having secured her support, and with his uncle briefed, Henry himself then found another potential supporter, but aware that wheels were in motion agreed to wait to see whether his uncle's contacts would bear fruit.

On the personal front, Uncle Godfrey and Aunt Elizabeth, together with their daughter Diana, paid a visit from their home in Newton Longueville, Bletchley, Bucks (Henry commenting that he found his aunt more irritating than ever!). Henry's Uncle Norman had joined the Home Guard.[262] The staffing situation had suffered a setback, with John Summers being called up, depriving Mrs Maudslay of valuable help around the house and estate. Henry returned to Salisbury by the night train. This time the carriage was crowded and sleep was impossible, although the mass of bodies proved beneficial when it was found that the train had no heating. Arriving back at Salisbury at 3.30 a.m., he discovered two colleagues on the platform. Reviving themselves with a cup of tea and a bun at the station kiosk, they collected the Beetle from the station yard as agreed (Henry possibly loaned the car to friends when he was not using it) and returned to the airfield.

The eiderdown requested from his mother arrived on 29 November. Writing to thank her, he thought that there was a chance that the detachment might be returning to Waddington for a brief period, giving him a chance to drive back via Fox Hill. He also told her that he had just heard from Ralph Allsebrook, still with No. 49 Squadron at Scampton, that the pilot of a Wellington whose exploits had been recently reported in the press was none other than his training companion Lucian Ercolani.[263]

There was still little activity at Boscombe Down. The early Lancasters were having teething problems, which limited flying, and their embryonic crews were restricted to ground instruction while the problems were sorted. The flight had only three Lancasters, the first, third and ninth production aircraft (L7527, L7529 and L7535), which were very soon reduced to two when, after only seventeen hours-flying, L7527 suffered an undercarriage failure and was damaged in a belly landing. These aircraft had started life on the production line as Manchesters, but had been upgraded during manufacture and completed as Lancasters. Each had detail differences, L7527 and L7529 having only four wing tanks containing 1,710 gallons, with the latter having no mid-upper turret, and L7535 being fitted with a six-tank fuel system for the standard 2,154 gallon load. At this stage there were no formal pilot's notes, and the crews were learning very much from each other and the information they could glean from the A&AEE test crews who had flown the prototype. Those, like Flying Officer Herring, who had piloted the Manchester were at an advantage with regard to the size and general layout of the aircraft and its systems, while the others, like Henry, used to the snug, fighter-style cockpit of the Hampden, marvelled at the spaciousness of the Lancaster cockpit, with its vast greenhouse canopy and provision for a second pilot (later to become flight engineer) alongside, not to mention the sophistication of its controls and well-designed instrument layout. Once the crews had learned the basics, they found that the aircraft handled well and was light and responsive to the controls under normal conditions. (Evasive action, such as performing the 'corkscrew', a climbing, diving and turning manœuvre designed to escape nightfighters, when fully loaded, would be a different matter. Some former pilots considered that the pull-out from the dive required the equivalent strength of an oarsman in the boat race, presumably something that gave Henry no cause for concern.)

It was not only the pilots who had new equipment to learn. The gunners, in particular those from Hampdens used to hand-held weapons, had to become familiar with the operation of hydraulically powered turrets mounting two, and, in the case of the rear turret, four .303 Browning machine guns. In the Hampden, the navigator was also the bomb aimer; in the Lancaster these were discrete roles performed by two separate crew men; the wireless operator, though trained as an air gunner, would no longer combine the two roles except in an emergency. With a second pilot to monitor fuel and engines, the Hampden's crew of four had become the Lancaster's crew of seven, whose lives were to depend largely on each performing his task to the very best of his ability, and on their captain's proficiency to mould them into a coordinated and efficient team.

Meanwhile, Henry was finding other social activities to help pass the time. On the last day of November he was out walking, exploring the locality, when he found a cart track that took him directly to the main Salisbury road. Delighted with this discovery, he decided to use it the next time he went to town. The following evening there was nothing to do in camp, so he put his new route to good use and went off to see a film. Salisbury had three cinemas; it is not known which appealed to him that evening, but he could have selected from *International Lady* supported by *King of the Zombies* at the Picture House, *Lady be Good* and *The Great Swindle* at the Gaumont, or *High Sierra* with *Conga Swing* at the Regal. The next morning, discussing his evening with colleagues, he was nonplussed to be warned that his newly found route was allegedly sown with landmines to deter would-be airfield invaders! His own practical experience caused him to doubt it.

On 2 December General Hill, an old friend of the family, phoned and invited him to go over and join him and his sister, Mrs Batey, who was acting as housekeeper, for dinner at the weekend. His niece from Ireland would be there; she was now driving a mobile canteen in Salisbury. Mrs Gibb, widow of the Revd Gibb, might also be staying, stopping off on her way back from Budleigh Salterton. The general was also forming a shooting party with a wing commander friend of his to help control the local pigeon population. Would Henry care to join them? Knowing that the wing commander was stationed at Boscombe Down, Henry did not think that this was a very good idea, but good manners prevented him from saying so directly. Aware that the senior officer was currently on leave, he resolved to phone the general back and arrange to visit before the former returned.

With such little activity, leave was obtained easily, and Henry drove to Broadway on 4 December for two more days at home, finding his mother in bed suffering from a bad cold, part of which he put down to her exertions trying to run the estate almost single-handedly. He most likely would also have heard about the Hampden that a week earlier had force-landed in a field adjacent to the local railway station at Honeybourne. Piloted by Sergeant Moss from his own squadron, it had run out of fuel on a cross-country flight. Setting off to return to his unit, Henry found the Beetle reluctant to start. After numerous attempts with the starting handle, he coaxed it into life, hoping that it would keep going until he reached base. It was touch and go for two hours and five minutes, but he made it, although the car was losing power for the last part of the journey. The next day he investigated further and found that the car totally refused to start. Diagnosing what he thought was a blown cylinder head gasket, he walked into Amesbury a few days later to discuss the situation with the local Standard agent. Wartime shortages meant that spares for civilian vehicles were in short supply, but the garage proprietor was confident that he soon would have the vehicle running again. (In the event the problem was traced to a seized valve, not the head gasket, and they also found that the crown wheel and pinion had worked out of adjustment.) Meanwhile, Henry looked on the bright side: at least he was saving petrol and taking extra exercise! There was a slow-moving convoy in the town, and Henry was most surprised to find a recent Etonian Captain of Cricket giving him a wave of recognition as a tank rumbled past.[264]

Henry had sent a telegram to General Hill to arrange a new date for his visit, and rang the general's home on 7 December to confirm arrangements, finding himself invited to tea that afternoon. Mrs Gibb had arrived and was looking extremely well after her break on the Devon coast. After a pleasant evening Henry was preparing to leave when the general tuned his wireless in for the nine o'clock news. The week's events had focused on the 8th Army, locked in conflict with Rommel's forces in the Western Desert and the Far East, where the Japanese were advancing through China and growing more menacing every day, but where and when they would attack was unknown. This evening provided the answer, with the stunning news that Japanese aircraft had attacked the US naval base at Pearl Harbor. The assembled group felt a sense of warm, if grim satisfaction. Now America would have to enter the war!

As if influenced by the latest events (although almost certainly coincidence), the next morning it was confirmed that flying was to recommence immediately. Listening to Winston Churchill on the wireless that evening announcing the expansion of the war with Japan and extolling war workers to even greater efforts, Henry wrote to his mother, 'There can be no complaining that the news is dull tonight!' Thanking her as usual for his enjoyable leave, he appraised her of the problems with the Beetle and recounted his visit to the general's home the previous evening. Security prevented him discussing his work, or mentioning the Lancaster by name, but he allowed himself the comment: 'We started flying properly today and I flew the aeroplane [sic] for a while – it was very pleasant after such a long time on the ground.'[265]

He flew for each of the next three days with Squadron Leader Nettleton in L7529, carrying out circuits and landings of quarter-hour and half-hour duration to familiarize themselves with the aircraft. Despite Henry's comment, his log-book makes no record of him actually taking the controls, each entry being made as second pilot. At this stage the Lancaster was not equipped with dual controls, and Henry's role would have been one of 'pilot's mate', holding the throttles open on take-off, operating the flaps and undercarriage and monitoring fuel while absorbing as much as possible about the aircraft's flying characteristics.

His mother's illness gave him incentive to write more frequently. He had very little personal news, and his letter of 10 December was confined to topical issues and family matters. It was good that she remained in bed, at least she was resting. She really could do with a complete break away from Fox Hill, but now the chronic shortage of domestic staff would make that very difficult; meanwhile, he recommended that she take Bemax, Adexolin and Vitamin C tablets, repeating their names in large print in the left margin so she should not overlook them. Tita was considering taking a job as a munitions worker, a decision Henry was strongly against, 'unless there is a chance of a good secretarial job going. Manual work is best left to those with more brawn and less brains.' War news from the Far East was depressing. The Japanese were closing on Singapore, and Winston Churchill had just announced to the House of Commons the news that the British battleships *Prince of Wales* and *Repulse* had been sunk by Japanese aircraft in the Gulf of Siam.

> The Americans seem to have been caught out rather badly and goodness knows how we managed to lose two such powerful ships. . . . I was sorry to hear that Captain Tennant was commanding the Repulse.[266] What bad luck that part of the family are having, no details of casualties, however, so there is some hope of survivors.
> . . . the situation in Libya seems fairly well in hand – though there is not much evidence of the annihilation of the Huns, which we were promised, either they are gradually disintegrating or gradually slipping away.[267]

Confidence in the new aircraft was growing, and they ventured further afield on the 11th, with their first true cross-country – a trip to Waddington and a return via Honington in Suffolk, totalling three hours' flying. It was a memorable trip, meeting the squadron again, catching up on the latest news, and no doubt extolling the virtues of the new aircraft to those not yet fortunate enough to have flown it. Two days later the visit would be remembered for a more tragic reason.

It was the last time they were to see their highly respected commanding officer. On 13 December Wing Commander Misselbrook failed to return from a hazardous daylight mining operation by three aircraft against Brest. By one of those strange twists of fate, Squadron Leader Burton-Gyles was attacked by fighters and nursed his badly damaged aircraft back to make an emergency landing at Boscombe Down.[268] It is not known whether he met any of the detached crews; if so they might have heard at first hand how their squadron commander, having objected earlier to the operation on the grounds that such attacks produced heavy casualties for scant gain, had deliberately included himself on the Battle Order. He placed himself third in order of attack, knowing full well that the defences would be waiting, alerted by the two previous Hampdens. His predictions proved tragically accurate, for none of his crew (which included Sergeant Leggett, Henry's gunner from Finningley days) survived, and all are commemorated on the Runnymede Memorial.[269] Four nights later the squadron was to operate again against Brest on what was to be its final Hampden attack. Thirteen crews were despatched and superstitious members of the squadron might have claimed their views vindicated, for Pilot Officer Therald Kaschula, from Guelo, south Rhodesia, failed to return, he and his crew becoming the squadron's last Hampden casualties.

Despite a relative increase in flying activity in the weeks before Christmas, Henry was able to turn his mind to the question of presents and cards for the family. He asked his mother to send him his Christmas card list, since without it he was certain to miss somebody. For his 2-year-old niece Annette he had bought a plate with a rabbit decoration. He had been harder pressed to think of something suitable for cousin Joanna, but had finally settled for a copy of a Kenneth Grahame omnibus, containing *Wind in the Willows* and two other stories. His mother had received the brooch from the Goldsmiths and Silversmiths Company, and Henry thought that she might want the sides taken off. It would be easy for her to send it back to be altered once she had tried it on. He also needed to select a wedding present for Derek Mond, but this was giving him more difficulty locally, so he went up to London on 15 December to see if he could find anything suitable, taking advantage of the opportunity to brief the jewellers about probable alterations to the brooch. While in town he also made enquiries about membership of the RAC Club, perhaps still unsure of the possibility of being accepted for the RAF Club: 'For the RAC I have to get two members to propose and second me, and wonder if anyone knows of someone who would do it, not that there's much hurry, or that I want to join the RAC. I've been to it once with Daddy and once with Uncle Rustat, and don't know any of the members.'[270] He added rather laconically that it was difficult to know which one to join, 'as you can't walk in and look round like a hotel, it's not easy!'

Christmas leave seemed unlikely, but he might be able to engineer forty-eight hours over the festive period. Just in case, would his mother please buy some bottles of fizzy lemonade, 'as we've got quite a lot of Pimms, and it's best made with lemonade'.

The Beetle was giving trouble again, being sluggish to accelerate and prone to stalling, but, already dissatisfied with the earlier servicing of the differential, Henry decided to look at the problems himself. Having checked the carburettor jet, only then did he subsequently spot that the throttle cable was jamming at its linkage with the carburettor – a relatively simple fault to rectify.

There were some brief local tests on 16 and 17 December with L7535, but it was not until Sunday, 21st, after a total of 5 hours and 10 minutes' flight experience of the type, that Henry was given his first feel of the bomber's controls, completing fifteen minutes' dual circuits with Squadron Leader Nettleton, again in L7535. The aircraft landed, and Nettleton clambered out. Any fleeting memories of his first solo at Brough must have been eclipsed instantly by the need for concentration, applying all the knowledge he had gleaned as he taxied out for his first Lancaster solo.

For a pilot of Henry's experience, flying the Lancaster would not have been difficult once he was familiar with the larger size and weight of the machine and the fact that there were four throttles to control rather than two. It was the detail that might cause the problems, the need to watch engine temperatures while on the ground and taxiing (the liquid-cooled in-line Merlins would overheat far more rapidly than the Hampden's air-cooled Pegasus radials), the fact that it was advisable to open up the port engines slightly ahead of the starboard to counter-act the tendency to swing on take-off, the change of trim as the flaps and under-carriage were raised. Each could catch the unwary novice. Trim changed again as flaps and wheels lowered for landing, and an eye had to be kept on the speed, the right hand juggling the throttles to keep the aircraft above 92 mph, making sure she did not stall (the Hampden lumbered in at a sedate 73 mph). Then came the heart-stopping moment crossing the runway threshold and cutting the throttles, waiting for the wheels to make contact with terra firma. The Lancaster stood much higher than the Hampden and, when lightly loaded, tended to float if brought in too fast; judging the precise moment required strong concentration and a steady nerve until with practice it became second nature. Nevertheless, all went well and after a quarter of an hour L7535 landed smoothly on Boscombe's grass, its pilot no doubt retiring to the Mess for a period of quiet reflection on the qualities of the thoroughbred he had just begun to master. Security precluded mention of the Lancaster by name, as he expressed his elation to his mother in a letter that evening: 'I have at last flown the aeroplane solo – not that I had any difficulty in doing it, but I never had the opportunity before, having had other jobs to do. It was great fun, and the first time I had flown an aeroplane myself for over a month!'[271]

Some of the crews were now deemed ready to return to Waddington. Henry hoped he might be able to obtain twenty-four hours' leave over the Christmas period and promised to go home to Fox Hill 'if it's humanly possible in any way'. But his mother was already convinced that he would not be back and had sent him money with a recent letter, much to Henry's surprise – he had understood that her Christmas gift was the cupboard that he had seen on his last visit home.

All hopes of getting back to Broadway seemed dashed a day or so later when the Beetle again refused to start. A quick inspection suggested further valve problems, which were likely to take more than a week to resolve. His sense of despair was expressed in a letter to his mother on 23 December:

> I don't know what has happened to the Beetle, last time I came back from leave I suspected that the gasket had gone, and found that a faulty valve had seized – now I think the same has happened again, since the symptoms are the same and I can't find anything else wrong. It's a bore, as one can't get off the station to have it repaired during the day without a good deal of trouble, one can't use service mechanics. I want to try and get it repaired this afternoon. I suppose one is bound to get some trouble using it under these rather difficult conditions for cars.[272]

The matter may have been less serious than anticipated, or perhaps luck was on his side, for, despite his fears, he was able to drive to Fox Hill, arriving at 6.45 p.m. on Christmas Eve, to the amazement and delight of his mother and assembled family members. With him he brought his navigator, Pilot Officer Desmond Taylor.[273] He was able to stay for only twenty-four hours, but it was certainly worth the effort, although Henry was dismayed to find his mother looking tired and drawn.

Meanwhile, others from the detachment had returned to Waddington on Christmas Eve, bringing with them the squadron's special Christmas present, their first three Lancasters. That same day command of the squadron passed to Wing Commander Roderick 'Babe' Learoyd, VC, who had been on a brief detachment to Boscombe Down in mid-December, but he was soon posted on temporary attachment to Headquarters Bomber Command, and it was left to Squadron Leader Nettleton to oversee the squadron, working with the new aircraft to achieve at least eight operational aircraft by the end of January. With a few exceptions for trials purposes, nearly every Lancaster produced by Avro's would be delivered to Waddington with the intention of bringing the squadron up to an operational strength of twenty-four aircraft as quickly as possible. Meanwhile, their twenty-two Hampdens were being transferred across the airfield to No. 420 (RCAF) Squadron, which had been formed on 19 December under the command of (now) Wing Commander Joe Collier to take the place of No. 207 Squadron, which had taken its temperamental Manchesters to Bottesford.[274]

For Henry, however, Boxing Day meant a return to Boscombe Down. He had left Fox Hill on Christmas evening, stopping off in Willersey to see Captain Arkwright and Ann (Mrs Arkwright was apparently resting, no doubt exhausted by the efforts of catering for her young evacuees), before setting out for Boscombe at about 6.30 p.m.. Navigation was no problem in the excellent visibility provided by the bright moonlight, and the journey was completed in about three hours. The Beetle was running well, returning a fuel consumption of some 40 miles per gallon, which was just as well, since Henry had forgotten to fill up before leaving Boscombe and had only $3^1/_2$ gallons in the tank! Food for the journey provided by his mother was sufficient for breakfast the following day.

There was little to do, although the evening of the 27th was livened up with a cocktail party. Henry had invited Mrs Batey's daughter and niece over from General Hill's, providing appropriate companions for the subsequent dance.

There was to be but one final flight before the year ended, accompanying Squadron Leader Nettleton on a twenty-five-minute local hop on the 28th. With Nettleton's impending return to Waddington, Henry now hoped that he would be able to form his own crew. He was beginning to find the situation rather a drag. Having been attached for a month and a half to the Intensive Flying Development Unit, Henry had flown in a Lancaster for only some six hours and actually been at the controls for a mere fraction of that time. The unit's title seemed to be a misnomer.

Plans were afoot to see the New Year in at a bottle party in Amesbury, organized by a friend of his cousin Joan. Returning to his room after the party on the 27th, he wrote to his mother, seeking supplies: 'I wonder if you could pack up one of my bottles of Pimms No. 1 which are in the cellar (I can get the lemonade to dilute it with here) and send it off.' The thought of alcohol must have raised a touch of conscience, for he added: 'By the way, the bottle of Plymouth gin in the Dining Room corner cupboard is mine – a present from John – but I've used so much of the household's – so if there is a need of gin, there it is.'

Henry had to miss the party in Amesbury, for two days later he was ordered back to Waddington. Packing the Beetle, he drove back, stopping off at Fox Hill for the night of the 29th. Such was the speed of his departure that he had no chance to notify the family, who by now, like many, were getting used to sudden un-planned arrivals and departures. At least it was another chance to try and persuade his mother to take things easy. Tita had planned to take up temporary residence at Fox Hill, which would provide an opportunity for Mrs Maudslay to take a break away from the house without having to worry about staffing problems. He also probably took advantage of the moment to collect a jar of a patent ointment known as 'Mrs Herbert's child', which he had requested in his last letter. This was used by Henry to alleviate the effects of periodic bouts of eczema from which he suffered; the name suggests that it may have been a concoction originating from either his maternal grandmother or his 'M'Dame' at Eton.

Henry arrived back at Waddington on Tuesday, 30 December. During his time at Boscombe Down the squadron had lost only three crews, and Henry was pleased to see many old familiar faces still in evidence as he arrived back in the Officers' Mess. He had relinquished his billet with the Hensons and was now to be housed back on the main camp, possibly in the Mess itself, where he had 'a very nice room to myself with radiator &c [sic] H & C (and) a good batman'.[275]

The New Year was ushered in at a party with Ralph Allsebrook and some other No. 49 Squadron colleagues from Scampton, but no sooner had 1942 arrived than it was rumoured that he would soon be sent on another attachment. As part of the induction course for the Lancaster, captains and flight engineers were to be sent to visit the organizations building the new aircraft. It was to be a dual-purpose activity, a mixture of formal education to instil correct handling procedures for airframe and engines and an opportunity for the workers to meet those who were to place their trust in their workmanship.

The concept appealed to Henry's engineering instinct. He wrote to his mother on 4 January:

> I'm going off on Tuesday on a course – two courses actually, one at Rolls, one at Avro's, about four days each – I don't know which will come first or what my address will be. Then back to Boscombe Down for a while and eventually back here. . . The courses should be interesting and hold quite a reasonable chance of promotion, with some luck! Anyway it will be a great thrill to see something of Rolls-Royce's factory.

He also enclosed an illustration that the Goldsmiths and Silversmiths Company had sent suggesting how the brackets from Mrs Maudslay's altered brooch might be remodelled to produce a second brooch. He wondered what she and Tita thought of it. 'Personally I think it's nothing wonderful as a brooch and not worth while.'

On 7 January Henry took the train to Derby to commence the first course with Rolls-Royce. The Beetle continued to give problems: 'She won't start again and is really not to be trusted for long at a time nowadays – although when the engine goes it goes well.' The three-day course outlined the Merlin's construction and concentrated on the finer points of engine handling, including the most efficient settings for revs and boost, maximizing the engines' power output for the minimum wear and fuel consumption. Later pilots would learn this information from the official Air Publication 'Pilots' Notes', but in these early days these still had to be written and experience was gleaned from the development technicians. On the 11th he transferred for a four-day detachment to A. V. Roe's Middleton Works. Feeling he might require a little relaxation, he obtained a copy of Sir George Antrobus's *Diary of a King's Messenger* from Boots Library, using the subscription given to him by Tita and Gordon as a Christmas present. Arriving in Manchester, he found himself accommodated at the Waverley Hotel, 14 Oldham Street, run by Mrs D. Nichols. Even discounting the pounding the city had received from the Luftwaffe the previous year, Henry was not too impressed by his surroundings. Writing to his mother on the hotel stationery, he added his own comment 'No stars!' underneath the printed 'AA Recommended' and remarked:

> Both Rolls and Avro booked our rooms for us at hotels which evidently were chosen with an eye rather to the scale of the Air Ministry allowances than to the dignity of the King's Commission. Financially I agree with them, as we pay for ourselves and get what we can from the Accounts Dept. afterwards, but it's pretty grim.[276]

He was also unimpressed by the intellectual abilities of others on the course: 'The course is quite interesting, my companions on it aren't that much fun, only one can talk about anything but beer, and not for long at that.'

Avro's were determined to demonstrate the full handling capabilities of the Lancaster. On the first day they were taken up for a 'no holds barred' flight with one of the Avro test pilots, who 'gave a very fine demonstration of what can be done with an aeroplane'. The flight went unrecorded in his logbook, but there were evidently a few chastening moments, as Henry added, 'The RAF is much safer!' Nevertheless, the excitement fired a desire to return to operational flying: 'I've had about enough rest now and would like to get back in the early spring and fly in the good weather again, it's much more satisfactory, but difficult to arrange.'

On 14 January, the course over, Henry was allowed to deliver a new production aircraft from Woodford to Waddington with Sergeant Stott as his flight engineer; later that day he went off for another local flight lasting nearly an hour with Sergeant Baxter and Sergeant Hardcraft.[277]

The following day, as he had anticipated, he was posted back to Boscombe Down. Despite bad weather, with snow in the air, he decided to risk the Beetle and motored down, calling in at Fox Hill to stay overnight, taking Tita to a dance at Gordon's Army Mess at Edgecote, near Banbury, the next day – 'a great success and most beautifully done. Almost like a dream in the middle of a nightmare.'[278]

The following morning he rose at 6.30, later than planned, to return direct to Boscombe, while Tita travelled back by train. The Beetle behaved itself, 'occasionally making sinister noises', and, despite icy roads as far as Marlborough, the journey was completed in under three and a half hours. On arrival he found himself detailed to fly almost immediately and by midday was airborne, completing fifty-five minutes' circuits and landings in L7535. Then the weather clamped down with snow and fog and he was stuck on the ground again for another five days. 'This weather is vile. I just hibernate, read books and walk round the aerodrome for exercise. It's not worth bicycling and the Beetle won't go again. I changed the coil, to no avail, but hope to get to a garage soon and that will help.'[279]

And there were other difficulties:

I think there's a spare ignition key in the drawer in the mirror opposite my room on the chest of drawers – can you send it please as I've just lost mine. I can't use it until the new licence comes anyway. I'd been using it unlicensed but didn't notice until I arrived here – neither did the police fortunately – however I'm sending for a new licence and post dating it – or should it be ante dating it? – so as to get this month's petrol. Please send a pc if you can't find the key and I'll get another one made here.

He also took advantage of the hiatus to pursue his efforts to gain entry to the RAF Club. During his brief spell at Waddington he had spotted a table notice placed by the president of the Mess committee inviting applications for membership. Henry wrote to him requesting further details and enquiring about sponsorship.

The weather broke on 22 January, and he was able to take L7535 on three longer flights, each lasting some one and a half hours, including his first experience of handling the new aircraft at night.

Several days of snow had been followed by an afternoon of persistent rain. Slush lay everywhere, making progress around the camp extremely uncomfortable if not difficult, as paths were churned into quagmires and supplies of duckboards ran out. Perhaps anticipating the weather, Mrs Maudslay had sent Henry a new pair of boots: 'They seem almost too super to wear and anyway I daren't wear them till I can go to Salisbury and get a boot jack, as they are VERY difficult to get off.'[280] But then necessity appears to have overcome practical considerations:

'I think I will wear the boots.'[281]

His mother's gift had arrived with a letter updating him on family affairs. Kelly had been ill, and Henry had received a letter from Mary Gibb that had suggested that her condition was giving cause for concern, but Mrs Maudslay had heard that a slow recovery was under way and that things were looking better for her. The seasonal weather had brought its inevitable coughs and colds; Tita was the latest to succumb, going down with a touch of flu. A land girl was now helping out with work at Fox Hill, assisted by the ponies, which were much better than mechanical transport on the steep hills in the ice and snow.

Despite the weather, Henry's writing had regained an optimistic note with regard to his flying: 'The job is going much better than the last time I was here and we have got in much more flying than you'd think possible in this weather. I'm just beginning to get the hang of the machine which is easier than a Hampden when you are used to it. I hope that isn't famous last words!'[282]

They might well have been. At 1615 on Saturday, 24 January, Henry took off for a local night-handling flight in Lancaster L7535. With the weather deteriorating and unable to land at Boscombe Down, he sought permission to land at Stanton Harcourt, a training airfield near Eynsham, Oxfordshire, but was unable to make contact. Instead he saw Cheddington, a new airfield still under construction by George Wimpey and Co. Ltd on low-lying ground some 5 miles east of Aylesbury. Rather than attempting to regain Boscombe Down he elected to land there.

The Lancaster touched down without incident at 1810 hours, but the concrete runway was shorter than the grass landing runs at Waddington and Boscombe and, unknown to Henry, was further curtailed by construction materials. While they were still travelling at reasonable speed, the aircraft's port outer engine struck a pile of concrete posts left by the contractors and swung round violently off the runway. The port engine was torn out and the port undercarriage collapsed, damaging the port inner propeller as the aircraft slid backwards into the mud. Climbing out after the aircraft had come to a rest, the crew were shaken but otherwise unhurt. L7535 was badly damaged, its tail unit completely wrecked, port wing fractured outboard of the inner engine and fuselage broken in half behind the transportation joint. Though initially categorized as repairable, it was fated never to join an operational squadron, being relegated to become a ground instructional airframe by August 1942.[283]

Writing home the next day Henry reproached himself for events:

I crashed an aeroplane the other day and have been hating myself hard ever since. However the fault was by no means entirely mine and so long as I don't get my logbook endorsed, it shouldn't be too bad a thing for me. Self and

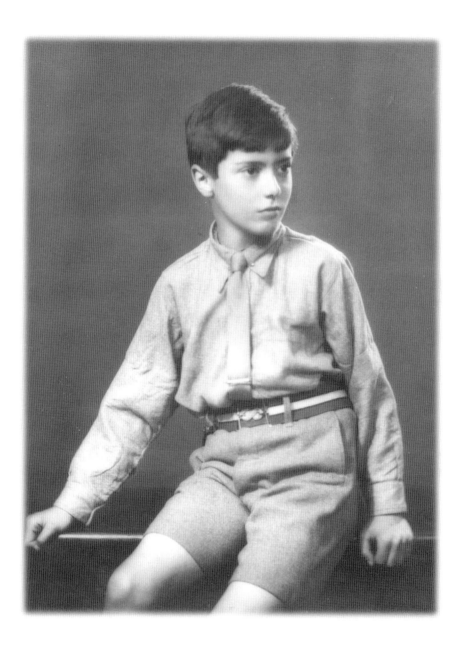

Henry during his days at Beaudesert. (*Maudslay family collection*)

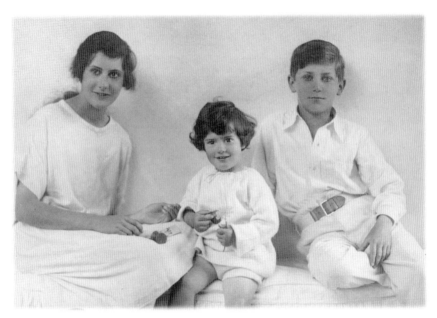

Margaret, Henry and John Maudslay. (*Maudslay family collection*)

Henry playing with a submersible diver in the garden at Sherbourne, with Beeny the terrier.
(*Maudslay family collection*)

Henry at the helm, Loch Shinn. (*Maudslay family collection*)

Henry and friends with his governess 'Kelly' – Emily Kellaway.
(*Maudslay family collection*)

Studio portrait of Henry. (*Maudslay family collection*)

Henry's mother Susan Gwendolen 'Gwen' Maudslay. (*Maudslay family collection*)

Henry and Colin Richardson in their plus-fours at a bridge on the Fiag Road, Shinness. (*Maudslay family collection*)

Henry out with a shoot on the moors at Shinness. (*Maudslay family collection*)

Henry's father, Reginald Walter Maudslay.
(*Maudslay family collection*)

**Tita and Henry on the garden terrace steps at
Fox Hill, circa 1938.** (*Maudslay family collection*)

Fox Hill Manor, Broadway, the family home from 1936. (*Maudslay family collection*)

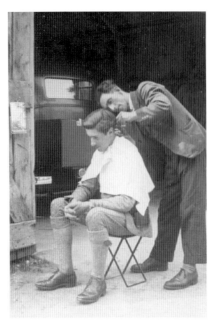

Above left – Henry getting a haircut at Shinness. Above right – Henry at the Jordan water jump, Eton College Steeplechase, October 1939. (*Maudslay family collection*)

Above left – Junior athletics at Eton College. Henry at the tape, circa 1936. (*Maudslay family collection*)
Above right – The Dunning Cup awarded outright to Henry for winning the School Mile in 1938, 1939 and 1940. (*Author's collection*)

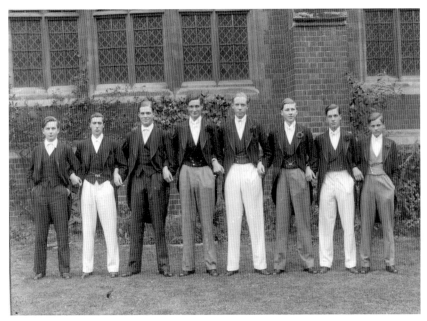

J. D. Hill's House, Eton College, 1939. L-R Michael Spears, Henry, Duncan Pearl, Geoffrey Jamieson, Richard Wood, David Quilter, Michael Chinnery, Peter Wake. (*Maudslay family collection*)

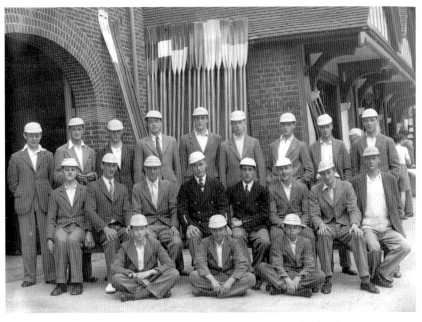

Henry (middle row, fourth from right) with the Trial Eights, Eton College boathouse, 1940. (*Maudslay family collection*)

Left – Henry as Captain of Boats, Eton College, 1940. Below – Skiing at Arosa, January 1939. (*Maudslay family collection*)

Below left – Henry's Eton leaving portrait photograph. Traditionally these were presented to Housemaster, Dame and friends.(*Maudslay family collection*) Below right – The second portrait produced after Henry's death by Cuthbert Orde, based on his Eton leaving photograph.

Above left – Henry and his brother-in-law Gordon Barker, autumn 1940. Above right – Henry circa 1942 wearing the brass VR badge on his epaulettes. (*Maudslay family collection*)

A recently enlisted Aircraftman Maudslay home on leave, autumn 1940.
(*Maudslay family collection*)

Above – No. 25 Operational Training Unit, Finningley 1941. Henry is second left front row, with Ralf Allsebrook to his left. Bottom right – Training in Canada. Henry, front row, left. Lucian Ercolani, centre rear, balances a beer on a fellow trainee's head. (*Maudslay family collection*)

Above – The Eder Dam as viewed from above Waldeck Castle, showing the line of approach for attacking aircraft. (*Author's collection*) Below – Vertical reconnaissance photograph showing the breach in the Eder Dam. (*Air Historical Branch*)

Above left – Reculver, May 1943. This sequence is believed to show Henry's aircraft being damaged by spray from an Upkeep released from below 60 feet. (*Imperial War Museum*) **Above right** – Damage to the parapet of the Eder Dam believed to have been caused by the premature detonation of Henry's Upkeep. (*Author's collection*)

Left – Henry's original temporary grave marker before reinterment in the newly created Reichswald Forest War Cemetery, 1948. Below – Henry's identification photograph, May 1943. Copies would be carried on operations to be used if necessary for false identity documents. (*Maudslay family collection*)

Henry's headstone, Reichswald Forest War Cemetery. (*Author's collection*)

crew completely unhurt by the way, but I'm just going to bed with what feels like a mild bout of flu, and I won't be surprised if it is.[284]

Trying to make light of the matter, he ended up with an oblique reference to the cost of his accident: 'I'm giving you all a bit more on the income tax I fear.'

The Court of Inquiry found that Henry was not to blame and his logbook was not endorsed, although, coincidentally, the page opposite the entry for his flight on 24 January was removed and the times for the flight together with other totals were added on to the next page in a different ink – that used for his February totals. Lest anyone should think that this had been done to remove an endorsement, a pencilled note was added to the right-hand page: '2 pages removed here as times were incorrect.'

Whether or not it had anything to do with the incident cannot be ascertained, but this was the last flight Henry made with the IFDU and his monthly total of nine hours was signed off by Flight Lieutenant Herring. Whatever misgivings he still had about the accident must have been eclipsed by the announcement published officially in the *London Gazette* of 30 January that he had been awarded the Distinguished Flying Cross. The citation made specific mention of his attack against shipping off the Dutch coast in poor weather the previous November and commended his keenness, determination and efficiency. Possibly on the strength of this, or because his cold still prevented him from flying, he was able to obtain a forty-eight-hour pass and return home to Fox Hill on the 31st to celebrate with his mother and Tita. The award would be publicized in the local *Evesham Journal* the following week, on 7 February, under the headline 'Outstanding example of keenness. DFC for Broadway pilot.' The *Eton Chronicle* of Thursday, 6 February, listed Henry and Flight Lieutenant D. A. Coke as recipients of the DFC, but the latter was already dead.[285] The following issue of the *Sunday Times* recorded:

In the lists of the honours recently won by Old Etonians is included the name of Pilot Officer Henry Eric Maudslay who has gained the DFC. He left Eton in the summer of 1940 to join the RAF after one of the most distinguished careers in modern times at the School. He was . . . [listing school positions and sporting achievements] a very distinguished wet bob.[286]

On his return to Boscombe Down, Henry found several letters of congratulations, including ones from those he had just seen, who had written immediately they heard the news, not knowing that he would be seeing them so soon. The Beetle's licence had arrived and he was 'legal' once again.

With the remainder of the squadron crews waiting to convert as more new

Lancasters arrived at Waddington, it was becoming obvious that the IFDU detachment would be better placed using their newly acquired expertise to instruct their compatriots. Poor weather was preventing flying and rumours grew daily that they would soon be posted back to Waddington. Henry took advantage of the inactivity and journeyed up to London to see Kelly on the afternoon of Wednesday, 4 February. He was pleased and relieved to find her up and about, and very much more her usual self, although still having to take things carefully. He stayed for tea, with toast made in front of the gas fire, no doubt recalling memories of his childhood and the schoolboy 'Mess' in the Hopgarden, while discussing the latest family news.

Rumour became fact and on Sunday, 8 February, Henry left Boscombe to return to Waddington, arriving at Fox Hill at 5.30 p.m. for his usual overnight stay. He left at 6.30 the following morning, only to be informed on arrival that he had been given a week's leave. He immediately retraced his steps and arrived back in Broadway at 11.30 p.m. the same day.

The week passed all too quickly, thoroughly enjoyable despite setbacks being reported in the Far East as Singapore surrendered, and the *Scharnhorst* and *Gneiseneau* made their dash through the English Channel from Brest. Returning to his unit on the 16th, Henry found yet more letters of congratulation, including one from Air Vice-Marshal Slessor and another very moving note from J. S. Herbert, signed by all in his House who remembered him. It was, in Henry's words, 'the most frightfully difficult thing to answer'. Meanwhile, the squadron adjutant had finally caught up with the recent awards, noting Henry's name in the squadron's Operations Record Book on the 13th in his list of 'awards for gallantry and devotion to duty in the execution of air operations'. The congratulations of his squadron colleagues were tempered by the receipt of news that Ralph Allsebrook had been forced to ditch off the Isle of Wight on return from an operation against Mannheim on 14/15 February, but was now safe. After a freezing twelve hours in their dinghy, he and his crew, three suffering from frostbite, had been rescued by an air-sea rescue launch.[287]

Chapter 13

Conversion Flight

At first it was thought it would be a comparatively simple matter to introduce crews to the new aircraft. But it was soon learned that a complete and thorough course . . . .was absolutely indispensable for the efficient handling of these more complicated aircraft.

(Air Chief Marshal Sir Arthur Harris, *Bomber Offensive*)

Henry now was officially an instructor with No. 44 Conversion Flight, his posting taking effect from 31 January 1942. The conversion flight was a shadow unit that had been formed on 16 January with two Lancasters and two Manchesters, under the administration of Headquarters, RAF Waddington, and commanded by Flight Lieutenant Herring. In addition to converting No. 44 Squadron's existing Hampden crews, the flight would also be responsible for the final training of new crews posted to the main squadron from Wellington or Hampden OTUs. These would start flying with the conversion flight immediately on arrival at Waddington. The training syllabus combined ground lectures with practical air experience and was intended to provide pilots with twenty-eight hours at the controls of a Lancaster, during which period they would also fly an average of five operations as a second pilot to a variety of the squadron's best and most experienced pilots. They would also have to complete the Beam Approach Course and attend the engine handling course run by Rolls-Royce at Derby. Observers, wireless operators and air gunners would similarly carry out a number of operations with experienced crews, concurrent with conversion training. In this way it was intended to dispense with the previous arrangement of freshman targets for novice crews and speed up the creation of operationally experienced crews.[288]

Flying resumed for Henry on Thursday, 19 February, when he served as check pilot for Warrant Officer Wright on a navigation training exercise, logging himself as a passenger in L7538, KM-B (one of the three initial Lancasters delivered to the squadron and fated to be written off the next day when Sergeant J. Rowan Parry overshot into a ditch on landing). Then the weather closed in again with

sleet and snow, and he did not instruct for a week, during which time he managed to sneak in a trip back to Boscombe Down on 24 February, piloting Anson
N9835 [289] with Flying Officer Taylor and Sergeant Miller as passengers. The same day
saw Henry's promotion to flying officer officially gazetted, with effect from 29 January. On return to Waddington, he contacted the Hensons to let them know he
was back in the area again and was invited over for a most enjoyable evening on
the 25th, catching up on the latest news.

On 26 February there was a half-hour local flight in L7544, followed by Henry's
first experience of the unreliable Manchester, when he took dual instruction from
Flight Lieutenant Herring.[290] The conversion flight had at least two of these aircraft, ex-No. 207 Squadron machines, which could be used as a 'halfway house'
between the Hampden and the Lancaster. They were unpopular, and cynics
maintained that these were the real rogue aircraft that even No. 207 had rejected.
Henry may have shared their beliefs, for on this occasion the airspeed indicator
of L7280 failed, necessitating Herring's experience of the type to judge their
approach after a quick circuit. Undeterred, the crew transferred to Lancaster
L7544 for a further three-quarters of an hour local flying. There were two more
local flights with Flight Lieutenant Herring in L7540 the next day, plus a trip in
Manchester L7280 with Herring and Pilot Officer Patten to Coningsby, home of
No. 97 Squadron, which was now also converting from Manchesters to Lanc-
asters, assisted by No. 44 Squadron personnel. After another half-hour with Flight
Lieutenant Herring in L7540 on the 28th, Henry went solo again, taking the
Lancaster on a short cross-country lasting an hour and ten minutes.

Early in March John Sauvage, wearing the ribbon of a newly awarded DFC and
now an instructor with No. 25 OTU at Finningley, flew down to Waddington to
deliver an aircraft, arriving in time for lunch and then staying the night, before
Henry drove him into Lincoln to catch a train back early the next morning. Henry
managed to get in two more familiarization flights with L7540 before the weather
closed in on the 4th, giving him time to catch up on his next letter home. Thanking his mother for a new pair of shoes that she had sent – 'I'd just worn one pair
to the leaky stage' – he confirmed that Squadron Leader Burton-Gyles was spon-
soring his application to join the RAF Club and expressed his relief at his growing familiarity with the Lancaster:

The weather isn't too kind, but we're getting some flying and I'm beginning
to get the feel of the new aeroplane – it's a long time before one becomes part
of the aeroplane. . . . I'm glad to hear that the Minister of Air has announced
the Lancaster at last, the speech on the estimates seemed good on the news
and I'm looking forward to reading it in the Times tomorrow morning, if I

can [get in] in time to bag our only copy of the Times![291]

The weather restricted flying for a week. A bitterly cold east wind brought sleet and snow, blanketing the airfield in deep drifts while the crews struggled to concentrate on ground training in huts equipped with only the barest form of heating. Meanwhile, Henry was kept busy as acting flight commander while Flight Lieutenant Herring attended an investiture at Buckingham Palace to receive his DSO. On 11 March personnel were shown a travelling exhibition of captured enemy technical equipment, including wireless sets, navigation instruments, bomb sights, guns and air-sea rescue aids. Training continued on the 12th, although Henry's logbook records a flight in the Anson[292] with Flying Officer Taylor and Sergeant Jess. The duty is recorded as being from Stoke-on-Trent, suggesting that he may have travelled there by rail and been collected later, possibly after attending another meeting with Rolls-Royce at Crewe.

Henry had planned to attend a dance arranged by Mrs Studd for the 14th, taking leave on Saturday afternoon and returning Monday afternoon after spending Sunday with the Herberts at Eton. He wrote to his mother on the 9th to ask if she could possibly meet him in London on the Monday, when they could take up an invitation received the previous month to have lunch with his cousin Ali Bond at her home at Eresby House, Rutland Gate, Knightsbridge. He would wire final details when he knew for certain he would be free. The following day he wrote asking for a pair of white canvas shoes and his running kit to be sent to him: black, rubber soled running shoes, white flannel shorts and light blue socks. Lest there should be any confusion: 'Don't send my rowing shorts – they have padded bottoms and D[enman] & G[oddard] labels in them.'

In the event he had to cancel the proposed visit to Eton and London. The conversion flight was short of experienced instructors, and he did not feel that it was in order to apply for leave at a time when the pressure to convert the squadron was mounting. His increased responsibilities were shortly to be recognized by the confirmation of his promotion to flying officer. The increase in rank was somewhat overdue, the official explanation being that while at Boscombe Down he had not been filling a flying officer vacancy, despite the added responsibility of handling the Air Force's latest aircraft. There was some consolation, however: at least he was not being punished for the mishap at Cheddington.

Despite the workload, there was still some time for recreation. His Uncle Jack, a keen fishing enthusiast, had sent him a *Black Bear* story and several books of fishing tales to while away his spare hours. The squadron was to hold a dance on 21 March; perhaps Tita would like to attend, if she wasn't seeing Gordon in Banbury? Henry would try to persuade Audrey Bates and Ralph Allsebrook to come too.

Alighting on the Mess copy of *The Times* on 13 March, Henry was saddened to see an announcement recording the death of Charles Pilkington while flying with No. 149 Squadron at Mildenhall. On the evening of 10 March he had taken off to attack Essen. Returning in the early hours of the following morning with battle damage, his Stirling overshot the airfield and crashed into trees at Holywell Row, killing all but a gunner. Fate had indeed dealt a cruel blow; the announcement of Charles's death coincided with the publication in the same edition of *The Times* of his engagement to WAAF Joanna Everard. 'I'm very much afraid that there is only one C. L. Pilkington and the world is now a much poorer place without him.'[293] There had been news too that John Harley, now a captain with the Coldstream Guards, had been wounded.[294] The war was closing in on his Etonian circle.

The weather improved and on the 15th, after nearly a fortnight on the ground, with the exception of the Stoke trip, Henry was given an hour's dual refresher with Flight Lieutenant Herring in Manchester L7280, followed by forty minutes' local flying on his own. The following day he took L7280 with Flight Lieutenant Herring and Flight Lieutenant McClure[295] to Oakington, near Cambridge, home to No. 7 Squadron.

Sight of their Stirlings may have rekindled thoughts of his late school friend, but there was little time for morbid reflection. Although he needed no reminding, the hazards of non-operational flying were reiterated again the following day. After a successful hour and forty minutes dual with Rhodesian Flying Officer Gerald Maclagan in Manchester L7280, the crew switched to Lancaster L7576, KM-E-bar (the bar over the aircraft letter showing it belonged to the conversion flight) to practise night take-offs, landings and local flying. No sooner were they airborne, however, than the starboard inner engine failed. Closing the throttle and feathering the propeller, Henry completed the circuit without difficulty, no doubt thankful that he was held aloft by three reliable Merlins rather than a single temperamental Vulture.

Mrs Maudslay and Tita arrived at Lincoln by train during the afternoon of Saturday, 21 March, booking into the White Hart as usual. They brought with them the clothes requested by Henry, a clock and a delicious home-baked cake. Arriving at Waddington, they enjoyed their first experience of an RAF Mess when they were entertained to tea by Monica Campbell, a WAAF friend of Henry's who worked in cyphers, before attending the evening's dance. At the end of the entertainment Henry escorted his mother and sister back to Lincoln, where he was able to spend the night at their hotel before returning to camp late on Sunday evening.

Flying intensified as new crews were transferred to the conversion flight, and the pressure increased. On 22 February 1942 Air Marshal Arthur T. Harris had taken over as Commander-in-Chief of Bomber Command. He was a former AOC of No. 5 Group, and his determination to press home the bomber offensive was well known, and No. 44 Squadron, equipped with the most potent weapon in Bomber Command's armoury, was fully aware of its new commander's expectations of his former group's squadrons.[296] The squadron had commenced Lancaster operations on 3 March, albeit on a limited scale, when four aircraft led by Warrant Officer Hubert Crum took off, watched by Air Vice-Marshal Slessor, to lay mines in the Heligoland Bight. All returned safely. Their first bombing operation was completed a week later, on the night of 10/11 March, when Flying Officer Peter Ball and Flying Officer Wilkins participated in a 126-aircraft attack on Essen (Charles Pilkington's fated operation). Both returned safely, although Ball had been hit by flak. The omens for the new aircraft looked good.

Henry's workload increased accordingly. While his mother and Tita made their way back to Fox Hill on 23 March, he was twice airborne in Manchester L7280 with Pilot Officer Lauderdale (who had survived the Hampden crash the previous June), completing nearly three hours of dual instruction before taking off with Flying Officer Maclagan, Pilot Officer Allen and Sergeant Upton for a further two and a half hours of local night flying in Lancaster L7576. After very little sleep he was up again, giving local dual to Pilot Officer Lauderdale in the Manchester and then flying with him and Wing Commander Learoyd, VC, to Alconbury, home to the newly formed No. 156 Squadron, which was about to commence operations. As if this were not enough, that evening Henry and Flying Officer Maclagan walked the three miles over to Boothby Graffoe to drink with Mr Henson and his friend Mr Daniels – 'a most amusing and very interesting man' – who talked at great length and with considerable knowledge about steel production, although he professed to be a farmer. Returning to his room exhausted, Henry still found time to pen his customary note to his mother, thanking her for her visit and apologizing for the letter's lateness and incoherence: 'I was flying last night so this is the first opportunity to write and say how absolutely splendid it was of you to come up here for the weekend . . . forgive this letter for being rather unintelligent as I've been in the air rather a lot – taking advantage of the good weather.'[297]

At almost the same time as Henry was completing his letter, the first Lancaster to be lost to enemy action was shot down, as South African Flight Sergeant Lyster Warren-Smith attempted to lay the squadron's mines in the waters off Lorient.[298]

On 25 March Henry flew a brief air test on L7280 to check adjustment and operation of the Manchester's flap indicator, and the following day took the aircraft to demonstrate overshoot procedure and single-engined flying to Pilot Officer Lauderdale. A similar exercise on the last day of the month was curtailed after twenty minutes by the failure of the Manchester's undercarriage warning lights. The last few days had seen a plague of technical problems, the most serious resulting in all the squadron's Lancasters being withdrawn from operations pending an examination of the wing-tip attachment points for failed rivets and rippled top skin. Aircraft exhibiting the problem were to be grounded immediately and those not affected were restricted to flying practice with a maximum fuel load of 580 gallons in the inboard tanks only. Two days later expediency dictated the restrictions be amended to allow aircraft with wrinkled skin to fly, provided it had not pulled through the rivets. Aircraft were to be inspected after every flight and grounded immediately any failure of the rivets was detected. There was one good thing to come out of the restrictions on flying: they enabled Henry to snatch his postponed weekend away and stay with the Herberts at Eton and meet old friends, including Geoffrey Gibbon, now with the Welsh Guards.

On 1 April Henry and the other three officers and seventy other ranks of the conversion flight were transferred to come under the direct control of the squadron. Bomber Command had now dispensed with the role of second pilot for medium and heavy bombers and introduced a new scheme involving the three core members of crew, to be known as the Pilot, Navigator, Bomb Aimer (PNB) Scheme. Henceforth pilots would have reached captaincy standard before being posted to the squadron. In the early evening all aircrew assembled for an address by the AOC, Air Vice-Marshal Slessor.[299]

The first two weeks of the month brought interesting diversions. On 5 April Henry piloted Flying Officer Maclagan down to Boscombe Down in Tiger Moth T6305, and five days later took the opportunity to record a flight of an extremely rare nature. No. 1426 Flight, based at Collyweston, near Wittering, specialized in the operation of captured enemy aircraft, touring airfields providing personnel with an opportunity to see the aircraft at close quarters and practise aircraft recognition from all angles. 'The Flying Circus' arrived at Waddington on the afternoon of 9 April, bringing with them a Junkers Ju 88, Bf 110 and Heinkel He 111. The following day Henry talked his way into a fifteen-minute flight as passenger in the Heinkel,[300] logging the trip as 'Familiarisation' and becoming one of the few RAF personnel to feature a German bomber in their logbooks. Unfortunately the Circus's demonstration that afternoon was marred by a fatal accident when two of the escorting Spitfires collided and crashed, killing one of the pilots and seriously injuring the other. The Tiger Moth featured again the next day, as Henry and Flight Lieutenant Herring went over to Coningsby to discuss the checking-out of No. 97 Squadron's pilots on the Lancaster.

Pilot Officer Lauderdale was now ready to progress from the Manchester, and Henry recommended instructional duties, converting his pupil to Lancaster

L7576 on the 15th and 16th, followed by a quarter of an hour's check flight with the recently promoted Squadron Leader Herring, ensuring that his instructors were keeping strictly 'to the book'.

There was considerable activity on the airfield during the morning of Friday, 17 April, as No. 44 Squadron's ground crews prepared seven of the unit's aircraft for operations. Security seemed tighter than usual, although the more observant noted that the squadron had been carrying out long-range low-level practice flights for the past week and that the bowsers were filling the Lancasters' tanks with maximum fuel. Seven crews were called to a briefing at 1130. Henry and those outside the select body of those in the know could only guess as to the location of the target. Everything pointed to a low-level deep penetration, but careless talk could cost lives and it was useless to speculate.

Led by Squadron Leader Nettleton, the aircraft took off shortly after three o'clock that afternoon, circling the airfield before setting course towards Grantham for their rendezvous with seven more aircraft from No. 97 Squadron. Over Selsey Bill the seventh reserve aircraft of each squadron would leave the formation and return to their base, leaving the remainder to head for their target –the MAN (*Maschinenfabrik Augsburg Nurnberg Aktengesellschaft*) works at Augsburg, 500 miles inside enemy territory, which manufactured U-boat diesel engines for the prosecution of the Battle of the Atlantic.

The aircraft were scheduled to return by 2300 that evening. The twilight became pitch blackness. The appointed hour passed. The late night air remained still, bereft of the reassuring sound of returning crews. There would be no aircraft returning to Waddington that night.

Saturday morning dawned revealing an emptiness and eerie silence across the airfield. News had come through that, of the six aircraft, only one, piloted by Squadron Leader Nettleton, had survived, landing shortly before 0100 at Squires Gate, near Blackpool, having flown off track on the return flight.[301] Of the thirty-five members of No. 44 Squadron who failed to return, only eleven, including Flying Officer John Garwell, who had been detached with Henry to Boscombe Down, would survive as prisoners of war. Among those killed was another Boscombe colleague, Flight Lieutenant Sandford, shot down by fighters at Ormes, near Evreux, leaving his mongrel, inherited from a previous pilot, to search again for a new master. For No. 44 Squadron's sole returning captain, Squadron Leader Nettleton, came the award of the Victoria Cross, for 'unflinching determination as well as leadership and valour of the highest order', together with an award for every member of his crew. But it was a high price for the squadron to pay and one that Bomber Command could ill afford to repeat.

The operation left the squadron short of both crews and aircraft. Of the

thirteen Lancasters on strength, only three were airworthy, and new crews were
needed desperately to replace those lost. The small resources of the conversion
flight were in urgent demand.

'I am very sorry not to be able to come home this weekend,' wrote Henry to
his mother on Saturday 18 April. 'You will realise the reason without my saying
more. My job is unfortunately doubly urgent just now. I haven't heard the news
today but they say that most of the story has been told. It was a very fine show and
a successful operation.'

Nevertheless, it appears he was able to pay a very brief visit to Fox Hill, possibly
as the result of having to go to London on official business on 22 April. While in
the capital, he found time to visit Mappin and Webb and obtain a wedding present
for his navigator before returning on the 1750 train, 'VERY comfortable and fast',
reaching Lincoln at 2115. On his return, he found conversation in the Mess centred
around the lucky escape of Flying Officer Gerald 'Mac' Maclagan and his flight
engineer, Pilot Officer Hubert Sturgess, who had been compelled to belly land one
of the conversion flight's Lancasters near Ashwell, Rutland, after engine failure
owing to fuel starvation, writing off the aircraft but without injury to the crew.

The following day official war artist Cuthbert Orde paid a visit to Waddington
to sketch portraits of the Augsburg survivors and others, including Henry, who
had just returned from Tollerton, where he had been to collect Manchester L7400.
'Captain Orde did a charcoal drawing of me this afternoon, which I believe is
pretty good – anyway people say so. He has done a good one of Nettleton and my
Flight Commander, Herring.'[302]

The sitting lasted two hours and twenty minutes, although to Henry it seemed
much longer. The portraits were photographed for the Air Ministry and reproductions sold for distribution to family and friends. The original sketch, about half
life size on buff paper with red highlights, was framed and offered to the subject
for the (then) princely sum of £6 10s (£6.50). 'I'll get you a photograph of it in about
a couple of months and that relieves me of having to get a photograph taken!'[303]

He was less enthusiastic about the fate of the painting of Hampdens that Sir
Frederick Handley Page had presented the previous September:

Our lovely picture of the Hampdens has been set up on a large mahogany
panel with a narrow and ugly gilt frame and diamond shaped moulding on
each side of the panel. One expects a cocktail cabinet on one side, a dart-
board on the other – the whole effect is that of a second rate roadhouse, and
the colour of the wood kills the delicate hue of the sky, a great pity.[304]

That night in conversation with a guest in the Mess, Mr Waller a Rolls-Royce engineer, Henry discovered to his delight that he was a keen skier and had been climbing with both Eton's headmaster and his old tutor. Henry's Etonian background also stood him in good stead when the station commander's 17-year-old brother-in-law, a pupil of the college, paid a visit to Waddington on leave between Halves: 'I met him in the Mess this evening, though I can't honestly say that I recognised him, however he is an excellent chap and went down very well in the Mess.'[305]

After a trip to Finningley in Tiger Moth T6305 with Flying Officer Taylor, Henry's instructional duties recommenced in full flow on the 25th with dual instruction for new pupils, Pilot Officer Stephens and Pilot Officer L. Tomkins, whom he continued to teach for the remainder of the month, using Lancasters L7576 and R5842. Travelling to Scampton by road on the last day of the month, Henry collected a No. 83 Squadron Manchester for use by the conversion flight.[306]

Under Air Marshal Harris, the RAF's offensive against German cities was growing in intensity. A raid on Lubeck on the night of 28/29 March killed 312 people and destroyed over 200 acres of the historic Hanseatic seaport. It was the largest loss of life from a single raid on a German target. Hitler declared the operation a *Terrorangriff* and promised reprisals. Accordingly the Luftwaffe began to mount attacks against the smaller British cities, adopting Bomber Command's tactic of concentrating the attack into a short length of time to saturate the defences. Known as the Baedeker raids, following a reference in the German press to the famous pre-war tourist guide, the raids caused proportionately high casualties and severe damage to historic town centres. Two consecutive raids were made on Bath during the nights of 25 and 26 April. Although poor navigation reduced the severity of the attacks, extensive damage was caused, compounded by low water pressure and strong winds, which hampered the firefighters. In all, 401 fatalities were caused and over 800 were injured.

Replying to two of his mother's letters on 29 April, Henry registered his concern for recent events and the threat they posed to Joan and Bobbie Rawstone, relatives living at Norton St Philip, Radstock, near Bath, and expressed optimism at the efficiency of Bomber Command:

> I hope none of our relations have suffered too badly from the Huns'
> attentions at Bath. The reprisal raids are bound to be unpleasant and bloody
> in the literal sense of the word. Their very name shows that we have now
> gained the initiative in the air war over Western Europe, and that there is
> more clearly defined evidence of the success of our strategic bombing than
> ever before AND the success is on a larger scale.[307]

He had now adjusted to the routine of training and obviously was enjoying himself:

> The job is going quite well, technical trouble is inevitable, but there is plenty
> of work to do, and it's all interesting. I'm beginning to feel really at home at
> the controls as I used to on the Hampden. Night flying on a clear night, with
> a full moon is very lovely. You see all the canals of Lincolnshire silver
> underneath. The sky is still faintly blue and the dark wings and engines look
> very fine against it. In fact they show up so well against it that one has the
> deepest sympathy for any Jerry who meets one of our own night fighters.
> Seriously, it's all very beautiful, but I'm not up to describing it on paper.[308]

Memories of Charles Pilkington were stirred yet again with the news that his
brother-in-law had flown as part of an inter-Service liaison programme: 'I'm so
glad Gordon has flown with a Stirling crew, they are a great aircraft and I wonder if it was Charles Pilkington's squadron? They are in this part of the world
[*sic*].[309] I don't believe that I ever told you that he was captain of a Stirling.'[310]

The first week of May saw intensive flying, commencing on the 1st with a flight
in Manchester L7430 with Flying Officer Maclagan to Skellingthorpe and returning with another Manchester, L7480, from No. 50 Squadron for the conversion
flight. That evening he supervised Pilot Officer Stephens's' night flying, sitting in
the flight engineer's seat of Lancaster R5508, KM-B – the Lancaster in which
Squadron Leader Nettleton had won his Victoria Cross a mere fortnight earlier.
The 5th was spent ferrying aircraft, Manchester L7400 to Tollerton, returning
with Manchester L7402 (neither of which was officially allocated to No. 44 Squadron Conversion Flight) and then taking Lancaster R5555, KM-P, to Squires Gate.
Henry was now averaging three flights a day as new crews were hastily converted
to bring the squadron up to strength.

Detailed as duty pilot on 7 May, after testing Sergeant Taylor in L7576, Henry
found time to catch up on outstanding correspondence:

> I have not written for over a week, I think. However I hope that you will for-
> give me if I say that at last there is a really hard programme of work for our
> flight, and I scarcely have time to think, flying all day. Operations would be
> quite a rest compared to this, but it's a job worth doing. . . At this moment
> I'm in the Mess waiting up for a crew on a night cross country. One has to be
> available in case of technical trouble, which is not likely, but once in a blue
> moon a pilot wants advice by wireless, and yours truly would have to give it;
> awful thought! All well so far, and he's due back in another hour.[311]

Meanwhile the conversion flight continued to assist other squadrons with their training requirements. On 9 May Henry took Wing Commander Richard Coad, DFC, up for an hour and a quarter's dual instruction in Manchester L7430. The wing commander would shortly take command of No. 61 Squadron and convert its crews from the Manchester to the Lancaster.

Friday, 8 May, saw a visit by Marshal of the Royal Air Force Viscount Trenchard to meet survivors of the Augsburg raid. The same day Wing Commander Patrick Lynch-Blosse, DFC, had taken over command of the squadron from Wing Commander Learoyd, who was posted to No. 25 OTU. That night seven aircraft, led by the new squadron commander, were despatched as part of a 193-aircraft attack on Warnemunde. Six of these were briefed to make a low-level attack at 500–1,000 feet. Arriving over the target five minutes late, they were met by intense searchlight and flak activity. Four crews were lost, including those of Wing Commander Lynch-Blosse and Flying Officer Maclagan (the squadron's first all-Rhodesian crew loss). Only one gunner survived as prisoner of war from the twenty-eight aircrew. Wing Commander Lynch-Blosse had been commanding officer for less than twenty-four hours.[312]

Over the previous three weeks the squadron had lost nine aircraft and sixty-six men. The squadron's strength was now reduced to eight fully experienced and two freshmen crews, with five more under training in the conversion flight. If called upon to operate normally, the same crews would find themselves on the Battle Order for every operation. It was suggested that the squadron should be stood down for a month to carry out extensive day and night training and regain full strength, but this recommendation was rejected. Instead the squadron was reduced to one operational flight and one training flight. Flying Officer Peter Ball, DFM was detailed to assist in flying instruction and ease the pressure on the flight's instructors.[313] As a consequence, Henry was able to write on the 10th that he had just been granted three days' leave, which could be taken when he wished. Increased petrol rationing had led Henry previously to suggest that his mother should apply for a 'country areas' ration and use the Beetle to collect essential supplies for the house, but he really wanted to have the car's rear axle serviced before returning it to his mother (the crown wheel and pinion were still causing problems). Staying long enough to witness the arrival of the squadron's new commanding officer, Wing Commander Kenneth Smales, DFC, on 11 May, Henry arrived back at Fox Hill on Tuesday, 12 May, where he was able to see the results of another artistic sitting, Miss Worsfold's recently completed portrait of his niece Annette.

Collecting a new uniform from Denman & Goddard, he caught a train back on the 15th, returning in time to have his hair cut by the station barber. En route he discovered to his annoyance that he had left his small Dunhill cigarette hold-er at home. It was either in the tray of the Beetle or in the pocket of one of his overcoats; he would have to write and ask his mother to look for it and send it on. Writing to her on 17 May his letter opened typically: 'My dear Mummy. Thank you very much for the very peaceful three days leave, it was simply grand and I only wish I could get on to "ops" when one gets it a week at a time.' Trying on his new uniform again, he found it was adequate, but would benefit from a few alterations.

The pace of training was undiminished. After a local test the following day in R5846 with Flight Sergeant Anderson, Henry's second flight was a forty-minute fighter affiliation exercise in R5556, KM-C (fitted with an experimental ventral turret intended to cover the notorious blind spot beneath the bomber's tail, although in practice it was found to be ineffective and soon deleted). Two Spitfires and a Boston of the Air Fighting Development Unit had been attached to the squadron since 10 May to instruct in evasive tactics for aerial combat. An arduous 'corkscrew' manœuvre of diving and climbing turns was designed to prevent the enemy obtaining a clear shot at the Lancaster. To be fully effective it needed to be executed as violently as possible, demanding all the pilot's strength and concentration. His stamina was further tested in carrying out an hour and a half's night circuits and landings that evening with Warrant Officer Dainty and Pilot Officer Young in L7576. Henry seemed to relish these demands: 'Things are much as usual here. I flew last night which was very pleasant. A lovely night and the pupil was a very good pilot so that I was able to appreciate the beauty of the night undisturbed by the anxieties that sometimes disturb one.'[314]

The remainder of the month saw continued dual instruction in both Lancasters and Manchesters with occasional night circuits and landings. There were still teething problems inevitable with a new aircraft. During the late afternoon of 20 May Warrant Officer Wright, one of the flight's pupils, was taking off on an air test when the leading edge of the port wing (hinged to provide access for servicing) blew back before the aircraft had reached flying speed. The Lancaster swung off the runway and collided with two of No. 420 Squadron's Hampdens, wrecking one and severely damaging the other, fortunately without any casualties.

Now that he had returned the Beetle to his mother, Henry sought another means of transport. Mrs Maudslay had recently acquired a small autocycle for local visits, which certainly made easier work of climbing Willersey Hill, and this may have prompted his own venture on to two wheels: 'I have got a second hand motorbike with new tyres and hope that you won't disapprove too strongly. They are going up in value so that I ought to be able to sell it fairly well at the end of the summer.'[315]

The motorbike, a Norton, appears to have been in need of some attention, but was quite within Henry's mechanical capabilities, and he was able to get it going for the first time on the 29th. Taking it for a test run, he paid the Hensons a visit in the late afternoon, noting on arrival that the smaller trees to the south-west of their drive had been cut down, opening up the view across the Vale of Trent from the front of the house. Mrs Henson greeted Henry warmly. Having shared a pot of tea with him, she insisted that he stay for dinner, even arranging to eat early to enable him to return to the airfield in time to carry out dual night-flying instruction that evening despite thundery conditions. It was a gesture greatly appreciated by Henry: 'They seem very well and are most hospitable always. It makes a tremendous difference to life to be able to drop in occasionally. Mr Henson was not at home which was a pity.'[316]

The next day saw considerable activity at Waddington. For several days there had been a sense of expectation in the air. That afternoon Battle Orders were posted and Henry saw that both himself and Squadron Leader Herring were required for operations that night. At 1900 hours thirteen crews, almost the squadron's entire complement, assembled in the briefing room to hear that they were to take part in the heaviest attack yet mounted by Bomber Command. By utilizing all his reserves, the Commander-in-Chief had assembled a force of 1,047 aircraft to mount an attack on a single target: the city of Cologne. The intention was to condense the raid into the space of ninety minutes, overwhelming the defences in an attempt to reduce losses. The crews of No. 5 Group were to take part in the final phase of the attack, between seventy-five and ninety minutes after the raid had opened, by which time it was hoped that the target would be well alight and the defences would have all but given up.

As they left the briefing room, the crews digested the full implications of the information they had just heard and reflected on the message from the Commander-in-Chief himself, which had been read to them:

The Force of which you are about to take part tonight is at least twice the size and four times the carrying capacity of the largest Air Force ever before concentrated on one objective. You have the opportunity therefore to strike a blow at the enemy which will resound, not only throughout Germany, but throughout the world. In your hands be the means of destroying a major part of the resources by which the enemy's war effort is maintained. It depends, however, upon each individual crew whether full concentration is achieved.

Press home your attack to your precise objectives with the utmost determination and resolution in the full knowledge that, if you individually succeed, the most shattering and devastating blow will have been delivered against the very vitals of the enemy. Let him have it, right on the chin.

The conversion flight would provide five aircraft, three Lancasters to be flown by squadron pilots, and two Manchesters captained by Henry and Squadron Leader Herring. While the latter would have two instructors in his crew, Henry's entire complement comprised those under instruction.

Wing Commander Smales was the first of the squadron to take off on Operation *Millennium*, at two minutes past midnight, flying a Lancaster of the conversion flight. Henry's turn came four minutes later, as he lifted L7430, KM-N-bar (the bar over the aircraft letter again signifying that it was from the conversion flight), off Waddington's grass and set course for the Suffolk coast between Aldeburgh and Orfordness.[317] Each of the Lancasters carried a 4,000-pounder and incendiaries loaded in eight Small Bomb Containers (SBCs), the Manchesters were restricted to only twelve SBCs of incendiaries.

Cloud over the North Sea gave way to clearer conditions as the force crossed the Dutch coast, with only slight cirrus over the target. Squadron records state that Henry identified his objective 'by map reading as there was a full moon and no low cloud', although this must have been superfluous, Cologne was already well ablaze and could be seen by crews while still over 70 miles away.

As they ran into the attack, the distinctive bend in the Rhine could be seen clearly, despite intense searchlight activity. By the time most of the squadron arrived, the flak had diminished considerably to allow fighters to enter the target area (although, owing to a misunderstanding, many fighters did not take off). The attack had commenced at 0047, and the target was now a sea of fire, estimated as 3 miles long by 2 miles wide.

The squadron had been allocated the southern aiming point in the district of Zollstock, and Henry had no problem in identifying his target and making his run in. The incendiaries were released from 6,800 feet at 0213, and then they turned for home. N-Nuts touched down at Waddington at 0520 after an uneventful trip. Inspecting the bomb bay at dispersal, however, Flight Sergeant Walker discovered that only eighty-four of their 30lb incendiaries had fallen on Cologne; twelve had hung up and remained in their container.

By way of diversion, the next day Squadron Leader Herring and Henry took Mr Rex Nicholson (the resident Rolls-Royce service engineer at Waddington) up on a height test in Lancaster L7537, KM-L. During the previous month a number of the squadron's aircraft had suffered engine failure owing to fuel starvation at altitude. Avro and Rolls-Royce engineers attached to No. 44 Squadron were working urgently to cure the problem.

Monday, 1 June, found Henry on the Battle Order again. While his large force was still intact, Sir Arthur Harris sought to deliver another blow against the Reich. Despite a less favourable weather forecast, 956 bombers were despatched against Essen, home of the Krupps armament empire. No. 44 Squadron was detailed to provide eleven Lancasters and one Manchester. Again Henry took the Manchester, this time L7480, KM-A-bar, recently repaired after suffering slight damage over Cologne. As before, the Lancasters would carry a 4,000-pounder and eight incendiary-filled SBCs, while Henry would carry twelve incendiary SBCs.

After an hour's night-flying test to check the aircraft, the crew retired for a rest before briefing and the usual pre-flight meal. Taking off at 2305, Henry reached the target area shortly before 0130, but found it covered by cloud between 3,000 and 5,000 feet, with additional ground haze. Most of the Lancasters had Gee, a new electronic navigation aid to assist them, but in the Manchester Sergeant Barr had to rely on his own calculations. Unable to identify the briefed aiming point, they located industrial buildings among scattered fires to the south of a canal junction and bombed at 0138 from 8,000 feet.[318]

The entire attack was disappointing. Bombing was scattered and Essen suffered relatively little damage, although Duisburg, Oberhausen and Mulheim recorded considerable bombing, and eight other towns in the area also reported varying degrees of damage.

As if to redress the balance, the squadron took part in smaller attacks on Essen again the following night and on the 5th. The latter operation cost the squadron Flying Officer Leslie Halls DFC, whom Henry had helped convert to the Lancaster only a month earlier.[319] By now the force assembled for the *Millennium* operations had been dispersed, and Henry and the conversion flight found themselves reverting to their routine training programme.

Perhaps in recognition of his efforts during the previous two operations, Henry was able to obtain a day's leave and travel to Eton for the 4 June celebrations. Arriving at 2.30 in the afternoon, he soon discovered many familiar faces: 'Esme Verney with Ann and Carol, June Harley with Christopher, Rex Whitworth and Daphne, Mrs Slessor and family[320] (I was on very best behaviour). Showed them the procession of boats, which was good to see again, arranged differently, but really much as ever.'[321]

The weather was perfect, and an added bonus was the presence of both his old tutors. John Hills had come over for the day from Bradfield, and Henry took tea with him in Mr Hartley's garden. Dinner was spent with Mr and Mrs Tait, with a lift back to London 'in time just to miss the 11.10 train back'. The next departure was not until 4.15 a.m. and the time was spent relaxing in a Turkish bath – 'a good thing after such a long sticky day'. Alighting at Grantham, he caught a bus and was back in the Mess in time for breakfast, concluding a quiet day without flying by writing to his mother while sitting in a deckchair on the Mess porch, sheltered from the evening breeze.

He had received a letter direct from Cuthbert Orde again offering to sell the portrait directly to him. The technique seems to have swayed him. In a postscript dated 8 June to the letter written three days earlier (which he had forgotten to post), he wrote: 'Would like to get the drawing and give it to you unless you see any reason for not doing so. Perhaps you'd like to see the copy first?'[322]

Henry was flying now on average twice a day, often with a night flight added for good measure. Occasionally a couple of local trips in the station's Tiger Moth and an Oxford added a little variety to life.

Production of the Lancaster had now reached the stage where the demand for crews was outstripping the ability of individual squadron conversion flights to train them. In addition, it was considered that the increased number of conversion crews flying in the vicinity of operational airfields created an unacceptable safety hazard. To overcome these problems it was decided to concentrate conversion flying at satellite airfields under the auspices of specialized Conversion Units (CUs) that had their own staff of instructors and aircraft. Two CUs had formed at the beginning of the year equipped with Stirlings and the first Lancaster/Manchester CU, No. 1654, had been formed at Swinderby on 16 May, taking crews from Nos 50 and 83 Squadron Conversion Flights. There was a possibility of Henry being posted to this unit. On 17 May he had written: 'I may get posted to another aerodrome, still on the same job, but it won't be much further from Lincoln, and if my guess is right, not a bad place so we can still forgather at the White Hart!'

According to his official Service record and the records of No. 1654 CU, Swinderby, Henry was posted to it from No. 44 Squadron Conversion Flight on 11 June, together with Squadron Leader Herring, but three days later Henry is recorded as being posted back to No. 44 Squadron Conversion Flight for a fourteen-day attachment. Whether he actually made the initial transfer is uncertain, but it may account for flights between Swinderby and Syerston on 14 June.

The conversion flight still used the Manchester, although more flying was being undertaken now in the Lancaster. Mishaps were still prevalent; on 6 June Pilot Officer L. Tomkins had written off a Lancaster during night-flying practice, overrunning the runway as a result of landing too fast. It made good sense to keep one's eye in. Six of the main squadron crews had been detached to Nutts Corner in Northern Ireland to carry out anti-submarine patrols[323] and instructors on the conversion flight might be called upon to operate. Possibly sensing this, on 19 June Henry flew day and night practice bombing sorties in Manchester L7430. On the 21st he made a one-off nostalgic return to the Hampden, taking up AE295 of No. 408 (Goose) Squadron, RCAF, for half an hour's local circuits.

At the request of the Air Ministry Public Relations Branch (PR II), Henry wrote an article about the Lancaster, which he duly submitted, receiving a reply on 24 June from the Branch's Director, author Hilary St George Saunders.[324]

Many thanks for your note on the Lancaster which was exactly what I wanted. I shall make every effort to include it as it stands if the aircraft is taken off the secret list before publication. It is most good of you to have taken so much trouble. You have produced a most satisfying result. I hope if ever you are in London you will not fail to let me know in order that we may have a meal together.[325]

(It has not been possible to identify the article in question, although the booklet *Bomber Command Continues*, published during the latter part of 1942 by the Ministry of Information/HMSO, contains an account of the Augsburg Raid entitled 'Maschinen Fabrik Augsburg'. Written by Hilary Saunders, the publication may conceivably have used material supplied by Henry.)

Mrs Maudslay visited Lincoln on the 24th and 25th, staying as usual at the White Hart. Henry was able to dine with her on the Wednesday evening, but the next night duties intervened and he was fully occupied in a battle for survival over Germany.

The target was Bremen, and 960 bombers had been assembled, again drawing heavily on the resources of training units and conversion flights. No. 44 Squadron would supply twelve crews, briefed to attack the Focke-Wulf factory. As he had taken a Manchester on the last two operations, this was to be Henry's first Lancaster sortie.

R5862, KM-G, lifted off from Waddington at 2345, carrying a load of six 1,000-pounders and 270 4lb incendiaries. The flight across the North Sea and northern Holland was uneventful. At 0131 they were approaching the target at 16,000 feet, some 12 miles south-west of Oldenburg. Suddenly heavy flak opened up on the aircraft with surprising accuracy. Shrapnel ripped into the aircraft, damaging the port centre wing tank and hydraulics and putting the rear turret out of action. There were several holes in the fuselage and cockpit. The oil temperature and pressure gauges for the port outboard engine ceased to function, as did the rev counter for the port inner.

Ascertaining that the damage was not critical, Henry carried on. At briefing the crews had been told that visibility would be clear over the target, but on approach it could be seen that thick layers of medium cloud were shielding the port from view. Pressing home his attack and aiming at the faint glow of fires caused by earlier aircraft, Henry commenced his run-in, only to find that the bomb doors refused to open. Repeated pulling of the lever to the left of his seat and even many minutes' strenuous hand pumping by a member of the crew failed to produce the desired effect. There was no option but to head for home. Meanwhile, the port inner engine had begun to run roughly and the vibration was becoming progressively worse. Crossing the coast, they attempted to open the bomb doors again. The flight engineer topped up the reservoir using oil drained from another part of the system, and Henry pulled the lever again. To their great relief the doors opened, enabling their load to be jettisoned safely 12 miles north of Borkum.

Shortly afterwards the vibration caused by the port inner engine grew worse and the decision was taken to shut down the engine and feather the propeller. Arriving back over England, Henry decided that, since the undercarriage, flaps or brakes might be inoperative, it might be better to divert to an airfield with better overshoot facilities. Flying a short distance beyond Waddington, Henry put down at Cranwell. The undercarriage held and the Lancaster rolled to a halt shortly after 0605. The crew's thoughts are not recorded, but all must have reflected on the fact that had they been in a Manchester they probably would not have survived.[326] (Four days later this view was reinforced. After half an hour's dual instruction with Rhodesian Pilot Officer Christopher Holland, engine trouble compelled Henry to make a forced landing at Wigsley in Manchester L7480, the aircraft he had taken to Essen four weeks earlier.)[327]

On return to his home base he found a letter dated 25 June, from Major W. Stockley, Secretary, Central Chancery of the Orders of Knighthood, St James's Palace, stating: 'The King will hold an investiture at Buckingham Palace on Tuesday, the 14th July, at which your attendance is requested.'

Despite the intention that Henry should return to No. 1654 CU on 28 June, he remained with No. 44 Squadron Conversion Flight, and training continued throughout July with little respite. With Squadron Leader Herring having been posted,[328] Henry found himself in temporary command. In a letter dated 6 July he made a rare reference to his operational flying:

> I haven't been flying far afield since you last saw me – my last operational
> flight removed a piece of my trousers and a good deal of the aeroplane, and
> was rather unsatisfactory generally. There is rather a lot of work to do now,
> as I've got a flight to look after by myself for the first time, until a new CO
> arrives, that is.[329]

In North Africa the Allied 8th Army under the command of Field Marshal Montgomery had halted the Axis advance only 60 miles from Alexandria at the Battle of El Alamein. Henry expressed his delight at the situation, showing his dismay at the lack of planning and practical application still prevalent among some of those responsible for weapons design:

> Things look much better in Egypt now – we might survive, always provided we don't rebound onto another wave of over optimism. Why the Directorate of Ordnance didn't INSIST on bigger guns for tanks immediately after the evacuation of the B.E.F. I can't imagine. We must have met the Hun tanks in France.
>
> It' all very well to say that things can't be done. The Air Force fighters were designed for .303 Brownings – at the beginning of the war there were no cannon in production – the Air Force technicians discovered that cannon were worthwhile – they didn't say that fighters weren't designed for cannon and couldn't take them – they simply said that they'd got to take them and they did.[330]

But even good design could not make total allowance for human fallibility. On 10 July Flight Sergeant N. Day, one of Henry's pupils on a solo night flight, repeated Pilot Officer Tomkins's error of the previous month and overran on landing after his third attempt, wrecking his Lancaster.

Travelling up to London the afternoon prior to his investiture, Henry arrived in time to meet his mother and Tita to have dinner and attend a show (most probably *The Man who Came to Dinner*). He was at Buckingham Palace promptly at 10.15 the next morning, with his mother proudly presenting her light blue admission ticket 2379 to witness the formal presentation by His Majesty King George VI.

Three days later another family event brought them together again. Derek Mond was to be married to Yvonne Victoria Seale, and Henry flew down in Tiger Moth DE422 to attend, bringing with him a clock as a wedding present. Landing at Honeybourne, a training airfield 5 miles north of Fox Hill, he stayed with his mother overnight and, borrowing £5.00 from her, travelled to Cheltenham the following day for the wedding, before flying back to Waddington in the evening.[331]

On 27 July Henry took up Lancaster R5846, KM-X, with Rex Nicholson and Pilot Officer Russell Suckling,[332] conducting another test to help determine a solution to the Lancaster's problem of fuel starvation at altitude.

Meanwhile, Henry's extended stay at Waddington was being reviewed, and as he celebrated his twenty-first birthday a decision was being made that would take him away from the sphere of an operational station for the next five months.

Chapter 14

Bumps and Circuits

It was quickly recognised that with this conversion, a definite stage of training
was reached which required the highest class of trained instructors . . . there
was for a long time an insufficiency of instructors to meet establishments,
and very hard work, long hours and long periods as instructors were put in
by a small number of personnel.
(Air Chief Marshal Sir Arthur Harris, 'Despatch on War Operations')

No. 1654 Conversion Unit (CU) had transferred to a satellite of Swinderby at
Wigsley on the Nottinghamshire–Lincolnshire border on 15 June 1942. Squadron
conversion flights, by now increased in strength to eight aircraft, were becoming
integrated into the expanded CUs, taking in additional experienced personnel
from other units to bring them to full strength. Although No. 44 Squadron
Conversion Flight would continue for several months until it formed the nucleus
of No. 1661 CU, under the command of Squadron Leader Nettleton, VC, Henry
was told that he was soon to be transferred to Wigsley along with another No. 44
Squadron pilot, Sergeant Knight. There they would join the air crew of twelve
officers and fifty-eight NCOs who made up the staff component of No. 1654 CU
under the command of Wing Commander A. D. T. Naish. The records conflict as
to the actual date. According to Henry's logbook, his posting to No. 1654 CU came
through on Monday, 3 August, but the records for this unit state that Henry
ceased to be attached to the conversion flight in July.

The move brought with it a certain culture shock. Wigsley was an expansion
airfield, built to wartime economy standards, with hutted accommodation and
widely dispersed sites as defence against enemy attack. Located to the south-west
of Wigsley village, two of its three runways cut across the road leading into the
settlement, while the bomb dump was concealed in Wigsley wood, to the north
of the airfield. A mixture of Manchesters and Lancasters stood dispersed around
the perimeter track carrying the unit's code letters 'JF' or 'UG' on their flanks.[333]
Airfields typically were built in remote locations, but the broad, flat expanse of

the Vale of Trent gave 'Wicked' Wigsley an extra air of forsaken desolation. There was no pub within easy striking distance, and even the Lincoln taxi drivers thought it was at the ends of the earth, charging premium rates to those unlucky enough to have missed the Service transport back to camp. The food was appalling, prompting some to raid nearby farms in search of sustenance. The prefabricated huts serving as officers' quarters were built beneath a runway approach, the unit's aircraft roaring low overhead at all hours, disrupting the sleep of those who were resting after either day or night flying. Sanitation and washing facilities were sadly inadequate, although as an officer Henry had the services of a shared batman to facilitate the provision of hot water. Nor was there efficient heating, even when sufficient fuel for the cast-iron tortoise stoves could be found. At least for Henry it was summer; in winter, on extreme days, personnel might rise to find their boots frozen to the concrete floors. It was bitterly cold in the winter and plagued by insects in the summer, and the squalor prompted one pupil to corrupt its location to 'Pigsley', describing it as a 'dunghill'. Wigsley was a far cry from the relative comforts of Waddington.

Henry's first flight with the unit was made on 4 August, ferrying Manchester L7419, UG-B, from Swinderby to Wigsley, followed that night with dual circuits with Pilot Officer John Harrad[334] in Lancaster R5734. The next day saw dual circuits with Sergeant John Dinning[335] and Sergeant Rickard[336] in R5893, with similar exercises for Flight Lieutenant G. Sweeny[337] the following day. On 9 August Flight Lieutenant George Smyth[338] and Squadron Leader Denis Clyde Smith[339] were given a demonstration of propeller feathering in R5730, UG-A. It must have seemed as if very little had changed for Henry, apart from location.

He wrote to say that he hoped soon to be granted leave, telling his mother that recently he had a reunion with a childhood friend:

Do you remember the picnic at Beaudesert when we cooked sausages with John and all the family – I think it snowed – and a boy called Spooner came out with us – I remember you liked him. Anyway, here he is as a Flight Engineer with one of the pilots that I'm training – amazing. He looks much the same – I recognised him immediately but couldn't believe my eyes. He left Bradfield [sic] early and went to a school nearer home in Yorkshire, so we hadn't met for about 11 years.[340]

Mrs Maudslay's pleasure at the thought of Henry returning home soon turned to delight during the morning of Sunday, 9 August. Not only was it gloriously warm and sunny, but a cable had arrived to say that her son would be back that evening for a week's leave. By 5.30 p.m. she was preparing for his arrival when the telephone rang. When she answered it, her expectations were shattered when she heard a voice announcing himself as Dr MacEvoy from Leicester Royal Infirmary, telling her that Henry had met with a serious accident and had been admitted to hospital.

The exact nature of Henry's accident is unrecorded, but it appears that he was riding his motorbike when he was in collision with a lorry and sustained a minor fracture of the skull along with other cuts and bruises. Mrs Maudslay set off for Leicester the following day to visit her son. On arrival she learned that Henry's injuries were not as severe as first feared. He was confined to bed in Apprice Ward, but was well able to receive visitors. Discussing the incident, Henry was concerned about the validity of his insurance, fearing that the cover note might have expired. Reassuring him, his mother promised to resolve the issue when she returned to Fox Hill. She was as good as her word, writing almost immediately that she had sorted things for him and he was not to worry.

A few days later, on Friday the 14th, Roland Lee, the owner of the lorry with which he had collided, called in to see him. He came in again the following afternoon, bringing various gifts that he hoped would ease Henry's time in bed, including several sheets of white lined paper, torn from an exercise book, which Henry used to write to his mother that evening, drawing comparisons with her own earlier accident:

I'm sorry to have been such a damned nuisance – falling off bicycles seems to be a family failing! . . . It's very good of you to arrange about the bicycle insurance – the police will find it's insured for a year even if the cover note has expired. I'm feeling very well now and had the stitches out this morning. There is one crack in my skull underneath the stitches – but it's a very slight one according to the X-ray.

. . . Mr Roland Lee, whose lorry I ran into, came in to see me yesterday and again this afternoon. We had tea together and get on very well. I asked him to bring me some odd sheets of paper to write to you on, and he insisted in bringing me two oranges, a bar of chocolate, a lot of butter-scotch as well, which was awfully hard. He says he runs a sweetshop as well as a lorry.[341] We find a lot to talk about as he's an amateur mechanic in his spare time. The bell on his shop rings when the customer walks through a ray of light, and so on.

Have no worry for my comfort. One lives in tremendous luxury here, with much better food than one can hope to eat. Milk in the middle of the morning. Fruit, butter and cheese ad lib. and so on. I still sleep like a log. Both eyes open and O.K. Am writing this in the cool of the evening with the windows wide open.

. . . The Doctor who picked me up came in and said hullo – as I was asleep at the time and woke up suddenly not knowing who he was – I was not at my brightest; thanked him for picking me up and that's about all.

 . . . considering it was all most probably my fault and that it's given everyone but me a lot of trouble I think that people are amazingly kind. It's given me a long rest which I'd no hope of getting any other way, and I'm feeling much better for it! [342]

As a postscript, to reassure his mother that he was suffering no visual effects he added: 'Read Sunday Times from cover to cover this morning – no eye strain at all.'

 With the stitches out and the necessary period of observation having shown no complications, there was discussion about moving Henry to a hospital at Oxford to convalesce. Henry hoped that this would be soon. The enforced bed rest was beginning to give rise to impatience, despite regular visits by his mother and Roland Lee. On 18 August, still using Mr Lee's paper, he wrote to his mother:

This summer weather is simply grand and I wish to goodness they'd let me go out of doors. However one can't hurry much I suppose.

 . . . I hope Oxford doesn't keep me long as I feel perfectly well and am sure I could recover much better sitting on the terrace than in a hospital bed. [343]

In common with many other hospital patients he had a list of requisites. He had ordered hair oil to be sent to Fox Hill; could his mother bring it on her next visit, 'as my hair is getting very dry and frizzy'? He needed another pair of pyjamas and books would help to pass the time: 'Please also bring. . . my two books by Peter Scott.'[344] If you happen to pass [W. H.] Smiths there's a book of light verse called 'Bells and Grass' by de la Mare[345] that I'd like very much to read – I got a copy and lent it to a chap who went missing, so never really read it.' Other clothing requirements, including extra pyjamas, could be obtained from LAC Bowrigg, his batman at Wigsley. Writing three days later, Henry exclaimed:

Great rumours are going round the hospital that we have invaded France.
 I do hope that they are true, can't help thinking that something is in the air. Anyway, will know soon. If it is an invasion the country will be in simply tremendous form as everyone seems to want it very badly, though how we are going to bust the Siegfried Line I can't imagine. One could take airborne troops over it, but not heavy equipment. [346]

The rumours were partly true, although the rejoicing of those who believed that the Second Front had opened was soon proven to be premature. In the early hours of that morning Allied troops, mainly from Canadian units, carried out an assault on the French port of Dieppe. Officially described as a 'Reconnaissance in Force', the operation was a costly investigation into the strength of German defences and the practicability of capturing a port area intact. Of the 5,000 troops engaged in the nine-hour operation, some 3,500 were killed or taken prisoner.

Henry was on the way to recovery: 'I'm feeling just too well to believe – and wish to goodness I could get up and out into this weather, lovely days although we had a tremendous thunderstorm last night.'

It had just been confirmed that he would be transferred by ambulance to Oxford at ten o'clock the following morning and was concerned that he had nothing suitable to give the staff who had shown him such kindness and consideration during his stay: 'Wish I could think of something to give the nurses here who have been more than kind. With chocolate rationed it's hard to think of any suitable colective [sic] present.' His mother was due to visit him in Oxford on Friday and Henry added one more postscript request, writing on the back of the envelope: 'P.S. Please bring my watch (the one from Lucerne) on Friday, as my flying one will have to go to London for overhaul.'

Henry's transfer to Oxford following his discharge from Leicester Royal Infirmary on Thursday, 20 August, proceeded as planned. His destination was the Military Hospital for Head Injuries located at St Hugh's College, to the north of the city between the Woodstock and Banbury Roads. Built in early eighteenth-century style, by H. T. Buckland, the main building ran east to west, with southern arms projecting into extensive gardens, the main entrance being beneath the cupola in St Margaret's Road. In October 1939 the majority of the academics had moved out to the Balliol College site at Holywell Manor for the duration. While the students retained use of the library in the main building, the remainder of the college had been transformed into a temporary military hospital. Single-storey utilitarian brick huts with flat concrete roofs, linked by brick corridors, had been constructed across much of the lawns and tennis courts, creating six wards for 300 beds, with an operating theatre and additional physiotherapy and occu-pational therapy units.[347]

The regime was relatively relaxed, and patients were permitted visitors from late morning, after the doctors' rounds, until dusk. Henry's first day there was celebrated by the visit of his mother. With her came Tita, who had been staying at Fox Hill and was now en route to London to meet Gordon. They arrived during the morning, bringing with them Henry's various requests for books and clothing. No sooner had they departed than Henry's brother John arrived from Kenilworth, with his companion, Betty Norton-Griffiths, whom Henry later remarked 'could hardly have been more ornamental'.[348] They brought gifts for the invalid, grapes and a copy of the newly published Thomas Armstrong historical novel, *Dover Harbour*; Kelly too had sent him 'a lovely book called the Snow White Goose'.[349] He was certainly not going to be short of reading matter.

On Saturday morning he was given a series of tests to ensure that he had suffered no deep-seated damage. To an outsider the procedure may have seemed somewhat bizarre. In a room on the ground floor of the main building he was seated on a chair placed inside a cage some 5 feet square, constructed of chicken wire and a timber frame. Electrodes were placed on his head to monitor his brain activity while the cage was earthed to minimize external electrical interference. Wires connected the electrodes to a terminal block behind his head, passing detected impulses to an electroencephalograph that printed out a graph on to a paper roll. (Henry described this to his mother as 'a thing rather like the recording barometer in the hall').

The results were encouraging for all appeared normal, although Henry admitted to feeling 'a bit weak in the legs', thereby displaying a typical symptom of concussion. With such cases, nursing staff were instructed to note any other signs such as headaches, lack of concentration or depression. The *Nursing Times* of this period recommended that treatment should comprise 'a judicious combination of encouragement, sympathy and firm management, together with some form of interesting and constructive work to occupy the mind and restore confidence'.

Returning to his ward, he found that the departure of another patient had allowed him to be moved to a bed near the window, with a view across the small remaining section of the ornate gardens. On Tuesday the 25th John paid another visit, driving over in his Avon-bodied Standard. By now Henry was allowed up and about from lunchtime until after supper. To update his mother on his progress, he had tried unsuccessfully to phone her the previous evening, finding that he could only reach the Oxford exchange. Instead he sent a letter requesting a spare shirt and collar and three pairs of black socks in anticipation of his being allowed out into the grounds.[350] He issued a mild rebuke, pointing out that the green pyjamas she had forwarded had not been washed and asking her to bring his red ones again when she next visited, 'as I've already changed and haven't any fresh ones at present'. Then, perhaps with a pang of conscience at his demands, added a final practical note: 'I seem to have asked you to bring over so many things that one of the small canvas suitcases would be most suitable, my haversack &c would go inside.'[351] (His mother was unable to deal with his requests immediately, since she arrived the next day, before receiving his letter.)

Derek and Yvonne Mond paid a visit on the Thursday, on their way for a long weekend at Sharnbrook, Bedfordshire.[352] He was also visited by Lieutenant Jiri Vranek, a Czech officer based near Dunsfold, an acquaintance of Kenneth and

Mary Chance, long-standing family friends. Seeing Derek reminded Henry that he still owed his mother for the £5.00 he had borrowed while attending the for-mer's wedding. Saying that he was enclosing a cheque for the outstanding amount, Henry wrote telling her that he would be transferred to a convalescent hospital at Middleton Stoney soon and warning her that he might require his golf clubs and tennis racquet, assuming the latter was still in a fit condition after a con-siderable period of non-use. Aware of the dangers of being presumptuous, he suggested that she should not send them until he phoned to request them. Henry posted the letter, then realized to his dismay that he had forgotten to put the cheque in the envelope!

The day before Henry was due to be moved, Robin Hamilton-Fletcher, who had been at the Hensons' with Peter Pritchard, arrived at St Hugh's, giving them both a brief chance to catch up on news of old acquaintances before Henry was transferred on Friday, 4 September.

It was only a short trip north out of Oxford on the Bicester Road, turning north towards Brackley. The car drove through stone and thatch settlements and past the glider training airfield of Weston on the Green, with its cumbersome combinations of Miles Master tugs and Hotspur gliders, their yellow and black striped undersides warning others in the vicinity to allow them a wide berth. Henry was taken by an ATS driver, who, learning that he had been based at Waddington, revealed that she was the sister of Pilot Officer John Ruck-Keene, one of his instructors at Finningley, who had been lost on operations with No. 207 Squadron during the previous October.

Middleton Park, Middleton Stoney, Oxfordshire, had been the seat of the 9th Earl of Jersey and his second wife, American film actress Virginia Cherill.[353] The original Georgian house had been demolished and rebuilt by Sir Edwin Lutyens and his son Robert in 1938 to reflect the needs of immediate pre-war country-house life, with accommodation for forty people, including servants. A great elm avenue, opening into a semicircle of cedars, flanked the entrance drive. Ahead a pair of piers surmounted with stone eagles between a group of four ser-vants' lodges formed an entrance into a forecourt area, with the main house, built to a neo-Georgian design in Clipsham stone, forming the left-hand side. A lack of windows on the ground floor of the forecourt side gave an imposing fortress-like illusion, with a modest front door opening to marble floored, vaulted entrance hall and interior corridors. At the time of completion it was seen as the height of 1930s luxury, with a cocktail bar and twelve guest bedrooms, each with en suite bathroom, together with Lady Jersey's own gilt, pink onyx and white marble bathroom. The house generated its own electricity, and there was an engine-driven service lift and refrigerated cold store. The terraced gardens, unfinished at the outbreak of war, contained an architectural swimming pool plus garaging for fifteen cars. The Jerseys had moved in only very briefly before departing for warmer climes. Requisitioned initially for use by an evacuated convent school, the house, with the exception of a few rooms, was now occupied by the Joint War Organization (a working partnership of the British Red Cross and Order of St John) as a Red Cross military convalescent hospital for officers with head injuries.[354]

Henry settled readily into his new surroundings. Hastily drafting a letter to his mother to send her the previously omitted cheque, he sketched his initial impressions: 'This is a glorious place and life is feeling much more normal every day. . . . The officers here I like as much as the ones at St Hugh's. . . . This house is lovely, VG, modern English style. . . . P.S. Can you send my tennis racquet please, but NOT my golf clubs?'[355] Five days later the tennis racquet arrived and he wrote to thank her, giving further details of his daily regime, quoting Emile Coué:

> Every day and in every way I am feeling better and better! I do wood cutting from 10 'til 11 every morning, no slave driving, so you do as much as you feel like, then P.T. from 11.15 to 12. Afternoon and evening are free to go for a walk, or play games or so forth. It's simply lovely country and I haven't felt so well since leaving home for Uxbridge. Also, all the officers are English, Scots or Irish. No Dominions by chance. The result is a definitely unstrained atmosphere, nothing definite, but no one is being polite, such a rest![356]

He had been told that he might be allowed out shortly for a day and had telephoned J. D. Hills at Bradfield with the hope that he might be able to make a brief visit. He had also been trying to obtain three RAF brooches with the astral crown for his mother and Tita and his cousin Diana, but had discovered to his dismay that jewellers were no longer permitted to manufacture them.

After a fortnight's convalescence, on Friday, 18 September, Henry was finally allowed home on fourteen days' sick leave, after which a medical board would assess his condition and fitness for return to duty. On 22 September, after four days at Fox Hill, Henry, with his mother, Uncle Reg and Tita, journeyed up to the family's Scottish summer retreat at Shinness.

It was an enjoyable break, visiting haunts familiar from his childhood, holding house parties and seeing old family friends. Boating, fishing, walking and a duck drive were all acceptable pursuits in the fine autumn weather. The estate Game Book records: 'Henry got a duck with a lovely shot standing at the mouth of burn.' All too soon it was over and Henry had to present himself before a medical board in London, who would assess his ability to return to flying.

Catching the train at Lairg on 30 September, he found himself sharing a compartment with 'a dear old boy of about 75 who had several nephews &c at Eton'. His travelling companion came from 'O'Hennery', the pink lodge opposite the railway line, by the River Shin. There was ample opportunity for conversation comparing notes about his school and discussing local gossip from Lairg. Changing trains, he took a third class sleeper to London, arriving so late that a planned breakfast with Mary Gibb had to be cancelled. Fortunately his mother had provided copious amounts of sandwiches, which were more than adequate for two meals. Assistance was also forthcoming from a small quantity of port in a bottle he had brought with him. Even so, Henry was glad that his three travelling companions in the sleeper had their own food and he felt no obligation to share his provisions.

Arriving finally at King's Cross Station, he reported to the Air Force Medical Board, a short distance from Tottenham Court Road. The initial assessment seemed good and Henry was confident that he would be passed fit to return to his unit.

Taking advantage of a lunch break, he was able to meet up with John, who looked tired but insisted that he was fine and enjoying himself. Thanking Henry for the gift of a fruit cake he had brought from his mother, John admitted that he had thought that his younger brother needed more time to recuperate and had attempted to get the authorities to extend his sick leave, without success. Lunch over, there was a further examination that afternoon, before spending an enjoyable evening with Mary Gibb. The next morning the medical authorities announced their verdict. He had been passed fit for duty and instructed to report back to Wigsley the following day. Catching an afternoon train to Lincoln, Henry spent the night of 2 October in the White Hart ('as good as ever') before returning to Wigsley the next morning. (Interestingly the No. 1654 CU records for this date state that Henry was posted in from No. 44 Squadron. His official Service record, which makes no mention of a posting to No. 1654 CU at the beginning of August, confirms 3 October for Henry's move to Wigsley, but from RAF Station Swinderby, to which for administrative purposes he had been 'posted' as 'N/E sick' on 10 August.)

When he reported for duty, Henry's first shock came when he was informed that as a result of his being unfit for duty for a period longer than twenty-one days he had lost his acting rank of flight lieutenant, which he had held from 12 June. Making light of it to his mother he wrote: 'However I have been promised mine back again as soon as the vacancy which there is for it is officially recognised. . . . One has less responsibility as a Flying Officer than as a Flight Lieutenant, and I think it's better for convalescence.'

On his first full day back, 4 October, fog restricted flying. Henry found himself occupied with ground instruction, giving a two-hour lecture in the morning, although by this time the unit's teaching arrangements were being formally re-structured to allow flying staff to concentrate on the practical aspects of training in the air. Ground tuition was to become the responsibility of a separate, dedicated officer.[357] Having overcome the first hurdle, Henry was rather nonplussed to discover that his flight commander was starting a course the following morning, leaving Henry to assume command of the flight.

On Monday, 5 October, Henry took to the air for the first time since 9 August to be checked out and given half an hour's refresher in dual instruction in Manchester L7457 by instructor Flying Officer Rupert Oakley,[358] followed by a local familiarization flight for his own benefit. His enforced spell on the ground seemed to have caused no ill effects: 'In the air for about two and a half hours and might have stopped yesterday for all the effect it has had, except that one feels fresher and better all round.'

While it might have been relatively easy for Henry to slip back into the routine of flying, domestic arrangements, in particular clothing and laundry, were giving a few problems. He had hoped to be able to send his suitcase with unwanted clothes back to his mother, and intended to use an aircraft of the communications flight to fly it back to Honeybourne. Unfortunately this opportunity was no longer available to him. In the interim he would send his new issue overcoat home as a registered parcel. His spare uniform was being returned to his tailors Denman & Goddard of Swallow Street, London, for repairs and alterations and would be sent on to Fox Hill when they were complete.

He also needed three more collarless shirts from home, plus a collar for each, together with a semi-stiff blue cotton collar, and two pairs of trousers; one a pair that had been too long and had been repaired at the bottom of the legs, the other a pair without a waistband strap bought in Doncaster while he was at Finningley.

The next few weeks were spent settling into the steady routine of dual instruc-tion in Manchesters and Lancasters. Henry was well suited to the task. Instructors needed to develop a keen analytical outlook and be clear and concise in their explanations, with quick and sincere praise when situations were well handled. Above all they needed to be understanding and tactful and avoid showing any signs of irritation that might further fluster and confuse a nervous pupil. Paced perseverance was needed with slow pupils, while capable ones, and perhaps those tending to overconfidence, required careful stretching to demonstrate and test their ability. The flying load was consistent although not great, usually only one flight a day lasting an hour and a half or so with some night flying. Occasionally there might be two, or possibly three, flights a day, but these were exceptions rather than the rule. With an increased number of squadrons converting to the Lancaster, the names of pupils passing through No. 1654 CU was beginning to read like a 'Who's Who' of No. 5 Group of the period. Henry's pupils included Canadian Sergeant Ken Brown, Australian Pilot Officer Robert Barlow and New Zealander Pilot Officer Les Munro fresh from Operational Training Units and destined for Nos 44, 61 and 97 Squadrons respectively. Notably Henry was to strike up a friendship with Flying Officer Bill Astell, who already held the DFC from Wellington operations with No. 148 Squadron in the Middle East and who would be posted to serve briefly with No. 1485 Bombing and Gunnery Flight before going on to No. 57 Squadron. Within six months all would be reunited at Scampton as founder members of No. 617 Squadron. Squadron Leader John Searby was also at Wigsley converting to Lancasters prior to a posting on 15 October to No. 106 Squadron as a flight commander under Wing Commander Guy Gibson.[359] He would take over the mantle of squadron commander when Gibson left Syerston to form No. 617 Squadron. On 15 October Henry collected Squadron Leader George Avis, whom he understood had been Charles Pilkington's flight commander at No. 20 OTU at Lossiemouth and had served on No. 44 Squadron towards the end of Henry's tour, bringing him from Swinderby to Wigsley to commence his conversion course.[360]

Wigsley's isolation seemed to rub off on to Henry, with the result that his usually frequent letters ceased for much of a very wet October. Training intensified as squadrons outside No. 5 Group began to convert to the Lancaster and the unit found itself with a fresh intake from No. 101 Squadron, a No. 1 Group unit. Additional pressure was placed on accommodation, as Wigsley now found itself home to 57 officer aircrew and 273 other ranks. During this period Henry never went more than a mile from the airfield, except for one visit to Lincoln to purchase a book to send to Kelly for her birthday. He ordered more books by post from Blackwell's in Oxford to serve as Christmas presents and had them addressed to him at Fox Hill. On the 23rd, prompted by the receipt of a parcel containing a cake from his grandmother, he finally put pen to paper. Apologizing profusely for his silence, he perhaps felt more guilty as he realized that his mother might now be feeling his lack of communication more acutely since Tita and Annette had now left Fox Hill in order to be nearer Gordon. Tita's assistance around the house was certain to be missed, although it was hoped that Olive, their land girl, would be allowed to stay on as an extra pair of hands.

Meanwhile, routine continued at Wigsley. There were the inevitable accidents, usually on take-off and landing. On 24 October Sergeant P. Wiltshire's Lancaster swung on take-off, Sergeant Smith collided with a gun post while landing on the 29th and there was another take-off swing two days later by Flight Lieutenant

McKenzie, recently attached from Rolls-Royce. The latter, a consequence of poor teamwork by the pilot and flight engineer, brought direct criticism to bear on the instructors of 'B' Flight. These relatively minor mishaps, resulting in damage owing to undercarriage collapse, caused few injuries but were a continual reminder against complacency – as if one were needed.[361] After his motorcycle accident, Lady Luck seemed to be favouring Henry, and he avoided any further misfortune.

During the final week of the month Henry was transferred to the other flight in order to support a newly arrived flight commander. No sooner had the transfer been executed than the latter went off on leave to be followed by a course, much to Henry's disgust, leaving him once again as surrogate flight commander for a fortnight. There was a brief respite between 28 and 30 October, as he nursed a sore throat exacerbated by the mists and fog that continued to cloak the airfield. A visit to the station medical officer set him on the road to recovery, the doctor concurring with satisfaction with Henry's decision taken after his accident to stop drinking. Apart from the purely medical (and financial) benefits Henry noted: '[I] certainly feel better I think because one gets to bed so much earlier instead of talking shop all night in the mess.'[362]

His new responsibilities demanded a few early nights. In a letter to his mother on 30 October, he told her: 'We have to parade once weekly at 8.30 so I've gone to bed early to stand a chance of being well enough awake to give the Flight the right orders at the right time. I hate it and my Flight Commander is going on leave so I have to do it.'

As late summer turned to autumn proper, the nights were drawing in, bringing with them further dank evening mists. For the time being Henry was still comfortable in his hut, where he had a single room heated by its own individual stove, 'luxurious on so crowded a camp as this'. Nevertheless he had an eye on the future: 'I will be sending my thin battledress and two pairs of thin pyjamas home quite soon for storage. . . .Can you please send my thick pyjamas with the green stripes and the last surviving pair of Vyella ones with the green stripes?'[363]

He had still not resolved the problem regarding the suitcase of clothes that he wanted to return to Fox Hill. With no other solution in sight, he told his mother that he intended to send it by rail, registered and insured.

A number of factors appear to have been causing Henry some frustration at the present time. His continuing duties as stand-in flight commander, executing a role that might have been his for real had his accident not occurred, was breeding discontent regarding his chances of early leave. He would try to obtain forty-eight hours in order to see Tita and Gordon when his flight commander returned. Otherwise the leave roster showed his next break was not due until 5–11 December. Compounding the issue was the fact that he had been invited by Elizabeth

Edwards and Phoebe Cresswell to attend Queen Charlotte's Ball on Saturday, 12 December. (The ball was held in support of Queen Charlotte's Maternity Hospital. Pre-war it had taken place on the anniversary of the patron's birthday in May, but wartime expediency had changed the date to December.) Initially enthusiastic about accepting,[364] Henry was now in a quandary; he wanted to attend the ball, but this would mean trying to extend his leave, and he also felt uneasy at accepting the girls' extensive generosity: 'I'm not quite sure what to do about things in this respect – these two girls have evidently got tickets for the whole party – I can only say thank you very much, but the hospitality seems a bit one-sided. I think I'd better try and get some tickets for a good show that will be over before the ball starts.'[365]

The thought of an overnight stay in London served to remind him that his attempt to join the RAF Club was still unresolved. Expressing his thoughts to his mother, Henry revealed some of his inner feelings on the situation. Usually generous in his comments where colleagues were concerned, he demonstrated uncharacteristic disdain for those who held sway over his present position:

Still haven't got a club. I know a few senior officers who even MIGHT belong to the RAF Club. My present CO I detest so much that I couldn't possibly ask a favour of him, and the same goes for the man who now commands my Squadron.[366] The only man I haven't tried is my late Station Commander, not being on a parent station I hardly know my present one. As a matter of fact, I'll probably try my CO. Although I don't like him he means well in many ways.

The shorter days and the late autumn weather with the onset of fog during the November evenings saw no let-up in training requirements and the pressures on the over-stretched CU staff. In addition to flying instruction, Henry was required to keep up to date with rigorous administrative chores, including the preparation of flying details and assessments of pupils' performance. There was little spare time for recreational activity, even had Wigsley been more favourably located. A lull in flying allowed him to pen a brief letter to his mother on the 10th. He had just finished listening to a broadcast of Winston Churchill addressing the Lord Mayor's Banquet at the Mansion House. Reviewing the progress of the war, the Battle of Egypt and the US Offensive in North Africa, the Prime Minister had made his prophetic remark: 'This is not the end. It is not even the beginning of the end. But it is perhaps the end of the beginning.' Henry's brevity and lack of news is indicative of the intensity of his work at this period:

Time is not on the side of correspondence at present as you may have noticed! I'm in bed at present, having listened to Churchill's speech in a friend's room, and returned to find that a spaniel with muddy paws had borrowed my bed, so it had to be re-made – by me. I'm off in a Tiger Moth very early tomorrow morning to take one of the Flight on a course[367] in Wiltshire, so may be over home. There will not be time to stop for lunch – much as I'd love to – because I'm very busy till the end of this week.[368]

Thanking his mother for continuing to send him copies of the *Eton Chronicle*, 'which I always like to see, though the casualty lists never bring good news', he asked her to open one parcel and forward the bill for the books he had ordered from Blackwell's.

In North Africa, Montgomery and the 8th Army were gaining control of the Halfaya Pass, pushing Rommel's forces out of Egypt and back towards Tobruk. Commenting on the news of recent events (Montgomery's knighthood and promotion to full general were announced on this day), Henry cautioned against any premature complacency: 'I fear that the Africa Corps is getting away without losing enough men. So long as that Army remains an intact fighting unit, we have plenty to worry about no matter how great our gains in territory may be.'[369]

Henry was again made up to the rank of acting flight lieutenant, backdated to take effect from 1 November. His new flight commander was Squadron Leader Hayter, 'a reservist who was on the purchasing commission in America, and had a flying job at Farnborough before that'. A quarter of an hour's flight to Waddington on 22 November with this officer in Manchester L7400 provided the excuse for a trip to Lincoln and a rendezvous with Monica Campbell and her friend Jean (the two WAAFs whom his mother had met during her tea party in Waddington's Officers' Mess some eight months earlier), followed by a party back in the Mess at Wigsley.

Since arriving back at the CU, Henry had been making regular visits to the camp dentist for root canal treatment (possibly a legacy of his accident?). The tooth had been drilled, and every fortnight the temporary crown was removed, the nerve exposed and treated to kill an infection. Despite the unpleasant-sounding nature of this treatment, Henry assured his mother that the process was 'quite painless and actually rather pleasant. He uses a very special preparation for dressing the nerve, made in Germany.'[370]

Henry's spirits were raised by the news of a friend's impending posting to Wigsley and the thought of forthcoming leave at the start of the following month, combined with good news of the Allied advance in the Mediterranean:

Things are good on the surface. I don't like the way the Luftwaffe is lying
quiet. Ralph Allsebrook is coming here for a course! So of course, I've
arranged for him to be posted to my flight. That will be fun.[371]

It's getting a gloriously short time from now to December 5th and I'm
just counting the days.[372]

The remainder of the month saw a regular mix of day and night instruction,
combined with a period of standing in for a flight commander away on leave:

I get moved from flight to flight always just before the flight commander
goes on leave and so am forever taking over and getting used to new people.
Good experience, but it takes all one's time.

The news is SUPERB, and if the Africa Corps can be annihilated, Africa
will be ours, then the Mediterranean will be open again, with endless
possibilities for us.[373]

The weather at the beginning of December was particularly fickle, the dampness
turning to sleet and snow. Henry's logbook records only one flight before he took
his extended nine days' leave, a 'dual and test' in Lancaster L7527, O, with Flight
Sergeant Ken Brown, who he discovered hailed from Moose Jaw.

It is not known whether Henry was able to attend Queen Charlotte's Ball at
the Grosvenor House Hotel on 12 December. Traditionally the occasion was seen
as one of the key events of the 'Season', where white-robed debutantes, chaperoned
by their mothers and maids of honour, circulated among eligible bachelors. High
point of the evening would have been the ceremonial entrance of the cake, bearing
197 candles (one for each year since Queen Charlotte's birth) pulled in by Guards
of Honour, girls presumably selected for their strength as well as their elegant
looks. The entrance effected, the young women gathered around and sank into
deep curtseys before it. Despite attempts to maintain pre-war appearances, there
were the inevitable concessions necessitated by the times. The debs' dresses,
restricted by wartime rationing, were bought with coupons, the young men were
all in uniform, and the cake, although cosmetically splendid, had false icing and
was made with powdered egg.

Arriving on leave at Fox Hill, Henry was able to learn further details of events
hinted at by his mother in her letters. He was pleased to hear that 'Uncle Alec has
replaced the time honoured Scottish tradition of drinking oneself to death on
whisky' sufficient to remember his mother's birthday, and that Uncle Norman
had recovered from his recent illness. His Uncle Godfrey had had a chance reunion
in Durban with Gwen Maudslay's cousin, Captain Bill Tennant. The other major

news from the locality was the visit on 7 November of Mrs Eleanor Roosevelt, the American First Lady, and her Secretary, Miss Dobson, to Wormington Grange as guests of Lady Ismay. Wormington Grange had become a wartime nursery for thirty-five evacuated babies. After inspecting the facilities and meeting Miss Berrow, the Matron, Mrs Roosevelt was invited to lunch before departing to see land girls at work on a nearby farm. Henry too was hoping to see the younger members of his family. Unfortunately, to his great disappointment, Annette and Joanna were not currently staying at Fox Hill.

Despite the warmth and jollity of the visit, Henry noted that his mother was still experiencing considerable difficulty maintaining Fox Hill. She was running it almost single-handedly since Tita had moved to Yorkshire to be nearer Gordon, now with the 4/7 RDG in the Keighley area as part of the 79th Armoured Division. The house and grounds were placing severe demands on her, and he was concerned about the strain she was experiencing looking after both the estate and his elderly grandmother. With increased rationing of food and fuel, the impending winter would exacerbate the situation, despite Henry's tongue-in-cheek suggestion that 'suet puddings are the only answer!' Did he not know that even suet was in extremely short supply?

Returning to Wigsley on 13 December, Henry wrote to his mother, thanking her as usual for her care and kindness during his leave and making a proposal that he had been mulling over during his visit but that he appears to have thought imprudent to voice directly:

> With the present shortage of domestics, would it not be possible to get a 'companion' (of an age just above the reserve limit) for Granny? I know that you will dislike the idea, but feel there should be quite a lot of people who would be only too glad of a job in the country – whatever the hardships involved. I may (of course) be quite wrong, and know that Granny detests the very idea. But you are so desperately overworked that I see no alternative.
>
> About the house, your difficulties are immense at finding a place that would suit you, but I cannot believe that the problem of storing is as great as you think that it is. . . . There should be a chance of dispersing your things over several places of storage, surely you might be able to let the house PARTLY furnished with your best things in store? Or else move into a smaller house with only your best things and store the rest? [374]

Henry knew that his mother had been to view several properties, finding each of them unsuitable in terms of size, location or repair, and suggested a house in nearby Weston-sub-Edge, which had been occupied by friends of theirs, although he did concede 'it's probably too much of a rabbit warren'. In an attempt to keep the thought alive he ended by saying that he would scan the papers carefully for anything in the district that might be any good. It is ambiguous whether this meant that he would look in the national press for property in the Cotswolds, or in local papers for an opportunity to move his mother closer to Lincoln.

As festivities approached he sent his mother the station Christmas card, a plain white embossed card, with the RAF crest in gold and a piece of RAF ribbon on the fold. Inside, it was as simple: 'Every Good Wish for Christmas and the New Year, from *Henry Maudslay*, Royal Air Force, Wigsley, Newark, Notts.' Meanwhile, Henry's hopes of being able to obtain a forty-eight-hour pass diminished. On 19 December he accepted the inevitable and wrote: 'I'm sorry not to be at home this Christmas, but think that one should probably give the Air Force a hand.' He added with a touch of irony: 'Ralph has finished his course and gone home with my flight commander for a weekend. Meanwhile I look after the flight!'[375]

He was certainly kept busy. The following day saw two daylight exercises followed by two night dual instructional flights totalling four hours, with a further half an hour's night instruction the following evening.

On Christmas Eve he was summoned to his commanding officer's room to find himself party to a meeting of senior officers discussing the formation and staffing of a new Lancaster CU. Henry was notified that he would be posted to it with the rank of squadron leader, but would serve as Chief Ground Instructor.[376] The thought of a ground instructional role did not appeal in the slightest, and Henry made his views known immediately, requesting an interview with either Wigsley's station commander, Group Captain William McKechnie, GC, or Group Captain Hubert Patch, station commander at Swinderby, Wigsley's parent station. 'Sam' Patch was a well-respected leader and an astute assessor of those under his command. After several phone calls Henry was granted an interview. Exactly what was said during the discussion is not recorded, but it appears to have been an amiable meeting. The result was that Henry's posting to ground instructional duties was to be cancelled henceforth and that he would be posted to an operational squadron, retaining his acting rank of flight lieutenant.

Whether or not the return to operations was at Henry's direct request, or part of a deal to ensure that he would remain flying, can only be conjecture, although the former would appear likely. Strange as it may seem, even by the end of 1942 there was still no formal agreement among the Air Staff as to the length of an operational tour, nor the time to be spent on non-operational duties between tours. The general consensus of opinion (to be formalized during the first half of 1943) was that the first tour should comprise thirty operations, followed by nine months at an OTU, before embarking on a second operational tour of twenty sorties. With the exception of the three operations made while with the conversion flight during May and June, as part of the *Millennium* force, it had been over twelve months since Henry had flown actively with an operational unit. During that period considerable changes and developments had occurred, in both the modus operandi of Bomber Command and the intensity of the German defences. As was common with many screened aircrew posted for instructional duties, Henry would have realized that there would come a point after which a return to operations would pose a degree of risk greater than that of the enemy opposition alone, owing to the erosion of the sixth sense for self-preservation acquired by the majority of operational crews. He was keen to avoid this risk.

Unable to return to Fox Hill for family companionship, Henry enjoyed the festive season with his colleagues. He booked into the White Hart with Rex Hayter and Ralph Allsebrook, and on Christmas Eve the three of them enjoyed an excellent dinner before retiring for the night. On Christmas morning Ralph and Henry attended the eight o'clock service in the cathedral. 'I have never seen anything look so superb.'[377]

They returned to Wigsley in time to continue the time-honoured Service tradition whereby officers entertain sergeants to drinks and then serve lunch in the Airmen's Mess. By devious means, and not without difficulty, Henry then arranged transport to attend a tea party in the WAAF Mess at Waddington, staying on for dinner that evening. As might be expected, everyone was in high spirits, and celebrations continued late into the night with no sign of abating.

Eventually the party broke up in the not so early hours of Boxing Day morning. Henry and his companions ended up with a breakfast of bacon and eggs in the kitchen at 4.30 a.m. 'It was a good party!'[378]

On 28 December a final dual instruction of one hour and five minutes with Sergeant Thomas in Lancaster L7575 brought Henry's total flying hours to 741.30.[379]

Sitting up in bed that evening, he wrote to his mother, apologizing for his handwriting and thanking her for the Christmas card and excellent cake that she had sent. The letter detailed his Christmas activities and advised of his imminent posting: 'from January 1st onwards my address will be RAF Skellingthorpe, Nr Lincoln AND I want my operational flying boots (Registered mail please), you have them in my boot cupboard.'[380] He added a postscript: 'PS Skellingthorpe is very close to Lincoln and the White Hart will (I hope) be used again by you and the family!' The style and content of the letter reflected Henry's good mood and obvious excitement at the thought of returning to operations. Whether or not Mrs Maudslay shared his enthusiasm is not known, although it would be natural to assume that it was not without a degree of trepidation that she packaged his foot-wear and despatched it to Skellingthorpe.

Chapter 15

Regaining the Offensive

Lie in the dark and listen,
It's clear tonight and they're flying high
Hundreds of them, thousands perhaps,
Riding the icy moonlight sky.
Men, material, bombs and maps
Altimeters, guns and charts,
Coffee, sandwiches, fleece lined boots
Bones, muscles and minds and hearts
English saplings with English roots
Deep in the earth they've left below.
Lie in the dark and let them go
Lie in the dark and listen.
(Noel Coward, 'Lie in the dark and listen')

Henry reported for operational duty with 'A' Flight, No. 50 Squadron, at RAF Skellingthorpe on New Year's Day 1943.[381] A satellite of Waddington, Skellingthorpe, like Wigsley, was of wartime construction. Sited to the south of Skellingthorpe village, 'Skelly', as it was popularly known, was built to the standard three-runway layout, the main one running north-east to south-west, ending adjacent to the B1190 Bracebridge to Doddington road, which was closed whenever heavily laden aircraft took off. At this time of year it was an uninviting setting. It was surrounded on two sides by dank and dripping plantations providing camouflage for the dispersals, bomb dump and some of the hutted sites, while water-filled gravel pits pockmarked the neighbouring countryside. Nevertheless, despite the apparent inhospitability, its location, only 3 miles west of the bars, cinemas and varied social life of the city of Lincoln, was far more conducive than that of his previous station.

No. 50 Squadron was another of No. 5 Group's pre-war squadrons. It had been Skellingthorpe's first operational unit, moving in with Hampdens in October 1941 and re-equipping with the Manchester in April 1942. While new runways were being laid during the summer, the squadron had transferred briefly to Swinderby, where it converted to Lancasters, returning again in October 1942 to become Skellingthorpe's sole occupants. As with No. 44 Squadron, a Victoria Cross was recorded among the decorations awarded to its crews. During the major attack against Cologne on 30/31 May 1942, 20-year-old Flying Officer Leslie Manser had remained at the controls of his burning Manchester over Belgium, enabling his crew to escape before he was killed when the aircraft crashed. Since October 1942 the squadron had been commanded by Wing Commander William 'Bill' Russell, DFC, who had maintained successfully high morale and a 'press on' reputation despite poor serviceability caused by a lack of facilities and equipment.[382] Only four aircraft had been lost on operations since returning to Skellingthorpe, and the squadron's strength included a number of highly experienced aircrew. Nevertheless, statistics show that at this period only about one in forty crews could be expected to survive two tours of operations.

In the six months since Henry had been on an operational station, Bomber Command had become increasingly sophisticated, in both tactics and the equipment it used. No longer did aircraft fly singly, or in small groups to the target. The *Millennium* operations had taught the benefits of concentration, swamping the enemy ground defences and overwhelming the target's firefighters and ARP services. Not only could the four-engined bombers carry a greater load for a greater range than the Hampden; the size of individual bombs had grown from the Hampden's 2,000-pounder to the Lancaster's 8,000lb 'Super Cookie'. New radio and radar navigation aids such as Gee and the forthcoming H2S would enable crews to navigate with increased precision across the night skies of a blacked-out Europe without having to rely on map-reading using occasional snatched glimpses of dubiously identified ground features. A new Group, No. 8 (Path Finder Force), had been formed in August 1942. Experienced crews would locate and mark targets for the Main Force, using a range of coloured pyrotechnics, enabling attacks to be conducted with increased accuracy, even when the ground was shrouded by cloud. No longer would crews be forced to bomb blind on ETA, or drop their loads on isolated fires, uncertain as to whether they were enemy decoys or the genuine target. In retaliation, the German defences had developed new measures and techniques to counter the ever-increasing weight of RAF attacks. The Reich was now defended in depth by interlocking radar co-ordinated searchlight and flak zones stretching from Belgium to the Danish border. The Luftwaffe nightfighters were increasing in number and becoming ever efficient with their *Lichtenstein* airborne radar, while electronic jamming created increased interference with Gee reception, hampering navigation. As each side gained a brief advantage with the use of new tactics, the other quickly developed countermeasures in a deadly game of technical cat and mouse.

On 2 January Mary Gibb married Lieutenant Robert Aikenhead of the Irish Guards at St Nicholas church, Saintbury, with a subsequent wartime ration reception for family and friends at Saintbury Close. Mrs Maudslay was present, but Henry was one of several potential guests prevented from attending owing to circumstances beyond their control. Mary's two brothers were also absent. Lieutenant Ivor Gibb of the Sherwood Foresters was serving in India, while her younger sibling, Alec, was still attending school in Canada.

The squadron operated twice before Henry was selected for a place on the Battle Order. On the night of 2/3 January aircraft were mining 'DEODARS' and 'FLOWERS', off the Biscay ports, and on 7/8 January a small force of three aircraft made up the squadron's contribution to a nineteen-Lancaster force sent by No. 5 Group to attack Essen. Henry commenced operations on the night of 8/9 January 1943 with an attack against Duisburg. He was to fly as second pilot to Squadron Leader Peter Birch, 'B' Flight Commander. From Leeds, aged 24 and married, Birch had been a pre-war apprentice with Blackburn Aircraft at Brough before joining the RAFVR. An experienced pilot and a popular leader, holding the DFC from a previous tour, he was a creative man who spent much of his spare time making models and sketching his impressions of bomber operations.[383]

The raid was to be a minor affair, comprising thirty-eight Lancasters from No. 5 Group, marking being carried out by three Pathfinder Mosquitoes. It would be Henry's induction to the new technique of 'skymarking', a fact confirmed by the comment '(PFF Flares)' in the duty column of his logbook. Attending the briefing, Henry would have noted that it was a far more formal affair than the earlier Hampden days. Rather than huddling around a table in the ops room, aircrew now were briefed on their parts individually; navigators by the navigation leader, gunners by the Gunnery Leader and so on, before gathering together for the final overall briefing when the curtains covering the map at the end of the room would be drawn back and the night's target would be revealed.

According to Henry's logbook, this was the first flight with his new squadron – seemingly without the benefit even of an air test. This may not have been so, since the entries for this operation show an uncharacteristic inaccuracy and a marked variance with the squadron records. Henry notes the aircraft as 'Lanc (ED) 442 S', whereas the ORB logs it as (W) 4380.[384] He also lists the target incorrectly as being Düsseldorf, rather than Duisburg.

After a cold but very bright day, at shortly after half-past five that evening, Squadron Leader Birch lifted the laden Lancaster off Skellingthorpe's runway, carrying a 4,000-pounder together with 870 4lb incendiaries. Despite snow showers over the North Sea, the initial part of the flight out was uneventful. Crossing the Den Helder peninsula, they reached Enkhuizen and turned across the Zuider Zee. Reaching their next pinpoint at Kampen, 10 miles north-west of Zwolle, they came under attack from an enemy fighter. Peter Birch's experience was again put to the test. Successful evasive action was taken and the fighter shaken off.[385] Almost immediately, however, the aircraft came under fire from about twenty flak guns. Among the explosions there was 'a rocket contrivance . . . which burst at about 21,000 feet, like the hub of a Catherine Wheel, 300–400 yards radius, bursting in white stars'. These may have been the 57lb shells from the heaviest of the German flak guns, the 12.8 cm, or special shells, which have been described variously as bursting like 'flaming daisies or Prince of Wales' feathers', fired to assist nightfighters locate their prey. Again they escaped unscathed.

The low cloud over which they had flown from the Dutch coast persisted right through to the target area, rendering the searchlights ineffective, but it did not deter persistent and heavy flak firing 'blind' up to heights of 27,000 feet. An unidentified aircraft was seen to be hit over the target at 21,000 feet and to go down in flames before exploding with a shower of red and green flares. (This led to the supposition in the No.50 Squadron ORB that it may have been a Pathfinder aircraft, but in fact all these returned safely. The aircraft was possibly a Lancaster from No. 467 Squadron or, more probably, one of No. 50 Squadron's own crews, that of Sergeant Joseph Kiernan, who crashed near Düsseldorf with no survivors.) Tracking over the preliminary green and secondary red warning flares dropped by the Pathfinders to indicate the approach of the target, the Main Force crews waited for sight of the Release Point flares. Dropped from 18,000 feet by the Pathfinders, their green and red stars would float down for two minutes before being backed up by white flares, burning for a longer period. Flying on a course of 185 degrees (Magnetic) the bomb aimers targeted the flares in order that their bombs would fall on the cloud-masked target. The familiar jolt and a lifting sensation accompanied Flying Officer Wood's call of 'Bombs gone' and Peter Birch eased the Lancaster on to the south-westerly course that would take them to Leeuwen, on the River Maas, from where they would head north-west to their coasting-out point at Noordwijk. Returning over the North Sea, they found that the weather had closed in over Lincolnshire and they were diverted to Tangmere, a fighter airfield near Arundel in Sussex, landing safely at 2137. There they stayed overnight, flying back to Skellingthorpe the following day.

On his return Henry wrote to his mother, crouching over a stove, writing pad on his knee, as he struggled to keep out the damp January cold that penetrated his room:

I am beginning to like this Squadron, cannot tell if I like my Flight

Commander because I have not got one, he's been on leave since I arrived and is due to be posted on coming back.[386] I like the CO and the rest of the Squadron and we are very well placed here geographically! So whenever you feel like it, do come up to the White Hart.[387]

Warning her that he did not expect to get any leave for at least eight weeks, he expressed his relief at being free of the tedium of the conversion unit:

However *that* I don't mind, being on a squadron is so much better than the other job.
    I know the other Flight Commander fairly well and did a trip with him not long ago, to get the hang of things. Enjoyed it a great deal, glad to find that I didn't get too cold at height, even in this weather. Am taking over the crew of the Squadron Leader who has been commanding the Flight that I'm in. Met them today and like them.[388]

Commenting that he was 'glad the wedding [Mary Gibbs] had been a success' and that he hoped 'Mrs Gibb is none the worse for the strain', he thanked his mother for sending glucose and chocolate and ended with a postscript demonstrating his dislike of pomposity and presumptuous attitudes: 'I did not pay Cutt's (?) bill as I object to being addressed as Mr M.ly [sic] by a man who made a great fuss over his own connexion [sic] with the RAF.'

    Recent snow turned to rain and the squadron continued to be active during the following nights, although Henry did not take part in immediate operations, which despatched small numbers of aircraft against Essen, on the nights of 11/12, 12/13 and 13/14 January. These were part of a series of seven minor raids inflicted on this industrial complex during the first fortnight of the new year by small forces of between fifty and seventy aircraft from No. 5 Group with Pathfinder support. The forces employed on these operations were of limited size, since the purpose of the attacks was to perfect the new marking technique, using the most experienced crews.

During this period Henry spent his time visiting various other Bomber Command airfields in Lancaster ED468, VN-A. On Wednesday the 13th he flew to Elsham Wolds, staying overnight and returning the following day, before taking off again to Holme on Spalding Moor, a Yorkshire Halifax station. His old home at Waddington was visited the next day. Life settled down into a pleasant routine. His application for membership of the RAF Club, supported by Squadron Leader Burton-Gyles, had been accepted, and Mrs Maudslay continued to send gifts:

packages of glucose and chocolate, together with a copy of Boswell's *Life of Dr Johnson*, selected by Uncle Reg, not that Henry had very much opportunity to relax, as he explained:

> I'm afraid that there has been no time for reading since I got here. I always seem to arrive at a Flight as a Flight Lieutenant where there is no Squadron Leader so have to do the work for both – not that it's any great strain, as we just spread the work out, but it leaves very little spare time, and one just subsides in an armchair with a flop and that's that![389]

Survival as a bomber crew depended to a great extent upon teamwork and trust in each other's reliability. 'I have an excellent crew (I think) very keen and I like them all. I have not done very much flying since coming here, mostly ground work, but will fly more later.'[390]

Between 17 and 20 January the crew flew air tests and a cross-country as they learned to respond to one another and work with the newly delivered Lancaster, ED475, coded VN-D, which had been allocated to them for operations.

Essen was again the target for a force of seventy-nine Lancasters and three PFF Mosquitoes on the night of Thursday, 21 January. This was to be Henry's first operation as a captain with his new crew. Attending briefing, he learned that again the Pathfinders were to use the skymarking technique he had experienced over Duisburg. Approaching the target on a course of 197 degrees (Magnetic), each bomber was to release its 4,000-pounder, sighting on three red and three white release flares and then, after waiting 10 seconds, release its 4lb incendiaries. It was not to be a successful night for the squadron. Taking off at 1715, Henry soon found that the winds along the route were greater than those forecast. Of the six aircraft despatched by Skellingthorpe, four experienced mechanical failures, forcing them to jettison their bombs and return to base before reaching the target. On arrival at the target, area crews found 10/10 cloud and thick haze that prevented observation of any ground detail, despite a full moon. The Pathfinders were scheduled to drop their flares at 1945, but after waiting for half an hour and seeing nothing, with the bomb aimer calling to him to 'go round again', Henry directed his bomb aimer to target what seemed to be a genuine fire burning in the Ruhr area. The poor visibility made the searchlights ineffective; nevertheless the defences were putting up a heavy flak barrage, and the Lancaster was hit several times, receiving damage to the rear turret and port wing, though no serious injury. With not a little relief, they touched down back at Skellingthorpe at 2155. It was a scenario that would have taxed many an experienced pilot, but Henry appears to have taken it all in his stride, later remarking casually: 'The flak was rather heavy tonight.' Other crews had fared no better; only thirteen of the entire force had attack as briefed, most bombing blind on their estimated time of arrival.

Perhaps prompted by the inclement weather and the anticipated threat of poor landing conditions at this time of the year, Beam Approach training was carried out on the 24th and 25th, followed by 55 minutes of low-flying practice on the 26th. Meanwhile, news from home was good. Tita and Annette were back at Fox Hill with Gordon, the latter albeit temporarily. His grandmother was now enjoying better health and his mother was seeking a companion for her. Nevertheless, Henry was still concerned about the strain running Fox Hill was imposing on his mother: 'Do try and simplify everything you can, pack my cup[391] if it is a nuisance to clean and so on.'[392]

He was optimistic about the war news and his own progress:

> Everyone should be thrilled with news of the 8th Army. I'm so glad they got to Tripoli before the Yanks got to Tunis! After all one has heard of the superb organisation of the aforesaid allies of ours – the First Army has to sit and wait whilst Eisenhower straightens out (or attempts to straighten out) the chaos behind it. . . .Have not done much more serious business yet but am getting plenty of flying with an excellent crew, a new aircraft of my own, which I enjoy a lot.[393]

He did not participate in an operation to Düsseldorf on Saturday, 23 January, but found himself included in the list of ten captains detailed to attack on the same target four nights later. This was to be a larger-scale operation, comprising 124 Lancasters, 33 Halifaxes and 3 Mosquito PFF markers employing a 'ground marking' technique. Using 'Oboe', a radio bombing aid, to ensure accuracy, Mosquitoes would drop salvos of three red markers at intervals throughout the raid. These would burst above the target and cascade to burn on the ground as a pool of colour. Lancasters dropping salvos of six green markers would then back up each Mosquito. The technique had the advantage that the markers would not be carried off target by any wind, as might be parachute flares. Bombing from a minimum height of 18,000 feet, crews were to aim exactly at the red markers if they were burning, or, if not, at the centre of the green concentrations. They were not to be distracted by other fires or ground features.

Again the squadron suffered from technical failures. Taking off at 1754, two minutes before Henry, Sergeant Alfred Kitching climbed into the medium level overcast, circling the airfield to gain height before setting course. A short while later his aircraft was seen to dive out of cloud at 2,000 feet, straight into the ground near Waddington, killing all the crew.[394] Two other aircraft returned early owing to mechanical problems.

The route out left the Norfolk coast at Sheringham and crossed into Holland at Noordwijk then directly to the target. Over Düsseldorf a thin layer of cloud at 5,000 feet obscured ground detail. An estimated fifty searchlights probed the sky, searching for gaps in the cloud, finally forming a cone north-west of the town on the bomber's approach path. At 2000 the initial red markers burst at 9,000 feet, and their glow could be seen clearly for several minutes through the cloud. Bombs were being concentrated on the southern districts of the town, the glow of fierce fires reflecting through the cloud as they took hold. After searching for a break in the cover, Henry released his load on the last green marker flare, seeing the bombs burst accurately near it. Again the heavy flak was intense and accurate, peppering both wings with shrapnel, fortunately causing no critical damage. The squadron records state 'an unsatisfactory trip', but German accounts suggest otherwise, with 10 industrial firms destroyed or seriously damaged, 21 lightly damaged, 456 houses destroyed or damaged and 2,400 lightly damaged. More-over, 66 people were killed and 225 injured, among the latter 169 members of the Wehrmacht caught in their train at the main railway station when it was hit by high explosives.

A day's respite and operations were on again, with an attack by a force of 148 aircraft against Hamburg on the night of 30/31 January. This raid was to mark the debut of another bombing aid, H2S, a self-contained radar aid carried by the Stirlings and Halifaxes that were to mark the target. In theory the river should have provided a good radar image to ensure accurate marking, but this night, possibly owing to inexperience or lack of later refinement to the equipment, results were disappointing. Nevertheless Henry reported that he found only 5/10 cloud over the target, with good visibility, which meant that he could see clearly the river and docks. The PFF red sky markers went down at intervals as briefed from 0300, backed up by greens on the ground, and were clearly recognizable. Making his run in from the south-west over the dock area with the Main Force, Henry held the aircraft steady while Flying Officer Wood released the 4,000-pounder, followed 10 seconds later by the incendiaries, which were seen to impact in a built-up area. On this occasion the No. 50 Squadron records state that there were 'several really good fires in the town. The operation was a complete success', although post-war German reports claim that, of the 315 tons of bombs dropped, most fell in the river or adjacent marshes. Opposition was reported as being relatively light. There were about 100 searchlights within an 8-mile radius of the city, but they and the flak were inactive until a few minutes after the opening of the attack, when it had become clear that Hamburg was the target. Aircraft bombing early had a relatively uneventful run. Five Lancasters failed to return, but all eight despatched by No. 50 Squadron came home safely.

February opened with a night flying test and gun tests. The crew had been operating with different combinations of gunners, but now Pilot Officer William John Tytherleigh teamed up with Sergeant Norman Burrows to provide what would become their permanent defence. On the 2nd, after a short trip to Waddington in ED491, Henry was briefed for an operation against Cologne. The squadron despatched eight aircraft, one of which was forced to turn back early with technical failure, its rear turret out of action. En route from Sheringham to their landfall at Oudorp, on the island of Overflakee in the Scheldt Estuary, there was convection cloud over the North Sea, towering to 22,000 feet in places, with disconcerting static discharges. Most of the aircraft, including Henry's, were experiencing icing conditions. By the time ED491 had reached the turning point at Julich, Sergeant Burrows reported from the rear turret that all his guns had frozen up and that they would be virtually defenceless should a nightfighter make an attack. Undeterred they pressed on, heading for the steady green flares marking the preliminary point 16 miles west of Cologne. There was no moon, and variable broken cloud lay over the target. Crews had been briefed to bomb either red ground markers dropped by the Oboe Mosquitoes or Release Point sky markers, red with green stars, dropped by H2S-equipped Halifaxes and Stirlings. In the event, both were used, but the subsequent green back-up markers were scattered. Nevertheless, returning crews reported good results with numerous fires illuminating the target area to such an extent that one pilot was able to distinguish clearly a factory and attack it. The defences were less intense than expected, the flak being mostly to the west of target. Searchlights were numerous and very active. Hampered by the cloud, they occasionally highlighted a bomber's condensation trail in the cold night air, tracking along it to pick up the aircraft, before others joined them, forming large cones to ensnare their unfortunate prey. Avoiding these, Henry bombed a group of markers from 19,000 feet, seeing the bombs burst, although he was unable to assess accurately their exact location. Fighters were active at 18,000–20,000 feet over the target and on the return route via Euskirchen and Endorp. They were to claim the squadron's sole casualty, Flying Officer David Power, RCAF, shot down near Hamont, Belgium.[395]

Five aircraft were sent to Hamburg the following night, but Henry was given a respite, finding himself one of five scheduled to make the first attack of the year on Turin, on the night of 4 February, while two other crews were detailed to attack the French port of Lorient. Trips to Italy involved a long, tiring and often uncomfortable flight, but the risks from the defences were considered to be less, the Italian targets putting up negligible opposition compared to those in Germany. (Some crews reflected this distinction by indicating the former with a symbolic ice cream cone rather than a bomb on their aircraft's ops tally.) In addition there was usually the breathtaking view of the gleaming peaks of the Alps passing just below, or occasionally alongside, as the aircraft threaded their way through the mountain range between France and Italy.

Lifting ED475 off Skellingthorpe's runway at 1835 hours, Henry set course for the Sussex coast on a route to join the other 187 aircraft detailed for this night's operation. The flight out over Cabourg and Aix-les-Bains was uneventful. The weather was good and there were no problems with icing. There was no moon to aid navigation, but the sight of red flares dropped by the Pathfinders over Lac du Bourget confirmed they were on track. Approaching the target, however, the crews were surprised to see considerably more opposition than had been expected. While this was nothing in comparison to the Ruhr targets, crews who had experienced the target before reported an increase in both the number of search-lights and the intensity of the flak.

Henry reported excellent visibility, enabling positive identification of the target, assisted by red target indicators that were burning in the centre of the city. Descending to 8,000 feet, a height that would have been suicidal over a German target, he located his briefed objective (Aiming Point E) and commenced his bombing run. Gentle pressure on the rudder bar nosed the aircraft to line up on two factory chimneys, which his bomb aimer had selected slightly to the north of the target. The aircraft reared as the bombs were released and below them the 4,000-pounder was seen to burst in a built-up area. Numerous fires were now taking hold, and as they turned for home the entire target was burning well, the glow being visible for a long way along the return route.

Landing at Skellingthorpe shortly before a quarter past two, after a flight lasting some seven and a half hours, Henry and his crew completed their debriefing, learning that all had returned with the exception of Sergeant Keith Johanson, a New Zealander with a predominantly Canadian crew. His wireless operator had sent a message to say that they had attacked the target successfully but would have to make a forced landing. At first it was rumoured they had managed to reach Gibraltar, but subsequent reports confirmed that the aircraft had in fact crossed the Mediterranean and crashed in Spanish Morocco with a total loss of life.

A day or so later Henry managed a reunion with John Sauvage, now with No.27 OTU at Lichfield, being joined by Ralph Allsebrook (still with No. 49 Squadron) and Bill Astell, DFC, whom Henry had known at No. 1654 CU, now back on oper-ations with No. 57 Squadron at Scampton. It appears to have been quite a wild evening: 'Bachelor Party and Rather Alcoholic!'[396]

Squadron Leader Douglas Street, DFC, had arrived on 1 February from No. 1654

CU to take command of the flight, but for the time being Henry's workload was unabated. On 7 February his new flight commander had landed heavily in a slight cross wind after a fighter affiliation exercise and the starboard undercarriage had collapsed. A subsequent medical examination revealed that Squadron Leader Street suffered from a minor visual impairment. Writing of events to his mother that evening:

> From Saturday last to Thursday I worked on the ground or in the air
> every night!
>   I now have a new Flight Commander. Nice chap but too old and has been
> behind an office desk for too long. The general impression is that he won't
> stay the pace, which is a pity – so I hope I'm wrong.[397]
>   Am very happy in my work – have splendid aircrew and ground crew, and
> find that although there have been great strides in navigational aids and com-
> fort and performance of aircraft. . . the general technique has not changed so
> very much. Feel very much in my stride – got well and truly perforated on my
> first efforts but nothing since.[398]

Among the duties connected with the flight were those of 'animal welfare officer': 'The Flight adopted a couple of dogs before I came here. One of them wasn't a dog – so now there's a family of puppies in a cardboard box in the Flight Office!'[399]

Low cloud and rain prevailed over the next few days, but, despite these un-favourable weather conditions, operations were on again on the night of 11/12 February, when ten crews were detailed for an attack on the naval facilities of Wilhelmshaven. This time three of the squadron's aircraft were compelled to return early owing to engine problems, other aircraft in the force experienced icing. Again the target was to be marked by the Pathfinders. When they arrived over the port, they found the target area to be completely covered by thick layer cloud and were forced to mark using H2S and releasing parachute flares as sky-markers that could be seen above the cloud layer. There was only moderate flak, and the searchlights were unable to penetrate the cover. Henry's bombing run was unopposed. With the markers floating as a compact red group dripping green stars in the bombsight graticule, the bombs were released from 13,000 feet on the briefed heading of 135 degrees (Magnetic), but no results could be observed. In keeping with many crews, Henry reported seeing the brilliant flash of an explosion on the ground at 2006, which lit up the sky and left a pale glow lasting for nearly 10 minutes. This was later attributed to a direct hit on the naval ammunition depot at Mariensiel, south of the town. The explosion devastated some 120 acres and caused severe damage in both the naval dockyards and the town. Several other fires could be seen, which by the end of the attack had merged into a single orange glow beneath the cloud.

In the letter written to his mother the previous Sunday Henry had expressed his concern about the U-boat threat:

> Only one trouble at present is the most serious one of submarines. I do not think that enough people realise that the F[leet] A[ir] A[rm] aircraft are designed for tactical use mainly in Fleet actions and to fuss about them and their obsolescence is necessary – but not directly related to the anti-sub war, which is Coastal Command's job. They have the right men and aircraft.[400]

Henry was only partially correct. Increasing numbers of U-boats were now operating in the Atlantic and sinkings had grown alarmingly, but Coastal Command's resources were already overstretched, as they were tasked to extend the range of their protecting convoy patrols. In response to Admiralty pressure, a directive was issued instructing Bomber Command to attack the Biscay ports of Lorient and Saint-Nazaire in support of anti-U-boat operations, denying the vessels a safe haven. This was a setback for ACM Harris, who was marshalling his force to deliver a major offensive against German industrial production. He knew that, when they were in harbour, the U-boats were protected by large concrete pens, impenetrable by any current bomb. The directive allowed for this, approving the devastation of the entire port and town, thereby denying the enemy fuel, water, repair facilities and other supplies vital for maintaining an underwater offensive. Harris accordingly, but with reluctance, switched targets to accommodate his new orders on nights when the weather prevented operations over the Reich.

Henry's opportunity to contribute to the U-boat war came on the night of 13/14 February, when Bomber Command despatched its heaviest attack on Lorient: 466 aircraft were to drop over 1,000 tons on the town, which had already suffered six large raids since the beginning of January. On this operation Henry would be carrying an additional crew member, bomb aimer Sergeant Michael Fuller, who had been posted to the squadron from No. 106 Squadron two days earlier and was shortly to replace Sergeant William Miller.

Despite near freezing temperatures at take-off, weather conditions improved along the route, with good visibility enabling the target to be seen clearly. There were only a few searchlights, the flak was spasmodic and overall the defences appeared ineffective. The attack was split into two half-hour phases, with Nos 4 and 5 Groups in the second. Routed out over Bridport and Brittany, ED475 arrived over the target, approaching from the north to avoid the smoke from the first wave attacks. Fires were burning throughout the whole town, and the crew's designated aiming point on the Keroman peninsula (Aiming Point Z) was already ablaze as they bombed from 6,000 feet, taking an aiming point photograph that would earn them another certificate. The intensity of the defences had diminished as the raid progressed, and there was relatively little opposition. As they turned for home, a searchlight tried to hold them as they crossed the coast. Three short well-aimed bursts from Sergeant Burrows extinguished the beam, sending the crew scattering for cover. They headed out to sea, reaching 5 degrees west before heading north-east to skirt the Breton peninsula and return to the English coast near Dartmouth. On arrival back they found that the defences had not been as impotent as they appeared. The force had lost seven aircraft, including the squadron's Flight Lieutenant Evan Davies. With a second navigator taken along for operational experience, his Lancaster had been carrying a crew of eight. All died as the aircraft came down in the sea, only three bodies being recovered for burial in French cemeteries.

The squadron's attention reverted to Italy the following night, and again Henry found himself en route to Milan. This time 142 aircraft were participating, with Pathfinder support. The route took them across cloud-covered France in bright moonlight, over Cayeux and Troyes to Aix-les-Bains, where green flares were burning as a navigational aid over Lac du Bourget. The northern slopes of the Alps were shrouded in medium cloud reaching up to 18,000 feet, creating icing conditions, but then they were through to clearer skies, with further red flares to mark the route near the southern tip of Lake Maggiore, gateway to the Lombardy Plain. By the time the squadron's nine aircraft had arrived over the target, several good fires were already apparent. With no cloud, visibility was excellent, enabling individual buildings and ground detail to be picked out with ease. The defences – between forty and seventy searchlights deployed in a circle around the city and about twenty heavy guns with occasional light flak – were weak and totally ineffective. Identifying the railway to the south-west of the city and pinpointing his position, Sergeant Miller, again with Sergeant Fuller observing, released ED475's load from 8,000 feet, aiming at the red markers burning in the city centre. As they left the target, the fires were spreading and Sergeant Burrows was able to see their glow for up to a hundred miles along the return route. Flying Officer Urquhart's observations were recorded in a statement published in the Canadian press a few days later: 'With the flares lighting the city so brightly we could see the streets and big gardens. We were able to give it an awful pranging.' This time the operation cost the force only two Lancasters,[401] all those despatched by Skellingthorpe returning safely.

There were to be no further operations and only two more flights for Henry during February. On the 16th he flew ED475 on a two-hour daylight anti-aircraft cooperation exercise and five days later a brief ten-minute hop with Sergeant Marriott to Waddington in W4823. On Wednesday, 24 February, Squadron Leader Street signed off his month's flying, and Henry drove down to Fox Hill for a week's leave.

Arriving home, he was pleased to learn that his mother had recruited a new cook to start the following month, which would ease some of her workload. Various members of the family were recovering from ill health. Brother John was reputedly confined to his bed at home in Leamington. From London the news was more serious; Kelly had been admitted to Hammersmith Hospital, a short distance from her home, suffering from gallstones and jaundice.

Henry returned to Skellingthorpe on 2 March, stopping off en route to see John, finding he too was 'far from well', before continuing on to Leicester and onwards along Watling Street. The Beetle was now behaving itself, 'but I think a new rear universal joint is necessary'.[402]

Entering the Mess shortly after 9 p.m. he learned that the squadron had despatched eight aircraft to Berlin for the night's operations. Two would not return. Henry's spirit was undaunted. He had enjoyed the break and returned very much refreshed and eager to recommence operations.[403] It was about this time that the crew acquired a new wireless operator, Canadian Sergeant Alden Cottam. Aged 30 and older than the majority of aircrew, Cottam had passed through No. 1654 CU the previous year and had been a member of Sergeant Kitching's crew, but had escaped their fate having been 'non-effective' owing to illness on the day of their deaths. Now lacking a permanent crew, he had not flown since an operation to Berlin on 16 January and expressed concern that he would be either sent back to conversion unit for recrewing, or placed with an inexperienced team – a prospect he did not relish at all. Demonstrating typical compassion, Henry invited him to join his crew as a permanent replacement for Sergeant Ken Lyons, who was now approaching the end of his tour.[404]

Thus, after a period with changes and substitutions, Henry's crew was now established, comprising a mix of officers and sergeants, most in their early 20s. All were English, with the exception of the Canadian navigator and wireless operator. From Chinley, Derbyshire, came their new flight engineer, John 'Jack' Marriott, well on his way to completing his first tour, having been posted to Skellingthorpe on 25 August 1942 after only four days at No. 1654 CU and who had flown twenty-three operations with Drew Wyness. Born in Reigate, Sergeant Fuller was 22 years old, his family home now being in Kent. Manning the turrets against fighter attack were 21-year-old Johnny Tytherleigh and Norman 'Bunny' Burrows. Energetic, and seemingly always doing everything at the double,

Tytherleigh was Norwich-born but his family now lived in Hove, Sussex. He was on his second tour with No. 50 Squadron, having previously flown in their Hampdens, before a spell with No.1654 CU. A 28-year-old Liverpudlian from Mosley Hill, Burrows was of slight build, thinning on top and always cheerful. Of the Canadians, wireless operator Al Cottam's home was Jasper Park, Alberta. With greying temples and a small 'cookie duster' moustache, he was of distinguished appearance and had a fine voice, often singing Western melodies on his way back to camp after a good night out. Well liked and with an honest, straightforward and happy disposition, he was very attached to a girl in Scotland with whom he seemed to spend most of his leaves. Navigator Robert Urquhart was another native of Moose Jaw. Quiet, reserved and methodical, he was, according to Squadron Leader Birch, 'one of the Squadron's most exceptional navigators. Keen and efficient.' Urquhart too had passed through No. 1654 CU the previous year and when he crewed up with Henry was halfway through his second tour, which had started with Squadron Leader Philip Moore the previous August.

The revised crew first appeared on the Battle Order for the night of 3 March. No. 50 Squadron was sending 8 of its most experienced crews as part of a force of 417 aircraft to attack Hamburg again. After a brief air test lasting a little over half an hour in their designated mount for the night, W4823, VN-F, Henry landed and penned a brief version of his usual 'Thank you' letter to his mother before he took off on the night's operation: 'Thank you for the lovely leave which I enjoyed very much. I really feel very well now and extremely ready to carry on with the job – which is just as well as it happens.'[405]

Take-off was at 1900 hours on a dark and cloudless night. Flying Officer Gilmore's crew were forced to jettison its bomb load and return to base early with a technical problem. The other crews crossed the North Sea to the north German coast at Husum, where white target indicators marked the turning point, provoking flak and searchlights. The force encountered further flak in the vicinity of the Kiel Canal, and north of Hamburg some 200 searchlights formed two large cones attracting intense heavy flak. To those fortunate to be flying outside these cones, including Henry, the flak seemed comparatively mild.

According to the squadron records: 'Visibility was good and enabled the pilots to identify the target visually and confirm the PFF markers.' Unfortunately, despite this apparently reassuring observation, the PFF were not on target. Notwithstanding the good conditions, they had released their markers using H2S, seeking to practise their technique. They were either deceived by the radar images of a decoy lake or mistook mud banks in the Elbe, exposed by a low tide, as part of Hamburg's docks. As a result, they incorrectly marked an area near to the small town of Wedel, some 13 miles downstream of their intended target, Hamburg's

Altona railway station. In the resulting attack the majority of the bomb loads fell upon Wedel, as fortune would have it severely damaging a large naval clothing store and harbour installations. A proportion of the force, however, was successful in locating the correct target, causing over 100 fires in Hamburg itself.

No. 5 Group squadrons were briefed to bomb in the closing stages of the raid, between 2135 and 2150. It seems likely that Henry attacked Wedel. He identified the River Elbe on his approach, but his bomb aimer led him on to target indicators, where there was a good fire sending up a large pall of black smoke. With the markers in the bomb sight, they released their load. Leaving the target and heading west, the bombers had to cross a heavily defended coastline with intensely active defences between Bremerhaven and Cuxhaven, where another white target indicator marked the bombers' exit route, and there were parting shots from the east Frisians. These appear to have given Henry and his crew little cause for concern, and ED475 returned safely to Skellingthorpe, landing at 0635.

Variable weather during the following week restricted operations, and, although the squadron sent crews to Essen and Nuremberg, Henry was not called upon to operate. Instead his duties involved a drive over to Waddington to collect a new Lancaster, ED693, on the 5th, and the following day he took ED478, VN-G, up on an hour and a half fighter affiliation, air firing and 'Tinsel' test.[406] The following day saw an air test, including a period of two-engined flying, shutting down various combinations of the Lancaster's Merlins to gain experience of the variations in handling and performance. Sometime during this period Henry sustained a minor sprain of his ankle. Although the injury did not curtail his flying, it is unlikely that any asymmetric flying would have been carried out in this condition. It is just possible that the heavy rudder loads imposed when flying with two dead engines on one side may have caused the injury. Though he was heavily bandaged for support, the sprain does not appear to have inconvenienced him greatly, and he was able to remove the strapping by 11 March.

Ops were on again on 9 March, when the target was the Bavarian capital of Munich – birthplace of the Nazi Party and administrative and industrial centre. During the day Henry flew another air test in Lancaster W4161, VN-J, although the crew would switch that night to a newer aircraft, ED415, VN-C.[407]

The attack involved a penetration deep into the heart of Germany, the long distance necessitating a relatively direct route that would leave the Germans in little doubt as to the bombers' objective. Departing England at Dungeness, the bomber stream encountered intense but ineffective heavy flak while crossing the French coast at Dieppe. Again technical failure dogged the squadron, causing two crews to jettison their bombs and make an early return. Over the continent the aircraft encountered headwinds stronger than forecast, slowing their progress, and any straying from the main route found themselves exposed to the defences of Metz, Saarbrücken and Augsburg. To assist with track keeping, white target indicators were dropped on the ground near Metz. Others with white and green flashes bursting at 20,000 feet over the northern shore of the Ammer See provided a datum from which the Main Force was to make a timed run-in to the target. Useful as they were to the navigators, these route markers also served as a focus for the German defences.

Over the target an estimated 200 searchlights formed cones of 10–20 beams north-west and south of the city, some highlighting the bombers' telltale condensation trails. Flak gunners were putting up a barrage of over 14,000 shells, mainly 88mm, mixed with heavier 105mm and strings of rapid-firing 20mm, but the intensity diminished as the raid progressed. Although a deterrent, and off-putting to those inexperienced or in close proximity, the flak over Munich was lethal to only one aircraft, a Lancaster of No. 61 Squadron, which exploded in the air over the target.[408]

The attack opened at two minutes after midnight. There was no cloud and only slight haze, enabling the Pathfinders to identify their target easily, but the strong easterly winds hampered accurate marking, with the result that much of the bombing fell on the western side of the city instead of the briefed central area. By 0015 the centre of the attack had shifted to the western suburbs south-west of Oberweisenfeld airfield.[409] As usual, No. 5 Group's Lancasters came in as the final wave, briefed to bomb between 0003 and 0015. Many of the squadron's crews, arriving late owing to the wind, failed to locate the target markers and bombed fires or built-up areas they could see. Henry arrived shortly before the last of the markers went out. Running in at 12,500 feet, he was aiming for a green target indicator nearest to his briefed aiming point, the central railway station. On this occasion the crew were carrying Flight Lieutenant Wood as bomb aimer. As squadron bombing leader and on his second tour of operations, he usually flew with Squadron Leader Birch and was extremely conscientious.[410] At seventeen minutes past midnight, two minutes before they bombed, the crew observed a large orange explosion to the south-west of the centre, which was later assumed to be a direct hit on the city gas works. The results of their own attack are unrecorded, but crews reported the burning city being visible for 200 miles. All the squadron's aircraft returned safely following the reciprocal of their inbound route, successfully evading nightfighter activity near Rheims.

In spite of the circumstances, German records report that the attack was very successful, much public and commercial property being damaged or destroyed, together with some 249 military buildings, including the local flak brigade headquarters. The BMW plant, producer of aero-engines for Ju 88 nightfighters, was severely damaged, disrupting full production for nearly six weeks. The squadron rested the following day, a number of crews having operated two nights in succession, but for some it was a brief respite, as nine crews (although not Henry) were sent to Stuttgart on 11 March.

He was now flying less frequently between operations. On 11 March he took his crew and Flight Lieutenant Reg Avis[411] up in ED478, VN-G, for an air-firing exercise, his gunners firing at drogue sleeves towed by Miles Martinets from the local Bomber Defence Training Flight. At one point Henry gave members of his crew, including Robert Urquhart, an opportunity to take the controls as they skimmed the crests of some billowing cumulus. As they did so a USAAF P-47 Thunderbolt fighter joined them, flying briefly in formation before peeling away, leaving them alone again to surf the cloud tops.

Oranges and orange juice were luxuries rarely seen in wartime Britain, although Henry appears to have found a supply. On 11 March he wrote to his mother: 'It will be good to hear when Kelly is off the danger list and out of pain. I have sent her two oranges and two cans of orange juice and another can is going off tomorrow – that should help a bit.'

The crew were back on the Battle Order for the following night. What was to become known as the Battle of the Ruhr had commenced on the night of 5/6 March, with a major attack by 412 aircraft on Essen and now, seven days later, another onslaught was to be launched against this industrial target. This time No. 50 Squadron was to contribute 10 aircraft to the 457 aircraft force.

Leaving Lincolnshire at Mablethorpe, they crossed the North Sea to Egmond, proceeding to a point north of Essen, where they turned south to the target. There was considerable opposition from the ground defences over Holland, especially in the proximity of Egmond, Alkmaar, Ijmuiden Amsterdam and Hilversum. North of Essen, along the line of approach, an estimated 150 searchlights formed three or four large cones, into which intense and accurate large-calibre flak was firing, capable of engaging aircraft up to heights of 20,000 feet. The Mosquito ground markers were accurate, with red target indicators backed up by reds. Bombing was centred on the giant Krupps complex, a little to the west of the city centre, creeping back to lay waste working-class housing in the north-west suburb of Berbeck as the raid progressed. Again No.5 Group's Lancasters were to close the attack. As they approached the city at about 2133, the target could be seen already burning fiercely, the shock waves of 4,000-pounders expanding across the fires like ripples in a pond. Suddenly a large explosion was seen in the centre of the inferno, with flames erupting many hundreds of feet into the air, the glare illuminating the many aircraft overhead. Selecting the red target indicators that identified his allotted target (Aiming Point C), Sergeant Fuller released ED415's load from 15,000 feet at 2139. As they turned for home, bundles of leaflets were pushed down the flare chute, reiterating Allied might and the futility of continuing the war.

Crossing the Dutch coast, returning crews could still see the glow of the fires burning out the heart of Essen. Reports at debriefing suggested a highly successful attack, a view confirmed by subsequent photographic interpretation, which indicated that Krupps had received 30 per cent more damage than had been inflicted on the previous raid. Nearly a third of the built-up area of Essen had been destroyed, and by now some 196,000 square yards – over a quarter – of the Krupp complex had suffered some degree of damage. There was inevitably a price to be paid. Twenty-three aircraft failed to return, including that flown by 22-year-old Sergeant Frederick Ward from Toronto, shot down by a nightfighter over Holland on his way to the target, with the loss of the entire crew.

One aircraft was detailed for mining operations in the 'SILVERTHORN' area of the Kattegat the following night, but then the threat of early morning fog formation at base caused the next few days' operations to be cancelled at the very last minute.

For the crews, having being briefed and geared up to operate, the strain was tremendous. There was a little respite. Good weather during the day enabled Henry to carry out air tests and participate in training exercises. The crew had managed to regain their trusted ED475, and there was further fighter affiliation on the 18th and a Beam Approach practice on the 22nd, following what seems to have been, for Henry, a rare practice bombing exercise at the Wainfleet bombing range on the Lincolnshire coast south of Gibraltar Point.[412]

That night Henry was detailed for what was to be his thirteenth and final operation with No. 50 Squadron. While continuing the Battle of the Ruhr, Sir Arthur Harris was still compelled to support the U-boat counter-offensive. Tonight the weather over the Ruhr would be unfavourable, and the target was to be the French port of Saint-Nazaire. Nos 3, 4, 5 and 6 Groups despatched 357 aircraft, although most of No. 3 Group's 63 Stirlings were recalled before reaching the target. Of the 12 aircraft detailed by No. 50 Squadron, Flight Sergeant Dennis had to return owing to intercom problems.

It was to be an easy operation, with excellent conditions, relatively clear with patches of cloud at 6,000 feet en route. There was a full moon and slight haze over the target. No. 5 Group was scheduled to bomb between 2134 and 2155, during the second half of the attack. There was little opposition of note: intermittent flak from a dozen heavy guns and between twenty-five and thirty light weapons mainly in the dock area, with fifteen searchlights forming two cones, dwindling to one or two solitary beams by the end of the raid. An elaborate smokescreen activated early on caused problems for some crews, but the green PFF markers were clearly visible to Henry and his crew, who were among the first of the 110 aircraft from No. 5 Group to attack. They were briefed to bomb Aiming Point C, and their bombs, released from 11,500 feet, were seen to explode across the submarine pens. On return the fog that had caused the cancellation of the previous nights' operations again confounded the Met men and cloaked Skellingthorpe, concealing the runways and necessitating the diversion of the squadron's aircraft to eight different airfields. Returning to base from the south coast, Henry found himself instructed to put ED475 down at Abingdon. After a snatched sleep, a check on the weather revealed that conditions at Skellingthorpe were clearing. While the crew devoured a much appreciated breakfast, the aircraft was refuelled, and they were able to depart for base during the late morning.

The weather deteriorated again; flying was severely restricted and the squadron did not operate for the next week or so. Henry remained on the ground, although there is no suggestion that this caused him any frustration. There were routine administrative chores to keep him occupied, combined with an active social life. On Wednesday, 17th, accompanied by Bill Astell, he attended a party at Waddington held to mark the posting to Southampton of his friend Monica Campbell, the WAAF who had hosted Mrs Maudslay to tea. The following day Henry took Monica for a more sedate reunion at the White Hart. She was also present at the Skellingthorpe Officers' Mess party on the 19th, along with Ralph Allsebrook and John Sauvage.[413] Bill Astell was unable to attend, being '*hors de combat*', the result of a wild forty-eight hours' leave in London. Earlier in the day Henry had booked a call to his mother. It was put through in error to a phone in the Mess anteroom while the party was in full swing, preventing Henry from holding a sensible conversation. 'I dared not transfer the call for fear of losing it.' Despite the noise and distractions, it was good to hear her voice again and to talk to his sister, who brought Annette to the phone to hear a few words from her favourite uncle.

A last-minute cancellation of flying the following evening removed him of the onerous duty of OC night flying, and after a lazy bath Henry put pen to paper to apologize for the quality of the call. After he had updated his mother on the last few nights' social activities, his thoughts turned to domestic matters. The introduction of the new cook to Fox Hill had caused friction between her and others in the household, causing Mrs Maudslay yet further concern: 'I do hope that it will calm down and you won't have that extra worry.' Henry shared his mother's frustration at the way in which even staunch supporters of the Home Front overlooked the struggle faced by the housewife in her efforts to keep home and family together with the meagrest of resources:

I often think that it is infernally bad luck that your war job [414] should consist
of deputising for the manpower (and womanpower) which has 'gone to war'.
There is no doubt that to wear a uniform or wave a flag – even on the dullest
of jobs – helps convince one that one is winning the war and so makes
life easier. [415]

Henry was still concerned about Kelly's health. It had been sometime since he had
been able to visit her and news of her condition since her recent hospitalization
did little to raise his hopes. With both his mother's and Kelly's welfare at heart,
he added:

I do hope that you can get up to see Kelly and stay at the Connaught in
comfort – even several hours at the hospital would be a rest after Fox Hill
for you. By my latest bulletin . . . it seems that the odds on recovery are not
so much better than evens and that there is a certainty of a slow recovery
even if we're lucky, with a long convalescence. [416]

Mrs Maudslay was able to heed Henry's advice and travelled to London to visit
Kelly. Talking to her by phone four days later, he was relieved to hear more
optimistic news. His mother thought that his old governess's condition had
improved and she would spend a few more days visiting her bedside before
returning to Fox Hill.

   On Wednesday, 24 March, Henry was surprised to receive notification that he
was to be posted. After thirteen operations with No. 50 Squadron, his second tour
was barely half completed. [417] The information given about this posting was
limited. He was to join a new squadron, where he would be promoted to squadron
leader and given formal command of a flight. At least it seemed to be formal recognition and reward for a job he had been doing by default now for several months.
He would be taking his regular crew with him. There was an additional benefit:
his new squadron would be based at Scampton and he could look forward to
sharing a Mess with Bill Astell. It was a pity No. 49 Squadron had moved out to
Fiskerton in January, otherwise Ralph Allsebrook would have been there too.

   He confided the information in a brief note to his mother that evening, ever
conscious of the wartime need for discretion: 'I could not tell you over the telephone that I am going to join Bill Astell at Scampton – tomorrow. My Wing
Commander here tells me that they are making me a Squadron Leader and giving
me a Flight but please don't take this too seriously yet – I'm not anyway.' [418]

   Adding a hasty 'PS 9.30 p.m. I'm just starting packing, the usual form!', he
placed the letter in an envelope addressed to his mother care of the family solicitor,

Eric Ellis at 1a Porchester Terrace, Hyde Park. It would not be posted until the 26th and reached London the following day, but his mother had already left for Fox Hill and it had to be redirected. By the time she received it on the 28th, Henry was already taking stock of his new posting, although the full explanation and implications of his sudden transfer and promotion had yet to be revealed.

Chapter 16

Practice to Perfect

If we are mark'd to die, we are enow
To do our country loss; and if to live,
The fewer men, the greater share of honour.
(William Shakespeare, *Henry v,* Act 4, Scene 3)

Henry and his crew made the short journey from Skellingthorpe to Scampton by road on Thursday, 25 March, finding on arrival seven crews for the newly formed squadron already in residence. They had begun to assemble on the previous Saturday, when their new commanding officer, Wing Commander Guy Gibson, DSO and bar, DFC and bar, arrived from commanding No. 106 Squadron at Syerston. Aged 24, Gibson had already completed seventy-one operations with Nos 83 and 106 Squadrons, together with an interim spell with No. 29 Squadron, equipped with Beaufighter nightfighters. A strong disciplinarian, he had the reputation of being an efficient and inspirational leader. As a commanding officer he was respected as one who led from the front and by the example he set, frequently listing himself on the Battle Order for more distant targets, rather than selecting less dangerous options. To some he could be disarmingly charming, to others, particularly non-commissioned ranks, he could seem brusque to the point of arrogance. Socially he preferred to mix with an 'inner sanctum' of pilots of proven ability. Those who displayed 'the right spirit' had little cause for worry, but he could be ruthless with those who failed to demonstrate commitment to the job in hand.

The squadron was already beginning to attract attention. A disproportionate number of the crews were obviously highly experienced, although, despite later accounts, not all had completed even their first tour, nor were the majority decorated.[419] Again contrary to later legend, those selected were not all personally known to Gibson or hand-picked by him, although Flight Lieutenant John Hopgood, DFC, Australian Flight Lieutenant David Shannon, DFC, and Canadian Flight Sergeant Lewis Burpee had served under him on No. 106 Squadron. Hopgood had given Gibson his initial introduction to the Lancaster when the latter was commanding No. 106 Squadron and had been poached from a brief sojourn at No. 1660 CU, to which he had been posted as 'tour expired'. Others, notably Australian Flight Lieutenant Harold 'Mick' Martin, DFC, who was to arrive later, were legends beyond their own units and had already earned a 'press on' reputation within No. 5 Group. Henry himself had never served under Gibson, or on the same station, and does not appear even to have met him before his posting to Scampton, although he may well have known of him by repute. Likewise it is unlikely that Gibson would have had cause to know of Henry directly until making the selection for his new squadron. It is possible that Wing Commander Collier, Henry's old flight commander now at the Air Ministry, via No. 5 Group Headquarters, brought Henry to his attention. AVM Slessor had long since departed, as had his successor AVM Coryton. No. 5 Group was now commanded by AVM the Hon. Ralph Cochrane, who had taken on his new role on 27 February. Previously commanding No. 3 Group in East Anglia, Cochrane may not have known of Henry, although it is likely that his senior Air Staff officer, Group Captain Harold Satterly, would have been aware of his experience and suitability for the new squadron that was being formed.

For Henry, looking round the assembled crews, there would have been a number of familiar faces: fellow No. 50 Squadron 'A' Flight member Australian Pilot Officer Leslie Knight and his crew, who had recently completed twenty-six operations – Flying Officer Sidney Hobday, Sergeant Bob Kellow, Sergeant Harry O'Brien, Sergeant Ray Grayston, Flying Officer Edward 'Johnnie' Johnson and Sergeant Fred 'Doc' Sutherland. Also from No. 50 Squadron came Flight Lieutenant Richard Trevor Roper, DFM, 'Trev', who had been with Peter Birch's crew and was able to utter the most profound Billingsgate vocabulary in the very best public-school tones. He would be joining the wing commander's crew as rear gunner and squadron gunnery leader.

On the crest of the Lincolnshire escarpment, alongside the A15, 5 miles north of Lincoln, Scampton was a pre-war expansion station like Waddington, signalling a return to a higher standard of accommodation and facilities. There was, however, one retrospective feature. Unlike the recently constructed Wigsley and Skellingthorpe with their concrete runways, Scampton still retained a grass-surface flying field, necessitating additional care with a heavy aircraft, especially while landing in wet conditions, when locked wheels could increase the risk of a ground loop and possible undercarriage collapse.[420] Although Henry had been promised promotion to the rank of squadron leader, nothing yet had been confirmed formally. Nevertheless, for the time being, in the absence of any other squadron leader or flight commander, he would be preoccupied with helping Gibson to structure the new squadron into flights and resolving the numerous administrative details to ensure the achievement of operational status as soon as possible.

The following day, Friday, 26 March, saw the formal arrival of Squadron Leader Henry Melvin Young, DFC, from 'C' Flight of No. 57 Squadron, already based at Scampton. Known as 'Dinghy' since he had survived two ditchings from his days flying Whitleys with No. 102 Squadron, he was to become senior flight commander commanding 'A' Flight, while Henry was to command 'B' Flight. Six years older than Henry, Young had read law at Trinity College, Oxford, and was also a keen oarsman, having rowed as Number 2 in the winning dark-blue crew of the 1938 inter-varsity boat race. With him from No. 57 Squadron came four more captains, including Flight Lieutenant Bill Astell, together with his flight engineer Sergeant John Kinnear and gunner Sergeant Richard Bolitho, who had been converted to the Lancaster at No. 1654 CU the previous October. Others too had arrived whom Henry would recognize from those days, including former pupils Flight Lieutenant Norman Barlow, Flight Lieutenant Les Munro and Flight Sergeant Ken Brown. In addition he probably recalled another 'A' Flight pilot, Flight Lieutenant David Maltby, who three years earlier had been in Henry's intake at Uxbridge, Bexhill and Paignton.[421]

The atmosphere was that of controlled, organized chaos. The squadron had been formed so rapidly that the official machine had not had time to grind into action. Furniture, typewriters, chairs, desks and a myriad of other administrative equipment had to be 'begged, borrowed or otherwise acquired', as had tools and other ground-servicing equipment. Ten Lancasters had been borrowed from units supplying crews, No. 50 Squadron providing ED437. To date the squadron had no formal identity or code letters, but on 27 March information was received that henceforth the new unit was to be known as No. 617 Squadron. Its code letters would be 'AJ' (although, since the aircraft being used were technically 'on loan', they continued to carry their previous unit codes for some time).

Gibson called his two flight commanders to a briefing in his office, where they found two Australians, the squadron navigation leader Flying Officer Jack Leggo, DFC, (ex-No. 50 Squadron) and bombing leader Flight Lieutenant Bob Hay DFC, also in attendance. Initial instructions had recently been received from No. 5 Group regarding the training regime that was to be established. The orders gave no mention of the target, merely that the squadron would be required to attack a number of lightly defended targets. The crews should practise accurate navigation at low level in moonlight and be able to release their bombs within 40 yards of a specified point. The final approach should be made at 100 feet and at a speed of about 240 mph. 'It will be convenient to practise this over water', and a list of suitable lakes and reservoirs was appended. Henry and Young were told to draw up a practice programme, liasing with Leggo, who would establish standard routes to make life easier for the Observer Corps and Anti-Aircraft Command.

Henry went away to review the status of his flight. By the end of the month he would have nine captains under his command. In addition to Pilot Officer Les Knight, Flight Sergeant Lewis Burpee and Flight Lieutenant John Hopgood, DFC, there were Sergeant Bill Townsend and Sergeant Cyril Anderson from No.49 Squadron; Flight Lieutenant Les Munro and Flight Lieutenant Joe McCarthy had arrived from No. 97 Squadron – Munro a New Zealander, and McCarthy a tall, blond American who had joined the RCAF before his country had entered hostilities. Flying Officer Kenneth Earnshaw from No. 50 Squadron would join Hopgood's crew as navigator and from Henry's first squadron, No. 44, came Flight Lieutenant Harold Wilson. On 31 March Flight Lieutenant Harold 'Mick' Martin DFC, arrived. Martin too had served previously with No. 50 Squadron and came from an instructor's posting at No. 1654 CU. He was an acknowledged low-flying specialist. All his flight's captains had arrived, although it would still be some time until these had their full complement of crew members.

Despite his responsibility, Henry was still awaiting formal confirmation of his rank as squadron leader. On 30 March he wrote home, the brevity of his letter confirming spare time was at a premium, although he obviously was pleased with his new situation:

> I am still a Flight Lieutenant! – although promoted the other rank at any moment . . . The job is very worth while and one which I will enjoy more than any other that I have had. However it is by no means easy and will mean a lot of hard work, but I have a Flight Sergeant from my original Squadron which is a help.[422]

He had recently received a letter from his mother, posted in Paddington and doubtless delayed by being addressed to Skellingthorpe. Her news was not good. She had visited Kelly in hospital, and it transpired that his old nanny was far from well and that her anticipated recovery had received a setback.

Formal implementation of the flying training programme began on Wednesday, 31 March, with crews being despatched on daylight cross-country flights of between two and three hours' duration with practice bombing at Wainfleet. To reduce the likelihood of accidents until the crews had accustomed themselves to low level, heights were restricted to 500 feet, descending to 100 feet over the bombing range. Henry himself took a Lancaster (recorded as ED309 but actually LM309, WS-X, a borrowed No. 9 Squadron aircraft) on a flight lasting 2 hours 58 minutes. His crew comprised Flying Officer Urquhart, Pilot Officer Tytherleigh and Sergeants Cottam, Marriott and Burrows. In place of his usual bomb aimer,

Flight Sergeant Fuller, Henry carried Flight Lieutenant Hay, the squadron bombing leader. At present without a pilot, Hay was no doubt anxious to sample the difficulties of the new training programme. In accordance with Gibson's original briefing, 11½lb practice bombs were released at a speed of 240 mph over Wainfleet range (which Henry persisted in recording as 'Waynfleete'). On the ground a plotting crew with theodolites assessed their accuracy.

Promotions were beginning to catch up with postings. On 1 April Bill Astell was notified of his promotion to flight lieutenant. Sergeants Townsend and Anderson became temporary flight sergeants and within Henry's crew Pilot Officer Tytherleigh became a flying officer, reflecting his role as the flight gunnery leader. Flying Officer Urquhart was flight navigation officer.

Further refinement had been made to the training structure. In the first week of April they would concentrate on low-level navigation and map reading, while Gibson identified a suitable stretch of water over which to carry out final training. By now the commanding officer had been told that his unit's target was to be a number of major dams east of the heavily defended Ruhr, but was under the strictest instructions that he should reveal this knowledge to no other member of the squadron. Between 8 and 15 April there was a switch to developing accurate flying at 150 feet at night over water. After this the crews would continue to rehearse aspects of the entire operation until it actually took place. The full moon around 20 April would provide ideal training conditions.

Gibson had already given thought to the difficulties of establishing the aircraft's height over smooth water at night. It would be a major problem, and he supported a method whereby a determined weight would be lowered from the aircraft on a wire, calculated to skim the water at 150 feet at the required airspeed. A jerk on the wire would confirm that the height had been reached, after which the pilot could set and fly by his barometric altimeter. The point of release would be determined, adapting a triangulation method established by Wing Commander Charles Dann from A&AEE Boscombe Down. The original sight comprised a wooden triangular-shaped base with a peephole at one corner and a pin at the others, which would coincide with specific points on the target when at the correct range. Some crews later adopted a development of this, using marks on the bomb aimer's Perspex panel.

Henry's next flight was on 2 April, taking W4926, AJ-Z, up for a quarter of an hour's circuits and landings with Sergeant Burrows and Sergeant Cottam,[423] possibly as an air test, or to gain familiarity with local landmarks. The following day saw a daylight cross-country at 500 feet in LM309 lasting 1 hour 55 minutes.[424] Henry was carrying both Flight Lieutenant Hay and Flight Sergeant Fuller in addition to his usual crew, and again practice bombing was also undertaken from

100 feet at 240 mph. Meanwhile, other members of the flight were venturing further afield on flights lasting up to five hours, taking them over Wales and down to Cornwall. By now the crews were becoming more familiar with low flying and descending to 100 feet for considerable parts of the route.

The hanging-weight method of determining height over water had proved to be impractical. Fortunately others had been debating the problem, and Benjamin Lockspeiser, Director of Scientific Research at the Ministry of Aircraft Production, recalled a concept originating from the First World War that had been resurrected in an attempt to assist Coastal Command. Two spotlights could be positioned underneath the aircraft with their beams angled downwards to intersect at the required height and visible from the cockpit. When the point of intersection coincided with the ground the aircraft would be at the correct height. Despite reservations by a few (including Sir Arthur Harris) that over glass-smooth water the lights would pass straight through the surface without being reflected, it was decided that the Royal Aircraft Establishment at Farnborough should fit a proto-type installation into one of the squadron's Lancasters. Accordingly, on 4 April Henry flew W4296 to Farnborough via Reading with Flying Officer Urquhart, Sergeant Cottam and Flight Sergeant Fuller, together with a member of ground crew, Aircraftman Chaplin. Two Aldis lights were rigged in the aircraft, the front one located in place of the bombing camera ahead of the bomb bay, on the port side, the rear one under the fuselage aft of the bomb bay, adjacent to the flare chute. Installation took three days. On 8 April, with the lights fitted, they returned to Scampton, and that evening Henry took off with Dr Picard and Mr Fieldgate (civilian observers from the Royal Aircraft Establishment) and Pilot Officer Urquhart, Sergeant Cottam and Flight Sergeant Fuller to give the equipment its first squadron practice, flying out to Skegness and carrying out low flying over the Wash just after sunset.

The sky was heavily overcast, with a cloud base at about 1,000 feet and the sea choppy with occasional white caps. Visibility was poor, and conditions were considered approximate to those of a full moon. The lights were fitted to shine downwards and outwards to starboard, the pools of light being visible by the wireless operator from the starboard window, by the bomb aimer and by the navigator from the cockpit blister. The navigator was selected to act as height observer. When the lights were switched on at about 200 feet, he would initially see two separate pools of light and would give the pilot 'down' instructions over the intercom in order to bring the lights together to touch and form a figure '8', indicating the correct height. A curt 'up' would suffice to make a correction if the aircraft descended past the point of intersection.

Henry's flight lasted an hour and a quarter. Dr Pickard and Mr Fieldgate took turns with Flying Officer Urquhart to try out the system. It took very little practice to perfect the technique and a number of runs were also made over the airfield to enable observers on the ground to check the accuracy of the height with theodolites. The system worked beautifully, with a maximum variation of plus or minus 10 feet of the desired height being noted – although reservations were voiced about the wisdom of flying into the attack against a (presumably) defended target while carrying lights. Accordingly measures were put in hand to find a means of screening them as much as possible.[425]

By 8 April the squadron had flown sixty-two low-level cross-country flights and dropped a total of 665 practice bombs with an average error of 50.5 yards. Despite his other commitments, Henry had flown two low-level sorties and dropped twelve practice bombs, achieving an average error of 63 yards.[426]

A letter from his mother dated 5 April had brought sad news. That day, after a valiant struggle to regain her health, Kelly had finally succumbed to her illness at the age of 63.[427] Replying on 11 April, Henry tried to see the event in a positive light, paying tribute to the person who had been a constant reference point throughout his life: 'I suppose that we couldn't have done more, and the only alternative was to be an invalid, which I know Kelly would not stand for. I do not think that we will ever know so true a friend, or one to who we owe so much.'[428]

Meanwhile, life at Fox Hill was becoming more difficult for Mrs Maudslay. Local petrol controllers were tightening up on the allocation of petrol 'for domestic purposes' – a ration that was already meagre enough for those in areas with little alternative transport, despite a rural allowance. Over the previous month she had had some altercation with the authorities, having also had problems over licensing her car. Henry's annoyance at the news is evident: 'Travel will be difficult for you now – it is unfair to deprive you of petrol and if you give me the address of the woman in Birmingham I'll write a line and see what I can do.'[429]

Telling her not to expect to see him for some time, he also warned her not to enquire as to his activities:

> Do not expect me on leave before June – one usually loses some when going from one job to another! My present one is well worth it. I have my old crew which is very pleasant. Please ask no more questions – letters can be opened even in this country, and a leading question can be a source of information.[430]

The following week saw Wing Commander Gibson visiting Reculver on the north Kent coast to attend the initial dropping trials of the squadron's new weapon. His whereabouts were a closely kept secret, neither Young nor Henry having any real idea of the activities of their commanding officer. Gibson's spasmodic absences placed additional demands on their duties as flight commanders. At Reculver the trials were only partially successful. While the weapon's design team strove to resolve their problems, the squadron continued to practise, taking advantage of a week of good weather.

A longer daylight cross-country and bombing detail of four and a half hours was completed with his usual crew in W4926 on 11 April. The following day saw only a brief quarter of an hour's air test of ED329, EM-T, with Sergeant Marriott, but on the 13th he was back on a short daylight cross-country and bombing detail in LM309. This was followed that night in the same aircraft by Henry's first long night cross-country, lasting nearly five hours. On the 15th there was a brief air test of LM309 and that night another four-and-a-half-hour cross country at 150 feet, this time taking ED437, N, up to the north of Scotland on a route designed to simulate the conditions expected during an operation. The moon would not be full until around 20 April, but already the quarter moon was highlighting rivers, canals and other vital pinpoints essential for accurate navigation.

Perhaps strangely, bearing in mind the nature of the operation for which they were practising, Henry did not fly during the nights of the full moon. This apparent limitation in his training may have been due to the fact that serviceability was restricting the number of available aircraft and a formal decision had been made to hold back the more seasoned crews and concentrate on those who were less experienced. Henry's next recorded flight was a brief twenty-minute air test of ED437 on 22 April. In the interim he may have had a brief meeting in the Mess with Ralph Allsebrook, still with No. 49 Squadron, who landed at Scampton at 0627 on the morning of 17 April, diverting on return from an attack against the Skoda works at Pilsen.[431]

The squadron's curiosity was aroused further on Thursday, 22 April, with the arrival of the first three of their new aircraft. Most apparent were the major modifications to the bomb bay. The bomb doors had been removed and replaced with fairings fore and aft, giving the appearance of a gutted fish. Strange V-shaped calliper arms carrying disc-like attachments were to be hung from the fuselage sides either side of the cut-out, the disc on the starboard side being linked by a drive belt to a pulley mounted on the front fairing. It was obvious that they would not be carrying a conventional bomb load. In addition, the mid-upper turret was removed and the hole faired over. On closer inspection of the interior, the crews found a strange hydraulic motor and a prominent rev counter. Still they were none the wiser, and questions went unanswered in a manner that made it very apparent that they were not to be voiced again.

On the ground, Henry was kept busy with administration, ensuring adherence to training schedules and the maintenance of discipline. On the 22nd Gibson had cause publicly to reprimand an officer who had telephoned his girlfriend to say that he could not see her one evening because he was doing special training. Each member of the air crew had a head and shoulders portrait photograph taken. Ostensibly for 'passports', in reality these were a further security measure. Periodic meetings were called among the crews of the flight to pool ideas and discuss specific problems.

The remainder of the month was taken up mainly with daylight bombing details, each of about an hour's duration. The usual ground targets at Wainfleet had been replaced by two white 'cricket boards', each 30 feet by 20 feet and spaced 700 feet apart. There were two bombing details for Henry on the 24th, this time with the height reduced to 60 feet and at a speed of 220 mph. After the second, having completed a normal landing at 2000 hours in W4926, Z, Henry was disconcerted to feel a thump from the rear of the aircraft and a marked reluctance for the aircraft to taxi properly. Scampton's rough mud surface had claimed another tailwheel failure. Damage was minimal and the aircraft was repaired within a week, no blame being attached to Henry. Another bombing detail during the late afternoon of the 25th saw Henry's crew in LM309 joined by Flying Officer Malcolm Arthurton, the squadron's medical officer. The weather was gusty and severe buffeting at low level caused Arthurton to write in his logbook: 'Low flying experience. Weather bumpy. Airsick after $^1/_2$ hour.' Future requests by aircrew for medication to alleviate nausea were received with greater sympathy.

A severe gale on the following day curtailed flying and blew down the target screens. They were re-erected. Trials of the intended weapon had revealed a need to reduce the height of release, and on the 26th crews were briefed to make all future runs at an altitude of only 60 feet and a speed of 210 mph. The lights were adjusted accordingly. Henry was airborne again on the 27th in ED437 for an hour's night-time 'tactical training', concentrating on navigation and probably with spotlight flying over the Wash at the new lower height, taking with him Sergeant Tom Jaye, Pilot Officer Burpee's navigator. The month's training ended for Henry on the 29th with another daylight bombing sortie with ED437 at Wainfleet. He had now completed a total of 19 hours 50 minutes' daytime training and 10 hours 20 minutes by night. The fact that this was only about half that completed by other crews is indicative of the heavy organizational burden he had to bear. Training had progressed so well that crews were now being released in rotation to take three days' leave over the first week of May in order to give them a beneficial break after the intensive period of training. On 30 April, Henry flew a modified aircraft for the first time when he took ED909, AJ-P, with Flight Sergeant Fuller and Pilot Officer Toby Foxlee, one of Martin's gunners, to Farnborough for further modification. No return flight to Scampton is logged, and evidence suggests that

Henry made a trip into London, where he paid a visit to Skinner and Co. to purchase one of their last Astral Crown brooches for his cousin, Diana Byrom. There was time too for a brief meeting with Cuthbert Orde at the RAF Club, before travelling to Fox Hill to take leave. He brought with him Flying Officer Urquhart (who may have been on leave, since the latter's logbook does not record any flying between 25 April and 4 May). Among the family subjects of discussion on this occasion may have been the news that Gordon was now stationed in Suffolk and Tita was expecting her second child.[432]

Henry and Flying Officer Urquhart returned to the squadron on Monday, 3 May, by train. Travelling up they met a large number of his mother's friends, including Mrs Gibbons and Lady Ismay and her daughter Sarah. Arriving just in time for lunch, Henry sat down with Bill Astell. Their conversation digressed from squadron issues. Astell had recently succeeded in gaining membership of the RAF Club, after having had similar difficulties to Henry. The topic strayed on to schooldays, and Henry mentioned his old housemaster, J. D. Hills, discovering that Astell had been a pupil at Bradfield, although he had left the school in July 1937, two and a half years before Hills took over as headmaster.

The following day Henry wrote his customary letter to thank his mother. The censor's continuing interest in Scampton's mail was again in evidence, the label of Examiner 1831 resealing the envelope. Henry's brevity was perhaps indicative of the pressures that were now mounting, combined with the fact that he would have returned to face a pile of his flight members' logbooks, for him to check and sign off their previous month's flying: 'It was lovely to get home and see you, for even so short a time, and I feel a thousand times better for it . . . I think Bob enjoyed his time at Fox Hill a lot and is much better for it.'[433]

More modified Lancasters had been delivered while Henry had been on leave, bringing the total number to date to seventeen. Among them was ED933, which was to become Henry's 'personal' aircraft. In keeping with the other new arrivals, the bombers had been taken into the hangar and was being checked over and the Aldis lamp installation and other modifications effected. The codes AJ-X were marked up in tall, thin, dark red letters on the fuselage side. While this work was being completed, Henry continued training with a standard aircraft. On 4 May he flew an hour's night tactics (probably spotlight runs), in ED909, AJ-P, although the flight is unrecorded in his logbook, and the following day he was up shortly after noon taking ED735, AJ-R, on a 2½ hour day cross-country, probably using 'two stage amber'. This synthetic training aid required the pilot to wear blue goggles while the aircraft Perspex was fitted with amber screens, simulating moonlight conditions while flying in daylight.[434]

By the beginning of May all crews in the squadron were able to navigate from pinpoint to pinpoint at night by map-reading at low level, bomb accurately using the rangefinder sight, and fly safely over water at a height of 150 feet. It was now important to coordinate these individual aspects into operational tactics. In order to achieve this, Eyebrook Reservoir, 4 miles south of Uppingham, was select-ed for training, and on 3 May the target screens were moved from Wainfleet to the earthen dam at Eyebrook. From 5 May it was proposed to conduct special practices over the lake at 60 feet, using ten aircraft at a time. Meanwhile, crews would continue to practise low flying and spotlight runs at dusk, together with simulated night cross-countries using the daylight two-stage amber.

On 6 May Gibson called a training conference, gathering all the captains to-gether, along with the squadron armament officer, Pilot Officer Watson, and engineering officer, Pilot Officer Caple, to announce the change from individual training to the development of full operational tactics. The target was still a closely guarded secret, known only to Gibson, Watson and a few senior Scampton officers. At this meeting, in answer to a question from Young, Gibson admitted that the operation would take place within the next fortnight, but stressed the utmost need for secrecy. Maximum serviceability was essential, and all weapons must be ready by 12 May. Young was given the task of calculating the all-up weight of operational aircraft, his figures to be checked by a flight engineer. That night Henry flew an hour and a quarter's cross-country, bombing and tactics exercise. ED933 was still not ready, and he took AJ-V, a standard aircraft.[435]

It was probably at about this period, possibly even at the meeting of 6 May, that the first insight was gained into the nature of the weapon they would be using, although the identity of the target remained a mystery. To breach a dam using a conventional bomb would require a weapon of greater weight than existing air-craft effectively could carry. Seeking a solution to this dilemma, Barnes Wallis,[436] the weapon's designer, had calculated that the weight of explosive required (and hence the gross weight of the bomb) could be reduced significantly if it could be detonated at a specific depth in direct contact with the dam wall. To position the weapon would require more than aiming accuracy, and Wallis had developed a bomb with peculiar dynamics that would achieve these requirements. The weapon, codenamed Upkeep, was shaped as a large cylinder, some 60 inches long and 50 inches in diameter, supported on its axis between the strange V-shaped arms that crews had seen on the modified aircraft. The belt drive, driven by the hydraulic motor in the fuselage, was to impart a backspin of some 500 rpm before release, when strong springs would force the arms apart allowing the weapon to fall. Upon striking the water, Upkeep would ricochet forward in a series of decreasing bounces (incidentally avoiding any anti-torpedo netting defending the target) until it ran out of momentum, or struck the dam parapet. There it would sink, the back spin causing the bomb to cling to the wall. At an optimum predetermined depth, calculated as being 30 feet, three hydrostatic pistols would detonate 6,600 lb of the explosive Torpex,[437] by which time the attacking aircraft should be some 300 feet beyond the 1,000-feet-high plume thrown up by the explosion. The unique characteristics of the weapon had dictated the nature of the squadron's training. To perform in the predicted manner it was essential that Upkeep be released at an accurate range within a narrow band of precise criteria of height and speed.

For success the operation would also require tactical control in the air by the force leader, who would direct individual aircraft to attack. Trials had confirmed that the Lancaster's standard wireless transmitter would not be suitable for communication between the participating aircraft, and a decision had been made to equip the squadron's aircraft with fighter-style, three-channel TR1143 VHF (Very High Frequency) sets. While in the hangar undergoing its acceptance checks, ED933 had been fitted with a prototype installation, which was tested on the ground on 7 May. At 1740 on the evening of 8 May Henry took his aircraft up to make the first air-to-air test of the new radio fit, carrying Flight Lieutenant Hutchison, the squadron signals leader, as a passenger to observe the trial. Airborne with him in a second aircraft, ED887, AJ-A, was Dinghy Young. Climbing to 500 feet, Henry steered a course of 180 degrees, due south from Scampton, while Young orbited the airfield at 500 feet. Voice communication was to be established between the two aircraft and maintained until extreme range was reached. Young would make flat turns around the circuit, calling out every 10-degree change of course in order for an observer flying with Henry to determine whether there were any blind spots in the transmission pattern. At 500 feet communication was good up to about 50 miles, although a degree of sound vibration was experienced. Attributed to propeller modulation, it was not serious enough to interfere with speech. The exercise was repeated at a height of 200 feet, and the range was found to have decreased by about 2 miles. One unexpected side effect of the installation was that Henry found the intercom was reduced in volume, and it was difficult to communicate within his own aircraft. The problem was addressed, and installation of the sets continued in the remaining squadron aircraft while wireless operators were trained in their use at specially constructed benches in the crew room.

On Monday, 10 May, Henry penned what would be his last letter to his mother. Despite the pressures on time posed by training and organization, the letter was longer than those sent recently. The envelope showed no evidence of the censor's interest. Had it been opened, its contents, discussing routine domestic issues, would have communicated an atmosphere of complete relaxation and normality, although the opening sentence suggests that preoccupation with his work had caused Henry to forget his brief note of 4 May:

My dear Mummy

I have not written since coming back from leave – all too short as it was – but I am already feeling a thousand times better for it. I hope that you got – and sent on – the brooch for Diana as I had stupidly left the address in my luggage when I got it and decided that the best thing was to send it to you.

Did I tell you that I travelled up with Lady Ismay and Sarah as well as Mrs Gibbons, Mrs White and Jill? Mrs Gibbons, out of the blue, has sent me the most lovely morocco leather wallet – strangely enough my own one was becoming worn, so the one which she has given me will be particularly acceptable.

I think that I've missed John's birthday,[438] which is a bad thing since he remembered my last one.

I saw Captain Orde again in the RAF Club – (perhaps I've said this before) – he was at pains to explain that he did not at all mind being told that you disapproved of his picture.[439]

I can think of no news that would interest you from here – except that I will probably send some socks home for darning soon! I wonder if you would mind sending the picture back to the Parker Gallery in Albemarle Street for framing. I ought to have taken it but somehow there wasn't quite time to collect it. The companion to it which was in store at Oxford[440] should have arrived by now.

It has been infernally cold again, and I hope that you are not suffering from it too much. Perhaps Mrs Fisher makes a good treacle pudding!

Bob is very much better for his leave.

Best love to you all from Henry.[441]

Training intensified. Henry was now to fly virtually every day until the operation. At 1135 on 11 May he took ED933 on a four-hour daylight exercise, presumably a cross-country, possibly encompassing Uppingham Lake. The following evening came a two-hour dusk exercise and Henry's first opportunity to release Upkeep. For the best part of a week selected crews had been releasing inert Upkeeps[442] on the Reculver range. In addition to providing final confirmation of the crew's ability to release the weapon at the correct height, speed and range, these drops also gave pilots a chance to feel how the aircraft handled with four and a half tons of bomb spinning beneath the floor.

Taking off at about 1820, Henry took ED933 down to the Thames Estuary and thence to the north Kent coast, flying in loose formation with Shannon, Munro and Knight. Shortly before 1930 the hydraulic motor was set in motion and gradually the cylindrical bomb started to turn. A growing vibration spread through the airframe as the bomb gathered rotational speed. A few minutes later the report came through that 500 revs had been attained. Making his run at right angles to the coast, Henry was watching for the two posts on the beach that indicated the aiming point. Further to starboard he picked out the twin towers of the ruined Reculver church, a landmark to sailors since Saxon times. A small group of official observers could be seen standing on the approaching beach, out of the line of shot. Everything seemed to be proceeding as briefed. He was perhaps a little low; without the spotlight altimeter it was more difficult to judge, but better this than being too high. Some 450 yards from the shore Pilot Officer Fuller pressed the release. The calliper arms sprang apart and the spinning cylinder began to fall, vibration easing as its bulk fell away. A gentle forward pressure on the control column resisted the tendency for the aircraft to climb.

The weapon hit the sea almost directly beneath the aircraft, its first impact with the water throwing up the forward plume of dense spray characteristic of Upkeep by now familiar to the observers on the beach. But the next few seconds' events held them spellbound. Keeping pace with the approaching Lancaster, the ascending column of water reached up, totally enveloping the fuselage and tail, the plume clearly being split by impact with the aircraft. As it emerged from the spray, several large sections were seen to break away from the underside of the centre section, but the Lancaster flew on, trailing a stream of water from the rear of the bomb bay and rear turret. Meanwhile, Upkeep continued its juggernaut progress towards the beach in a series of diminishing bounces.

In the Lancaster Henry would have felt a hammer blow as the rising mass of water struck the aircraft like a gigantic fist. A combination of luck and airmanship enabled him to maintain control and keep the aircraft level as he overflew the sea wall and headed inland, seeking to assess the degree and nature of the damage before making any significant manœuvre. The engines were undamaged, but the aircraft had obviously sustained major damage to the rear fuselage, tail and possibly the underside of the mainplanes. Observation by a very wet rear gunner confirmed that both fins and rudders were still attached, if somewhat bent, as were the elevators. The aircraft was still responding to the controls, and, possibly recalling Gibson's remarks of a week earlier about serviceability, Henry opted to return to Scampton rather than land at nearby Manston. Repairs would be easier at the former, avoiding undue delay. Landing safely, Henry no doubt had to explain events to a concerned Gibson while the ground crew assessed the full scale of the damage.

The following day ED933 was officially classified as being damaged Cat. Ac – the damage being beyond unit repair, but repairable on site by another unit or contractor. It was estimated that repairs would take five days, but the need to have every possible aircraft available for operations set work in progress immediately. Meanwhile, Henry reverted to the standard AJ-V for an exercise during the night of 13/14 May. The ground crews' labours to repair ED933 would continue around the clock until a few hours before the operation, when it would be admitted finally that the aircraft would not be ready. An inquiry into the incident described the cause officially, if inaccurately, as being due to 'L[ow]-L[evel] Bombing. Underside of aircraft damaged by spray from explosion of special mine dropped by the aircraft.' Gibson had attributed this to the fact that the 'Pilot mis-judged his height', but since the station commander and Court of Inquiry were aware of the special training being carried out no further action was to be taken.[443] That same afternoon, at a progress meeting held in London to monitor Upkeep development, those assembled were told of the squadron's progress:

> Successful test trials are being carried out . . . using cylinders. Squadron pilots have carried out several successful drops at Reculver. It has been found that if pilots drop the store from below 50 feet the aircraft are likely to suffer damage from spray. With the use of the spotlight altimeter at night no difficulty is anticipated in keeping at the correct height of 60 feet.[444]

Both Martin and Munro also suffered similar, though less severe, spray damage while carrying out training drops. Their aircraft were repairable. Writing *Enemy Coast Ahead*, some nine months later, Gibson commented:

> Aircraft were very seriously damaged by the great columns of water set up when their mines splashed in. They had been flying slightly too low. Most of the damage was around the tails of the aircraft; elevators were smashed like plywood, turrets were knocked in, fins were bent. It was a miracle some of them got home. This was one of the many snags that the boys had to face while training. On the actual show it wouldn't matter so much because once the mines had been dropped the job would be done and the next thing would be to get out of it, no matter how badly the aircraft were damaged by water or anything else. But the main thing was to get the mines in the right spot.

Only twenty-three Lancasters had been modified to carry Upkeep. Three were being used currently for trials and now nineteen had been delivered to the squadron. The final aircraft to be converted, ED937, had been delivered to No. 39

Maintenance Unit, an aircraft storage unit at Colerne, on 6 May. On 14 May it was transferred to the squadron, seemingly already having undergone modification to bring it up to the operational standard of the other Lancasters. Carrying the codes AJ-Z, this now became Henry's replacement aircraft. Soon after its arrival Henry took off at 1915 for a twenty-minute night-flying test and bombing detail, although the short duration of the flight would suggest that no bombing was carried out.

With practice drops of the actual weapon now taking place and the moon nearly full, the squadron knew that the operation was imminent. It could only be a matter of days. Possibly encouraged by Gibson or by their own intuition that this could be a 'dicey do', a number of the aircrew who had not already done so made their wills. Among them was Bill Astell, whose brief statement leaving all to his father was duly witnessed by Henry and Australian Robert Barlow.

That night saw a full-scale exercise, taking in Uppingham and Colchester reservoirs. Again, Flying Officer Arthurton joined Henry's crew in ED937, ignorant of the fact that this would be a final rehearsal before the actual operation. Before take-off he issued Cloretone capsules to crew members as a precaution against airsickness.

> We took off at 21.50 hours and flew for four hours. I have not the foggiest notion where we were nor exactly what we were doing except that we were doing low flying . . . people said very little and I did not embarrass them with very difficult questions as I realised there was something in the wind.[445]

Arthurton's preventative measure was successful. He wrote in his logbook (recording the aircraft incorrectly as ED906): 'Result – no nausea or airsickness among crew.'

There was very little flying on 15 May. During the morning, as the crews at Scampton embarked on another day's training, the teleprinter at Bomber Command Headquarters chattered, printing a coded signal from the Air Ministry, Whitehall. Within a few hours the signal was retransmitted to No. 5 Group Headquarters at Grantham: 'OPERATION CHASTISE. IMMEDIATE ATTACK OF TARGETS X, Y AND Z APPROVED. EXECUTE AT FIRST SUITABLE OPPORTUNITY.'

AVM Cochrane, AOC No. 5 Group, travelled to Scampton to meet Gibson. If the weather was right, the attack would take place the following night. Gibson was to brief his flight commanders and deputies that afternoon.

At about 1600 a white-painted Coastal Command Wellington landed at Scampton, bringing Wallis and Major Hugh Kilner of Vickers, while Cochrane and Gibson discussed final details of the operation. Gibson had summoned

Henry to a meeting in the station commander's residence at 1800. On arrival he was joined by Squadron Leader Young, Flight Lieutenant Hopgood and Flight Lieutenant Hay. When they had assembled, Gibson made the announcement that the squadron would be operating the next night. No record was taken of the meeting, and none of those present was to survive the war, so the exact discussion cannot be known. After the initial revelation and perhaps expression of relief that the waiting and uncertainty were over, Gibson would have taken them through the draft operation order, detailing the plan of attack, the routes, key timings and other essential information. Final allocations of crews to targets were made, and oversights identified and corrected. Hopgood noted that the route north of the Ruhr took them very close to a defended rubber factory at Huls. The route was amended. The meeting broke up towards midnight. As they were leaving, the station commander, Group Captain John 'Charles' Whitworth, took Gibson aside to inform him that Nigger, his black Labrador, had been run over and killed outside the camp that afternoon.

The morning of Sunday, 16 May, dawned, heralding a bright, clear and warm day. After an early breakfast, Henry would have gone down to the hangar to review his flight's aircraft serviceability and crew fitness in preparation for the night's operation. It was looking increasingly as though ED933 would not be repaired in time, and Henry would have to take his replacement ED937. Under normal circumstances this would have created a shortage of aircraft, but Flight Lieutenant Harold Wilson's crew were non-effective owing to sickness, conveniently resolving the potential problem. Meanwhile, out at dispersals around the airfield ground crew were taking covers off engines and canopies and making final checks. Bowsers toured the aircraft in turn, fuelling them with 1,740 gallons of fuel and topping up their 150 gallons of oil. With Upkeep weighing 9,250 lb, each Lancaster would be taking off at maximum load of 63,000 lb. In the bomb dump and armoury the armourers were preparing each Lancaster's offensive load. Every gun would be loaded with 100 per cent daylight tracer, 18,000 rounds per aircraft. The tracer would cause tremendous wear on gun barrels but was deemed most effective for terrifying enemy flak gunners. It took about half an hour to load each Upkeep, ensuring that it was held securely between the retaining arms and then spun to check free movement and serviceability of the driving mechanism.

Shortly before noon the wireless operators received a separate briefing on code words and signals procedure from Wing Commander Wally Dunn, No. 5 Group signals officer. A little later Gibson and Wallis briefed all pilots and navigators. Some two hours later the groups broke up, before individual crews re-formed to study models and photographs of the targets and discuss navigation and pin-points. As a member of the first wave, Henry would need to be familiar with details for the Mohne, Eder and Sorpe Dams. Meanwhile, Wallis went around each aircraft discussing last-minute issues with the ground crews.

All crews were called to Scampton's large briefing room on the upper floor of a building on the station headquarters site at 1800 hours. Entry was restricted to aircrew and senior personnel only, and passes were scrutinized closely. Once inside, 133 airmen sat expectantly on the wooden benches. They rose as Gibson entered and walked down the central aisle, accompanied by Cochrane, Whitworth, Wallis and Dunn, mounting the dais at the front of the room. Behind him was a map of Europe, the routes to and from the target marked by red tape. Motioning them to sit, Gibson began the final briefing.

After introducing Wallis, Gibson sat down while the designer explained the nature of the weapon, the difficulties encountered during development and the reasons for selecting the dams as their objective, occasionally illustrating his points with sketches on a blackboard. Much was familiar to Henry from the mini-briefings of 15 May and earlier that morning. After Wallis had concluded his presentation, Cochrane addressed the crews. He was certain that the operation would be successful and cause a tremendous amount of damage to the Ruhr and German war machine. He predicted that the attack would become 'historic', stressing that it was imperative that all details of the weapon remained secret; it was intended to use it against other targets in the future. (There also was the possibility that a last-minute adverse weather report could delay the operation.)

Gibson then reconfirmed the operational details. The attack would comprise nineteen aircraft, in three waves. One wave of nine aircraft would take off in groups of three at ten-minute intervals – Henry would lead the third group. These would be routed initially to attack the Mohne Dam. After this was breached, Gibson, his deputy and other aircraft still carrying Upkeep would continue to the Eder Dam. Any Upkeep remaining after this had been attacked successfully would be taken to the Sorpe. Another wave of five aircraft would fly individually to attack the Sorpe, being routed along a separate route for part of their track. A third wave of five Lancasters would serve as a mobile reserve, either to reinforce the initial waves or to attack other smaller dams in the area. The latter would take off two and a half hours after the first aircraft and be directed to individual targets by radio communication from No. 5 Group Headquarters at Grantham.

All aircraft were to remain at low level for the entire operation. Aircraft attacking the Mohne and Eder Dams would release Upkeep from 60 feet, having spun it to 500 rpm, after a run made at a ground speed of 220 mph and at 90 degrees to the dam wall. The Mohne and Eder Dams were gravity dams, relying on their weight to retain the water, but the Sorpe was an earthen dam, with sloping banks extending away from a central core. It was not an ideal target for Upkeep, and a different method of delivery had been devised. Crews attacking this target were not to spin their mine, and were to make their run along the length of the dam at 180 mph and at the lowest practicable height. They were to aim to release their weapon into the lake about 20 feet out from the centre of the dam, where it would roll down the sloping bank to explode at a depth of 30 feet.

As far as could be determined, the Mohne was the only target to be defended by flak, with guns located on the towers and others below the dam. The Germans thought that the hills surrounding the Eder precluded any need for defences. Nevertheless, light flak posed a severe risk along the route, and adherence to planned tracks was essential to avoid known defended areas. That still left any new and unplotted guns.

The crews then broke into smaller groups and gathered to study the target models, together with photographs and maps, confirming the location of defences, line of attack and rechecking numerous other details.[446] By 1930 they had adjourned for their pre-flight meal in their respective Messes. Security and a sense of self-preservation decreed that as far as the remainder of the station was concerned the squadron would be carrying out yet another night-flying programme. Even so, sharp-eyed personnel noted that the aircrew menu that evening comprised the traditional 'pre-op' meal of bacon and eggs, and that operational flight rations were being issued. Others noticed a gradual increase in tension as the appointed hour approached. After eating, the crews went back to wash and change, some taking the opportunity to complete a final letter home to be lodged with the adjutant or other trusted confidant to be posted should they fail to return.

Shortly after 2000 crews began to assemble in the crew rooms alongside the squadron hangar to don their flying clothing, collect their parachutes, escape kits and flight rations and check other essential items before wandering out into the warm evening to await transport out to the aircraft. Some took advantage of this time to have a final cigarette, others chatted in small groups or lounged in a scatter of chairs.

Transport arrived just before 2030. Gibson called the crews to action and they climbed aboard the assortment of vans and buses to be driven out to dispersal.

Arriving at Z-Zebra's hardstanding, Henry and his crew walked round the aircraft checking control surfaces, the condition of tyres and undercarriage and the security of panels, and looking for any traces of oil or fuel leaks. The routine pre-flight external inspection completed, Henry signed the Form 700, formally accepting serviceability of his aircraft. It was the responsibility of the bomb aimer, Pilot Officer Fuller, to inspect the bomb bay and confirm the stowage and safety of the bomb load. On this occasion the remainder of the crew probably joined him as they took a final look at the unconventional weapon before climbing the short ladder up to the aircraft's rear entrance door.

Ascending the familiar uphill slope of the fuselage, the crew negotiated the cramped confines of the main spar (at least the Upkeep specials did not have the usual additional obstacle of the mid-upper turret). Settling themselves into their respective positions, stowing their parachutes and kit, they organized themselves ready for start-up. At 2110 a red Very light soared up from Gibson's aircraft – the signal for the first-wave aircraft to start engines. Across the airfield there was a spluttering cacophony as the Merlins fired one by one, settling down to a steady rumble.

Flight Lieutenant Barlow had taxied to the southern end of the runway strip in use and was waiting on the perimeter track. After a brief pause a green Aldis lamp winked from Flight Sergeant Frank Wade in the runway controller's caravan. Barlow advanced the throttles, moving on to the grass, and at 2128 (double British summer time) E-Edward became airborne. One by one aircraft began to move around the perimeter to the marshalling point, where they were cleared for take-off. Munro, Byers and Rice followed at one-minute intervals, completing the departure of the second wave, with the exception of McCarthy, who had been delayed by problems experienced during his pre-flight checks, forcing his crew to change to the single spare Lancaster.

Aircraft of the second wave began to start their engines, running them up to check the magnetos, oil pressures and coolant temperatures. Instrument and other internal tests completed, the crews awaited their turn to take off. On board Z-Zebra final checks were carried out. Calling around the aircraft from nose to tail, each member of the crew tested his intercom, the gunners rotating their turrets as they did so, to ensure that communication was maintained at all positions. Sergeant Cottam checked his radio equipment, Sergeant Marriott satisfied himself that the fuel tank contents and engine temperatures were correct. Watches were synchronized throughout the crew and hatches checked 'secure and locked'.

At 2135 Gibson, Hopgood and Martin, the first group of the second wave, had taken off in a loose Vic of three, followed at 2147 by Young, leading Shannon and Maltby. Now, his checks completed, Henry indicated all was well and he was ready to move. The ground crew pulled the wooden blocks away and ran out to the edge of dispersal ahead of the wing tips, where he could see they were clear. Releasing the brake lever, with the inner engines running at about 800–1,000 rpm and using bursts of the outer engines, he began to taxi from dispersal, steering with brakes and differential throttle. Rudder and aileron trimmers were set to zero, with a little up elevator trimmer to help the aircraft climb after take-off. When he arrived at the end of the runway, the green Aldis flashed; he taxied a short distance forward to ensure the tailwheel was straight and waited while the other two aircraft formed up on either side, Knight in N-Nuts to port and Astell's B-Beer to starboard. Final take-off checks were completed: propeller pitch fully fine, mixture controls to 'Rich', fuel pumps on, brakes on and flaps set at 25 degrees. The engine noise increased as the throttles were opened. Leading initially with the port engines and helped by a subconscious application of starboard rudder to counteract any tendency to swing, they were rolling. With a full load, the aircraft gained pace, slowly at first across Scampton's undulating grass, but then the controls becoming more responsive as the speed increased. At an indicated airspeed of 110 mph, with the engine gauges showing +9 psi boost and some 2,850 rpm, contact with the ground became tentative as the wings took the load. At 2200, after using the maximum available run and with the northern boundary hedge looming perilously close, the three aircraft lifted slowly into the air; a dab on the lever to brake the wheels as they folded into the inboard nacelles and the airspeed built up. With a slight reduction in boost and revs, the flaps were raised in increments, elevator trim being adjusted accordingly to maintain longitudinal stability while the aircraft were kept down to little more than treetop height.

Chapter 17

Final Flight

We were off on a journey for which we had long waited, a journey that had been carefully planned, carefully trained for, a mission that was going to do a lot of good if it succeeded: and everything had been worked out so that it should succeed. We were off to the Dams.
(Wing Commander Guy Gibson, VC, DSO, DFC, *Enemy Coast Ahead*)

As the Lancasters settled down into a loose Vic formation, navigators set their Air Position Indicators (API), some switching on the Identification Friend or Foe (IFF), registering the aircraft as friendly to UK radar.[447] At 2208, after a circuit of the airfield, the formation turned onto a heading of 125 degrees True (135 degrees Magnetic), establishing the track to their exit point at Southwold, on the Suffolk coast. Although the Operation Order permitted climbing to a maximum of 1,500 feet over England, the crews remained close to the ground. Flying at 100 feet and an airspeed of 180 mph, with no appreciable wind, it would take them forty minutes to reach the North Sea.

Seven minutes later they were over the flat fenland of Kesteven, passing low over the town of Woodhall Spa, nestling among its silver birch and pine woods. The sun was astern on the starboard quarter in a cloudless sky as they headed towards the darkening south-east, where a faint moon was beginning to rise. Another five minutes brought them to the mudflat coastline of the Wash, where many of the crews had practised spotlight flying during the previous weeks. It might almost have been another training flight. Recrossing the coast near Snettisham, the Lancasters swept over the flat expanse of Norfolk, reaching West Raynham by 2230. As they headed south-east, a light easterly wind began to affect their course, with a tendency to push the formation slightly south of track, but at this stage it was not critical, and bomb aimers found the map-reading easy. They reached the coast near Southwold at 2248, giving the navigator an accurate pinpoint with which to compare his API reading. A quick calculation and a new course was given: 119 degrees True (128 degrees Magnetic), which, with the light wind, would enable them to make good a track of 120 degrees to the first waypoint (Position A) over the North Sea. Maintaining height at 100 feet, the formation was still cruising at an indicated airspeed of 180 mph, the wind reducing their groundspeed to 173 mph.

Skimming the almost flat sea, the pilots settled down to methodical flying, eyes transiting between the distant horizon, the altimeter and key instruments of the blind flying panel. IFF was switched off as the aircraft receded from English radar cover. Some navigators released flame floats,[448] enabling rear gunners to check drift, which was established as being 1 degree to starboard. For as long as possible, until prevented by enemy jamming, the aircraft's position would be plotted using Gee in conjunction with the APIs. (In Knight's aircraft Flying Officer Hobday was able to maintain Gee readings well beyond expected range and well into Europe.) Five minutes after leaving the coast they reached position 52 degrees 14'N, 01 degree 59'E. The aircraft descended to 60 feet using the spotlights, partly to ensure they were working and also to enable pilots to reset their barometric altimeters. Flight Sergeant Sutherland, flying with Knight, later reported that Sergeant Grayston remarked that one of the other aircraft, possibly Henry's, appeared to be some 20 feet lower than them when this was done.[449] All crew members kept a sharp look out, quartering the horizon and sea for any shipping or sign of fighters. The fusing switch to activate Upkeep's 90 second self-destruct pistol was clicked 'on'. The weapon's three hydrostatic pistols had been 'live' since being loaded at dispersal, but these could be activated only by the pressure of 30 feet of water. The 90-second fuse was intended to ensure the destruction of the weapon should these fail to function for any reason, or should the aircraft come down on land. Until this point in the flight the weapon could have been jettisoned 'safe' over land or, in theory, should have survived a belly landing. Now, no matter whether the aircraft was forced to ditch, or Upkeep was torn off as the aircraft hit the ground, the weapon would be destroyed, preventing the enemy from learning its secrets.[450]

By 2301 they were at position 52 degrees 05' N, 02 degrees 28' E. Ahead of them, Gibson, Martin and Hopgood were four minutes from their landfall. They too had experienced the stronger wind and crossed the Dutch coast flying over Walcheren, a few miles south of track, but they were lucky and caught the defences unawares. Already the aircraft of the wave that was flying a more northerly route, had begun to run into trouble as they approached the Frisian Islands. Pilot Officer Vernon Byers was shot down by flak over Texel, crashing into the Waddenzee at 2257. At the same time, as he crossed Vlieland, Flight Lieutenant Munro was engaged by flak, which damaged the aircraft, destroying the compass master unit and putting his intercom out of action, leaving him little option but to turn for home with his mine. Ten minutes later, Pilot Officer Geoff Rice, having slipped undetected past the islands, descended too low and hit the water. Miraculously he was able to drag the Lancaster back into the air, but it was heavily damaged and his Upkeep had been torn off. He too turned for home, leaving Flight Lieutenant Joe McCarthy, twenty-one minutes late owing to his technical problems, as the sole survivor of this wave.

Dusk was turning to night, but with the rising full moon visibility was excellent as the approaching Lancasters skimmed over the highlighted wave crests. At 2310 Henry and his formation arrived at Position A (51 degrees 51' N, 03 degrees 08' E). They now had an estimated twelve minutes to run until they reached the coast. Gradually an almost imperceptible dark line on the horizon marked the approaching islands of the Scheldt Estuary, and the three Lancasters spread their formation, creating a larger target for any flak. Front gunners began to rotate their turrets ready to respond to any defences that might open fire. The intercom crackled as each crew prepared to cross into hostile territory: enemy coast ahead.

Position B off the north-west of Nord Beveland was reached at 2321, a minute ahead of their revised ETA, but still slightly behind their briefed schedule on account of the wind. The formation had made a better track than Gibson's group and achieved an accurate arrival over the Scheldt Estuary between Schouwen and Walcheren. Pilot Officer Fuller began consulting his maps ready to identify key features and commence navigation to the target. Flying Officer Urquhart called out the course alteration to 103 degrees True (111 degrees Magnetic) that would take them on a more easterly track of 102 degrees True for the next twelve-minute leg to the town of Rosendaal. Henry gently eased the Lancaster's nose the few degrees to port, maintaining height at 100 feet and a speed of 180. Reflections on the water ceased abruptly as surf and beach flashed beneath the aircraft. Over the land, buildings, roads, canals and even people could be seen clearly in the moon's bright illumination. At this stage of the flight, Young's second wave had been forced to take evasive action as light flak had opened up, suggesting that they had been taken slightly south, following Gibson's path in, and had passed over defences alerted by the latter's formation. Henry's formation, probably on the briefed track slightly to the north, appears to have encountered no opposition and began threading its way through the known defences.

Rosendaal was reached at 2334, clearly identified by its railway junction. A further adjustment was made onto a due easterly course of 090 degrees True (098 degrees Magnetic), which would lead them between the two German night-fighter bases of Gilze Rijn and Eindhoven. They were now flying directly into the wind, and there was no need to allow for drift. As they passed low to the south of Breda and Tilburg, all eyes kept an intense watch. Unknown to them, this was an area where the second group, led by Young, had encountered brief flak and searchlight activity only a short while earlier. Henry's formation may also have met slight opposition here. Although none is recorded in surviving records, there is a suggestion that, when seen at the Eder, Henry's aircraft showed possible signs of damage, which could have been received either here, or later on, north of the Ruhr. The flatness was deceptive, for the countryside was crossed by high-tension power lines, a potential death trap for the low-flying aircraft. The crews had learned to split the task of observation, pilots watching ahead and to port, the flight engineer ahead and to starboard. Training had taught them how to differ- entiate between insects and dirt on the Perspex and approaching obstacles; if they moved their heads slightly, the former would move, while distant objects remained still. Front gunners kept alert for defences, and the bomb aimer, his quarter- million charts marked with power lines and other key features, picked up pin- points and passed them on to the navigator at his position back in the fuselage. Navigators had limited visibility outside, but were otherwise fully occupied mon- itoring their position and calculating course and speed. The next pinpoint would be the Wilhelmina Canal.

The canal came into sight, joining their route from the north-west, before turning east along the desired track. The aircraft followed the straight silver ribbon, leaving it briefly as it made a slight twist north at Oirshot, regaining it to pass a few miles to the north of Eindhoven. Hurdling the several power lines crossing their path, the aircraft covered the remaining 11 miles to the next turning point: south of Beek en Donk, where the canal ended abruptly as it met the Zuid– Willemsvaart canal running north-east–south-west. Approaching this critical pinpoint at 2352, Henry would most likely have climbed to some 300 feet, from which the unmistakable T-shaped junction could be identified clearly, before descending back down to a lower level.

The wind had increased slightly, necessitating a bank to port on to a course of 067 degrees to give the desired track of 064 degrees True (075 degrees Magnetic), taking them on to the Rhine. Crossing the Maas south of Boxmeer, the formation passed on into Germany. Numerous water features in this area showed up well, greatly assisting navigation. A distinctive bend in the Rhine, with the makings of an oxbow lake near Rees, provided the next turning point onto 085 degrees True (092 degrees Magnetic). The wind would give them a track of 0840 True, and, having arrived at the turning point at 0004, a minute ahead of ETA, Knight reduced his ground speed to 172 mph.[451] Crossing the Rhine, they passed over the main Wesel–Arnhem rail line with its parallel autobahn. They saw the attendant line of pylons and skimmed the invisible cables strung between them. Ten min- utes earlier the wires had snared Barlow's aircraft, as he joined this track from the longer northern route. Barlow simply may not have seen the pylons, or may have been damaged by flak and unable to avoid the power line. His Lancaster came down at Heeren, with the loss of the entire crew. Henry's group must have passed close to the spot, although there is no record of their observing the burning wreckage.

Ahead of them Gibson's formation was encountering greater opposition from small pockets of flak. This was of significant danger to following aircraft, so Gibson ordered his wireless operator, Flight Lieutenant Hutchison, to transmit a flak warning to No. 5 Group Headquarters at 0007, indicating a concentration of guns at 51 degrees 48' N, 07 degrees 12' E. Group rebroadcast this to all aircraft a few minutes later. By this time Henry's formation had reached 51 degrees 39' N 06 degrees 31'E, south of Bocholt, and was about to enter the hostile area. A slight course adjustment would take it south of the guns. Until the last pinpoint at the Rhine, Henry, Knight and Astell appear to have maintained good formation, but now the aircraft were strung farther apart. Knight's slight change of speed may not have been reciprocated by Henry, and Bill Astell appears to have been uncertain of a pinpoint, either at the Rhine or a little further on. He hesitated to turn at a waypoint and fell behind, so that the three aircraft were now in effect separated and proceeding in line as individuals.[452] As they passed slightly north of Raesfeld, south of Borken, Knight's wireless operator, Flight Sergeant Bob Kellow, looking back from the astrodome reported seeing two lines of tracer rise to intersect on an aircraft about 2 miles astern. The target's gunners appear to have replied with vengeance, but Kellow saw the aircraft become engulfed in flames, followed by an explosion on the ground.

The interpretation was that Astell's aircraft, possibly having climbed to check position, had been engaged by light flak. German witnesses, however, assert that there was no flak in this locality, and that his aircraft flew into power lines running north to Borken. The Lancaster collided with the top of a 90-foot-high electricity pylon and continued descending on fire for some 500 yards, passing over farm buildings and clipping the tops of trees, obviously doomed. It is possible the bomb aimer jettisoned the Upkeep moments before the aircraft hit the ground and exploded in open country, or that the mine was torn off on impact. Ninety seconds later the weapon detonated in an adjacent field.

As John Sweetman records in *The Dambusters Raid*, there are a number of conflicting accounts of these events. The official aircraft loss card attributes its failure to return as being 'Light flak'. The apparent 'tracer' observed from a distance may have been the ensuing arcing of the high-tension cables, as the aircraft collided with the pylon, or may have been from a battery out of sight from the subsequent German witnesses. The No. 617 Squadron Operations Record Book suggests that Astell, rather than Henry, was leading the formation at this time and 'appeared uncertain of his whereabouts, and on reaching a canal crossing actually crossed at the correct place, turned south down the canal as though searching for a pinpoint. He fell about half a mile behind his accompanying aircraft doing this and got slightly off track.' The use of the terms 'canal' and 'turned south' would place the break-up of the formation back at the junction at Beek, unless 'canal' refers erroneously to the Rhine. It also raises the question as to whether the other two had become separated from Henry at an earlier stage. Other records suggest that Astell was shot down over an airfield, although no airfield existed in this area. At least one post-war account appears to have confused the loss of Astell with the later loss of Lewis Burpee, who crashed on the perimeter of Gilze Rijn airfield. Regardless of these uncertainties and errors, German records confirm that Bill Astell, whose will Henry had witnessed only three days earlier, was killed, along with all his crew, when ED864, AJ-B, came down on Herr Thesing's farm in the rural community of Marbeck at fifteen minutes past midnight on Monday, 17 May.

Four minutes later the navigation log of AJ-N records a further course correction to take them to Ahlen. With a ground speed of 170 mph, the aircraft banked 12 degrees to starboard, taking it on a more east–south-easterly heading of 097 degrees True (102 degrees Magnetic). Tension mounted as the aircraft tracked around the area that had given Gibson cause to despatch the flak warning. Two minutes later Knight's navigator recorded their position as being 12' east of that given for the warning, on the same latitude, but with no indication that they had experienced any difficulties. Nevertheless, it may have been at this stage of the route that (unconfirmed) damage occurred to Henry's aircraft. A further minor correction three minutes later, at 0024, maintained the course to Ahlen. Henry would now have been less than fifteen minutes from the Mohne Dam. At 0028 a final turn to starboard brought AJ-N round on to a course of 153 degrees True (160 degrees Magnetic), the drift taking it onto the required track of 155 degreesTrue. Shortly beyond this point, some 10 miles from the target, the Operation Order required the leader of each section to climb to about 1,000 feet and listen out on VHF, Channel 'A', which would remain on until an hour after they had finally left the target area. Henry presumably carried out this order and would have heard Gibson, who had by now reached the Mohne lake. Soon the remainder of the preceding aircraft of the second wave were arriving at the target and beginning to orbit, making an initial reconnaissance. Already the defences were active, but the aircraft rarely ventured within lethal range.

It appears that Henry and Pilot Officer Knight would have been still some six minutes away from the target when Gibson opened the attack. Although they would not be able to see events, they could hear of their progress over the VHF. Making the first run at 0028, Gibson passed through the defending flak unscathed, his Upkeep exploding within 50 yards of the dam without causing a breach. Some five minutes later, as Flight Lieutenant John Hopgood (who had already been damaged by flak east of Dulmen on the route to the target) made his approach, he was hit by flak and a wing set alight. His mine, released fractionally too late, bounced over the dam parapet. As Hopgood climbed away, struggling for enough height to enable his crew to escape by parachute, the Lancaster exploded at 500 feet. Three got out, but only two survived.[453] On the ground the self-destruct pistol detonated Upkeep, destroying the 6,000-kilowatt powerhouse below the dam wall. Very shortly afterwards Les Knight arrived over the target at 0034. There is no recorded timing of Henry's arrival, although it is believed to have been within minutes or so of Knight.

On reaching the target, crews had been briefed to fly left-handed circuits. Henry's first objective would have been to ensure that he kept clear of both the attacking aircraft and those circling to await their turn. Evaluating the defences, he positioned himself to remain out of range, hugging the contours of the surrounding hills. In doing so he would have identified the key topographic features, familiar from the models, maps and photographs studied at briefing, orienting himself in preparation for his turn to bomb.

Calling Martin in to make his attack, Gibson announced that he would run in with him and attempt to draw off some of the defences. This action was only partially successful. Martin succeeded in releasing his bomb, despite his aircraft being hit in the starboard wing. Although damaged, the aircraft remained flyable and would return safely to base. Martin's Upkeep detonated with a tremendous plume of water, but had veered off to the left and was some 80 yards from the dam. After a wait of five minutes to allow the water to subside, Young was ordered to attack. Supported by Gibson to the north, this time seeking further attention by flashing his navigation lights, and with Martin to port, Young's run was accurate, and the mine hit the dam after three bounces. Water was thrown over the parapet by the explosion and for a moment Gibson and Young thought the dam had gone. As the spray cleared it still appeared to be intact.[454] Again supported by Gibson and Martin, who were now circling near the dam to concentrate their fire on each of the towers, Maltby ran in and released his mine at 0049. It was assessed as accurate, but by now spray from the attacks was hanging in the air and settling on aircraft canopies, hampering visibility. Gibson called the next aircraft, Shannon's, preparing him for his run. As he did so, a exultant shout came over the VHF. Banking round in front of the target, Martin had seen the dam wall crumble under the pressure, and a jet of water burst through, becoming an irresistible torrent pounding down the valley.

Out of range and at low level over the upper reaches of the Mohne lake, the crew of Z-Zebra concentrated on remaining out of trouble until their call came. They probably saw very little of the action other than the tracer being fired around the distant dam, although they could hear the progress of the operation over the VHF. Hearing Gibson calling Shannon, 'Cooler 6', Henry would have known that it was to be his turn next, and may have commenced spinning his Upkeep in preparation. He would have been orbiting for nearly a quarter of an hour when he heard Martin's shout, followed by Gibson's urgent instructions for Shannon not to attack. After confirmation that the dam had been breached, the circling crews drew closer to look at the awe-inspiring sight There was little danger now; only one gun was firing, soon silenced by a well-aimed burst from one of the air gunners. The R/T was alive with excited chatter as the elated crews viewed the spectacle below. Crouched over his Morse key in Gibson's G-George, Flight Lieutenant Hutchison tapped out the code word 'NIGGER', informing No. 5 Group Headquarters of their success.

After some five minutes Gibson called for silence and ordered Martin and Maltby home, while the three remaining aircraft carrying Upkeep, together with Young, who was to act as deputy leader, were to accompany him to Target B. Should anything happen to Gibson, Young would take over as leader. In this eventuality, or should anything happen to Young, Henry would assume the role of deputy leader. At about 0058 Flying Officer Urquhart gave Henry his new course of 112 degrees True (128 degrees Magnetic). Leaving the southern tip of the emptying Mohne lake and cruising over the treetops of the Arnsberger Wald at 180 mph, the aircraft should have needed a little less than a quarter of an hour to reach the Eder. The undulating countryside near the Mohne gave way to steeper wooded hillsides, forming marked valleys interspersed with rivers and lakes. Pinpoints here were few, which placed greater emphasis on time, distance and heading for navigation. After three and a half hours of solid concentration, stress and physical effort, combined with the mixed emotions experienced at the Mohne, it was becoming a greater effort for the pilots to haul their laden Lancasters over the contours. Early morning mist was now forming in the valleys, effectively homogenizing both those with and without lakes and hampering navigation.

With their ETA approaching, the crews strained to identify recognizable features. Gibson reached the Eder lake towards its western end and spent five arduous minutes following the water searching for the target. He eventually located the dam, finding the area in the immediate vicinity to be relatively free of mist. Young arrived very soon after, but there was no sign of the other three aircraft orbiting the target, Gibson called them on the R/T. Shannon, who had flown from the Mohne with his Upkeep still spinning, answered, saying that he thought he was in the vicinity, but could not positively identify the dam. Gibson then fired red Very lights over it, in the hope that Shannon and the others would be able to see their glow and position themselves. The tactic worked, and soon all five aircraft had established themselves in a left-hand orbit of the target.[455] At least briefing had been correct – there was no flak. The Germans believed that the terrain was sufficient deterrent for any attacker, and the dam was guarded only by two sentries with rifles.

Even at briefing it had been apparent that executing an accurate approach would be far more difficult than at the Mohne and would require a higher degree of flying skill. The reservoir was cradled in a steep-sided serpentine valley, with hills rising some 600 feet above the lake level. Some three-quarters of a mile in front of the dam, a spur projected, masking sight of the dam from any aircraft attempting a straight run in along the lake. Instead it had been agreed that the best approach would be a complex dog-leg. Approach was parallel to the dam over the hills, heading on about 225° Magnetic towards the readily identifiable Waldeck Castle, situated on a summit to the north-east of the dam opposite the spur. On reaching the castle, the attacking aircraft should commence a dive towards the promontory, executing a sharp turn to port as they reached the lake at a height that still allowed them to clear the spit, while maintaining descent to 60 feet. Straightening out on a heading of 150° Magnetic, the aircraft should then be on the correct line for the final run-in, with the moon on the starboard beam. A little more than 300 yards beyond the dam, the valley swept around to the right, presenting the pilot with a steep hillside, rising to 1,000 feet directly ahead of the aircraft, necessitating a steep turning climb out at full power. As if this were not difficult enough, speed would be another critical factor. Losing 500 feet in under a mile, the Lancaster could easily build up speed in excess of that specified for release, reducing the time available for final positioning and imparting an additional release velocity on Upkeep, with unpredictable effects on its range and bounce.

It was now 0130, and a faint glow in the east signalled the first signs of dawn. Conscious of the need to be clear of the enemy coast before daylight, Gibson ordered Shannon to make the first attack. The Australian made three or four runs without being able to position himself correctly for release. Suggesting that Shannon hold off for a while, Gibson then called on Henry, who tried twice with the same results. A short conference was then held over the R/T, as recorded by Gibson in *Enemy Coast Ahead*: '[Henry] said he found it very difficult and gave the other boys some advice on the best way to go about it.'

It is at this point that accounts conflict as to the order of attack. In *Enemy Coast Ahead*, Gibson says that, having made his two abortive attempts, Henry then called up and announced that he was going to make his final run. This view is echoed by Fred Sutherland, Knight's front gunner, who says that, after Henry had made two abortive runs, 'Gibson was getting a bit irritated. He said, "Henry, that's very nice flying, but you will have to do better than that." Henry said, "Sorry sir. I will try again.'"[456] Other evidence, cited by John Sweetman,[457] suggests that Shannon was then called in and made two dummy runs before releasing his Upkeep on the next run at 0139. The weapon bounced twice and sank against the dam wall. Shannon, with his landing light on to illuminate the approaching hillside, cleared the obstacle, as the now familiar explosion rent the water behind the dam wall, sending up a column of water 1,000 feet high. From their positions, Gibson and Knight could see no apparent damage, although Shannon was certain that he had made a small breach in the eastern end of the dam, and his wireless operator sent a coded message to No. 5 Group Headquarters to this effect.[458] Strangely this was not logged until 0206, by which time events had overtaken it.

Gibson then called on Henry to try again. Records are corrupt, but the available evidence would suggest that the time was about 0140. To one observer, something appeared to be hanging down from Henry's aircraft, thought to be indicative of damage sustained on the flight to the target.[359] In Gibson's account of Henry's final run, although there is no specific detail, he does allude to a possible problem:

We could see him running in. Suddenly he pulled away; something seemed to be wrong, but he turned quickly, climbed up over the mountain and put his nose down, literally flinging his machine down the valley. This time he was running straight and true for the middle of the wall. We saw his spotlights together, so he must have been at sixty feet. We saw the red ball of his Very light shooting out behind his tail and we knew he had dropped his weapon. A split second later we saw someone [sic] else; Henry Maudslay had dropped his mine too late. It had hit the top of the parapet and had exploded immediately on impact, with a slow yellow vivid flame, which lit up the whole valley like daylight for just a few seconds. We could see him quite clearly banking steeply a few feet above it. Perhaps the blast was doing that. It all seemed so sudden and the flame seemed so very cruel. Someone said, 'He has blown himself up. . . .'

Trevor Roper made the suggestion that Henry's bomb aimer must have been wounded. This possibility, though remote, cannot be discounted and, if correct, could conceivably account for the earlier record that at the time of his loss Astell had been leading the formation. If Pilot Officer Fuller had been injured, he might have had difficulty in assisting with navigation, and leadership of the formation may have been delegated to Astell. Nevertheless, Henry made no mention of any such damage or injury during his earlier R/T conversation, nor is there any firm confirmation that the formation came under fire during the outward journey.

With no other evidence, such an assumption can only remain speculation.[460]

If the possibility of significant and influential battle damage is discounted, the available evidence suggests that the aircraft may have built up excessive speed during its dive, reducing the reaction time for Pilot Officer Fuller to confirm the range and release Upkeep. With a greater forward velocity, possibly combined with a fractionally late release, the weapon would have impacted on the dam free-board with far greater force than design tolerances had anticipated. Such an excessively violent impact would have been sufficient to distort and detonate the charge while the aircraft was still in close proximity.[461]

Gibson called Henry over the R/T: 'Henry – Henry. Z-Zebra – Z Zebra. Are you OK?' There was no reply. Gibson repeated his call. This time he heard a faint reply, which was also confirmed by members of Shannon's and Knight's crews: 'I think so, stand by. . . .' The voice sounded very tired and weak. Gibson record-ed: 'It seemed as though he was dazed and his voice did not sound natural.'

Concurring, Sergeant O'Brien thought it very faint, unnatural and almost dehumanized. Sergeant Sutherland's recollection is that he also heard a very faint, almost imperceptible, 'Returning to base.'[462]

As far as the four crews circling the Eder Dam were concerned, this was the last that was ever heard or seen of Henry and his crew. There was nothing they could do except wait for the smoke from the detonation to clear and hope that Knight's remaining Upkeep would be sufficient to breach the dam. 'Henry had disappeared. There was no burning wreckage on the ground; there was no aircraft on fire in the air. There was nothing. Henry had disappeared. He never came back.'[463]

But there was little time in which to dwell on Z-Zebra's fate. The glow in the eastern sky fast heralded the approaching dawn. The smoke cleared, and at 0150 hours Knight made his first attempt to attack the dam. He too found extreme difficulty in attaining the correct conditions for release, but made a second run and was successful in releasing his Upkeep at 0152. In the rear turret O'Brien felt grave concern that their run might emulate that which they had just witnessed. His fears were unfounded. After three bounces their weapon sank just to the right of the dam centre. Knight hauled his aircraft round and out of the valley. The seconds ticked past until the Upkeep detonated. As the plume began to rise from the surface, a great hole appeared in the dam wall itself, 'as if a giant hand had pushed a hole through cardboard' was Gibson's subsequent description. A solid jet of water spurted through the void, then the parapet crumbled into the widening breach, releasing a maelstrom that boiled and churned down the valley. At 0154 Hutchison sent the code 'DINGHY', signifying the attack's success. Every aircraft in Gibson's wave had released its Upkeep and now the sole objective of each of the captains who had witnessed the Eder's destruction was to return safely.

Chapter 18

Point of No Return

Here dead lie we because we did not choose
To live and shame the land from which we sprung.
Life, to be sure, is nothing much to lose;
But young men think it is, and we were young.
(A. E. Housman, 'Diffugere Nives', xxxvi)

Contrary to the belief of observers in the accompanying aircraft, the fate of Z-Zebra
and its crew was far from sealed at the Eder Dam. The aircraft had survived the
explosion, and the Lancaster would set course for Scampton, remaining airborne
for another fifty minutes until a cruel twist of fate brought its flight to an end. The
full details of this flight may never be known, but, by combining limited evidence
with the plans detailed at the briefing, it is possible to outline a scenario that may
account for this final period.

German evidence records that Henry's Upkeep struck the parapet above the
third main discharge sluice to the east of the centre of the dam. Although appearing to have caused no significant damage to the dam wall itself, the blast demolished some 150 feet of wall running along the crest. A number of masonry blocks
at the point of detonation were shattered, but most were broken apart at their joints,
shearing off at road level. The roadway itself was relatively undamaged. Debris
was hurled over the dam to fall on to the 60,000-volt power line running from the
Hemfurth 1 Powerhouse at the eastern foot of the dam, causing it to short out with
a tremendous blue flash.

Gibson's account initially maintains that the Upkeep detonated immediately
beneath Henry's aircraft. Shannon and his crew saw only the sudden flash, but
Knight's navigator and bomb aimer believed that the Lancaster was beyond the
explosion. Their view is supported by Gibson's next statement, witnessing that
the wireless operator had fired a red Very cartridge, thus signifying that the aircraft was crossing the dam having released its weapon. Assuming that the Lancaster
had been travelling at over 220 mph and the range of release was still in the region

of 450 yards, the aircraft should have been beyond the dam at the moment of impact. Even allowing for modification of these figures, the fact that the aircraft survived would suggest strongly that it was in fact beyond the explosion and travelling away from it. Nevertheless, the detonation of 6,600lb of Torpex a relatively short distance below and behind the Lancaster would certainly have been felt by the aircraft and its occupants. Without the tamping effect of the water, the full force of the blast would have radiated upwards and outwards in all directions from the centre of detonation. The dam parapet would have offered scant protection from the mass of rapidly expanding air.

Blast can be extremely capricious, and its effect upon the aircraft would depend on a number of factors. Eyewitnesses report that the aircraft was seen banking steeply in the aftermath of the explosion, possibly as a result of the blast, or more likely as Henry hauled it round to starboard to avoid the approaching hillside. If the aircraft were still flying straight and level, the rising air under the tail surfaces might be expected to cause a sudden nose-down pitch, whereas, if the Lancaster was already starting to bank and turn, the effect could be to accentuate the aircraft's attitude. Again, dependent upon the force of the blast, the aircraft may possibly have suffered structural damage. If so, the tail unit would be the most likely area to be affected and, by fateful coincidence, Henry may have found himself in a similar condition to that experienced in ED933 at Reculver only five days earlier. Damage to the elevators would hamper lateral control, adding to the hazards of low-level flight, while that to the rudders could cause difficulties in maintaining an accurate course, effectively increasing the time taken to clear enemy territory. The master gyro compass was also located towards the rear of the aircraft and may have suffered damage. In the rear turret, Sergeant Burrows would have been at the very least severely shaken, his night vision temporarily destroyed by the intensity of the flash. He may possibly have been injured by fragments of Perspex if his turret had yielded to the force of the blast. The engines, mainplanes (including fuel tanks) and front crew compartment are unlikely to have suffered damage, and there was no major fire on board. Possible damage incurred during the outward flight, as suggested by Gibson, might also have contributed to the aircraft's difficulties.

Apart from the very faint reply to Gibson's second request, R/T contact was lost immediately after Henry made his run. While this may have been the result of damage, it is more likely to have been caused by topographical factors. If Henry's route away from the vicinity of the dam took him down the valley, rather than an immediate steep climb over the adjacent hill, then the intervening spurs could have disrupted communication and may also have accounted for the poor reception of his response.

After a prompt survey of damage and a check on the state of his crew, Henry's overwhelming objective would have been to take his aircraft away from the Eder Valley and the path of any potential flood. Had the aircraft been badly damaged to the extent that it was unlikely to remain airborne for much longer, he would have been faced with two choices: either to climb to a height sufficient to allow the crew to abandon the aircraft, or (less likely given the local terrain) to seek a suitable stretch of ground on which to attempt a forced landing. However, there is nothing to suggest that either of these options was attempted, reconfirming the assumption that although possibly suffering some degree of damage, ED937 was still considered to be controllable and capable of remaining airborne for some time, if not for the entire flight back to base.

The briefed return route from the Eder followed the reciprocal of the inbound track until north of the Ruhr. From there individual aircraft were designated to follow one of three differing routes back to the coast in order to avoid running into flak positions that had been alerted earlier. The briefed route around the Ruhr was both the shortest and the safest; any aircraft flying south of this ran the risk of running into more intense defences, as was to happen to Pilot Officer Warner Ottley later that night.[464] There was no better option open to Henry, and it would seem logical that this was the route taken.

The operation order required aircraft to set course for base as soon as their attack was completed. On this basis Henry would have left the vicinity of the Eder by 0150. If he followed the briefed route, he would have followed a heading of 295 degrees True (302 degrees Magnetic). It was 45 miles back to the Mohne and at 0157, shortly before reaching the lake, Warrant Officer Cottam sent No. 5 Group Headquarters the coded Morse W/T message: 'Goner 28B', signifying: 'Weapon released. Overshot dam. No apparent breach.' This was three minutes after Gibson's wireless operator had sent the code confirming that the Eder Dam had been breached, but neither this anomaly nor the later signal received confirming Shannon's release seems to have been questioned by Group Headquarters. They were already too preoccupied with allocating targets to the third-wave aircraft. Additionally, they were ignorant of the fact that, as far as the other attacking aircraft were concerned, Henry and his crew had already perished.

With a reduced petrol load, without Upkeep and assisted by a slight following wind, the returning aircraft were able to increase their speed to 220 mph. If Henry adhered to his briefed return route, the distance flown during the last fifty minutes of his flight gives an average speed of only 183 mph. It has been suggested that this may have been caused through damage to the aircraft. Alternatively, Henry may have taken a longer route, either because of damage hampering directional control, or because he deliberately took himself further from the Ruhr defences while maintaining the higher speed. Either way, the Mohne would have been reached at about 0200. By this time the lake level had already dropped signifi- cantly and below the dam a new lake of expanding dimensions was forming. It was still also a potential danger area. Returning along the same route a short time later at 0208, Les Knight discovered one flak gun was still active and was forced to take evasive action as tracer curved towards him. A German police report records that at 0230 hours 'several aircraft' flying over the Mohne attacked flak positions, incendiary bullets from the second group setting fire to a farmer's barn at Gunne, on the side of the Mohne Valley below the dam. This presumably refers either to aircraft returning from the Eder or to Flight Sergeant Brown of the third wave en route to the Sorpe.

From the Mohne the planned route threaded back between Soest and Werl to Ahlen, a distance of 22 miles on a heading of 337 degrees True (344 degrees Mag- netic) before turning west on to 279 degrees True (307 degrees Magnetic) for the long leg of some 62 miles north of the Ruhr to the Rhine. This was the area that had presented the strongest opposition on the outbound route. Aircraft of the third wave passing outbound through this area shortly before 0230 en route to their targets were given a hot reception by small pockets of flak and searchlights. Henry may have deviated to the north here to skirt this area. Two of the alterna- tive return routes headed off before reaching the Rhine, but Henry had been briefed for Route 3, which, given the circumstances, seemed fortuitous, being the shortest track.

No. 5 Group tactical notes provided advice regarding defensive measures to be employed against light flak. Experience had shown that navigational difficulties were greatest on routes back from the target, when correct map-reading was even more essential. Accurate navigation, however, was difficult below 1,000 feet, while light flak was claimed to be most effective at heights between 250 feet and 2,500 feet. Above this height, in bright moonlight, nightfighters at higher levels were deemed to be a greater threat than the light flak lower down. Overall it was con- sidered that achieving accurate navigation was the most important, 'as it ensures that an aircraft does not fly over known defended areas'. On routes where there was no danger of straying from the planned track and light flak was anticipated, it was recommended that aircraft should keep as low as possible, otherwise it was advocated to fly at 2,000 feet. If fired upon, pilots were advised that variations of height or course were of little use as evasive action, since light flak was sighted visually without the use of a predictor. It was best to rely upon high speed to take them out of range. If flying below 2,000 feet on bright moonlit nights, air gunners should open fire on flak positions with the object of putting the gunners off their aim. Given the circumstances, it is likely that Henry would have sought to stay as low as possible, but his ability to do so may have been restricted by damage sustained by the aircraft. Unwittingly, this could have created a situation that conspired against him – low enough to hinder accurate navigation, but not low enough to defeat the flak.

Shortly before 0230 Z-Zebra was approaching the Rhine and searching for the turning point at Rees where the third briefed return route turned north to cross into Holland and pass by Harderwijk on the southern shore of the Zuider Zee. Whether Henry was on track and turned correctly, but then strayed slightly off course, or whether he was already north of track cannot be confirmed, but five minutes later he was heading directly towards Emmerich, 20 miles north-north-west of Rees and only a mile or so from the Dutch–German border. The small town had suffered only two significant attacks by the RAF since 1940, but its functions as a Rhine port and oil refinery centre, combined with its location on the approaches to the industrial Ruhr, gave it sufficient importance to be defended by several light *Heimat* [465] flak batteries. The locality had seen action only recently, when a Lancaster, coincidentally from No. 57 Squadron at Scampton, returning from an attack on Duisburg, had crashed in the early hours of 13 May, killing five members of the crew. [466]

Gun crews in the area had already been brought to readiness earlier as the Lancasters of No. 617 Squadron passed by on their outbound flight. Now, in the early hours of Monday morning, they were alert again for the opportunity to engage the enemy aircraft as they returned to base. Should any pass within range, they would be ready. The night was silent apart from the occasional sounds drifting across from the river port. Then gradually above this background an aircraft was heard approaching at low level from the south-east. The gunners trained their sights, peering into the night. Visibility was good, and the sky was marginally lighter in that direction. They should have been able to detect the silhouette of the machine in time to allow them to take accurate aim. The sound of engines grew louder and the dark shape of a four-engined bomber could be discerned. It was flying low and would come within the range of the 20 mm batteries to the south and east of the town. Theoretically each gun could fire 400 4-ounce rounds per minute along a low-angle elevation range of some 6,500 feet. Under operational conditions this reduced to some 120 rounds per minute with an effective range of 3,500 feet. Fired over open sights, using intermittent tracer to correct aim, the weapons were best suited against a target either approaching directly towards them or flying away from them. Flying at 220 mph, or 322 feet per second, such a target would be in range for approximately 20 seconds.

The battery in Der Ward was the first to open fire, soon to be joined by other triple 20-mm sites along the Nierenbergerstrasse and near the river port. The plane banked and turned away to the right in an attempt to evade the phalanx of shells that was curving towards it. As it did so, the rear gunner returned fire, with continuous streams of tracer directed at the battery near the river lock of the harbour area. The plane was now under accurate fire from about a dozen guns firing at maximum depression, their fire cutting through the tops of nearby poplar trees. At first the shells seemed to have no effect, but then suddenly there was a flash as either an engine or the fuel tank was hit, followed by a burst of flame. The aircraft continued for a short distance, heading in the direction of Klein Netterden, to the east of the town. Witnesses could see the fire was spreading rapidly, and the aircraft lost height, until it hit the ground in a ball of flames.

The aircraft had crashed at 0236, coming down in a flat field close to Osterholt, a short distance before the Dutch border, between Kleine Netterden and 's Heerenberg. Later that morning German officials came out to inspect the smouldering wreckage that lay in meadowland to the east of the Industria Brickworks alongside the Osterholtweg. The machine was identified as being a British Lancaster bomber. Searching through the debris, the authorities recovered the remains of the crew, all of whom must have been killed instantly as the aircraft hit the ground. After an attempt at identification, they were placed in coffins and taken for military burial in graves 35–41 of Section IIIc of the Nord Friedhof (Northern Military Cemetery) at Düsseldorf.[467]

Squadron Leader Henry Eric Maudslay 62275, DFC, RAF(VR)   Pilot
Sergeant John Marriott 1003474, RAF (VR)   Flight Engineer
Flying Officer Robert Alexander Urquhart J9763, RCAF   Navigator
Warrant Officer II Alden Preston Cottam R 93558, RCAF   Wireless Operator
Pilot Officer Michael John David Fuller 143760, RAF(VR)   Bomb Aimer
Flying Officer William John Tytherleigh 120851, RAF(VR)   Front Gunner
Sergeant Norman Rupert Burrows 1503094, RAF(VR)   Rear Gunner

Dinghy Young was also taking Route 3 home and, assuming he was making a speed of 220 mph, would have been close to Emmerich at the time Henry was shot down. Whether or not he witnessed the demise of his fellow flight commander will never be known. Young himself was to survive for only another twenty-two minutes. He too was brought down by flak at the very last moment as he crossed the Dutch Coast. ED887, AJ-A, crashed into the North Sea off Castricum at 0258. There were no survivors.[468]

Chapter 19

Missing

The attacks were pressed home from a very low level with great determination and coolness in the face of fierce resistance. Eight of the Lancasters are missing. (Air Ministry communiqué, 17 May 1943)

Of the returning aircraft that had flown to the Eder, Flight Lieutenant Shannon touched down at Scampton at 0406, Pilot Officer Knight at 0412, followed three minutes later by Wing Commander Gibson. There they found that Flight Lieutenant Martin and Flight Lieutenant Maltby, who had started back after the attack on the Mohne, had both returned safely. Flight Lieutenant Munro and Pilot Officer Rice were also back already, after their enforced abandonment of the operation, the former's aircraft having been damaged by flak, the latter flying too low and hitting the water of the Zuider Zee, tearing off his Upkeep. Flight Lieutenant McCarthy, the only member of his wave to reach the Sorpe Dam, had also returned to base. There were still eleven aircraft outstanding. The crews already knew for certain that three would not be coming back. Witnesses could confirm the loss of Flight Lieutenant Astell and Flight Lieutenant Hopgood and, as it was believed, Henry. There was initially less concern for the crews of the third wave, since they had departed only around midnight, but fears were growing for those detailed to attack the Sorpe, and for Squadron Leader Young, who had left the Eder at the same time as Gibson, Shannon and Knight. Three other aircraft had been seen by surviving crews to explode on the ground, but their identity could not be confirmed. It appeared that the operation had cost at least six aircraft.

By 0615 a further three Lancasters had returned, Flight Sergeants Anderson, Brown and Townsend, all from the mobile reserve. By now it was daylight, and any aircraft still in the air would stand little chance of survival over enemy territory. At debriefing Townsend and his crew, the most recent to land, gave a graphic account of how they had picked their way across Holland as dawn broke. The time passed, until none of the outstanding aircraft could have fuel enough to remain airborne. There was always the chance that some had diverted to other airfields, but this hope soon faded, and the surviving crews faced the grim reality that Townsend and his crew were perhaps the last of the survivors. Out of the nineteen aircraft that had left Scampton the previous night, eight would not return. Of the principal and two witnesses to the will of Flight Lieutenant Astell only four days earlier, all were missing.

The atmosphere was a strange mixture of elation and deep sorrow. The operation had succeeded in destroying two of the three main objectives. The third, the Sorpe Dam, attacked by only two aircraft, appeared to have been seriously damaged. Against this was the stark fact that in all probability fifty-six aircrew had died. Very few believed that anyone could have escaped from their doomed aircraft at such low level.[469] For Barnes Wallis, the losses were a tragedy for which he felt directly responsible. He was completely distraught at the news that so many of the young men whom he had faced the previous afternoon, and with whom he had shared a common objective, were now no longer alive.

As messages of congratulation arrived at Scampton, Wing Commander Gibson and Flight Lieutenant Harry Humphries, the squadron adjutant, sat down to the difficult task of despatching telegrams to next of kin.[470] By the afternoon of Monday, 17 May, the telegraph messenger had delivered to Mrs Maudslay the envelope that she had fervently hoped she would never receive. Its contents were brief and followed the standard format:

PRIORITY MRS S. G. MAUDSLAY FOX HILL BROADWAY

DEEPLY REGRET TO INFORM YOU THAT YOUR SON S/LDR H. E. MAUDSLAY IS MISSING AS A RESULT OF OPERATIONS ON NIGHT 16/17TH MAY 43 LETTER FOLLOWS PLEASE ACCEPT MY PROFOUND SYMPATHY — OC 617 SQUADRON.

Twelve miles away in Cheltenham, Rachel Studd had awoken after a troubled night's sleep. According it no significance, she went as usual to her work as a secretary for the US forces. The following day she received a telephone call from her mother to tell her that Henry had failed to return from a flight made two nights earlier. Recalling her disrupted sleep and reflecting on the nightmare, which had had no element of premonition, Rachel told herself that it could only have been mere coincidence rather than anything paranormal. Meanwhile, in the absence of further news, hope for his survival remained.

Over the next three days Gibson would send confirmatory letters to the relatives. Most were written according to the approved formula, but with the inclusion of an individual, personal paragraph from Gibson briefly outlining his personal knowledge of the individual. Most were probably dated 20 May. The text of the

letter written to Henry's mother does not appear to have survived, but its opening and final paragraphs would have been similar to those letters that do, so an
approximation of its structure may be attempted.[471]

Reference:–   No. 617 Squadron, RAF Station,
DO/ x / 43   Scampton, Lincs.

20 May 1943.

My Dear Mrs Maudslay

It is with great regret that I write to confirm my telegram advising you
that your son Squadron Leader H. E. Maudslay is missing as a result of
operations on the night of May 16/17th, 1943.

[Personal paragraph(s), probably stating Gibson's high opinion of Henry
as a captain and flight commander and also that the aircraft had been seen
to make an attack on the target.[472]]

It is possible that the crew were able to abandon the aircraft and land
safely in enemy territory, in which case news will reach you direct from the
International Red Cross Committee within the next six weeks.

Please accept my sincere sympathy during this anxious period of waiting.

I have arranged for your son's personal effects to be taken care of by the
Committee of Adjustment Officer at this Station, and these will be forwarded
to you through the normal channels in due course.

If there is any way in which I can help you, please let me know.

Yours *very sincerely*

(Signed) Guy Gibson

Wing Commander,
Commanding, 617 Squadron, RAF.

Mrs S.G. Maudslay
Fox Hill
Broadway, Worcs.

(The letters were typewritten, although the opening salutation, final close and
signature were in Gibson's own hand.)

Already the Committee of Adjustment was taking over, visiting the aircrew quarters and gathering up each man's personal belongings, making the statutory five copies of inventory and removing the items to a secure place. Within a few days a further letter was received, written on behalf of Group Captain Whitworth, Scampton's station commander, offering his 'deepest sympathy during this time of anxiety' and advising her:

> In order to ensure the safe keeping of your son's personal effects, they have been carefully checked and packed and are being despatched to:–
> The Central Repository
> RAF Colnbrook
> Slough, Bucks.
> where they will be held for some little time prior to their release by Air Ministry on completion of the necessary formalities. All further communications regarding the effects should now be addressed to the Central Repository.

The day following the operation, No. 5 Group Headquarters had sent a message to Group Captain Whitworth commenting: 'In the first Augsburg raid four of the crews out of the five shot down were uninjured.' Although this was intended to provide hope for the safety of those missing, Whitworth seems to have noted that the Augsburg raid had taken place in daylight when crews would have had a better chance to execute a successful forced landing. Not wishing to raise false hopes, he did not relay these sentiments in his letters to next of kin.

Within fourteen days any financial documents, such as bank books, savings and share certificates found among Henry's possessions, would have been forwarded to Air Ministry Accounts, Whittington Road, Worcester. RAF-issue clothing would have been returned to store. His flying logbook (which Henry had last completed at the end of April to obtain Gibson's monthly signature) was made up in respect of the month of May and signed off by Flight Lieutenant Martin, as the officer commanding 'B' Flight. It was then countersigned by Flight Lieutenant Maltby, now the new commander of 'A' Flight and acting squadron commander in the temporary absence of Wing Commander Gibson. The 'Remarks' column for 16 May read starkly: 'Operations – Eder dam – Missing'.

In completing these entries for May, presumably using details from the 'B' Flight Authorization Book, the compiler omitted Henry's flight of 4 May and did not enter a duration for the night of 16/17 May, thus attributing a total of 8.05 hours (day) and 10.35 (night) for the month of May. Allowing another 4 hours 37 minutes (night) for *Chastise* and another 30 minutes (night) for 4 May, Henry's total flying hours should have totalled 8.05 day and 15.42 night. His entire flying career had encompassed 910 hours 17 minutes. The logbook was then forwarded to the Air Ministry Repository at Hayes. As an official service document and technically still 'Restricted', it could not be returned to the family, at least for the duration of the war.[473]

On Tuesday, 27 May, the survivors were presented to Their Majesties King George VI and Queen Elizabeth, who paid a visit to Scampton as part of a tour of RAF stations. Recommendations for thirty-four decorations had already been submitted and approved, including the award of the Victoria Cross to Wing Commander Gibson for his 'inspiring leadership' of the operation. Recipients would meet the Queen again when they attended their investiture en masse at Buckingham Palace on 22 June. There was a certain grim irony the day following the royal visit to Scampton; while the *London Gazette* and the press were recording the awards for those who had returned, *Aeroplane* listed Henry's official promotion from flying officer to flight lieutenant (war substantive), with effect from February 1943.

With military efficiency, action was already being taken to bring the squadron back to operational strength. Replacement Lancasters were delivered to Scampton direct from Avro's, EE150 becoming the new Z-Zebra on 6 June after acceptance checks.[474] New crews began to arrive as early as 20 May, when, by coincidence, Flight Lieutenant Ralph Allsebrook, DSO, DFC, and his crew were posted in from No. 49 Squadron at Fiskerton. During the following summer months No. 617 Squadron would carry out only limited operations and Allsebrook would fly two 'shuttle' raids, landing at a North African base after attacking Italian targets. On the night of 15/16 September 1943, after an abortive attempt the previous night, he was captain of one of eight Lancasters despatched on a low-level attack against Dortmund–Ems Canal at Ladbergen, near Munster. His aircraft was one of five from the force that failed to return, crashing at Bergeshovede, near the target area. There were no survivors.

Meanwhile, the relatives of those who had failed to return from Operation *Chastise* could only wait and hope that the next day might bring some encouraging news. Henry was officially posted missing from No. 617 Squadron and transferred for administrative purposes (non-effective) to No. 1 RAF Depot, Uxbridge, with effect from 17 May 1943, pending further confirmation as to whether he had been killed, or survived as a prisoner. Communication with next of kin transferred to the Air Ministry Casualty Branch, based at 73–77 Oxford Street, London W1, where an army of clerical staff, under the auspices of the Director for Personal Services, coordinated all information regarding missing aircrew. On 30 May I. A. Smith of this branch wrote to Henry's mother, conveying the Air Council's great regret and offering the glimmer of hope that her son may have survived as a prisoner of war. The department assured her that they were conducting enquiries through the International Red Cross Committee and would inform her as soon as any news was received. In the meantime, should she hear any information from any source she was requested to inform the Air Ministry immediately.[475]

Three days later, having made enquiries with a Colonel Elwes at the War Office, Henry's uncle, General Norman Herbert, was put in contact with the Air Ministry Casualty Branch. He was anxious for news and asked whether he might be informed of any information that might emerge relating to any of his nephew's crew. He was assured that this would be done, but in the meantime all they could do would be to wait.

Replying to I. A. Smith's letter of 30 May, Mrs Maudslay wrote to the branch on 4 June:

> I shall very anxiously wait for news you may have of my son, or any of his crew, the names you no doubt have, but I will add them in this letter. I will let you know at once should any news reach me. Thanking the Air Council for their kind sympathy.

On 7 June AVM Cochrane submitted the official report of Operation *Chastise* to Bomber Command Headquarters. In its description of the attack on the Eder Dam it maintained that Shannon had attacked first, 'causing a breach about 9 feet wide on the eastern side of the dam'. Of Henry's attack:

> The second aircraft to attack, S/617 [sic] reported an overshoot by W/T. It is believed that this aircraft was damaged by its own Upkeep which hit the parapet and detonated instantaneously. He was subsequently heard in weak R/T communication with the Squadron Commander but was not heard again afterwards.[476]

Norman Herbert and Gwen Maudslay paid a personal visit to the Casualty Branch on 23 June, where they discussed the possibilities of Henry's fate with Wing Commander R. Burges. Although they had been told (most probably in Wing Commander Gibson's letter) that Henry's aircraft had been seen to leave the target, Wing Commander Burges felt obliged to tell them that the squadron's report had made no mention of this. This inexplicably maintained that nothing had been heard from the aircraft after take-off. Perhaps in an attempt to suggest a degree of normality, or seeking to maintain hope, he informed them that to date no definite news had been received of any of the crews missing from the operation.

Tita also visited the branch on 28 June and enquired on behalf of her mother 'whether there was any point or harm in writing to him as a supposed Prisoner of War'. She was advised it would be better not to do so. They should hear from him 'at once' if he had been captured. (The official view was that, had any of the crew survived and not been captured, such communication might compromise any attempt at evasion.)

Other members of the family were also expressing their concern to the official channels. On 1 June Henry's cousin, Diana Byrom, wrote to the Home Office from Woodleys, Woodstock, near Oxford, enquiring about Flying Officer (sic) Henry Maudslay, DFC, 'a relative of mine', whom she thought was stationed in North-amptonshire and was missing from the raid on the Mohne and Eida (sic) Dams in Germany: 'Naturally I am very worried and anxious to know if you had news. If so, could you please let me know immediately and what address if he is in a pris-oner of war camp.' Expressing the branch's 'deep sympathy with you in your anxiety', I. G. Shreeve replied on 14 June, regretting that no news had been heard since Henry was reported missing.

The first official public announcement that Henry and the other members of his crew were 'Missing' appeared in Air Ministry Casualty Communiqué No. 259, published in The Times, Wednesday, 21 July 1943, appearing subsequently in other titles, including Flight of 29 July and Aeroplane the following day. Under the head-line of 'Missing Airmen', the Daily Telegraph of 21 July carried an erroneous editorial comment to the list:

> Squadron Leader H. E. Maudslay is also reported missing. At Eton he was President of the Eton Society,[477] Captain of Boats, Captain of Athletics and won the mile three years in succession, the steeplechase twice running and also the half mile.
>
> His name is among 133 reported missing in an Air Ministry Casualty Communiqué issued today. It also states that 155 have lost their lives.

On Saturday, 29 July, under the headline 'Squadron Leader Maudslay missing', the Evesham Journal stated: 'Squadron Leader Henry Eric Maudslay DFC son of the late Mr R. W. Maudslay and Mrs Maudslay of Willersey was reported miss-ing after the raid on the German dams on the night of May 16. Squadron Leader Maudslay who is 21 joined the RAF straight from school (Eton) in 1940 and was awarded the Distinguished Flying Cross in the early part of last year.'

During the following days and weeks, the shock and sense of great loss spread around relations and friends. Numerous inhabitants from the villages around Fox Hill expressed their sorrow and sent condolences either in person, or by letter.

Outside the immediate family circle, three who must have been deeply saddened by the news were his Eton mentors: Claude Elliott, John Hills and John Herbert. On Sunday, 1 August, Vera Brittain, the active pacifist and supporter of the Peace Pledge Union, paid a visit to Eton to discuss the possibility of her son John attending the school.[478] During her visit she met John Herbert. News of the recent concentrated RAF and US 8th Air Force joint offensive against Hamburg had been reported in the day's edition of the *Sunday Express*. The article's morale-building speculation regaling the tremendous destruction and appalling death toll in the city prompted her to write in her diary: 'I hope they include Sir Arthur Harris among the war criminals.' One can only speculate the tension, or possibly sympathy, that existed between the pacifist and the schoolmaster during their meeting.[479]

Meanwhile, the wait for news continued. During the second week of August a telegram from the International Red Cross Committee provided Air Ministry Casualty Branch with their first indication of the fate of Henry and his crew. Quoting from German sources, it referred to a Lancaster that had crashed on 17 May with seven dead, identified as Sergeant Marriott, Sergeant Cottam and five unknown. These were assumed to be Squadron Leader Maudslay, Flying Officer Urquhart, Pilot Officer Fuller, Flying Officer Tytherleigh and Sergeant Burrows, the remaining members of the crew.[480]

On 11 August I. G. Shreeve of Casualty Branch despatched an 'immediate' priority telegram to Mrs Maudslay:

DEEPLY REGRET TO ADVISE YOU THAT ACCORDING TO INFORMATION
RECEIVED THROUGH THE INTERNATIONAL RED CROSS COMMITTEE YOUR SON
S/LDR HENRY ERIC MAUDSLAY DFC AND THE REST OF HIS CREW ARE BELIEVED
TO HAVE LOST THEIR LIVES AS A RESULT OF AIR OPERATIONS ON THE NIGHT
OF 16/17 MAY 1943. THE AIR COUNCIL EXPRESS THEIR PROFOUND SYMPATHY.
LETTER CONFIRMING THIS TELEGRAM FOLLOWS. PRESUME YOU WILL INFORM
HIS SISTER AND GENERAL W. N. HERBERT.[481]

Norman Herbert paid another visit to the branch's Oxford Street offices on 16 August to see Wing Commander Burges. He was shown the Red Cross telegram and the 'missing, believed killed' assumption was explained. He also saw a draft of the confirmatory letter that was to be sent to his sister the following day:

I am commanded by the Air Council with great regret to confirm the telegram in which you were notified that in view of information received through the International Red Cross Committee your son, Squadron Leader Henry Eric Maudslay DFC Royal Air Force is believed to have lost his life as a result of air operations on the night of 16 May 1943.

The Committee's telegram, quoting official German information states that the seven occupants of the aircraft in which your son was flying on that night were killed on 17 May. It contains no specific information regarding the place of their burial or any other details.

Although there is unhappily little reason to doubt the accuracy of this report, the casualty will be recorded as 'missing, believed killed' until confirmed by further evidence, or until, in the absence of such evidence it becomes necessary, owing to the lapse of time, to presume for official purposes that death has occurred. In the absence of confirmatory evidence death would not be presumed until at least six months from the date when your son was reported missing.

The Air Council desire me to express their deep sympathy with you in your great anxiety.

I am, Madam, your obedient servant,
(signed) Charles Evans.

With virtually all hope extinguished that Henry night have survived, Gwen Maudslay issued a notice to be published in *The Times* on Saturday, 21 August 1943, in the 'Deaths' column under the heading 'ON ACTIVE SERVICE':

MAUDSLAY – Killed in Action May 1943 in Ruhr Dam operations. Squadron Leader HENRY ERIC MAUDSLAY, younger son of the late R. W. Maudslay and Mrs Maudslay, Fox Hill, Broadway, Worcestershire, aged 21 years.

The *Evesham Journal* echoed the entry on 28 August under the heading 'Squadron Leader Maudslay killed. Rhur [*sic*] dam operations', which essentially repeated the details published a month earlier in *The Times*.

Ralph Allsebrook read *The Times* notice at Scampton, prompting him to write immediately:

Dear Mrs Maudslay.

I have seen the Times today and know that you have heard the German report. I myself had heard it three days before, and was told that you would have been informed at once, and so I did not write then.

This is just the briefest of letters – and I will be honoured if you will do me the compliment of not answering – to tell you that my hopes and prayers which were for you and for Henry are now for you, to bear this terrible news. I know that nothing can be said that is of any use, but perhaps I may tell you that often I feel – and I think Henry felt – a fear of death only so far as it will bring such sadness and despair to one's parents. Against it we can do nothing, but one fears for those you love more than for oneself.

You can perhaps help yourself a little for the time in the immediate empty future by knowing how he or I or anyone hopes and prays that you will find strength to bear the sorrow.[482]

I will write again, I hope, in a month or so, when it is possible I may have leave.

With less than a month of his own life remaining, fate decreed that Ralph Allsebrook's closing intention would remain unfulfilled.

Further letters of sympathy and support arrived at Fox Hill. On Thursday, 9 September, the Revd Arthur Fletcher, Rector of Willersey and Saintbury, wrote to Mrs Maudslay from Willersey Vicarage, enclosing a cutting from the previous day's *Manchester Guardian*. The clipping reported a lunchtime address at Christ Church, Down Street, London, by Air Chief Marshal Lord Hugh Dowding, an active spiritualist supporter. After reading a letter from a dead seaman, dictated through a medium, Dowding affirmed that he had a great many such communications from those killed during the war: 'The tone of these messages is: "Don't grieve for us. We are the lucky ones. We have never been so happy as we are now."' In his accompanying letter Revd Fletcher suggested that the cutting might be of interest, citing as it did the beliefs of a senior Air Force officer. Admitting that he too was a firm believer in an existence beyond death he wrote: 'I believe that Henry is very happy, rather as Auberon Herbert was happy in the poem of Maurice Baring's I am sending you. The comfort of these words is in the deep truth of them. I trust you may find it.'[483] Enclosed was a copy of 'In Memoriam, A.H.', written in memory of Captain Auberon Herbert, 8th Baron Lucas of Crudwell, RFC, killed in combat over the Western Front on 3 November 1916.[484] The poem records the uncertainty and sense of loss experienced by relatives awaiting confirmation of the fate of those they loved:

That night I dreamt they sent for me and said
That you were missing, 'missing, missing – dead':
I cried when in the morning I awoke,
And all the world seemed shrouded in a cloak;
But when I saw the sun,
And knew another day had just begun,
I brushed the dream away, and quite forgot

The nightmare's ugly blot.
So was the dream forgot. The dream came true.
Before the night I knew
That you had flown away into the air
Forever. Then I cheated my despair,
I said
That you were safe – or wounded – but not dead.
Alas I knew
Which was the false and true.

And after days of watching, days of lead,
There came the certain news that you were dead
You had died fighting against the odds,
Such as in war the gods
Æthereal dared when all the world was young;
Such fighting as blind Homer never sung,
Nor Hector nor Achilles never knew;
High in the empty blue.

High, high above the clouds, against the setting sun,
The fight was fought, and your great task was done. . .

This is in contrast to the heavenly reunion of the warrior with his comrades and
others who had sacrificed their lives for a just and righteous cause:

In that high place;
You met there face to face
Those you had never known, but whom you knew;
Knights of the Table Round,
All the very brave, the very true,
With chivalry crowned;
The captains rare,
Courteous and brave beyond our human air;
Those who had loved and suffered overmuch,
Now free from the world's touch.
And with them were the friends of yesterday, who went before and pointed
    you the way;
And in that place of freshness, light and rest,
Where Lancelot and Tristram vigil keep

Over their King's long sleep,
Surely they made a place for you,
Their long expected guest,
Among the chosen few,
And welcomed you, their brother and their friend,
To that companionship which hath no end.

The Times of Tuesday, 21 September 1943, carried a personal tribute by Henry's former housemaster, John Hills, which was reprinted in the *Evesham Journal* three days later:

  J. D. H. writes:

Henry Maudslay compelled life to give him the best things in her store. He had neither the robust strength of the oarsman nor the swinging grace of the athlete; but at 18 he was Captain of Boats at Eton and had won school mile for three times in succession. He was denied the reckless daring of the born fighting man and was in fact so sensitive as at times to seem nervous; but at 21 he was a squadron leader in Bomber Command, captain of a Lancaster, and picked for one of the toughest exploits yet undertaken by the RAF. He and his crew were all killed on that great dam-busting expedition.

  Many will recall his triumphs on the river or the running track; his victory in school pulling or that marvellously judged mile against the Achilles Club in the spring of 1939; but no one ever heard him talk of these things. Each new success made him more and more modest. And when last year he visited his beloved Eton soon after winning his DFC, he wore his overcoat throughout a hot day to hide the medal ribbon. His unselfishness and self-effacement were almost embarrassing. But there was no false modesty. On mechanical subjects of which he had an inherited mastery, on details of training for a race or for an expedition which he had mastered for himself, he spoke with a certainty that admitted no argument.

  He was so clearly master of himself that could easily master others. This made him a great leader. He combined as so few men do, a love for his fellow-men with a love for his machines. On leave he would talk with enthusiasm of his Hampden or Lancaster and of the various members of his crew; once or twice he spoke of navigational difficulties over Germany. But I never heard mention of his own exploits, and he certainly never gloried in the destruction wrought by his bombs. He had, too, a way of making friends feel that their affairs were much more important than his own. He was always the same, at his mother's lovely home in the Cotswolds, with a crowd of

Eton friends, or walking over the country with a single companion, courteous, cheerful, loyal, sincere. With his many friends and admirers, old and young alike, his memory will never die. It will be an ever fresh inspiration to aim at the highest and best in life.

The *Eton Chronicle* carried its tribute on Thursday, 30 September. On the front page, under the heading '*Etona non immemor*' were the names of nineteen more Old Etonians who had given their lives for their country. The list also recorded 21-year-old Second Lieutenant Roger Peek, 1st Royal Dragoons, RAC, a contemporary of Henry in Mr Hills's House and another keen athlete.[485]

Meanwhile, seeking positive action helping to alleviate the stress of bereavement, members of the family and those mourning Henry's death addressed themselves to necessary administrative tasks.

On 7 September, Messrs Ellis, Peirs & Co. wrote to the Secretary of State for Air on behalf of the executors of Henry's will, stating that no steps could be taken to prove the document until a certification of death had been issued and requesting clarification of the position. With uncharacteristic delay an acknowledgement would not be received until 4 October. They were advised of the date and place of burial of Henry's presumed remains and that 'action is now being taken to presume for official purposes the death of this officer and upon completion a certified notification of death will be forwarded to you'.

General Herbert paid a further visit to Casualty Branch on 9 September, to enquire about the early return of Henry's personal effects. Sympathetic to his request, Wing Commander Burges authorized their immediate release. By half past five that afternoon a signal had been sent to the officer commanding the RAF Repository at Colnbrook confirming an earlier telephone instruction that the items should be packed and sent immediately by passenger train to Mrs Maudslay at Fox Hill.

Further confirmation came in a letter from I. G. Shreeve of the Casualty Branch, dated 30 September. This referred to a report received from the International Red Cross Committee detailing the grave locations of Sergeants Marriott and Cottam and the remaining five crew interred on 19 May. Expressing 'bitter regret' that it was not possible to state which was Henry's grave, it nevertheless recorded that, since 'the correct number of crew had been given there can be no doubt that he [Henry] is one of the (at present) unidentified airmen'.[486]

Referring to this letter the branch was again in contact with Mrs Maudslay on 13 November. D. Bent, writing on behalf of the Director of Personal Services, confirmed: 'I am directed to inform you that action has now been taken to presume for official purposes that your son, Squadron Leader H. E. Maudslay

DFC lost his life on 17 May 1943.'

Four days later Messrs Ellis, Peirs & Co. received the formal certified notification of Henry's death, acceptable to the Principal Probate Registry:

NOTIFICATION OF DEATH

Certified that according to the records of this department

No.   62275
Rank: Squadron Leader
Name: Henry Eric Maudslay DFC
Service: Royal Air Force Volunteer Reserve

was reported missing and is presumed for official purposes to have lost his life on the seventeenth day of May 1943 as a result of air operations. Information received through the International Red Cross Committee states that this officer is buried in Section IIIc of the North Military Cemetery, Düsseldorf, Germany.

(Signed) A.P. Le M Simpkinson
for Director of Personal Services.

Dated at the Air Ministry London this 17th day of November 1943.

In accordance with official procedure, it was exactly six months since Henry and his crew had failed to return.

Chapter 20

In Memoriam

Others will fill our places,
Dressed in the old light blue;
We'll recollect our races,
We'll to the flag be true;
And youth will be still in our faces
When we cheer for an Eton crew.
(William Cory, 'The Eton Boating Song')

Official confirmation of Henry's death permitted the final process of mourning and readjustment to begin. With no funeral on which to focus grief, the reading of Henry's will and the settlement of his estate served as the final act. A Grant of Probate was issued on Monday, 6 March 1944, when the Principal Probate Registry in Llandudno[487] assessed Henry's estate at £21,536 15s 8d (£21,536.79). The executors were named as Henry's mother and Eric John Wykeham Ellis, the family solicitor, of Messrs Ellis, Peirs & Co. (Solicitors), 17 Albemarle Street, London W1.[488]

Henry left all his personal effects to his mother, with a request that she dispose of them as she thought fit. When drafting his will in July 1941, Henry had sought to ensure that his childhood governess, Kelly, would be provided for in her advancing years. In addition to receiving an outright sum of £100, she was also to receive an annuity of £52 for the remainder of her life, payable each quarter. This was to be made available from an annuity fund, in the form of either investments or an insurance policy that his trustees were to establish. In the short time between Kelly's death and his own fate, Henry had not amended his will, with the result that such funds as would have been used for this purpose were retained as part of his residuary estate for division among the other named beneficiaries.

Four-fifths of this estate were divided between Tita and John. They were not to receive lump-sum payments, but the amounts were to be held in trust and invested to provide an annual income, which would pass on to any of their surviving children upon their death. The remaining fifth was also to be held in trust for cousin Joanna until she came of age, or married, whichever was the sooner. Echoing his father's will, Henry left detailed instructions as to acceptable modes of investment for these trusts. Stocks or securities of the British government, or local government, either at home, or in the Dominions, including India, were permissible, as was debenture stock of limited companies. Alternatively, investment could be made in property, either freehold or leasehold, although the latter must have at least sixty years' unexpired lease.

Formal public acknowledgement of Henry's death appeared in Air Ministry Casualty Communiqué No. 355[489] published in *Flight* dated 9 March 1944, recording officially that Squadron Leader H. E. Maudslay, DFC, 'Previously reported Missing' was now 'Presumed Killed in Action'.

Accordingly Henry's official service record would be inscribed with the following, in accordance with a recommendation made by Air Marshal Harris on 29 June 1943: 'On the night of May 16/17 1943 this officer took part in the extremely hazardous and highly successful raid on the Mohne, Eder, Sorpe and Schwelme [*sic*] dams, from which operation he failed to return.'[490]

Mrs Maudslay was discussing how her son's sacrifice might be remembered on the anniversary of his death. On 1 May General Herbert phoned the WAAF receptionist at Casualty Branch on his sister's behalf to request details of the names of Henry's crew, their rank and positions in the aircraft, explaining that Mrs Maudslay was having a memorial erected and required the information for the inscription. The request was passed to Flight Lieutenant Willishaw, who replied the following day enclosing the relevant details. Acknowledging their receipt, Mrs Maudslay stated her intention to place a notice in *The Times* and hoped that she would be permitted to include the names of her son's crew.

The notice was one of two commemorating the squadron's flight commanders appearing among the Roll of Honour entries on Wednesday, 17 May 1944:

MAUDSLAY – In memory of SQUADRON LEADER HENRY ERIC MAUDSLAY DFC RAFVR and his gallant crew FLYING OFFICER W. J. TYTHERLEIGH, FLYING OFFICER R. A. URQUHART, PILOT OFFICER M. J. D. FULLER, SERGEANT N. R. BURROWS, SERGEANT A. P. COTTAM, SERGEANT J. MARRIOT who died gloriously in the historic breaching of the Ruhr Dams, May 17, 1943.

YOUNG – In memory of SQUADRON LEADER HENRY MELVIN YOUNG DFC and all the gallant crew of his Lancaster bomber who lost their lives off the Dutch coast when returning from the raid on the German Dams on the night of May 16–17 1943.

Consideration continued as to a suitable permanent memorial. With no grave or headstone in England, Mrs Maudslay felt that a commemorative tablet in a suitable location would be appropriate and commissioned Gilbert Ledward, RA, the sculptor who had created her late husband's headstone, to produce a design that centred on an inscription:

To the glorious memory of Henry Eric Maudslay DFC, Squadron Leader RAFVR. Killed in the attack on the Mohne Dam 16/17 May 1943, aged 21 years.[491]

This was surmounted by the Royal Air Force crest and supplanted by a motif depicting the sun rising over water, symbolizing the hope of resurrection and eternal life. In each quadrant were representations of the constellations of the Great Bear, Little Bear, Pole Star, Cassiopeia and part of Leo, portrayed in their relative positions as seen in the July sky, at the time of Henry's birth. A wreath of laurel leaves encompassed the design, Ledward going to Kew Gardens to make studies of the plants from life.

Cast by the Morris Singer Bronze Foundry, Dorset Road, South Lambeth, SW8, in May 1944, the 2-foot-diameter plaque was placed originally on his father's grave in Sherbourne. Exposed to the elements, it began to discolour, much to Mrs Maudslay's concern. After cleaning, the patina was restored, the surface was sealed with lacquer and the bronze was remounted inside All Saints church, on the north wall of the nave near the organ.

Responding to an announcement in the national press, Mrs Maudslay wrote to the Ministry of Pensions applying for a memorial scroll to commemorate Henry's service. The department's bureaucratic response caused her to write to the Secretary of State for Air on 19 August 1947, submitting that she considered their wording to be '*most* unfortunate'. She accepted that there might be some delay in receiving the scroll, but insisted that it must, however, be on record that he had been killed in action and that as his mother she was next of kin. There should be no need for her claim to have to be 'very carefully considered'. She felt that many other next of kin would experience similar feelings about this standard 'form' letter and hoped that her concern would be brought to the attention of the Ministry of Pensions.

The scroll was duly despatched. Surmounted by the royal crest, flanked by the cipher 'G VI RI', it formally recorded her son's sacrifice:

This scroll commemorates
Squadron Leader H. E. Maudslay DFC
Royal Air Force

held in honour as one who
served King and Country
in the World War of 1939–45
and gave his life to save
mankind from tyranny. May
his sacrifice help bring
the peace and freedom for
which he died.

At Beaudesert, Henry's old prep school, a memorial was commissioned to recall old boys who had given their lives in the service of their country. On the after-noon of 3 February 1947 Canon Sidney Bush, Rector of Amberley, conducted a service, including an address by the Right Revd Clifford Woodward, Lord Bishop of Gloucester, in the school gymnasium. He then led those assembled to the front hall, where the school's founder and former headmaster, Arthur Richardson, unveiled the two wooden panels outside the 'Big Room', revealing the thirty-four names, including those of his son Colin,[492] and Henry Maudslay.

A short distance away in the Cotswolds, Henry's memory was also to remain fresh in the minds of his family and neighbours. On 29 July 1947, the day after what would have been his 26th birthday, Mrs Maudslay donated to the Royal Air Force Benevolent Fund the sum of £14 3s 0d (£14.15), which had been collected in memory of her son by members of the village of Willersey. Henry's name was added to the village's war memorial built on top of the wall to the right of the entrance to St Peter's churchyard. Two faces of the base recorded eleven sons of Willersey who had died in the earlier conflict. On the third side was inscribed:

TO THE MEMORY OF THE
MEN OF WILLERSEY WHO
GAVE THEIR LIVES IN THE
SECOND WORLD WAR
1939–45
EDWARD LOUIS FOLKES
ANTHONY KAYLL
HENRY MAUDSLAY
EDGAR WILLIAM PROCTOR

Inside the church a further brass plaque on the north wall of the chancel hon-oured their sacrifice:

IN MEMORY OF THOSE WHO

LOST THEIR LIVES IN THE WAR

1939–1945

EDWARD LOUIS FOLKES

ANTHONY KAYLL

HENRY MAUDSLAY

EDGAR WILLIAM PROCTOR[493]

Some nine months earlier, towards the end of 1946, the Dean and Chapter of Lincoln Cathedral had been approached by Air Vice-Marshal R. S. Blucke, CBE, DSO, requesting that the Memorial Books of Nos 1 and 5 Groups Bomber Command might be deposited in the cathedral. This had stimulated activity by the Friends of the Cathedral to make available a £500 grant towards the refurbishing of three chapels in the North Transept associated with the Armed Forces. The first work to be undertaken was to the Airmen's Chapel of St Michael, which had been rededicated in 1923. Contributions came from the Cathedral Friends, combined with other donations from RAF associations, RAF stations, ex-aircrew, WAAFs and relatives of those who had given their lives. Open-work white bronze metal grilles were installed, carrying the badge of the two Bomber Groups and on the walls were mounted the crests of the RAF, Bomber and Fighter Commands, together with the heraldic shield of the RAF College, Cranwell.

A number of special gifts were made by individuals, including altar cloths and candelabra. Mrs Maudslay and Tita decided that the chapel would be a fitting location for a further tribute to Henry and his comrades. With the approval of the Dean and Chapter, they commissioned a set of silver ornaments for the altar from George Hart of Campden, comprising a cross and two short candlesticks. In the enamelled centre boss of the cross a halo-surmounted lamb carries the flag of St George, each arm of the cross having panels depicting a new moon in a dark blue starlight sky. They were engraved with the simple inscription: 'In memory of Squadron Leader Henry Eric Maudslay, DFC, and his gallant crew.'

Two Memorial Books, each bound in Morocco leather of Air Force blue with the badge of the RAF in silver-gilt on a sunken panel, were produced by Messrs Waterlow. These contain the names of 25,611 personnel killed flying from airfields in or near Lincolnshire during the Second World War, including those of Henry and his crew.

With work on the refurbishment completed, the books and the furnishings were dedicated by the Bishop of Lincoln, the Right Revd Maurice Harland, himself an observer in the RFC and RAF during the First World War, in a service held on 8 November 1949. The bishop met Air Marshal Sir Aubrey Ellwood, AOC.-in-C.

Bomber Command at the cathedral's west door and together they processed down the nave, through the 3,500 members of the congregation, accompanied by Wing Commander K. P. Smales, DSO, DFC, and Wing Commander R. D. Stubbs, DSO, DFC, former commanding officers of Nos 44 and 49 Squadrons respectively, bearing the Memorial Books. In his sermon the bishop pronounced: 'It is right and proper that the names of these gallant men should be recorded and the books containing their names be deposited in this glorious cathedral church over which they flew and which was their last and loveliest sight of England.'

The books were then taken to the Airmen's Chapel and handed over to the sub-dean, Canon Arthur Cook. After the dedication, 'Regard their loyalty and devotion, forgive their frailties and sins . . .', trumpeters of the Central Band of the RAF sounded the Call of the RAF, the Last Post and reveille as the chapel's small congregation, including aircrew aggregating nearly 500 operations, stood silently to attention.

(Henry's name was also recorded in one of the Books of Remembrance listing over 125,000 RAF personnel who gave their lives, placed around the walls of the nave of the historic Wren church of St Clement Danes. Situated in the middle of London's Strand, the church had been destroyed by bombing in May 1941, but was restored and rededicated as the church of the Royal Air Force in October 1958.)

At Eton College Old Etonians who had fallen in the First World War had been commemorated on bronze panels mounted in the colonnade beneath Upper School, which had been damaged by bombing in 1940. On 27 May 1943, ten days after Henry's death, it had been mooted by Viscount Cranbourne that, when the time came to restore Upper School, the names of those killed in the current conflict should be incorporated on an adjoining set of panels. An initial meeting to set up the Eton War Memorial Fund was held at Barings Bank on 4 June 1943, although it was acknowledged that little could be finalized until the cessation of hostilities. In 1946 a committee was formed under the chairmanship of the Hon. Sir Jasper Ridley to raise and administer funds. By 1948 it was recorded that most of the contributions to the War Memorial Fund had been allocated as bursaries and a new appeal was made in the *Eton Chronicle* on 17 June.

The loss of so many of their contemporaries had a profound effect on many of those Eton pupils from the immediate pre-war era who were fortunate to survive. Michael Bentine, the unconventional genius whose unique gifts were to contribute much to the surreal humour of the 1960s, reflected:

How can you have a sentimental attachment to a school where you are probably one of eight survivors of all the boys you knew? Your mind automatically blanks off because you think to yourself, 'Oh Jesus, how I wish they were around.' Because they were very, very nice blokes. So many of my year were killed, who left around 1938, we had about 70–80% dead, never mind gravely injured or missing. I lost good friends like Henry Maudsley [*sic*] who was killed on the Sorpe [*sic*] and every two or three months you would hear of another friend gone. The chaps I knew were very positive people with fine minds and extraordinarily outgoing personalities who could have done so much for the world, and they were just massacred, totally massacred. I suddenly see in my mind this boy and think: 'Gee, wouldn't it have been marvellous if they had survived, what good they would have done in the world; they would have been great doctors, great engineers and great scientists.' I feel very sad when I think of Eton.[494]

A more fatalistic view was held by actor Patrick Macnee, a near contemporary of Henry in the ECOTC, who served as navigation officer aboard Motor Torpedo Boat MTB 434. He himself had narrowly evaded the hand of destiny by being confined to a hospital bed with bronchitis the night his boat was lost attacking a German convoy off Cap d'Antifer in the summer of 1944:

When I think back to my Eton days, I think about how many Etonians were killed – much more than anything else. We were all trained for that. We went blazing into battle with complete sense of folly and bravery, and very little intelligence, because we were trained to do that. That's why we're all such good officers. . . . A lot of the people I knew are dead – most of them are dead, in fact. A lot of them were killed in the war almost immediately afterwards. At least 15 members of my house (Mr Sladden's) were killed within two years of the beginning of the war in action of some form or another. I always get the feeling that we were being trained in the OTC for a war, and in fact, I left just two months before war was declared.[495]

Reconstruction work was begun on Upper School and the memorial panels in early 1949 by Messrs Bowyer of Slough, under the supervision of William Holford, MA, FRIBA, MTPI, Chartered Architect and Planning Consultant. At a cost of £6,582, the new panels were cast in statuary bronze by Messrs Adrian Stokes Ltd and erected by Messrs Seely and Paget. Alongside a quote from Milton's 'Samson Agonistes', 'Nothing is here for tears', they recorded the names of the 748 old boys killed during 1939–45. In addition to that of Henry Maudslay, the lists contain the names of two other Old Etonians who were killed flying on later operations with No. 617 Squadron.[496]

With the re-establishment of peace across Europe, the RAF Missing Research and Enquiry Units set about their sorrowful task of accounting for the British and Commonwealth dead, ensuring that they were laid to rest in marked graves in consecrated ground. Those who had fallen liberating German-occupied territory would generally remain in local churchyards and cemeteries, where they had been buried, remembered and cared for by those whose freedom they had gained. Perhaps believing that it was unrealistic to expect such consideration from the newly defeated former enemy, the British and Commonwealth governments had decided that those buried within the German borders would be exhumed from isolated cemeteries throughout Germany. They would be concentrated and reinterred in newly created regional military war cemeteries, selected for their natural beauty and peace of their surroundings, 'the soil of which would forever be British' and which would be tended in perpetuity by the Imperial War Graves Commission.[497]

One such regional cemetery was the Reichswald Forest British Military Cemetery situated three miles to the south-west of the German town of Kleve, some $2^{1}/_{2}$ miles from the Dutch–German border, 9 miles from Emmerich, and coincidentally close to the track taken by the aircrews on their flight to the dams. The skies and fields of this area had borne witness to the six years of conflict. In local cemeteries throughout the region lay the bodies of aircrew, many killed during the costly Battle of the Ruhr, together with members of the 6th British Airborne Division who had fallen taking part in the final spring offensive to cross the Rhine and carry the fight into the heart of Germany.[498] With due reverence, these would be exhumed during 1947–48, reidentified and brought to their final resting place – 3,985 airmen being laid to rest to the left of the entrance, 3,647 Army personnel to the right.[499]

On 16 April 1948 G. M. Haslam of the Casualty Branch wrote to Fox Hill notifying Mrs Maudslay of the removal of her son's grave from Düsseldorf to Reichswald and confirming that his crew were interred nearby. The letter explained that this reburial was in accordance with agreed policy and stated that a photograph of the grave would be sent to her, 'although this may not be for some considerable time'. The War Graves Commission would consult her regarding the inscription to be placed on the headstone that would be erected. The letter was forwarded to Gwen Maudslay, who was staying at Shinness. In her reply of 20 April she noted:

> In the letter I had from the Air Ministry at the time my son was killed I was told that only one [sic] of the crew had been identified and that was not my son. Has it been possible since then to identify him and all his crew? I shall be most grateful for anything you can tell me.

Three days later a reply was received confirming:

> When the graves of your son's crew were exhumed from Düsseldorf Cemetery
> to the Reichswald Forest Cemetery your son was identified by the name on
> his tunic.[500]

> Sergeant Marriott, Sergeant Cottam and Sergeant Burrows were also identified
> individually, but the remaining members, Flying Officer Tytherleigh, Flying
> Officer Urquhart and Pilot Officer Fuller, could not be identified and their
> graves are registered collectively.

Expressing her appreciation, Gwen Maudslay replied on 25 April:

> I am most grateful to you for all you have told me and trust that some day
> I can visit the cemetery where my son's remains and those of his crew are
> laid. What a [sic] wonderful work you are doing.

In total, the bodies of sixty-one members of No. 617 Squadron killed during operations against the dams in May 1943, the Dortmund–Ems Canal in September
1943, or while serving later with other squadrons, were brought to Reichswald.
Air Ministry Casualty Records dated 28 October 1948 noted that the crew of
Z-Zebra had been laid to rest in Plot 5. The grave locations indicate they were not
as a complete crew side by side, but split between two adjacent rows:

Squadron Leader H. E. Maudslay, DFC	Row C, Grave 3
Sergeant J. Marriott, DFM	Row C, Grave 4
Flying Officer R. A. Urquhart, DFC, RCAF	Row B, Collective Graves 16–18
Warrant Officer A. P. Cottam, RCAF	Row C, Grave 1
Pilot Officer M. J. D. Fuller	Row B, Collective Graves 16–18
Flying Officer W. J. Tytherleigh, DFC	Row B, Collective Graves 16–18[501]
Sergeant N. R. Burrows	Row C, Grave 2

Reichswald also became the final resting place for two of Henry's closest comrades
in arms. Flight Lieutenant Ralph Allsebrook, DSO, DFC, and Flight Lieutenant Bill
Astell, DFC, were interred alongside their crews in Plots 24 and 21 respectively.[502]

During the summer of 1949 Mrs Maudslay moved to Barn House, Broadway. On
19 September of that year Fox Hill Estate, now totalling some 41½ acres, was sold
for £12,200 – the exact sum of the amounts she had paid for the original estate,

plus the additional land on Little Hill.[503]

On 10 October she received a letter on behalf of the Under Secretary of State for Air enclosing photographs of the temporary marker for Henry's new grave erected by the Army Graves Service at Reichswald. Until a permanent headstone could be erected by the Imperial War Graves Commission, the grave would be marked with a plain white pressed metal cross bearing the simple black-painted words '62275 S/LDR H. E. MAUDSLAY (DFC)' on the cross bar, with 'RAF 17.5.43' on the upright beneath.

With the burials completed, the landscaping began. Wide avenues of manicured lawn converged on the Stone of Remembrance, a simple block designed by Sir Edwin Lutyens bearing the words from the Book of Ecclesiasticus: 'Their name liveth for evermore.' At the end of the south-east avenue Sir Reginald Blomfield's white stone Cross of Sacrifice, with its bronze sword. was positioned to contrast against the dark forest background. Near to the cemetery entrance two shelters were constructed, with steps to the upper floors permitting extensive views of the cemetery. On piers at each entrance were set Portland stone carvings of a lion and unicorn by Gilbert Ledward, providing an unwitting link between Sherbourne and Henry's final resting place.

Headstones conforming to the standard War Graves Commission pattern in Portland stone replaced the original crosses marking the graves. Beneath a carved badge of the relevant Allied Air Force (RAF, RAAF, RCAF, RNZAF, etc.) an inscription recorded name, rank, number, crew position and date of death. If they so desired, relatives were permitted to select a short personal epitaph, which would be carved at the base of the stone. Four of Henry's crew would be so remembered by their families. Flying Officer Tytherleigh's parents requested 'Goodnight son. God bless. We shall see you in the morning.' Those of Warrant Officer Cottam: 'He gave his life that we might live. Ever in our thoughts. Mum, Dad and Sisters.' For Pilot Officer Fuller: 'We have gained a peace, unshaken by pain for ever.' Recording the event that had resulted in her son's death, and correcting the inadvertent error on the plaque at Sherbourne, Mrs Maudslay requested the unique inscription: 'He died gloriously in the breaching of the Eder Dam.'

Wartime publicity and propaganda had championed the success of the Dams Raid, but censorship and security had restricted many of the details from being revealed. A series of articles by Wing Commander Gibson in the American publication *North Atlantic Weekly* during late 1943 were subsequently incorporated into Gibson's account of his wartime Air Force career, *Enemy Coast Ahead*, written during 1944 and published posthumously by Michael Joseph in 1946.[504] This account provided the public with their first detailed record of the operation that had so captured their imagination. Describing the problems that had beset the development of the weapon and training of No. 617 Squadron, the book provided a first-hand, eyewitness account of the actual attack on the dams. Many of the survivors who had been commended for their skill and courage in this and subsequent operations were by now familiar names, but *Enemy Coast Ahead* served to remind readers of those whose valour and courage were no less, but whom fate had decreed would die without experiencing the public acclaim afforded to their contemporaries. In his foreword and dedication, Gibson lists 'the following pilots who fought with me against our enemy' from the three squadrons with which he had flown and who had failed to return from operations. Henry's name appears second among those for No. 617 Squadron, below that of Squadron Leader Melvyn (*sic*) Young, recorded as 'Missing – Believed killed'.

It was Gibson who introduced Henry to a wider public: 'Eton gave us Henry Maudslay, the other Flight Commander. A champion runner at school, he was one of the best pilots from 50 Squadron. He was standing there quiet and suave, and not drinking too much. Later on Henry became one of the mainstays of the squadron in supervising our training.'

In the final pages of his book, Gibson merges his impressions of the return from the dams with reflections on the morality of war and its human cost, relating it to his comrades who would not be coming home: 'Bill, Hoppy, Henry, Barlow, Byers and Ottley had all gone. . . . They had all gone quickly, except perhaps for Henry. Henry, the born leader. A great loss, but he gave his life for a cause for which men should be proud. Boys like Henry are the cream of our youth. They die bravely and they die young.'

By 1951 the Australian author Paul Brickhill, himself a fighter pilot and ex-prisoner of war, had completed a commission to write the wartime history of No. 617 Squadron. Drawing heavily on Gibson's work for the account of the squadron's first operation, but including additional recollections by surviving squadron members and revealing, with permission, more about the nature of Upkeep, *The Dam Busters* has become a classic among war literature. With economy of style, paraphrasing Gibson, Brickhill portrayed Henry as 'ex-50 Squadron, ex-Eton, an athlete, polished and quiet, not a heavy drinker'. Like Gibson, and despite official knowledge to the contrary, Brickhill perpetuated the belief that Henry and his crew had disappeared into the night sky over the Eder Dam.

On 8 May 1954, almost the eleventh anniversary of her son's death, Mrs Maudslay was again in Lincoln Cathedral, as an official guest attending the Dedication of the Bomber Command Memorial Window. In attendance alongside her were a number of senior RAF officers, including Marshal of the Royal Air Force Sir Arthur Harris, former Commander-in-Chief, Bomber Command, Air Vice-

Marshal John Whitley and Air Vice-Marshal Edmund Hudleston, the then current Air Officers Commanding Nos 1 and 3 Groups RAF respectively and The Rt Hon. Lord De L'Isle and Dudley, Secretary of State for Air. Mrs Maudslay and Mrs Katie Creevy represented the Families of Fallen Officers and Airmen respectively.[505]

The window, painted by Harry Stammers of York, depicts the Archangel Michael slaying the dragon. Flanking the badge of Bomber Command are the arms of the British Isles and the Diocese of Lincoln, beneath which are figures representing both air and ground crew. In a lower panel Lancasters are depicted against a background of searchlights.

Unveiling the window, Air Marshal Sir George Mills, AOC.-in-C. Bomber Command, echoed the thoughts of those in the congregation: 'This window expresses in a truly personal way the deep pride and gratitude of great numbers of past and present members of the RAF and its friends for the unsurpassed courage and devotion of those who fell.'

During 1953–54 the playwright R. C. Sherriff adapted the works of Gibson and Brickhill into a screenplay for Associated British Pictures. Seeking to achieve as much accuracy as possible within the confines of security (the exact appearance and full workings of Upkeep were not to be revealed until 1962), the director, Michael Anderson, worked closely with Scampton's station commander at the time of the Dams Raid, Group Captain John Whitworth, as technical adviser. In casting the central characters, considerable attention was played to physical appearance, with Richard Todd and Michael Redgrave providing masterly performances as Gibson and Wallis respectively. Copies of the script were sent to those who had taken part in the operation, and to relatives of those to be depicted who had failed to return, in order that they would be represented as accurately as possible.

Henry's role was played by actor Richard Thorp. Although he appears in relatively few scenes as a key character, mainly meetings between Gibson and his flight commanders and the pre-raid briefings, he is soon established as a recognizable face among the squadron crews. His credentials are set out in the scene where Gibson is with Whitworth at No. 5 Group Headquarters selecting crews:

GIBSON: There are two I'd like as my Flight Commanders. Henry Maudslay and Dinghy Young.
WHITWORTH: I know Young well . . . he was a rowing Blue. Henry Maudslay's a darn good athlete too. He's a miler I think. Yes, you couldn't have picked two better chaps.

Prior to the raid itself scenes depict selected crew members preparing for their night's work. A lack of words communicates heightened tension. Henry is seen brushing his hair in front of a dressing-table mirror. He puts the brushes down and looks at his watch. Picking up a travelling alarm clock from the dressing table, he winds and sets it, before placing it down alongside a small athletics cup and medal. In the closing scenes, as the cost of the raid becomes apparent, the room is seen again. This time, in the emptiness, the silence is even stronger, broken only by the persistent ticking of the clock, now showing five minutes past six, concentrating thought on the events of the intervening hours.

The film *The Dam Busters* was premiered at the Empire Theatre, Leicester Square, in the presence of Her Royal Highness Princess Margaret and survivors of the operation on 16 May 1955, the twelfth anniversary of the raid, and was heralded with great acclaim. With the production well on its way to becoming the highest grossing British film for 1955, the producers had their sights set on overseas box offices. The US distributors Warner Brothers were less than enthusiastic, insisting on a re-edited version, incorporating a number of changes to make the film more acceptable to North American audiences. The changes were minor, and today some would be seen as an early attempt at political correctness.

The soundtrack was redubbed where necessary to change the name of Gibson's dog from 'Nigger' to 'Trigger', the former no doubt being seen as having racist overtones of which it was in reality totally innocent.[506] In addition, some non-action scenes, presumably considered 'too British', were cut, reducing the running time by some twenty minutes. Less comprehensible were the changes made to the sequence depicting Henry's attack on the Eder Dam. In the original, British, version, the attack was shown from a distance, using model work to depict the run-in and the explosion on the parapet, overlain by a suitable narrative soundtrack spoken by a member of one of the observing crews. It was felt that to show only the explosion and hear the faint radio reply would leave the audience uncertain as to the fate of the aircraft. Instead the decision was made to confirm its loss by including in the sequence the subsequent sound of an aircraft diving and then showing a second explosion on the horizon to mark its impact. For the American edition of the film, however, an additional sequence was inserted that would cause a question to be raised in Parliamentary Session.

After the sound of the aircraft diving, the editor had added another very brief model shot showing an aircraft crashing through trees before cutting back to the explosion on the horizon. This might have been acceptable had the aircraft been a Lancaster, but inexplicably the model was that of an American Boeing B-17 Flying Fortress.

On Wednesday, 16 November 1955, members present in the House of Commons heard Stephen Swingler, Labour MP for Newcastle under Lyme, question George

Ward, the Under-Secretary of State for Air: 'Is the Under Secretary aware that this excellent British film. . . in the American export version . . . has been grossly distorted in Hollywood, particularly by the introduction of a Flying Fortress into the raid sequence?' Mr Ward was unable to comment on whether a complaint should be made to the US authorities, but the issue was taken up by the following week's edition of *Flight* magazine, which quoted Robert Clark, the film's producer, as saying inexplicably: ' "it was just a flash for two seconds . . . to make things clearer for American audiences". Only a trained viewer could have spotted the aircraft and he thought that "It would go undetected by half the R(oyal) O(bserver) C(orps)"'. *Flight* did not share his belief in the cinema audience's ignorance.

Gwen Maudslay died on 9 February 1974 and was laid to rest in the same grave as her husband, her name and dates added to his headstone. Tita died in 1979, and her ashes were scattered near the home they had enjoyed at Shinness. At Sherbourne a memorial tablet was placed adjacent to her parents' grave:

Margaret Kate Barker
18 February 1910–9 July 1979
Their daughter in loving memory.

Her husband Gordon was to survive her by a further six years, until his death on 6 January 1985.

In late 1985 the No. 617 Squadron Aircrew Association agreed plans for their own memorial to the squadron's dead at Woodhall Spa, home to the squadron from January 1944–June 1945 and from where the squadron flew the majority of its wartime operations. Fund-raising began early the following year and had succeeded in accumulating £13,500 by November 1986. It was still some £6,500 short of the total required when 'Chan' Chandler, an ex-air gunner with the squadron who completed a total of ninety-eight operations during his wartime career, offered to auction at Sotheby's his unique collection of nine medals including the DFC and Soviet Medal of Valour. At this juncture, millionaire John Paul Getty II offered to fund the entire memorial, an offer that the association most gratefully accepted.

The memorial, designed by Keith Stevens, RIBA, stands in Royal Square Gardens, in the centre of the village. Constructed in buff York stone, it takes the form of a breached dam, 10 feet high. The water of the breach is represented by blue-grey Westmorland slate, engraved with the squadron crest that inspired the memorial's design. This stone is also used for the spillways that carry the names of the 204 members of the squadron who were killed while serving either with the squadron, or subsequently with other units during 1943–45. Along the crest is the inscription: 'They died for your freedom'.

In pouring rain and in front of an assembled crowd of some 1,500 onlookers, the memorial was unveiled on Sunday, 17 May 1987. One hundred ex-squadron members, including seventeen of Henry's contemporaries from the original squadron, stood as Group Captain Leonard Cheshire, VC, DSO, DFC, the squadron's commanding officer during the period November 1943 until July 1944, read the lesson.[507] As he finished, Air Chief Marshal Sir David Craig removed the RAF ensign that covered the squadron crest and dedicated the memorial:

> They shall not grow old as we that are left grow old,
> Age shall not weary them, nor the years condemn,
> At the going down of the sun, and in the morning,
> We will remember them.

Trumpeters of the Band of the Royal Air Force College Cranwell sounded the Last Post. After two minutes' silence the steady drone of Merlin engines once again echoed through the air of Woodhall Spa as the Battle of Britain Flight Lancaster, based at nearby Coningsby, made a symbolic low pass, followed by four Tornados from the present-day squadron. As their sound died away, the trumpeters sounded reveille. Wreaths were laid by representatives from the Dominions, including Air Marshal Sir Harold Martin and Colonel Joe McCarthy, both ex-members of Henry's flight during 1943. Thoughts focused as Richard Todd read from the Funeral Oration of Pericles, 429 BC:

> Each one, man for man, has won imperishable praise. Each has gained a glorious grave. Not that sepulchre of earth wherein they lie, but the living tomb of everlasting remembrance wherein their glory is enshrined.
>
> For the whole earth is the sepulchre of heroes; monuments may rise and tablets be set up to them in their own land, but, on far off shores there is an abiding memorial that no pen or chisel has traced. It is graven, not on stone or brass, but on the living heart of humanity.
>
> Take these men for your example. Like them remember that posterity can only be for the free; that freedom is the sure possession of those alone who have the courage to defend it.

Citation for the Award of the Distinguished Flying Cross

London Gazette, 30 January 1942
(Extract from Air Ministry Bulletin 6201, Serial 336)

'Pilot Officer Henry Eric Maudslay, 62275, RAFVR, No. 44 Squadron.'

'Pilot Officer Maudslay on one occasion attacked shipping off the Frisians when the cloud base was only 800 feet and continued his task when the cloud was down to 300 feet. He has shown an outstanding example of keenness and determination and has been exceptionally persistent in locating and bombing his target. His efficiency as a pilot and the interest and energy he has displayed in operational efforts deserve the highest praise.'

The Air Ministry Bulletin also contained brief biographical details for the benefit of the editors of local newspapers, enabling them to identify recipients from their area. That for Henry read as follows:

'Pilot Officer Maudslay was born in 1921 at Leamington. His home is at Broadway, Worcs. He was educated at Eton and enlisted in April 1940. He was commissioned in January 1941 and was trained in Canada under the Commonwealth Joint Air Training Plan.'

Operations Flown by Squadron Leader Henry Eric Maudslay, DFC, RAFVR

No. 44 Squadron

10/11 June 1941	Mining GORSE, off Quiberon	Hampden AD747 KM-O
Pilot:	Pilot Officer H. E. Maudslay	
Observer:	Sergeant Edmondson	
Upper Gunner/W/Op:	Sergeant Wayland	
Under Gunner:	Sergeant Beattie	
Take-off: 2340	Land: 0550	Bomb load: 1 x 1,500lb sea mine

Released mine at 0128 hours. Height 500'. One ordinary vegetable successfully planted in allotted position and parachute seen to open and vegetable to strike the water.

13/14 June 1941	Brest: Bombing cruisers	Hampden AD747 KM-O
Pilot:	Pilot Officer H. E. Maudslay	
Observer:	Sergeant Edmondson	
Upper Gunner/W/Op:	Sergeant Wayland	
Under Gunner:	Sergeant L. D. Leggett	
Take-off: 2310	Land: 0440	Bomb load: 4 x 500lb and 2 x 250lb SAP

Bombed at: 0152. Height: 12,000'. Attack made from south to north. Bomb flashes not seen owing to thick haze. Approximate position of cruisers identified by a river, which was plainly seen. No photograph taken owing to unsuitable weather conditions.

15/16 June 1941	Cologne	Hampden AD747 KM-O
Pilot:	Pilot Officer H. E. Maudslay	
Observer:	Pilot Officer Wood	
Upper Gunner/W/Op:	Sergeant Wayland	
Under Gunner:	Sergeant Edwards	
Take-off: 2250	Land: 0530	Bomb load: 4 x 500lb and 2 x 250lb SAP

Bombed at: 0145. Height: 14,000'. Target identified by flak and searchlight concentration and bombs dropped through 10/10 cloud. No flashes seen or results observed. Main target not attacked owing to inability to locate because of weather conditions.

17/18 June 1941	Cologne	Hampden AD904 KM-[?]
Pilot:	Pilot Officer H. E. Maudslay	
Observer:	Pilot Officer Wood	
Upper Gunner/W/Op:	Sergeant Wayland	
Under Gunner:	Sergeant L. D. Leggett	
Take-off: 2318	Land: 0535	Bomb load: 1,000lb, 2 x 500lb

Bombed at: 0220. Height: 13,000'. Aiming Point B. Stick south-east to north-west. Bomb flashes seen in target area, results not observed.

20/21 June 1941	Kiel	Hampden AD930 KM-L
Pilot:	Pilot Officer H. E. Maudslay	
Observer:	Pilot Officer Wood	
Upper Gunner/W/Op:	Sergeant Wayland	
Under Gunner:	Sergeant L. D. Leggett	
Take-off: 2325	Land: 0455	Bomb load: 4x 500lb and 2 x 250lb GP

Bombed at: 0150 hours. Height: 6,000'. Main target not attacked owing to dense cloud. Target estimated Aiming Point A, Kiel. Aircraft searched for target at 1500', impossible to penetrate cloud. Bombs dropped through 10/10 cloud, no bursts seen or results observed.

23/24 June 1941	Düsseldorf	Hampden AD975 KM-J
Pilot:	Pilot Officer H. E. Maudslay	
Observer:	Pilot Officer Wood	
Upper Gunner/W/Op:	Sergeant Wayland	
Under Gunner:	Sergeant L. D. Leggett	
Take-off: 2300	Land: 0415	Bomb load: 2x 500lb, 2 x 250lb GP and 120lb Inc.

Bombed at: 0120 hours. Height: 12,000'. Haze prevented identification of actual aiming point. Bomb flashes seen in target area. Haze prevented observation of results.

26/27 June 1941	Düsseldorf	Hampden AD975 KM-J
Pilot:	Pilot Officer H. E. Maudslay	
Observer:	Pilot Officer Wood	
Upper Gunner/W/Op:	Sergeant Wayland	
Under Gunner:	Sergeant L. D. Leggett	
Take-off: 2300	Land: 0410	Bomb load: 1x 1,000lb, 2 x 500lb GP

Bombed at: 0140 hours. Height 8,000'. Bombed Haren aerodrome, Brussels. 1 burst seen near the flare path, but no results observed. Main target not attacked owing to weather conditions.

29/30 June 1941	Emden	Hampden AD975 KM-J
Pilot:	Pilot Officer H. E. Maudslay	
Observer:	Pilot Officer Wood	
Upper Gunner/W/Op:	Sergeant Wayland	
Under Gunner:	Sergeant L. D. Leggett	
Take-off: 2315	Land: 0515	Bomb load: 4x 500lb, and 2 x 250lb GP

Dock area Emden. Bombed at: 0240 hours. Height 12,000'. Identified Emden docks by river junction and dropped bombs in a stick, which all seemed to burst. Main target not attacked owing to inability to pick out detail because of concentrated searchlight and flak activity.

2/3 July 1941	Cologne	Hampden AD930 KM-L
Pilot:	Pilot Officer H. E. Maudslay	
Observer:	Pilot Officer Wood	
Upper Gunner/W/Op:	Sergeant Wayland	
Under Gunner:	Sergeant L. D. Leggett	
Take-off: 2300	Land: 0525	Bomb load: 1x 1,000lb, 2 x 500lb GP

Target attacked: estimated aiming point COLOGNE. Bombed at: 0205 hours. Height: 12,000'. Identification of individual targets impossible owing to cloud and haze. COLOGNE located by ETA and route followed. Bombs dropped in a stick on fires already started. No results observed.

(No. 44 Squadron ORB Appendix: Entry D350. Summary of operations carried out by RAF Station Waddington 2/3 July 1941. States that Henry was flying a/c 'O'.)

4/5 July 1941	Lorient	Hampden AD975 KM-J
Pilot:	Pilot Officer H. E. Maudslay	
Observer:	Pilot Officer Wood	
Upper Gunner/W/Op:	Sergeant Wayland	
Under Gunner:	Sergeant L. D. Leggett	
Take-off: 2310	Land: 0525	Bomb load: 4x 500lb, 2 x 250lb SAP

Target submarines at LORIENT. Bombed at: 0210. Height: 8,000'. Bombs dropped in a stick from north-east to south-west, straddling the naval barracks and Privet (?) Ecole. Only one bomb seemed to burst.

7/8 July 1941	München–Gladbach	Hampden AD975 KM-J
Pilot:	Pilot Officer H. E. Maudslay	
Observer:	Pilot Officer Wood	
Upper Gunner/W/Op:	Sergeant Wayland	
Under Gunner:	Sergeant L. D. Leggett	
Take-off: 2205	Land: 0415	Bomb load: 1x 2,000lb HC bomb

Aiming point MÜNCHEN–GLADBACH. Bombed at: 01.50 hours, Height: 8,000'. Target located by first flare, subsequently lost. Bomb thought to have fallen in the centre of town, very near to the main target. One big burst followed by several blue flashes.

11/12 July 1941	Wilhelmshaven	Hampden AD975 KM-J
Pilot:	Pilot Officer H. E. Maudslay	
Observer:	Pilot Officer Wood	
Upper Gunner/W/Op:	Sergeant Wayland	
Under Gunner:	Sergeant L. D. Leggett	
Take-off: 2310	Land: 0450	Bomb load: 2x 500lb, 2x 250lb and 120x 4lb Inc.

Target attacked, main railway station WILHELMSHAVEN. 0127 hours, 12,000'. Estimated that the bombs fell in the main target area. Bomb flashes were seen, but results not observed. Photograph attempted of target area.

21/22 July 1941	Frankfurt	Hampden AD930 KM-O
Pilot:	Pilot Officer H. E. Maudslay	
Observer:	Pilot Officer Wood	
Upper Gunner/W/Op:	Sergeant Wayland	
Under Gunner:	Sergeant Austin	
Take-off: 2251	Land: 0545	Bomb load: 1x 1,000lb and 2x 500lb GP

Target FRANKFURT. Bombed at: 0200 hours. Height: 6,000'. Bombs dropped over town at point estimated just south of river opposite centre of town. Two bursts observed.

24/25 July 1941	Kiel	Hampden AE218 KM-[?]
Pilot:	Pilot Officer H. E. Maudslay	
Observer:	Pilot Officer Wood	
Upper Gunner/W/Op:	Sergeant Wayland	
Under Gunner:	Sergeant Hayes	
Take-off: 2245	Land: 0525	Bomb load: 1x 1,000lb and 2x 500lb

Target GR3589. Bombed at: 0200 hours. Height: 16,000'. Attack made from south-east to north-west. Bombs seen to burst in target area. No further results observed.

27/28 July 1941	Gardening ARTICHOKE and Lorient U-boats	Hampden AD966 KM-R
Pilot:	Pilot Officer H. E. Maudslay	
Observer:	Pilot Officer Wood	
Upper Gunner/W/Op:	Sergeant Wayland	
Under Gunner:	Sergeant Atkinson (Henry's logbook records Sergeant Hayes)	
Take-off: 2250	Land: 0540	Bomb load: 1 mine and 2x 500lb GP

Target 1: GARDENING ARTICHOKE AREA. 1 ordinary vegetable successfully planted in allotted position at 0240 hours from 400'. Target 2: Submarine base in docks at LORIENT. Time: 0300 hours. Height: 8,000'. 2 x 250lb bombs. Bomb flashes seen but results not observed.

30/31 July 1941	Cologne	Hampden AD975 KM-J
Pilot:	Pilot Officer H. E. Maudslay	
Observer:	Pilot Officer Wood	
Upper Gunner/W/Op:	Sergeant Wayland	
Under Gunner:	Sergeant Bagley	

Bombs failed to release. (This operation is not recorded in the squadron Operation Record Book.)

5/6 August 1941	Heilbronn	Hampden AD920 KM-[?]
Pilot:	Pilot Officer H. E. Maudslay	
Observer:	Pilot Officer Wood	
Upper Gunner/W/Op:	Sergeant L. D. Leggett	
Under Gunner:	Sergeant Bagley	
Take-off: 2210	Land: 0620	Bomb load: 2x 500lb 2x 250lb GP bombs and 120x 4lb Inc.

Target town of HEILBRONN, approximately 40 miles south-east of MANNHEIM. Bombed at: 0130 hours. Height: 9,000'. Estimated that bombs fell in centre of town. No results seen as cloud obscured target immediately after bombing. Overshot main target while flying over cloud. HEILBRONN attacked by mistake for KARLSRUHE. Two tins of DECKERS dropped over wooded country near MANNHEIM.

19/20 August 1941	Kiel	Hampden AD975 KM-J
Pilot:	Pilot Officer H. E. Maudslay	
Observer:	Pilot Officer Wood	
Upper Gunner/W/Op:	Sergeant L. D. Leggett	
Under Gunner:	Sergeant A. Cursett Sutherland[508]	
Take-off: 2100	Land: 0440	

Target: None attacked. Unable to identify target owing to 9/10–10/10 cloud, approximately 8,000', although estimated to be near target area. 1 x1,000lb and 2 x 250lb bombs brought back to base.

22/23 August 1941	Mannheim	Hampden AD975 KM-J
Pilot:	Pilot Officer H. E. Maudslay	
Observer:	Pilot Officer Wood	
Upper Gunner/W/Op:	Sergeant L. D. Leggett	
Under Gunner:	Sergeant A. Cursett Sutherland	
Take-off: 2200	Land: 0450	Bomb load: 1x 1,000lb and 2x 500lb

Target MANNHEIM. Bombed at: 0100 hours. Height: 12,000'. (Bombs) estimated to have fallen south-east of the town on the east bank of the river. One burst seen, two large fires from previous sorties seen in south of town on east bank.

8/9 September 1941	Kassel	Hampden AD930 KM-W (540 states AE290 'W')
Pilot:	Pilot Officer H. E. Maudslay	
Observer:	Pilot Officer Wood	
Upper Gunner/W/Op:	Sergeant L. D. Leggett	
Under Gunner:	Sergeant Stirk	
Take-off: 1955	Land: 0430	Bomb load: 1x 1,000lb and 2x 500lb

Target attacked: GN3819. Bombed at: 0005 hours. Height: 12,000'. Bombs estimated to have straddled target, which was clearly identified. Numerous fires started by other sorties seen in the target area. One especially large fire at the railway station, west of target. Dense white steam followed our bombing as if a boiler house had been hit. One package of EH510(15) was dropped over KASSEL.

12/13 September 1941	Frankfurt	Hampden AD975 KM-J
Pilot:	Pilot Officer H. E. Maudslay	
Observer:	Pilot Officer Wood	
Upper Gunner/W/Op:	Sergeant L. D. Leggett	
Under Gunner:	Sergeant Stirk	
Take-off: 2240	Land: 0550	Bomb load: 1x 1,000lb and 2x 500lb

Main target GH577 attacked. Bombed at: 0200. Height: 8,500'. Bursts not seen. One photograph attempted, unsuccessful.

15/16 September 1941	Hamburg	Hampden AD975 KM-J
Pilot:	Pilot Officer H. E. Maudslay	
Observer:	Pilot Officer Wood	
Upper Gunner/W/Op:	Sergeant L. D. Leggett	
Under Gunner:	Sergeant Stirk	
Take-off: 1830	Land: 0145	Bomb load: 1x 1,000lb and 2x 500lb

Main target GR3587 attacked. Bombed at: 22.00. Height: 10,000'. Bombs dropped and flashes seen in target area. 3 fires seen to burst, one medium fire seen approximately 3 miles west of primary target.

20/21 September 1941	Berlin	Hampden AD975 KM-J
Pilot:	Pilot Officer H. E. Maudslay	
Observer:	Pilot Officer Wood	
Upper Gunner/W/Op:	Sergeant L. D. Leggett	
Under Gunner:	Sergeant Stirk	
Take-off: 2020	Land: 0215	Bomb load: 4x 500lb GP

Main target not reached when recalled. Target attacked Sylt aerodrome. Bomb flashes seen on Sylt Island.

28/29 September 1941	Frankfurt	Hampden AD975 KM-J
Pilot:	Pilot Officer H. E. Maudslay	
Observer:	Pilot Officer Wood	
Upper Gunner/W/Op:	Sergeant Leggett	
Under Gunner:	Sergeant Copsey[509]	
Take-off: 2230	Land: 0700	Bomb load: 2x 250lb and 360 Inc.

Target attacked: Position believed to be on the RHINE, 20 miles south-west of FRANKFURT. Bombed at: 0315. Height: 10,000'. Bombs dropped and seen to burst. 2 tins of DECKERS distributed in wooded country in neighbourhood of FRANKFURT. Unable to locate primary target owing to haze and poor visibility.

10/11 October 1941	Essen	Hampden AD975 KM-J
Pilot:	Pilot Officer H. E. Maudslay	
Observer:	Pilot Officer Wood	
Upper Gunner/W/Op:	Sergeant L. D. Leggett	
Under Gunner:	Sergeant Copsey	
Take-off: 0005	Land: 0800	Bomb load: 1x 1,000lb and 2x 500lb.

Target attacked: the town of ESSEN. Bombed at: 0330. Height: 8,500'. Bombs estimated to have fallen in the town. One large red fire was observed in the area of the town. One package of Nickels dropped over the target area.

12 October 1941	Huls	Hampden AE130 KM-[?] (44 Sqn ORB) (Henry's logbook states AD975)
Pilot:	Pilot Officer H. E. Maudslay	
Observer:	Pilot Officer Wood	
Upper Gunner/W/Op:	Sergeant L. D. Leggett	
Under Gunner:	Sergeant Copsey	
Take-off: 0110	Land: 0810	Bomb load: 1x 1,000lb and 2x 500lb.

Target attacked: Military encampment 1 mile south AMBLETEUSE, south of Cap Gris Nez. Bombed at: 0600 hours. Height: 800'. 3 bursts were seen among huts and buildings and 3 medium fires were observed after leaving the target. Main target not attacked owing to 10/10 cloud. Similar conditions over ESSEN. Aircraft was damaged by anti-aircraft splinters.

21/22 October 1941	Bremen	Hampden AE399 KM-[?]
Pilot:	Pilot Officer H. E. Maudslay	
Observer:	Pilot Officer Wood	
Upper Gunner/W/Op:	Sergeant L. D. Leggett	
Under Gunner:	Sergeant Copsey	
Take-off: 1820	Land: 0130	Bomb load: 1x 1,000lb and 2x 500lb GP.

Unable to maintain accurate run-up to bomb main target owing to intercom failure. Town of BREMEN bombed at 2125. Height: 10,000'. No bursts observed owing to violent evasive action. One fire seen to west of river near target area.

24/25 October 1941	Frankfurt	Hampden AE868 KM-[?]
Pilot:	Pilot Officer H. E. Maudslay	
Observer:	Pilot Officer Wood	
Upper Gunner/W/Op:	Sergeant L. D. Leggett	
Under Gunner:	Sergeant Copsey	
Take-off: 1810	Land: 0230	Bomb load: 1x 1,000lb and 2x 500lb

Main target not attacked owing to 10/10 cloud. Target attacked estimated railway junction at BABENHAUSEN, 10 miles south-east of FRANKFURT. Bombed at: 2240. Height: 8,500'. Bombs dropped through gap in clouds and estimated to have fallen in vicinity of railway junction, but clouds obscured target immediately after bombs were released and prevented accurate observation. No bursts seen.

3/4 November 1941	Shipping off the north coast of Holland	Hampden AE399 KM-[?]
Pilot:	Pilot Officer H. E. Maudslay	
Observer:	Sergeant J. M. Rickard[510]	
Upper Gunner/W/Op:	Sergeant L. D. Leggett[511]	
Under Gunner:	Sergeant Howard	
Take-off: 1800	Land: 2350	Bomb load: 4x 500lb and 2x 250lb GP

Aircraft detailed to locate and destroy enemy shipping skirting the FRISIAN ISLANDS. Bombing height: 300–1,000'. Time: 2025 hours. (1) 53 30N, 05 30E: 2 stationary trawlers attacked with 3 x 500lb and 2 x 250lb bombs. One 250lb bomb dropped about two lengths astern of one trawler, and the second 250lb bomb dropped about a boat's width of the bow. Unable to see where the 500lb bomb fell. No bursts observed. (2) 53 47N, 07 12E: 4 ships of 400/600 tons heading west at about 10 knots, attacked with 1 x 500lb bomb. Target well in sights but did not observe bursts owing to a thick barrage of light flak fired from the ships. Wireless operator and rear gunner used his guns to good effect on convoy attacked after they had opened fire on us and silenced some of their guns.

No. 44 Conversion Flight

30/31 May 1942	Cologne	Manchester L4730 KM-N-Bar
Pilot:	Pilot Officer H. E. Maudslay DFC	
F/E:	Sergeant D. Skinner[512]	
Nav:	Sergeant A. R. Barr	
W/Op:	Sergeant W. D. Scott	
B/A:	Flight Sergeant D. Walker	
MU AG:	Pilot Officer D. L. Cowling	
RG:	Sergeant R. E. Gladwish	
Take-off: 0006	Land: 0520	Bomb load: 96 x 30lb Inc. (ORB says 80 x 30lb)

Main target attacked (Cologne). Bombed at: 0213. Height: 6,800'. Bombed estimated south-west aiming point, which was well alight. Target identified by map-reading, as there was a full moon and no low cloud. 12 incendiaries hung up. Pilot's remarks: The enemy defence system appeared to be quite ineffective by the time we arrived.

1/2 June 1942	Essen	Manchester L7480 KM-A-Bar
Pilot:	Pilot Officer H. E. Maudslay, DFC	
F/E:	Pilot Officer S. R. Young[513]	
Nav:	Sergeant A. R. Barr	
W/Op:	Sergeant W. D. Scott[514]	
B/A:	Flight Sergeant D. Walker	
MU AG:	Pilot Officer D. L. Cowling[515]	
RG:	Sergeant R. E. Gladwish[516]	
Take-off: 2305	Land: 0437	Bomb load: 12 SBCs (96 x 30lb Inc.)

Alternative target attacked at 0138 hours. Height: 8,000'. Target identified by obvious industrial buildings and canal junction in Ruhr. Incendiaries fell in built-up area, 300 yards south of blazing factory sheds on south bank of canal. Position not pinpointed. Fires seen to start. Numerous fires in area on approach. Fires a good guide. Pilot's report: Ground defences not at all effective.

25/26 June 1942	Bremen	Lancaster R5862 KM-S (or possibly G)
Pilot:	Pilot Officer H. E. Maudslay, DFC	
F/E:	Flight Sergeant W. H. Day[517]	
Nav:	Pilot Officer R. V. Allen	
W/Op:	Flight Sergeant A. S. Jess	
B/A:	Pilot Officer D. L. Cowling	
MU AG:	Sergeant R. E. Gladwish	
RG:	Sergeant W. D. Scott	
Take-off: 2345	Land: 0605	Bomb load: 6x 1,000lb and 720 x4lb Inc.

No target attacked owing to aircraft being hit by flak approximately 12 miles south-west of OLDENBURG at 0131 hours. Height: 16,000'. Aircraft approached within target vicinity but on reaching this bomb doors failed to open by any recognized means. Bombs jettisoned safely 12 miles nort- east of BORKUM. Pilot's remarks: Bomb doors finally opened over sea and jettison action taken after filling with oil and pumping open. Damage by flak put hydraulics, oil temp and pressure gauge on port outboard, rev counter on port inboard, port centre tank and rear turret u/s following which port inboard engine vibrated badly and was feathered. Landed at Cranwell.

No. 50 Squadron

8/9 January 1943	Duisburg	Lancaster W4380 VN-N - (ORB)
Pilot:	Squadron Leader P. C. Birch	
2nd Pilot:	Flight Lieutenant H. E. Maudslay, DFC	
F/E:	Sergeant G. Harrison	
Nav:	Flight Lieutenant T. W. Gray (W/Op and Nav may be transposed and this may be W. T. Gray?)	
W/Op:	Flight Sergeant S. Allen	
B/A:	Flying Officer E. C. Wood	
MU AG:	Flying Officer R. D. Trevor Roper, DFM[518]	
RG:	Sergeant J. M. Hartman	
Take-off: 1732	Land: 2137	Bomb load: 1 x 4,000lb HC. and 12 SBCs of 4lb Inc.

This aircraft made an easy journey out to the target, but was attacked by an enemy aircraft over KAMPDEN. Successful evasive action was taken and the aircraft carried on to the target. Very heavy flak was experienced in this area from about 20 guns bursting at about 21,000'. Then a rocket contrivance was experienced, which burst at about 21,000', like the hub of a Catherine wheel, 300–400 yards radius, bursting in white stars. Bombs were released over the target, but no results were observed. An unidentified aircraft was seen hit over the target at 21,000', and the aircraft was seen to explode. This was believed to be a Pathfinder aircraft, as red and green flares were seen to explode. Definitely a completed operation.
(The white and green stars were reported as rockets bursting by Flying Officer K. Johansen's crew.)

21/22 January 1943	Essen	Lancaster ED475 VN-D
Pilot:	Flight Lieutenant H. E. Maudslay, DFC	
F/E:	Sergeant R. Clarke	
Nav:	Flying Officer R. A. Urquhart, RCAF	
W/Op:	Sergeant K. M. D. Lyons	
B/A:	Sergeant W. A. Miller	
MU AG:	Pilot Officer C. W. Gray (sic Form 540)	
RG:	Sergeant N. R. Burrows	
Take-off: 1715	Land: 2155	Bomb load: 1 x 4,000lb GP and SBCs of 4lb Inc.

This aircraft was detailed to attack ESSEN. No PFF flares were seen, and it was impossible to identify any ground detail owing to the thick haze. The aircraft bombed what appeared to be a genuine fire in the Ruhr area after waiting for PFF flares for 30 minutes. Scattered fires were left burning. The rear turret and port wing were damaged by flak and the trip was most unsatisfactory.

27/28 January 1943	Düsseldorf	Lancaster ED475 VN-D
Pilot:	Flight Lieutenant H. E. Maudslay, DFC	
F/E:	Sergeant R. Clarke	
Nav:	Flying Officer R. A. Urquhart, RCAF	
W/Op:	Sergeant K. M. D. Lyons	
B/A:	Flying Officer E. C. Wood[519]	
MU AG:	Flying Officer C. W. Gray[520] (sic Form 540)	
RG:	Sergeant N. R. Burrows	
Pass:	Sergeant F. G. McGrath, RCAF[521]	
Take-off: 1756	Land: 2234	Bomb load: 1 x 4,000lb. and SBCs of x 4lb Inc.

The trip out to the target was uneventful, but on arrival no ground detail was available and the aircraft bombed on the last green marker flare after searching for a break in the cloud. The bursts from this aircraft were observed. No results were seen. Incendiaries were rather widespread and were burning, but no fires were reported. Flak over the target was rather heavy and both wings were holed. An unsatisfactory trip.

30/31 January 1943	Hamburg	Lancaster ED475 VN-D
Pilot:	Flight Lieutenant H. E. Maudslay, DFC	
F/E:	Sergeant R. Clarke	
Nav:	Flying Officer R. A. Urquhart, RCAF	
W/Op:	Sergeant K. M. D. Lyons	
B/A:	Flying Officer E. C. Wood	
MU AG:	Flying Officer M. D. Hicks	
RG:	Sergeant F. C. Greening	
Take-off: 0020	Land: 0635	Bomb load: 1 x 4,000lb HC and 1,080 x 4lb Inc.

The weather was good with only 5/10 cloud and good visibility. The dock area and the river were clearly seen and the PFF flares were on time and correctly placed. The dock area was in the sights and the bomb was seen to burst and the incendiaries to burn in a built-up area. Also several really good fires in the town. The operation was a complete success.

2/3 February 1943	Cologne	Lancaster ED491: VN-[?] (Henry's logbook records ED475 VN-D)
Pilot:	Flight Lieutenant H. E. Maudslay, DFC	
F/E:	Sergeant R. Clarke	
Nav:	Flying Officer R. A. Urquhart, RCAF	
W/Op:	Sergeant K. M. D. Lyons	
B/A:	Sergeant E. Hough[522]	
MU AG:	Pilot Officer W. J. Tytherleigh	
RG:	Sergeant N. R. Burrows	
Take-off: 1820	Land: 2320	Bomb load: 1 x 4,000lb HC and 1,080 x 4lb Inc.

This aircraft identified the target by the marker incendiaries, which were in the sights when the bomb was released. The attempt was made from a height of 19,000' and a burst was seen but could not be pinpointed. Five or six good fires were seen in the target area and some accurate flashless flak was reported over the target. All guns in the rear turret were u/s owing to freezing, otherwise nothing unusual experienced. Completed operation.

4/5 February 1943	Turin	Lancaster ED475 VN-D
Pilot:	Flight Lieutenant H. E. Maudslay, DFC	
F/E:	Sergeant R. Clarke	
Nav:	Flying Officer R. A. Urquhart, RCAF	
W/Op:	Sergeant K. M. D. Lyons	
B/A:	Pilot Officer G. A. Coops	
MU AG:	Pilot Officer W. J. Tytherleigh	
RG:	Sergeant N. R. Burrows	
Take-off: 1835	Land: 2320	Bomb load: Probably included 1 x 4,000lb and 4lb Inc.

Aiming Point E: TURIN. Visibility was excellent and the target was clearly identified. Target indicator incendiaries were burning in the centre of the town. The bombs were aimed at two factory chimneys north of the aiming point from a height of 8,000' and the burst of the 4,000lb bomb was seen in a built-up area. Numerous fires were burning, and as the aircraft turned for home the whole target was well alight. A completed operation.

11/12 February 1943	Wilhelmshaven	Lancaster ED475 VN-D
Pilot:	Flight Lieutenant H. E. Maudslay, DFC	
F/E:	Sergeant R. Clarke	
Nav:	Flying Officer R. A. Urquhart, RCAF	
W/Op:	Sergeant K. M. D. Lyons	
B/A:	Sergeant E. Hough	
MU AG:	Pilot Officer W. J. Tytherleigh	
RG:	Sergeant N. R. Burrows	
Pass:	Sergeant H. L Rutherford	
Take-off: 1743	Land: 2305	Bomb load: 1 x 4,000lb and ? x 4lb Inc.

On arrival the PFF Target Indicator flares were concentrated on a small area. No ground detail was visible, but the TI flares were in the sights when the target was attacked. Bombs were released from a height of 13,000', but the results were not seen. Many aircraft were seen attacking the target, and one brilliant flash was observed, followed by a terrific pale glow. A further orange-coloured glow could also be seen beneath the cloud. The trip appeared to be compled successfully, and the return journey was made without incident.

13/14 February 1943	Lorient	Lancaster ED475 VN-D
Pilot:	Flight Lieutenant H. E. Maudslay, DFC	
F/E:	Sergeant R. Clarke	
Nav:	Flying Officer R. A. Urquhart, RCAF	
W/Op:	Sergeant K. M. D. Lyons	
B/A:	Sergeant W. M. Miller	
MU AG:	Pilot Officer W. J. Tytherleigh	
RG:	Sergeant N. R. Burrows	
Pass:	Sergeant M. J. Fuller	
Take-off: 1901	Land: 0142	Bomb load: 1 x 4,000lb and ? x 4lb Inc.

Aiming Point Z. Conditions were ideal. Visibility was very good, and the target was clearly identified. The whole town was well alight, and there were definitely fires on the aiming point when this aircraft attacked. The bombs were released from a height of 6,000', and the fires were raging fiercely on leaving the target and turning for home. The rear gunner of this aircraft extinguished a searchlight on the coast with three short bursts. This operation was a complete success.

14/15 February 1943	Milan	Lancaster ED475 VN-D
Pilot:	Flight Lieutenant H. E. Maudslay, DFC	
F/E:	Sergeant R. Clarke	
Nav:	Flying Officer R. A. Urquhart, RCAF	
W/Op:	Sergeant K. M. D. Lyons	
B/A:	Sergeant W. M. Miller[523]	
MU AG:	Pilot Officer W. J. Tytherleigh	
RG:	Sergeant N. R. Burrows	
Pass:	Sergeant M. J. Fuller	
Take-off: 1835	Land: 0320	Bomb load: Possibly included 1 x 4,000lb

Visibility was very good, with brilliant moonlight and no cloud. The railway was identified just south-west of the town and the built-up area by the light of PFF flares. Bombs were released from a height of 8,000' on the TI flares, and good fires were left burning in the centre of the town. Defences proved very ineffective, and fires could be seen burning when well over the Alps on the return journey. The raid was a definite success.

3/4 March 1943	Hamburg	Lancaster W4823 VN-F
Pilot:	Flight Lieutenant H. E. Maudslay, DFC	
F/E:	Sergeant J. Marriott	
Nav:	Flying Officer R. A. Urquhart, RCAF	
W/Op:	Sergeant A. P. Cottam RCAF	
B/A:	Sergeant M. J. Fuller	
MU AG:	Pilot Officer W. J. Tytherleigh	
RG:	Sergeant N. R. Burrows	
Take-off: 1905	Land: 0014	Bomb load: 1 x 4,000lb and ? x 4lb Inc.

There was no cloud in the target area, and the target was identified by the River Elbe on the way in. The TI markers were seen, and bombs released on a good fire. Large palls of black smoke were seen, and the operation was successfully completed.

9/10 March 1943	Munich	Lancaster ED415 VN-C
		(or possibly VN-N)
Pilot:	Flight Lieutenant H. E. Maudslay, DFC	
F/E:	Sergeant J. Marriott	
Nav:	Flying Officer R. A. Urquhart, RCAF	
W/Op:	Flying Officer A. Howarth	
B/A:	Flight Lieutenant E. C. Wood	
MU AG:	Pilot Officer W. J. Tytherleigh	
RG:	Sergeant N. R. Burrows	
Take-off: 2036	Land: 0425	Bomb load: 1 x 4,000lb
		and ? x 4lb Inc.

This aircraft located the target and attacked same from 12,500' at 0019 hours. There was no cloud and only slight haze, and bombs were released on the green target indicator nearest the aiming point. A tremendous orange explosion was observed at 0017 hours in the area estimated to be south-west of the suburbs. Numerous fires burning well were gaining a good hold as the aircraft turned for home. A completely successful operation.

12/13 March 1943	Essen	Lancaster ED415 VN-C
		(or possibly VN-N)
Pilot:	Flight Lieutenant H. E. Maudslay, DFC	
F/E:	Sergeant J. Marriott	
Nav:	Flying Officer R. A. Urquhart, RCAF	
W/Op:	Sergeant A. P. Cottam, RCAF	
B/A:	Sergeant M. J. Fuller	
MU AG:	Pilot Officer W. J. Tytherleigh	
RG:	Sergeant N. R. Burrows	
Take-off: 1930	Land: 2351	Bomb load: 1 x 4,000lb
		and ? x 4lb Inc.

Aiming Point C. Visibility was quite good. The aircraft attacked the primary target at 2139 hours from 15,000', and the red target indicator markers were seen in the sights when the bombs were aimed. The actual bursts were not recognized. Fires were good and plentiful and bombing was well concentrated. One very large explosion was seen in the centre of the fires shortly before arrival at the target. There were no incidents and the fire could be seen from the Dutch coast on the return journey. Nickels were dropped on this operation, which was successfully completed.

21/22 March 1943	Saint-Nazaire	Lancaster ED475 VN-D
Pilot:	Flight Lieutenant H. E. Maudslay, DFC	
F/E:	Sergeant J. Marriott	
Nav:	Flying Officer R. A. Urquhart, RCAF	
W/Op:	Sergeant A. P. Cottam, RCAF	
B/A:	Sergeant M. J. Fuller	
MU AG:	Pilot Officer W. J. Tytherleigh	
RG:	Sergeant N. R. Burrows	
Take-off: 1917	Land: 2330	Bomb load: [N/A]

Aiming Point C. Visibility was good. This aircraft attacked at 2137 hours from 11,550' (or 11,500'?). Bombs were released on PFF markers, which were in the sights and seen to explode on the target. The pilot states that conditions were excellent, opposition was negligible, the PFF were very good and the operation was a real success. No incidents to report.

(NB Crew positions may be corrupt in No. 50 Squadron records, and individual aircraft bomb loads are not specified.)

No. 617 Squadron

16/17 May 1943	Eder Dam	Lancaster ED937 AJ-Z
Pilot:	Squadron Leader H. E. Maudslay, DFC	
F/E:	Sergeant J. Marriott	
Nav:	Flying Officer R. A. Urquhart, RCAF ('B' Flight Navigation Officer)	
W/Op:	Warrant Officer A. P. Cottam, RCAF	
B/A:	Pilot Officer M. J. Fuller	
FG:	Flying Officer W. J. Tytherleigh ('B' Flight Gunnery Leader)	
RG:	Sergeant N. R. Burrows	
Take-off: 2159		A/c shot down 0236
		Bomb load: 1 x 9,250lb UPKEEP
		(released at approx. 01.46)

Eder Dam (NB No. 617 Squadron ORB states Mohne Dam). The aircraft is believed to have been damaged on the way to the target, as something that could not be identified was seen by the light of the moon to be hanging underneath it. The mine overshot and struck the parapet, detonating instantaneously. The pilot was spoken to afterwards by R/T and was heard to reply once, when he sounded very weak.

Notes

1. Marshal of the Royal Air Force Sir John Slessor, *The Central Blue: Recollections and Reflections* (London: Cassell, 1956).
2. David Wentworth Stanley.
3. Edward Johnson, ex-Nos 50 and 617 Squadrons.
4. Fred Sutherland, ex-No. 50 and 617 Squadrons.
5. Baptism No. 292, Parish Register, St Mary Magdalene, Lillington.
6. The vicar of Sherbourne, the Revd. John Harold Gibb, had been blinded in the First World War and had chosen to move to a smaller property. Revd Gibb and his family would remain lifelong friends of the Maudslays.
7. Attending Eton between September 1924 and December 1930, John Maudslay was a near contemporary of future author Ian Fleming, Middle Eastern and African explorer Sir Wilfred Thesiger and, of more notorious note, subsequent Communist spy Guy Burgess. He played junior cricket for his House, won the 100 metres in March 1930 and in his final year served as secretary of the Eton College Photographic Society. An account of Eton and McNeile's House at this period may be found in Michael Asher, *Thesiger* (London: Viking, 1994).
8. Peter Giffard, Christopher Maude, Eric Warburg, Graham, Bruce Metcalfe, Francillon, Parker and Hunt. All with the exception of Henry would survive the war.
9. Enid Richardson taught French and Art. In 1932 she was to marry Vincent Keyte, a newly arrived master and himself a Beaudesert Old Boy, and would continue to play an important part in the running of the school until she and her husband retired. Their son would subsequently become a headmaster of Beaudesert. She died on 13 November 2000, aged 94.
10. Early nights were encouraged by the fact that night-time illumination continued to be gas lighting until a year after Henry had left.
11. At this time all the athletic events were short distances, any longer being considered to put too great a strain on a boy's heart. Later Henry would prove himself as a middle- or long-distance runner rather than a sprinter.
12. For sports and other events the school was divided into four teams, A, B, C and D.
13. The masters' view was that it regulated the boys racing their cars across the wooden floors and along corridors.
14. Timothy Vigors, a stockbroker's son from Hertfordshire, was of Irish stock, his family being landowners in County Carlow. His enthusiasm for aircraft was encouraged by his godmother, an air enthusiast herself.
15. Vigors states that the ticket was sold to an old lady in the village, who drew a horse perhaps appropriately called Tipperary Tim and won £25,000.
16. Colin Richardson visited Shinness on three occasions: 14–29 August 1932, 31 August–13 September 1933 (accompanied by his elder brother Austin) and 15–25 August 1936.
17. Such an expedition from Shinness to the West Coast was written up by John Maudslay as an article for the *Standard Motorist* in 1935. At about this period it appears that John was also a keen participant in Scottish motor rallies.
18. Henry is recorded as attending Shinness shoots during August and September 1933–36. His next recorded participation in 1939 appears to have been only for the period 15–23 August, the family's holiday perhaps being curtailed owing to the imminent threat of war.

19. An Eton King's Scholar, Colin Richardson would be granted the ultimate accolade of Captain of School in 1938.
20. At this period it was not necessary to register boys at birth for entry to Eton.
21. In 1934 the average male salaried worker's weekly earnings were £3 18s 7d (£3.93) or £204.36 per annum.
22. Archibald McNeile died in 1937.
23. The internal arrangement of the Hopgarden has been altered since Henry's time, although some of the features still remain.
24. The school year was divided into three terms, each known as a Half: Michaelmas, Lent and Summer.
25. These included two of Henry's contemporaries from Beaudesert, M. Kemble and H. R. F. Luttrell.
26. A; First Hundred, B: Fifth Form Upper Division, C: Fifth Form Middle Division, D: Fifth Form Lower Division, E: Remove, F: Fourth Form. Blocks A–D comprised Upper School and Blocks E–F Lower School. Blocks C–F were each divided into three removes. Note the term Division can refer to a sub-unit of the Fifth Form, the placing of a pupil within his Remove, or even more confusingly the classes into dividing the Block for schoolwork.
27. Unfortunately Henry's reports have not survived. The school did not keep copies.
28. Patrols were based upon Houses, thus some Patrols were very small, others, like the Kangaroos, mustered so many that they had to be split into two.
29. Sometimes boys attended scout meetings and carried out fieldcraft dressed incongruously in their tailcoats and top hats. Peter Wake (whose birthday was nine days before that of Henry) was the fifth child and third son of Major General Sir Hereward and Lady Wake of Courteenhall, Northampton. He was a keen historian and talented artist.
30. Charles Blount was brother of Catherine Tennant.
31. Henry Streatfeild would remain a Housemaster at Eton until 1939. He died in 1974. His son, Richard Ambrose Streatfeild, aged 4 at the time of Henry's arrival at the Hopgarden, would also pursue a career as a pilot in the RAF. By coincidence he too would serve as a squadron leader with 617 Squadron, flying Vulcans between 1958 and 1960.
32. A popular pastime for Eton masters, but demonstrably dangerous. In August 1933 four of them had been killed climbing in the Alps.
33. J. F. Lever, QC, recalling J. D. Hills as headmaster of Bradfield School, in John Blackie, *Bradfield, 1850–1975* (published privately, 1976), 162.
34. Later Lord Pym of Sandy, one-time Secretary of State for Northern Ireland, Defence Secretary, Leader of the House of Commons, Lord President of the Council and Foreign Secretary.
35. 'Wailing Well' had been written for the Eton College scout troop and was first read at their camp fire at Worbarrow Bay in August 1927. The story of a haunted well in a Dorset field, it features the names of Eton masters William Hope-Jones and Aubrey Beasley Robinson.
36. Lady Hills was a keen Guider; the members of her company were girls from Eton town.
37. Recounted by Patrick Macnee in his autobiography *Blind in One Ear: The Avenger Returns* (Mercury House, 1989).
38. It is quite possible that the property was brought to her attention by the Revd Gibb who was acquainted with Mr Scott. The Revd Gibb retired from the living of Sherbourne in 1936, and moved to the village of Saintbury, a mile from Fox Hill, taking with him a gift from his parishioners of an antique grandfather clock.
39. Reputedly with a sprung floor for dancing, although this cannot be confirmed.
40. The sitting room floor contained a trap door giving access to a storage area, used during the war by Gwen Maudslay for storing emergency rations.
41. As described in H. J. Massingham, *Wold without End* (London, Cobden-Sanderson, 1935).
42. Previously Alexander Hardinge had been Assistant Private Secretary to King George V. Five months later, on 12 May 1937, George Hardinge would attend King George VI's Coronation in an official capacity as a trainbearer. His father continued to serve the Royal Household as Private Secretary to the new monarch.
43. Housemasters were expected to meet the cost of food out of their lodging income. It was widely rumoured that Houses with a bachelor Housemaster enjoyed better food than those who were married and had a family to feed.
44. G. C. A. Doughty was Captain of Boats in 1937.
45. Tim Vigors, *Life's Too Short to Cry: The Compelling Memoir of a Battle of Britain Ace* (London: Grub

Street Publishing, 2006)

46. Long Leave was the equivalent of half-term.

47. Henry's 'discovery' by Vigors and Harley and their bet on the Junior Mile is recounted in Vigor's autobiography: Tim Vigors, *Life's Too Short to Cry* (London: Grub Street Publishing, 2006) pp.37–8.

48. At the next managers' meeting the vacancy left by Mrs Maudslay was filled by Dr Orton, proposed by Lady Drummond.

49. Until this time Henry seems to have had little time for girls – being quoted as saying to Tim Vigors at Beaudesert: 'All girls are soppy and a waste of time, and anyway they don't like aeroplanes' (Vigors, *Life's Too Short to Cry*, p.28).

50. R. Beresford-Peirse, letter, 31 December 2001.

51. His lack of directional control caused Henry to be dubbed 'Henry the navigator'.

52. However, it is known that on at least one occasion Henry went and stayed with Tim Vigors and his family at their rented holiday home, Sheen Falls, at the head of the Kenmare Estuary, County Kerry. There Henry would enjoy the river and the hills as he did at Shinness.

53. Patrick MacNee was later to achieve fame as an actor in stage, cinema and television roles, notably as the urbane John Steed in *The Avengers*.

54. Christopher Howard was the second son of Geoffrey Howard of Castle Howard and destined also to be killed flying on operations with No. 617 Squadron.

55. Ian Fleming, creator of James Bond, an Old Etonian and twice victor ludorum, had won the Junior Mile in 1924 in a time of 4 minutes 54 seconds.

56. Gordon Barker's family lived at 'Watchbury' in Barford, adjacent to Sherbourne, and his aunt, Edith, was wife of Colonel Bob Negus. Educated at Wellington School, Captain Barker had attended the Royal Military Academy, Woolwich, 1924-25. Qualifying as a gunner, he transferred to the cavalry and in 1926 was posted to the 4/7th DG in India, returning to England in 1930. A keen horseman, he rode with the Warwickshire, Grafton and South Staffordshire Hunts, participating in steeplechases, point to points and hurdle races. Badly injured in a riding accident at the end of 1931, he spent the next three years undergoing treatment, rejoining his unit at Tidworth in 1935, a year before they were granted the 'Royal' title. After a further riding accident he had been seconded from the 4/7 DG and appointed as Garrison Adjutant at Colchester in 1937. He would rejoin them again as second in command in 1941.

57. The Revd Gibb had been chaplain to Gordon's regiment during the First World War.

58. *Windsor, Slough and Eton Express*, Friday, 13 May 1938.

59. Having 'attacked' Datchet, the aircraft is believed to have turned too soon and missed Eton.

60. Son of Lord Melchett, chairman of ICI. His younger brother Julian also subsequently boarded in the Hopgarden.

61. Captain R. A. P. Lewis, Henry Maudslay, R. O. Scott, Merriam, Chadwick, Bourne, D. J. H. Mond, C. J. G. Howard (i.e. Kit Howard), Cox, Nicholson.

62. Wine crates were used once all the proper bags had been used up. Slit trenches were dug in the college gardens, but during the summer of 1939 concrete shelters had been erected for each House in time for the commencement of Michaelmas Half.

63. Michael Beauchamp de Chair would be killed serving as a captain with the 16/5 Lancers in North Africa. By remarkable coincidence he succumbed to his wounds on 16 May 1943, aged 22.

64. John Hills became a father for the third time on 16 May 1939, when Lady Rosemary gave birth to a son. They already had two daughters, Jean, born on 22 August 1933, and Margaret, born 25 September 1934.

65. The secret was for the boat to be moving rapidly, thus aiding stability before the crew stopped rowing to stand up.

66. Bow: J. Wilson, 2: Maudslay, 3: W. Jeudwine, 4: L. H. Vickers, 5: P. M. Gell, 6: P. E. C. Nugent, P. H. A. Bowman, Stroke: A. N. Dodd, Cox: D. A. Hoy.

67. John Wilson would be killed on 23 January 1942, serving as a second lieutenant in Libya with the 10th Royal Hussars, Royal Armoured Corps.

68. All things considered, this was a fine performance. Eton had last won the Ladies' Plate at Henley in 1921.

69. If Henry was present at Northolt that May, he might have seen one of the RAF's front-line bombers when Handley Page Hampdens of No. 83 Squadron attended the annual air exercises. Among No. 83 Squadron's pilots taking part was a 20-year-old pilot officer by the name of Guy Gibson.

70   Son of Lord Halifax, the Hon. Richard Wood left Eton in the winter of 1939. After a year as Hon.

Attaché at the British Embassy, Rome, he enlisted in the King's Own Yorkshire Light Infantry in 1940. He was commissioned in early 1941, joining the 2nd Battalion 60th Rifles as a lieutenant. Posted to the Middle East, he succumbed to jaundice, thereby missing the Battle of El Alamein. Rejoining his regiment, he came under dive-bomber attack near Sirte, Libya, on 30 December 1942. As he sheltered in a crater, one bomb fell directly on him, miraculously failing to explode but crushing both his legs, which were subsequently amputated. His obituary in the *Daily Telegraph* recorded that he attributed his stoicism to his disability, as having had had such a rough time at Eton in his early years that nothing could be as rough again. Regaining his mobility on artificial limbs, he attended New College, Oxford, 1945–47, before entering politics, becoming Member of Parliament for Bridlington 1950–79 and a champion for many disabled causes. He was created Baron Holderness in 1979 and died aged 81 in 2002.

71. Michael Chinnery would leave shortly to join the Welsh Guards. His brother H. M. Chinnery, two years his junior (and a year junior to Henry), would join the RAF in 1941. He subsequently commanded No. 138 Squadron with Vickers Valiants during 1960–62 and retired as a group captain in March 1965.

72. During one year's visit Walter Howard is reputed to have fallen into a patch of extremely boggy ground, sinking up to his armpits, only avoiding total inundation by placing his gun across the ground and holding on tightly until he could be hauled out.

73. Sir A. J. C. Meyer, Bt, had inherited the title at the age of 15 on the death of his father, Sir Frank Meyer, MP. Leaving Eton, he went up to New College, Oxford, before serving with distinction with the Scots Guards in 1941–45. Joining the Treasury in 1945, he subsequently developed his career in the Foreign Office, stood as the 'stalking horse' against Margaret Thatcher in the 1989 contest for leadership of the Conservative Party and is now a committed European. His wife, Lady Burbrulée Meyer (née Knight), recalls meeting Henry at Eton: 'He was a great character, full of purposeful vitality.'

74. Other sources attribute the name 'Pop' as being derived from the Latin word *popina* (a pastry-cook's shop).

75. Old Etonian Andrew Callender in *Eton Voices*, ed. Danny Danziger (London: Viking, 1988).

76. Henry Maudslay, letter to Gwen Maudslay, 13 December 1939.

77. Eric Ellis, solicitor and family friend, partner of the law firm Ellis, Peirs & Co.

78. This comprised five double-sided shellac records together with comprehensive textbook exercises.

79. Henry may have been granted special dispensation in this respect. John Hills usually forbade boys owning wireless sets, the only set being in the Library, which also housed the House gramophone.

80. E. M. Wells & Son were upholsterers at 135 High Street, Eton, selling furniture and soft furnishings, including curtains.

81. John Hills had accepted this post only after considerable hesitation. Replacing E. E. A. Whitworth MC, MA, he remained at Bradfield until his retirement in 1955. He died on 14 July 1975. Lady Hills died in April 2004.

82. John Herbert was an assistant master at Eton, 1928–59, and a Housemaster 1940–55. During the war, while still teaching at Eton, he was to assist in the development of a floating roadway codenamed 'Swiss Roll', used in the Normandy landings.

83. Henry had been a member of the Library since the summer of 1939, when his fellow members had been A. J. A. Spears, D. J. Mond, W. W. D. Pearl, G. J. E. Jameson, Hon. R. F. Wood, D. C. Quilter, M. J. B. Chinnery and P. Wake. By Christmas 1939 Spears, and Chinnery had been replaced by C. Pilkington and W. Birkbeck.

84. Rhys Williams subsequently became a captain in the Welsh Guards and was killed in North Africa on 9 April 1943. MacAndrew was the son of Sir Charles MacAndrew, MP for Largs and Rothesay, and played the drums for Humphrey Lyttleton's band. He was to serve as a pilot with the RAF in Europe, flying Beaufighters with No. 141 Squadron, being awarded the DFC in June 1944 and finished the war as a squadron leader in the Far East. He was to die tragically in a shooting accident on 18 April 1946, only five days after returning to England and being demobilized, while cleaning a shotgun at his wife's parents' home in Devon, aged 24. Of the twenty-four members of Pop during Lent Half 1940, a quarter were from Mr Herbert's House: W. Birkbeck, G. J. E. Jameson, Henry, C. R. Muir, W. W. D. Pearl and C. L. Pilkington. Although an American national, Warren 'Hank' Pearl was to serve with the RAFVR until his death as a flying officer serving with No. 2 Glider Training School. Known as 'Slow Flying Pearl', he was killed when his Miles Master stalled and spun in while he was making a circuit of Weston-on-the-Green airfield on completion of a cross-country exercise

on 26 March 1943. (Originally interred in the American Extension to Brookwood Military Cemetery, his remains were exhumed post-war and repatriated to the USA.) Charles Pilkington too would be killed serving with the RAF.

85. The letter, not surprisingly, prompted strong representation from Eton tailors. Claude Elliott countered by saying that without such measures the number of boys attending the college would inevitably decline, to far greater detriment of the Eton economy. An interesting sequel was that this story was seized upon and broadcast by 'Lord Haw Haw' (William Joyce) on 4 March 1940. However, as he made his broadcast on stations Hamburg, Bremen and D. J. A, it appears that RAF aircraft were approaching, causing the Germans to fade out this story of apparent English class conflict.

86. Dunning had been victor ludorum in 1912 and 1913, although his fastest time for the Mile of 4 minutes 34 seconds was in 1911.

87. Home of Lieutenant Colonel Hon. Glyn Keith Murray Mason, DSO, MP, father of K. A. H. Mason, who was a year below Henry in Mr Colquhoun's House and a fellow member of the Upper Boat crews.

88. Identity unconfirmed, but possibly Mr Bond, butler and handyman at Fox Hill.

89. Henry Maudslay, letter to Gwen Maudslay, postmarked 24 April 1940.

90. A Harrovian, King's Cadet at Sandhurst and formerly of the Queen's (Royal West Surrey Regiment), Air Vice-Marshal Blount had strong Army connections and had pioneered tactical air support for troops after having been seconded for flying with the Royal Flying Corps in 1916. During the Battle of the Somme, a reconnaissance by Captain Blount, then a newly appointed flight commander with No. 34 Squadron, resulted in the change of a divisional objective only a few hours before the launch of a night offensive. Awarded the MC in 1916 and promoted, Major Blount had gone on to command No. 34 Squadron between June 1917 and April 1918, operating in France and Italy. Post-war he transferred to the RAF with a permanent commission as squadron leader and commanded No. 4 Squadron at Farnborough (30 April 1920–May 1925) and attended the RAF Staff College (4 May 1925–April 1926). As Wing Commander Blount, OBE, MC, he commanded No. 7 (Bomber) Squadron (1 May 1926–11 March 1927). After three years in the Air Ministry at the Directorate of Operations and Intelligence (April 1927–October 1930), he was posted to the Middle East, as officer commanding No. 70 Squadron (10 October 1930–21 April 1932). Following a period on the engineering staff at HQ Iraq Command as a group captain, he returned to the UK in April 1933 as commandant of the School of Army Cooperation at Old Sarum. He joined No. 2 Group as Senior Air Staff Officer in August 1936, being promoted to Air Commodore; subsequently commanding this group from 2 December 1937 (replacing Air Commodore A. T. Harris (later C.-in-C. Bomber Command)). On 25 May 1938 he was transferred to command No. 4 (Bomber) Group, a post held until 26 March 1939. A keen cricketer, he was one-time captain of the RAF team.

91. Harrovian John Blount had joined the RAF as a flight cadet with 'B' Squadron at Cranwell in January 1938 and trained on the Avro Tutor, Hawker Hart and Airspeed Oxford. Graduating and commissioned in October 1939, he had initially been posted for a month to the School of Army Cooperation War Course at Old Sarum before transferring to an enigmatic unit forming at Heston, which was to become the Photographic Reconnaissance Unit, flying Spitfires and Blenheims (see Chapter 11).

92. Henry met Air Commodore Fletcher twice. First, pre-war to discuss the relative merits of joining either Imperial Airways or the RAF, the second time, after the outbreak of war, to accelerate his entry into the latter.

93. Henry Maudslay, letter to Gwen Maudslay, 15 May 1940. Eventually Mr Dunning presented a replacement trophy for the event, which he stipulated on the inscription was never to leave Eton. It is now presented for 1,500 metres and retained for the year by the winner's House.

94. Eden's son Simon was a current member of Mr Herbert's House. On leaving Eton in 1944 he joined the RAFVR and was sent to Canada under the Commonwealth Air Training Scheme to train as a pilot. Assessed as below standard, he retrained as a navigator, and by 1945 was with No. 62 Squadron engaged on supply missions to Allied forces in Burma. He was killed at the age of 21 when Dakota III KN455 flew into high ground in poor weather near Sumsen village, Burma, on 23 June 1945. A few days later confirmation was received of his commission.

95. The contingent would become part of the 6th Battalion, South Bucks Home Guard. Although visually impressive, the Bren gun was marked 'For Drill only' and would fire only single shots, regardless of being set to 'Automatic', or even 'Safe'!

96. Henry Maudslay, letter to Gwen Maudslay, undated, probably written on 21 May 1940.

97. Henry Maudslay, letter to Gwen Maudslay, undated, probably written on 21 May 1940.

98. Their efforts were appreciated. At a meeting of Eton Urban District Council on 4 July, a report by the committee dealing with waste utilization praised the efforts of Mr Tait and the Eight. Henry's involvement with this activity has not been confirmed.

99. It does not appear that Henry remained at Eton long enough to become a formal member of the LDV and that his activities were under the auspices of the ECOTC/JTC.

100. Henry Maudslay, letter to Gwen Maudslay, 27 May 1940.

101. The Eton College Home Guard also protected the environs of the college, including the manning of sandbag and moveable barbed-wire barrier in Common Lane, adjacent to the Hopgarden.

102. Robert J. M. Harley, who had left Eton in 1938, was subsequently promoted to the rank of captain. He was killed in Italy serving with the 3rd Battalion Coldstream Guards on 14 September 1943 during the Salerno landings.

103. Tim Vigors had recently joined No. 222 (Spitfire) Squadron at Duxford, Cambridgeshire, shortly to move to Hornchurch. By the first week of June he had scored his first victories over Dunkirk, becoming wingman to Douglas Bader. He scored eight victories before being posted to No. 243 Squadron, Kallang, Singapore, in March 1941.

104. Henry Maudslay, letter to Gwen Maudslay, undated, but believed to be 24 May 1940.

105. Michael Crossley had been a visitor to Shinness during August–September 1931. After leaving Eton he had studied aeronautical engineering and eventually joined the RAF in 1935. Pre-war he had served as ADC to the Governor of Aden. Awarded the DSO and DFC for his part in the intensive air battles during the summer of 1940, by September he had twenty victories to his credit. In 1941 he was sent to the USA as a test pilot for the British Air Commission, returning in 1943 to European operations, which were curtailed when he contracted tuberculosis. Awarded the OBE in 1946, he took up farming in South Africa and died in September 1987.

106. After Dunkirk Captain Tennant joined his new command, HMS *Repulse*, subsequently having an eventful war, playing significant roles in the Far East and Normandy theatres.

107. MTB 102 survives as a member of the Little Ships of Dunkirk Association, and also featured in the 1976 film of Jack Higgins's novel *The Eagle Has Landed*.

108. Born 1880. Served in the South African War 1902 (Queens Medal and five clasps), N. Nigeria 1906 (Medal with clasp), Mentioned in Despatches and awarded DSO and bar in the First World War. General Staff Officer 1st Grade, Northern Command 1930–32. Commander of the 10th Infantry Brigade 1932–4. Commander 50th (Northumbrian) Division TA 1935–9. He had retired in 1939 but was quickly recalled as commander of the 23rd (Northumbrian) Division 1939–40. Mentioned in Despatches 1940.

109. Henry Maudslay, letter to Gwen Maudslay, undated, possibly 21 May 1940. Henry's own decision to join the RAF was influential on other boys: Robert Beresford-Peirse, some months younger than Henry and member of the VIII, recalls: 'His action had some influence on me joining the RAF in preference to the Welsh Guards.' In all 512 Old Etonians were to serve with the RAF during the war.

110. C. L. Pilkington and C. R. Muir were also both fellow members of Pop. Robin Muir occupied a room at the end of the upper-floor corridor, opposite Henry.

111. Henry Maudslay, letter to Gwen Maudslay, undated, May 1940.

112. Gordon Barker had been posted to the War Office as a staff officer in 1939, Tita moving with him to London.

113. Until this time 68-year-old General Maurice Gamelin, France's youngest divisional commander in the First World War and now Commander-in-Chief of the French Army, had been seen as one of the world's leading military commanders. He was a firm believer in the invincibility of the Maginot Line.

114. Henry Maudslay, letter to Gwen Maudslay, undated, possibly 21 May 1940.

115. Henry wrote to his mother from Eton on 3 June 1940 and could not have left before this date.

116. *Eton Chronicle*, 11 July 1940.

117. Promotion was not rapid and commissions almost non-existent. In the *Eton Chronicle* of 21 March 1940 Henry's friend Charles Pilkington laid rather dubious claim to the title of being the oldest private in the ECOTC, having not been promoted since his enlistment at Easter 1937.

118. Derek Mond, Henry's rowing partner, had won the Pulling and also the School Sculling in May 1939, as well as being stroke to the Eton Eight at Henley that year. In 1940 prior to Henry's departure he had been Captain of Lower Boats. His tenure of the position would be short-lived, as he too would leave Eton at the end of the Half term to join the Royal Naval Volunteer Reserve.

119. About 150 of the older boys were now giving up their half days and time for organized sports to work either on local farms and allotments, or in Slough factories and warehouses, coordinated by Science Master Mr Robert Weatherall.

120. Some 152 boys would leave Eton at the end of Half term 1940, 9 of them from Mr Herbert's House: F. C. H. Fryer (Grenadier Guards), D. F. Gilliat, G. J. E. Jameson (Kings Royal Rifle Corps), P. W. Lloyd, Henry (RAFVR), D. J. H. Mond (RNVR), C. R. Muir (RAFVR), C. L. Pilkington (RAFVR) and J. G. Quicke (New College, Oxon and Royal Artillery).

121. This suggests that Henry had attended an earlier selection board at Uxbridge. It is possible that he had been sent to the enlistment the previous April to be assessed as to an appropriate trade or branch of the Service.

122. The hotel building on the corner of Devonshire Road and Marina was bombed later in the war, the remains demolished in 1954 and new shops and flats erected on the site in 1961.

123. Initially recruits were introduced to the phonetic alphabet and taught to read Morse by buzzer at a speed of four words per minute. Practical half-hour sessions once or twice a day developed this into an ability to send and receive by both buzzer and Aldis lamp at a minimum of four wpm by the end of the course. Much spare time practice was required to achieve this standard.

124. Henry Maudslay, letter to Gwen Maudslay, 27 June 1940.

125. The RAF still retained a presence in the town, with the RDF (radar) station at nearby Wartling. Today there is little evidence of the RAF in Bexhill. In 2001 £6,000 was raised through public appeal and a window placed in St Mark's Church, Little Common, Bexhill, depicting a radar tower, contrails and the RAF cap badge. The inscription records: 'In remembrance of personnel of RAF Wartling and No. 4 Initial Training Wing, Royal Air Force, who served in Bexhill on Sea, 1939–64.'

126. In 1944 the Palace Hotel was to become the headquarters of the Canadian armed forces assembling for D-Day.

127. Mary Gibb subsequently joined the FANY, serving with the 2nd (Hants) MT Company at Aldershot.

128. Henry Maudslay, letter to Gwen Maudslay, 4 July 1940.

129. Henry Maudslay, letter to Gwen Maudslay, 7 July 1940.

130. Henry Maudslay, letter to Gwen Maudslay, undated, probably written 14 July 1940.

131. Henry Maudslay, letter to Gwen Maudslay, undated, probably written 14 July 1940.

132. Two other recipients of the Military Division of the 3rd Class or Companion of the Most Honourable Order of the Bath on 11 July 1940 were Air Vice-Marshal Arthur Travers Harris, CBE, AFC (later C-in-C Bomber Command) and Air Vice-Marshal Trafford Leigh-Mallory, DSO (later C-in-C Fighter Command). Major General Hastings Ismay was Chief of Staff to Winston Churchill and Deputy Secretary (Military) to the War Cabinet 1940–45.

133. Henry Maudslay, letter to Gwen Maudslay, 21 July, 1940.

134. George Hardinge went on to serve with distinction, surviving a torpedo attack, attaining the rank of lieutenant commander and remaining with the Service until 1947. He became senior editor of Collins, Longmans, Macmillans publishers, also writing crime fiction under the pseudonym 'George Milner'. On the death of his father in 1960, he inherited the title 3rd Baron Hardinge of Penshurst. He died in July 1997.

135. Henry had written out a copy of this evocative poem, which Mrs Maudslay kept among his effects after his death. *High Flight – The Life and Poetry of Pilot Officer John Gillespie Magee*, Cole, R. (Fighting High, 2013).

136. During a brief stay at Fox Hill while travelling to his new posting, Henry and his mother had consulted a road atlas, but erroneously identified the location as Brough, near Newark, Notts.

137. An early type of flight simulator for practising instrument flying.

138. Henry Maudslay, letter to Gwen Maudslay, 25 August 1940.

139. Henry Maudslay, letter to Gwen Maudslay, 25 August 1940.

140. Rupert 'Tiny' Cooling, in *International Air World* (November 1996), p.47.

141. Henry Maudslay, letter to Gwen Maudslay, 2 September 1940.

142. Henry Maudslay, letter to Gwen Maudslay, 2 September 1940.

143. In The *Eton Chronicle* of 18 July 1940 'Odd Man' had penned a discourse that correct etiquette when eating peas was to balance them on the knife. The following week a reply by 'Old Evansite' had cited this ditty to 'Odd Man'.

144. Major-General G. Le Q. Martell had taken command of the 50th (Northumbrian) Division TA in 1939.

145. Henry Maudslay, letter to Gwen Maudslay, 8 September 1940.

146. Everthorpe Hall is now used by the prison service.

147. *Hull Daily Mail*, 7 September 1940.

148. Henry Maudslay, letter to Gwen Maudslay, 14 September 1940.

149. Henry Maudslay, letter to Gwen Maudslay, 14 September 1940.

150. Although by 1941 there were numerous evacuees and troops billeted in Broadway, with her own mother, and occasionally her brother Norman, his daughter Joanna, Tita and baby Annette in residence, Mrs Maudslay was not required to provide accommodation.

151. Of the fifty members of No. 26 Course, September 1940, most were destined to go to Bomber Command, a few to Coastal Command. It is believed that only half survived the war. Eighteen would be killed before the end of the following year, the youngest, Sergeant Ernest Peacock, aged 19, lost with his crew on 17 May 1941 when his Wellington crashed into Spey Bay on what should have been his final flight with No. 20 OTU before being posted to an operational squadron. Three would die in 1942, three more in 1943, and the final loss, Wing Commander David Wilkerson, DSO, DFC, (attaining the highest rank and being the most decorated; one time commander of Nos. 51 and 578 Squadrons), was killed on 16 September 1944, aged 27, in a flying accident while being 'rested' as an instructor after his period of command, having survived forty-six operations, including three to Berlin. The Martin Baltimore of the Empire Central Flying School in which he was a passenger suffered loss of rudder control and crashed immediately after take-off from Hullavington airfield.

152. Although this sounds onerous from a modern perspective, it should be noted that, prior to the widespread adoption of central heating, thick clothing was often worn indoors, and even the best-dressed man would wear several layers of clothing underneath his business suit. Indeed, the itch and scratch of good quality woollen underwear was considered by some to be character forming.

153. Old Haileyburian Michael Foulis was to reach the rank of squadron leader. Posted to the Mediterranean and serving with No. 38 Squadron, he would be awarded the DFC in June 1942 for attacking an Italian naval force and a bar to this the following August for a night attack on enemy shipping. He was a flight lieutenant with No. 221 Squadron Coastal Command, when his Wellington failed to return to its base at Luqa, having taken off at 2130 hours on 18 April 1943 for a shipping search in the Maritimo area. He and his crew were presumed lost at sea and are commemorated on the Malta Memorial.

154. Earlier research published in Francis K. Mason, *Battle over Britain* (McWhirter Twins Ltd, 1969) states that the attack was by a Dornier of Ku. Fl. Gr. 606, which dropped a single 1,000kg GG mine, having become lost during an attempt to bomb Birmingham.

155. The practice was at 11 Vine Street, run by S. Shovelton, L. Shovelton and A. Shovelton. At the time of writing, the premises are still a dental practice.

156. Sergeant Forty would be killed serving with No. 106 Squadron. On 27 May 1941, returning from a mining operation off Brest, his Hampden crashed when it ran out of fuel trying to land at Wellesbourne Mountford airfield, Warwickshire. The remainder of his crew survived, although injured. Sergeant Forty had married his fiancée, Vera Hartwell, only nine days earlier, on 18 May.

157. On 1 July 1940, after his return to the UK, AVM Blount had been given command of No. 22 (Army Cooperation) Group. He had intended to fly himself in a Tiger Moth to Belfast to discuss Army cooperation exercises with the GOC Northern Ireland, but was persuaded by a fellow officer to take a regular transport flight. De Havilland Hertfordshire R2510 of No 24 Squadron, piloted by Flight Lieutenant Edward Jeffries, took off from Hendon at 0945 but crashed only a minute or so later into private houses in Woodland Way, Mill Hill, bursting into flames. Of the three crew, two ground crew and six passengers on board, all were killed except for one civilian passenger. Subsequent investigation suggested that the aircraft's elevator controls had jammed. As a result, all No. 24 Squadron's de Havilland Flamingos (the civil variant of the Hertfordshire) were grounded pending inspection, which resulted in a local modification being implemented. An Air Ministry press release issued the following day stated: 'The Air Ministry regrets to announce that AVM Blount, CB, OBE, MC, has been killed on active service as a result of a flying accident. It is requested that no further details should be published regarding this accident.' He is buried in the south-west corner of St Mary's churchyard, Essendon, Hertfordshire. Further details of AVM Blount's exploits in France can be found in Air Marshal Sir Victor Goddard, *Skies to Dunkirk: A Personal Memoir.* (London: William Kimber, 1982).

158. In July 1940 the British government had offered free passage for children to Canada and the USA, receiving 211,000 applications. Only 2,600 had been sent when the liner *City of Benares* was torpedoed and sunk by a U-boat on 17 September 1940. Of the ninety children on board only nineteen survived. Although the government scheme was stopped, nearly 11,000 children would be evacuated privately to friends and contacts across the Atlantic. John Hills had been director of the School's Canada Tour in 1932, and his wife had visited the country twice before, her grandfather having been one-time governor general. Even so it was not without considerable reservation that Lady Hills and her three children had sailed for Canada. After residing with a family friend a short distance from Montreal for two years, Lady Hills and her children returned by sea to Britain to rejoin her husband at Bradfield.

159. The summary in the back of Henry's logbook states that he ceased to be attached to No. 10 SFTS on 19 October.

160. Launched on the Clyde in 1928 for Canadian Pacific Steamships, the twin screw *Duchess of Richmond* had introduced a higher standard of cabin-class accommodation only slightly inferior to other ships' first class. She had commenced her duties as a troop transport in January 1940, but was not fully converted for trooping until December 1940, after this her fifteenth transatlantic round trip. Subsequently sailing mainly southern routes to the Mediterranean, Africa and India, she survived the war, being upgraded in 1947 and renamed the *Empress of Canada II*. During a refit at Liverpool's Gladstone Dock on 25 January 1953, she was badly damaged by fire, heeled over and sank. Salvaged, she was towed to Italy and broken up the following year.

161. Also on board was another RAF contingent from the School of Air Navigation at St Athan, who would join with an earlier party from their unit to form No. 32 Air Navigation School at Port Albert, Ontario.

162. This was one of the 'Winston Special' convoys. Vessels bound for a variety of destinations would depart in convoy, gaining protection for the initial part of the voyage, after which they would separate and proceed in smaller groups, or as individuals to their eventual port of call. WS 4, the largest such convoy to date, comprised seventeen ships, forming up on 2 November 1940 off Orsay, most of the vessels being bound for Suez, via Freetown.

163. HX 84 scattered after its armed merchant cruiser escort *Jervis Bay* had been sunk. *Admiral Scheer* also sank the merchantman *Fresno City* and steamers *Maidan*, *Trewellard*, *Kenbane Head* and *Mopan*, and then pursued the *Beaverford*, which was armed only against submarines. Battle commenced at sundown, and the gallant *Beaverford* continued to engage the battleship's attention until nearly an hour before midnight, when the cargo vessel blew up with no survivors.

164. Henry Maudslay, letter to Gwen Maudslay, 9 November 1940.

165. On leaving Eton in 1939, Peter Wake had travelled to Canada 'to experience life', working in logging camps.

166. Back in Broadway, Mrs Maudslay would have been spending a restless night listening to enemy aircraft passing overhead en route to attack targets in Coventry, including her late husband's works. The dull thump of explosions could be heard and the glow from the fires caused by the 'Moonlight Sonata' could be seen from nearby hilltops. Henry's letter to her written on this day took one month to reach Fox Hill, being received on 14 December. News of the attack on Coventry reached the cadets at Moose Jaw on 15 November, though Henry made no comment on it in his letters home.

167. Henry described the club to his mother in his letter of 14 November.

168. Henry Maudslay, letter to Gwen Maudslay, 27 November 1940.

169. Henry Maudslay, second letter to Gwen Maudslay, also dated 27 November 1940.

170. Henry Maudslay, letter to Gwen Maudslay, 6 December 1940.

171. Although the RAF Schools in Canada came under RCAF administrative control, they were not considered part of the Empire Air Training Plan, and nearly all the instructors and staff at Moose Jaw were RAF personnel.

172. One of the Ansons flown by Henry is still extant. R9725 was one of eight Anson Is sent to Moose Jaw with the initial contingent of No. 32 SFTS on 16 September 1940 and taken on strength by the RCAF on 12 October. Flown by Henry on 17, 19 and 28 December 1940 and 1 and 5 January 1941, it subsequently served with No. 1 CNS, No. 6 Air Observers School and No. 33 SFTS. Declared war surplus in 1946, it was purchased privately and remained on a farm until it was transported back to Moose Jaw in 1986 to be restored by Vintage Aircraft Restorers. It is now preserved as a static exhibit in the Moose Jaw Western Development Museum.

173. In a letter to his mother, Henry wrote: 'Thank you for your lovely Christmas Box with the pineapple and gorgeous cigarettes – we can't get anything like that here' (Henry Maudslay, letter

to Gwen Maudslay, 29 January 1941). Pineapples would soon become a rarity in England as shipping losses mounted. The letter was never posted and Mrs Maudslay found it in a suitcase after Henry's return to the UK.

174. Henry Maudslay, letter to Gwen Maudslay, 29 December 1940.

175. Henry described a typical day in a letter to his mother, remarking that the catering had not improved: 'The Mess is vile so I'll be quite ready for more rationing on coming home...' (Henry Maudslay, letter to Gwen Maudslay, 10 January 1941).

176. It is believed that Henry sent his residual Canadian currency to assist Lady Rosemary Hills.

177. The RAF List records seventeen members of this course being commissioned as pilot officers w.e.f. 29 January 1941. The remaining successful pupils would have graduated as sergeant pilots.

178. Debert Camp was a recently completed divisional depot of wooden huts capable of holding 15,000 troops.

179. Completed in 1930 in Amsterdam, the *Johan van Oldenbarnevelt* was owned by N. V. Stoomvaart Maatschippij 'Nederland', Batavia, Java, and plied routes to the Dutch East Indies. At the outbreak of war she became a cargo carrier, but in January 1941 was converted by Harland and Wolff to carry 4,000 troops, being operated by the Orient line but retaining her Dutch crew. Her taste of the cold North Atlantic was short-lived, and soon the vessel returned to warmer routes. She survived the war and returned to the Nederland Line in 1946, sailing on the Amsterdam–Indonesia service before being refitted in 1959 for round-the-world service. She was purchased by the Greek Line in March 1963 and renamed *Lakonia*. On 22 December of the same year she caught fire on a cruise from Southampton and was subsequently abandoned, although faulty and badly maintained safety equipment and a poorly trained crew resulted in the loss of 128 lives.A week later the fire-ravaged hulk capsized and sank while under tow to Gibraltar. The tragedy resulted in stringent new international legislation for maritime safety, SOLAS ('Safety Of Lives At Sea').

180. This may have been a relief to Mrs Maudslay. In his letter from Canada, dated 10 January 1941, Henry had warned his mother that, on returning to the United Kingdom, 'there is no reason why we should not get pushed out East'.

181. Henry Maudslay, letter to Gwen Maudslay, undated, believed to be *c*.6 April 1941.

182. Flying Officer Coton had already served operationally with No. 144 Squadron. On 22 May 1940, while attacking Krefeld, his aircraft had been hit by flak, and his crew had baled out. Regaining control, Coton flew his Hampden back to the Essex coast. Approaching Dagenham, the damaged aircraft was illuminated by searchlights and fired upon by anti-aircraft guns, forcing Coton to take to his parachute. On 26 April 1941, while practising night landings with pupil pilot Sergeant Church in one of No. 25 OTU's Ansons, the aircraft ran into the Chance Light (a floodlight used to illuminate the landing area) and was written off, without injury to its crew. Subsequently Coton was to fly No. 97 Squadron's first Lancaster mining sortie on 20 March 1942.

183. Henry Maudslay, letter to Gwen Maudslay, 25 March 1941. John Maudslay is believed to have been engaged in a reserved occupation, presumably connected with engineering.

184. On completion of his course on 3 May 1941, Peter Wake was commissioned as a Second Lieutenant and went to Winchester to join the King's Royal Rifle Corps, of whom his father was colonel commandant. Peter's elder brother Toby was a company commander with No. 1 Battalion in the Western Desert, and, although his father did his best to prevent Peter from joining him, he managed to reach North Africa in the summer of 1942. There he commanded a motor platoon in B Company and participated in the opening stages of the Battle of Alamein. By 1943 he had become a signals officer in Tunisia, transferring with his unit to Italy in May 1944 as a captain, and second in command of A Company. He was wounded in action on Monte Lignano in July. Recovering from his injuries, he rejoined his unit, but contracted pneumonia in September 1944. After a period in hospital, during which he was allegedly prescribed a bottle of champagne each day, he was evacuated back to the UK in March 1945. He was to suffer from poor health for the remainder of his life, although this did not prevent him from pursuing a distinguished career as a merchant banker. In retirement he was equally active in local government, the Church and the British Legion, until his death after a short illness on 24 November 1993.

185. Claude Elliott, letter to Gwen Maudslay, 28 March 1941.

186. Claude Elliott, letter to Gwen Maudslay, 10 April 1941.

187. Henry was almost correct in his assumptions. Austin Matthews was a talented all-rounder, initially playing club cricket for Cardiff and rugby for Penarth in the mid-1920s while still a student. He joined Northampton RFC in 1927 and, while remaining a member of this team, also played

first-class cricket for Northamptonshire. After a brief spell away from the crease in 1936, to coach for Cambridge University and Stowe School, he returned to play professional cricket for his home county Glamorgan in 1937. A mere three weeks later he was selected as a fast swing bowler for the England team in the 1937 Test Series against New Zealand. Apart from a wartime break, he remained a member of the Glamorgan side until 1947.

188. Henry Maudslay, letter to Gwen Maudslay, 30 March 1941.

189. Henry Maudslay, letter to Gwen Maudslay, 30 March 1941.

190. The constant speed propeller levers were connected with an adjustable nut to maintain synchronization of engine speeds, fine in theory but impracticable in practice without the pilot continually making adjustments. Hydraulic power was selected by means of a 'power bolt'. Without operating this, systems would fail to operate.

191. Henry's logbook records the aircraft as P4074, a Fairey Swordfish serial. The correct number should be L4074.

192. There is no record of Henry completing any Link Trainer at Finningley.

193. Unknown to Henry, another member of his course at No. 32 SFTS had been killed before reaching an operational unit. Sergeant Ernest Peacock, one of those who had not been commissioned at the end of the course, had been posted to No. 20 OTU at Lossiemouth. On the afternoon of 17 May, he and his crew took off on an air-sea firing, bombing and photographic exercise, marking the completion of their training course. During this their Wellington inexplicably flew into the sea 4 miles north-east of Buckie. There were no survivors.

194. Pilot Officer Salazar was the son of Portuguese nobility, Count and Countess Demetrio Salazar, who at this time were resident in Malvern.

195. Henry Maudslay, letter to Gwen Maudslay, 22 May 1941.

196. Squadron Leader Collier had joined the RAF in 1936, being posted to No. 83 Squadron, where he became a contemporary and friend of Pilot Officer Guy Gibson. He served with distinction, being awarded the DFC for leading a low-level attack on an oil refinery at Bordeaux, before being posted to No. 44 Squadron in March 1941.

197. Henry Maudslay, letter to Gwen Maudslay, 23 May 1941.

198. The two boys were usually away at school, Richard at Stancliffe Hall, Derbyshire, and William at Harecroft Hall, Cumbria, billeted airmen occupying their rooms.

199. Henry Maudslay, letter to Gwen Maudslay, 24 May 1941.

200. Subsequently he was able to obtain a retrospective ration card, which was sent to his mother on 6 June in order to reimburse her for some of the food.

201. Captain Arkwright was one-time hon. treasurer of the North Cotswolds Hunt. On his return to Waddington, Henry's consideration for the evacuees was expressed in a letter sent on 2 June requesting his mother to ask his sister to seek out any old wooden toys at Fox Hill that would not be wanted by Annette. Recalling his old train set: 'I wonder if the "puff-puff" is still in being, it stopped puffing a long time ago I fear.' A week later he learned the engine had gone, but that the guard's van had been found, although 'there was always trouble with its wheels'.

202. Revd Gibb was buried at Sherbourne at 3 p.m. on Saturday, 31 May, his grave only a few yards from that of Reginald Maudslay. Mrs Maudslay was unable to attend, but the family was represented by her brothers, General Norman Herbert and Reginald Herbert, together with Gordon and Tita, who met many of her former neighbours among the mourners. Mrs W. B. Scott, wife of the former owner of Fox Hill, was also in attendance, representing Sir Hastings and Lady Ismay.

203. Since her mother's death in 1933, when not at school, Joanna had spent much of her time living with Mrs Maudslay. Her later acquisition of a polo pony would be a further addition to Fox Hill's animals.

204. Henry Maudslay, letter to Gwen Maudslay, 1 June 1941.

205. Henry Maudslay, letter to Gwen Maudslay, 6 June 1941.

206. Henry Maudslay, letter to Gwen Maudslay, 7 June 1941.

207. Situated on the east side of High Street, south of the Stonebow, the Saracen's Head Hotel closed in 1959, and the site was redeveloped as shops, although elements of the facade remain. In May 1993 a plaque was unveiled on an adjacent building commemorating the pub's memorable wartime role as 'a favourite watering hole for thousands of RAF and Allied airmen and women who served on Lincolnshire airfields'.

208. Peter Pritchard had been in the same year as Henry, in Mr Huson's House, but left Eton in July 1939. Entering the RAF in October 1939, he qualified at No. 16 OTU as an operational Hampden

pilot the following August.

209. Henry Maudslay, letter to Gwen Maudslay, 10 June 1941.

210. Squadron Leader Burton-Gyles had been one of the first pilots sent to the Aeroplane and Armament Experimental Establishment at Boscombe Down to experience the Avro Manchester and introduced it into service with No. 207 Squadron in February 1941, flying eleven operations on the type before being transferred to its companion unit at Waddington, No. 44 Squadron.

211. Henry Maudslay, letter to Gwen Maudslay, 10 June 1941.

212. Flying Officer John Hubert Lempiere Blount, son of AVM Charles Blount, had followed his father's exploits in aerial reconnaissance. His operational career commenced at PRU on Spitfires in June 1940, after which he transferrd to No. 3 Photo Reconnaissance Unit at Oakington in November 1940. That month he was responsible for taking post-raid photographs of Mannheim from Spitfire X4385, which showed widely scattered and erratic bombing, giving, according to AVM Slessor, AOC No. 5 Group, 'the first of any real evidence we have as to the general standard of bombing accuracy'. He flew sorties over a range of targets, including the Ruhr, Cologne, Osnabrück, Hamm, Bremen, Emden, Hamburg, Hanover, Frankfurt, Magdeburg, Rotterdam, Amsterdam, Arnhem and Brest. At 1120 on 9 April 1941 (the No. 3 PRU ORB incorrectly records 8 April) he took off from Alconbury (used in wet weather) to fly sortie B/133 to Bremerhaven in Spitfire PR III X4712 (which the previous month had been the first RAF aircraft to fly over Berlin in daylight). He did not return, being shot down on his return route over Texel by a Bf 109 flown by Fw. Mickel of 1./JG 1. On 26 April a telegram from the International Red Cross reported they had received a card from him saying that he was safe and held by the Germans at Dulag Luft. After spending the war as prisoner of war No. 3682 in Oflag VIB and Stalag Luft III Sagan and Belaria, he arrived back in the UK on 7 May 1945, being awarded the DFC. In October 1945 he attended a month's course at No. 21 (Pilots) Advanced Flying Unit, Wheaton Aston, followed by another with No. 1517 Beam Approach Training Flight at Chipping Warden, before being posted to No. 21 (Wellington) OTU at Moreton-in-the-Marsh. Promoted to squadron leader, after a conversion course at the Lancaster 1651 CU, North Luffenham, in the autumn of 1946 he was posted as officer commanding No. 214 Squadron, Upwood. He was seriously injured on 23 April 1947 when his Lancaster (TW873) crashed at Burgh-next-Aylsham, near Coltishall, Norfolk, while performing a low-level demonstration flypast on two engines for members of the ATC. Recovering, he was posted to command No. 15 Squadron, flying Avro Lincolns until December 1949, when he was posted as a wing commander to the Officers' Advanced Training School, Bircham Newton', and thence to No. 75 School of Recruit Training, Bridgnorth. The start of 1952 saw him at the RAF College, Manby, mastering Meteor and Vampire jet fighters, after which he served with No. 34 Wing, Gütersloh, Germany, until the end of 1954. Returning to the UK, he spent a year at the RAF Staff College, Bracknell, before being attached to the Cabinet Office for two years. In November 1957 he was promoted to group captain and given command of RAF Syerston. This was followed in April 1960 by another overseas posting to New Zealand as air adviser to the British High Commission, returning in September 1962 to become deputy director of Air Staff Plans. He was promoted to Air Commodore, and on 2 August 1964 became captain of the Queen's Flight. On the morning of 7 December 1967 he took off from Benson as a passenger in Wessex HCC 12 helicopter XR487 to attend a meeting with Westlands at Yeovil to discuss the proposed VVIP Wessex. He and the three other crew aboard were killed when manufacture-induced fatigue caused failure of the main rotor shaft and the head sheared off, the aircraft crashing at Malthouse Farm, Brightwalton, 5 miles south of Newbury.

213. Semi Armour Piercing to help penetrate the cruisers' plates.

214. Lighting laid out in farmland to simulate an airfield and attract attackers away from a genuine target.

215. He may have received a set of materials from his mother. In a letter to her dated 12 June Henry wrote: 'I have started work on the water colours and am enjoying it more than I had believed possible, it's simply grand fun.'

216. General Purpose.

217. Henry Maudslay, letter to Gwen Maudslay, 21 June 1941. The navigator and gunner to whom he referred were Pilot Officer Wood and Sergeant Leggett.

218. Instrument repairer Sid Green (ex-No. 44 Squadron) cited in Ray Leach, *An Illustrated history of RAF Waddington* (Bognor Regis: Woodfield Publishing, 2003).

219. Selected letters from Peter Pritchard are reproduced in *Last Letters Home*, ed. Tamsin Day-Lewis (London: Pan Books, 1995). According to his sister Rosemary, 'Peter's last letter to his mother has "no special significance". It was a hastily written note written as he rushed off to meet a friend' – most probably immediately prior to his meeting with Henry. Details of his funeral are included in Harry Moyle, *The Hampden File* (Woodbridge: Air Britain, 1989), pp.83–85.

220. On completion of his Junior Staff Course at Camberley in April 1941, Gordon had qualified as a general staff officer, 2nd grade, and had been posted to Royal Armoured Corps Headquarters in London. He would shortly return to 4/7th RDG, being promoted to major and becoming second in command to their new commanding officer, Lieutenant Colonel Geoffrey Byron in August 1941.

221. Born in Allahabad, but now from Gloucestershire, Pilot Officer Denzil Biggane had been educated at Uppingham and Sidney Sussex College, Cambridge. After a period with No. 408 Squadron during the autumn of 1941, for which he was awarded the DFC for minelaying and anti-shipping attacks, he subsequently returned to No. 44 Squadron but was fated to be killed attacking Munich on 21 December 1942.

222. Henry Maudslay, letter to Gwen Maudslay, 10 July 1941, written 'on notepaper with every side printed, but the Mess has run out of the other sort'.

223. Henry Maudslay, letter to Gwen Maudslay, 20 July 1941, written on white lined foolscap with an 'Official Stationery' crest embossed at the top: 'I can't at the moment get hold of my pen or any writing paper.'

224. Henry Maudslay, letter to Gwen Maudslay, 20 July 1941.

225. This may have been the inspiration for the poem 'No Trace' by Herbert Corby, an armourer with a No. 5 Group Hampden squadron during this period.

226. Henry Maudslay, letter to Gwen Maudslay, 26 July 1941.

227. Henry Maudslay, letter to Gwen Maudslay, 26 July 1941.

228. Henry Maudslay, letter to Gwen Maudslay, 26 July 1941.

229. 'Blow Thou Winter Wind' and 'A Lover and His Lass' were recorded in 1940 by Al Bowlly with Ken 'Snakehips' Johnson and his West Indian Orchestra and the Henderson Twins. 'Yes My Darling Daughter' was a Jack Lawrence adaptation of a Yiddish song from the musical *Crazy with the Heat* and the first hit for Dinah Shore in 1940, selling over a million copies. 'Down Argentine Way' was from the 1940 film of the same name.

230. Henry Maudslay, letter to Gwen Maudslay, 30 July 1941.

231. Joseph Henri Jean Sauvage came from the Seychelles, having served with the Seychelles Defence Force before being commissioned in the RAF in 1939. Despite Pilot Officer Sauvage's French heritage, with English being his second language, Henry usually referred to him as an Anglicized 'John'.

232. Pilot Officer John Stewart Robinson would be posted subsequently to the Far East and was killed as a flying officer on 14 February 1942, aged 21. His was one of three Lockheed Hudsons from a depleted No. 62 Squadron that took off from a jungle airstrip P2 at Palembang, Sumatra, to attack Japanese invasion vessels entering the Banka Straight. As he approached his target, his aircraft was shot down by a Japanese A6M Zero-Sen fighter. With no known grave, he is commemorated on the Singapore Memorial. Pilot Officer Prescott Decie was to be posted later to No. 106 Squadron, under the command of Wing Commander Guy Gibson, where he would fall victim of the ill-fated Manchester, being taken a prisoner of war during an attack on Rostock on the night of 23 April 1942.

233. Henry Maudslay, letter to Gwen Maudslay, 2 August 1941.

234. Henry Maudslay, letter to Gwen Maudslay, 5 August 1941.

235. Hampden X2917, KM-R, the aircraft that Henry had air tested on 3 and 4 August.

236. Henry Maudslay, letter to Gwen Maudslay, 18 August 1941.

237. Sergeant Anthony Cursett Sutherland would be killed flying with No. 61 Squadron during an attack on Frankfurt, 24/25 August 1942.

238. Henry Maudslay, letter to Gwen Maudslay, 10 September 1941.

239. The formal description of the crest: 'On a mount an elephant with the motto "Fulmina Regis Iusta" – The King's thunderbolts are righteous.' The elephant was seen as symbolic of the weight of the squadron's attacks, and had a historical precedent. In 1895 Queen Victoria had presented a seal to acknowledge the loyalty of King Lobengula of Matebeleland (the southern portion of southern Rhodesia), who described himself as 'Her Majesty's thunderbolt of Matebeleland'.

240. Henry Maudslay, letter to Gwen Maudslay, 24 September 1941.

241. Later Major John Henry Wiggin, MC.

242. Henry Maudslay, letter to Gwen Maudslay, 24 September 1941.

243. C. W. O. Parker had been a member of Mr Butterwick's House and had competed with Henry in

the 1938 School Mile. Leaving Eton in 1939, he had become a lieutenant in the Royal Artillery before being invalided out of the Essex Yeomanry.

244. Henry Maudslay, letter to Gwen Maudslay, 8 October 1941.

245. Henry Maudslay, letter to Gwen Maudslay, 8 October 1941.

246. On the night of 20/21 October 1941 Pilot Officer Ruck-Keene took off to lay mines in the Baltic and crashed in the North Sea 18 miles off Great Yarmouth on return, cause unknown. Despite two days of searches for their dinghy, nothing was found of the crew, although the flight engineer's body was washed up later on the French coast and buried at Boulogne. Pilot Officer Ruck-Keene was the son of Admiral W. G. E. Ruck-Keene, MVO, JP, who lost two other younger sons, Charles and Francis, on active service with the Royal Navy.

247. Only the bodies of Pilot Officer Budd and one of his gunners were found. They are buried in separate cemeteries near Bremen.

248. Pilot Officer Wood was posted to No. 14 OTU, Cottesmore, on 8 November 1941.

249. Henry Maudslay, letter to Gwen Maudslay, 27 October 1941.

250. New batteries supplied in January 1942 appear to have resolved the problem.

251. Henry Maudslay, letter to Gwen Maudslay, 7 November 1941.

252. Two strands linked the Slessors to the Maudslay family: John Slessor had succeeded Charles Blount as officer commanding No. 4 Squadron in 1925, and the Slessors's son John, then 16, was at Eton, where he had been four years below Henry. He would subsequently join the RAF, gaining his commission in October 1945. In 1962, as a wing commander, he commanded No. 83 Squadron, operating Blue Steel-equipped Avro Vulcan B. Mk 2s. He retired as a group captain in 1993.

253. Retitled No. 1524 Beam Approach Training Flight from the end of October 1941.

254. At this time pilots converting to the two other four-engined heavy bombers (the Halifax and Stirling) were required to have a minimum of 350 flying hours before joining an operational squadron.

255. The request was made in his letter of 23 November.

256. Henry Maudslay, letter to Gwen Maudslay, 20 November 1941.

257. George Weston was a red-haired New Zealander who always wore a bright blue polo neck sweater and flew his aircraft as if it were a fighter. In March 1942 he became seriously ill with tuberculosis and meningitis, but after a period of convalescence in Torquay he returned to operations with No. 61 Squadron as a squadron leader with the DFC. On the night of 1 October 1942, while just becoming airborne from Syerston for an operation against Wismar, the aircraft's dinghy came out of its stowage and fouled the tailplane. Too low for the crew to bale out, the aircraft descended gradually, only for the bomb load to detonate as it hit the ground, killing all on board.

258. *Fantasia* was released as a wide-screen presentation requiring special projection facilities, together with multi-track stereophonic sound – 'Fantasound' – enabling the music to swoop across the screen in synchronization with the animation.

259. Henry Maudslay, letter to Gwen Maudslay, 23 November 1941.

260. It is possible, however, that the letter was written following his recorded flight to Waddington on 11 December.

261. The brooch appears to have been a remodelling of an existing item of jewellery.

262. Having retired from active service at the end of 1940 at the age of 60, Major General Herbert went to join his sister and daughter Joanna at Fox Hill. Post-war he moved to Manor Farm House, Stanton, near Broadway, and died on 26 April 1949.

263. Henry's previous contact with Pilot Officer Ercolani had been on return from Canada, when the latter was posted to No. 21 OTU Moreton-in-Marsh to continue his training on Wellingtons. He had been operating from Stradishall as part of No. 214 Squadron's contribution to the ill-fated attack against Berlin on the night of 7/8 November 1941. On his twenty-sixth operation, his Wellington, X3206, BU-O, was hit by flak, which set fire to the incendiary bomb load, and soon the fire was raging out of control, making the aircraft an illuminated target for further flak batteries. As they were unable to jettison the burning bombs, a distress call was sent out, and Ercolani then flew the burning aircraft for some three hours until eventually an engine failed at 1,000 feet from lack of fuel, at which point he ditched successfully in heavy seas off the Dutch coast. Ercolani and his five crew boarded their dinghy and spent fifty-seven hours in appalling conditions, drifting for nearly 100 miles until they were brought ashore exhausted but safe at Ventnor, Isle of Wight, where he was admitted to the Royal National Hospital. For his fortitude Ercolani would be awarded the DSO on 6 January 1942.

264. Second Lieutenant David Colman, who had been a member (and auditor) of Pop with Henry, and Captain of the Eleven during 1939/40, scoring a commendable ninety-two runs in that season's annual Eton vs Harrow match. He was subsequently killed on 5 November 1942 fighting at El Alamein with the 2nd Battalion, the King's Royal Rifle Corps.

265. Henry Maudslay, letter to Gwen Maudslay, 8 December 1941.

266. Captain Tennant, by now with the reputation of being the Navy's finest navigator, had built a strong bond of loyalty with the crew of *Repulse*, many of whom referred to him affectionately as 'Dunkirk Joe'. Once, while at sea on his birthday, he was surprised to find a vase of fresh flowers in his cabin – a gift from the stokers, aware of his love of nature. At 1100 hours on 10 December 1941 *Repulse* was attacked by Japanese aircraft off Kuantan on the eastern coast of the Malay peninsula. After successfully avoiding bombs and torpedoes, she was hit by three torpedoes, which left her able to steam only in circles. At 1233 Captain Tennant gave the order to abandon ship. As the vessel heeled over, he climbed over the side of the bridge until he was standing on what had been a vertical surface. The rate of roll increased rapidly and Tennant was engulfed by the sea. Everything became very dark and he had to fight an overwhelming desire to take in water and drown quickly. Fighting to hold his breath, he was pounded by debris until he saw the water getting lighter and he came to the surface of the swirling water near to a Carley float, whose occupants hauled him aboard, still wearing his steel helmet. The survivors were soon rescued by the destroyers *Vampire* and *Electra* and taken to the temporary safety of Singapore. William Tennant was promoted to rear admiral in 1942 and commanded a cruiser squadron until January 1943, when he was placed in charge of the Mulberry Harbour project for D-Day, becoming flag officer in charge of both Mulberry and Pluto (PipeLine Under The Ocean – supplying fuel to the Allied forces in France). He ended the war as a vice-admiral and retired in 1949 holding the rank of admiral. By coincidence, Etonian Flight Lieutenant Tim Vigors, DFC, now flying Brewster Buffalo fighters as temporary commanding officer of No. 453 Squadron, had taken off leading ten aircraft to provide air cover for *Repulse* and *Prince of Wales* when they were sunk, arriving to see only survivors in the water. Two days later Vigors himself was shot down and badly burned but managed to struggle through the jungle to find Malays who would assist him. After five weeks in hospital in Singapore, Vigors was able to leave just as the Japanese invaded. Travelling to India via Java, he spent the remainder of the war on staff and training duties before returning to the UK in time to take part in the Battle of Britain flypast over London in September 1945. He retired as a wing commander in November 1946 to enjoy a highly successful and flamboyant career breeding racehorses and founding an aviation company, one-time holding the UK agency for Piper Aircraft. Vigors died on 14 November 2003.

267. Henry Maudslay, letter to Gwen Maudslay, 10 December 1941. This suggests that Henry may have spoken to his mother by telephone on this date.

268. Wing Commander Burton-Gyles DSO, DFC and bar, was subsequently posted to Malta in September 1943 as commanding officer of No. 23 Squadron, flying de Havilland Mosquito intruders in support of the Italian offensive. He was killed on 10 December 1943. No trace of his aircraft was found, and both he and his navigator are commemorated on the Malta Memorial.

269. On 6 October 1942 details were published of the award of the DFM to Sergeant Leggett (with effect from 12 December 1941 – the recommendation having been made before his death). The citation made reference to his part played in Henry's crew: 'Since June 1941 this airman has taken part in numerous operational sorties against most of the important enemy targets. He is a most efficient Wireless Operator/Air Gunner. On a number of occasions he has machine gunned ground targets and shipping and his fearlessness combined with his determination have won the confidence of his captains.'

270. Henry Maudslay, letter to Gwen Maudslay, 16 December 1941.

271. Henry Maudslay, letter to Gwen Maudslay, 19 December 1941.

272. Henry Maudslay, letter to Gwen Maudslay, 23 December 1941.

273. Pilot Officer Taylor, from Bulawayo, had been awarded the DFC at the same time as Henry, his citation praising his 'high standard of navigation often in extremely adverse weather' and stating that 'he is a keen and efficient officer whose exceptional coolness over the target has set a good example to his crew and the Squadron as a whole'.

274. Wing Commander Collier, DFC, went on to command No. 97 Squadron in March 1942, being awarded the DSO. In early 1943 he was posted to the Directorate of Bomber Operations at the Air Ministry, where he helped plan the bomber offensive, including the Dams Raid. Retiring from the RAF in 1959, he regained his pre-war career as a land agent, in later life performing much voluntary work for Dr Barnado's. He died aged 83 in November 2000.

275. Henry Maudslay, letter to Gwen Maudslay, 31 December 1941.

276. Henry Maudslay, letter to Gwen Maudslay, 11 January 1941.

277. Details of this flight and the serial number of the aircraft are not recorded in Henry's logbook. However, it is likely that the aircraft was one of the following, which were all taken on RAF charge on 11 January 1942 and delivered to No. 44 Squadron shortly afterwards: L7541, L7544, L7545, L7548.

278. Henry Maudslay, letter to Gwen Maudslay, 20 January 1942.

279. Henry Maudslay, letter to Gwen Maudslay, 21 January 1942.

280. Henry Maudslay, letter to Gwen Maudslay, 24 January 1942.

281. Henry Maudslay, letter to Gwen Maudslay, 24 January 1942.

282. Henry Maudslay, letter to Gwen Maudslay, 24 January 1942.

283. L7535 had flown only 73 hours 35 minutes. After this accident the unit abandoned its intention of flying each aircraft for 150 hours and concentrated on L7529.

284. Henry Maudslay, letter to Gwen Maudslay, 25 January 1942.

285. Son of the 4th Earl and Countess of Leicester, Flight Lieutenant the Hon. David Coke of Holkham, Norfolk, was killed flying Hurricanes with No. 80 Squadron in Libya on 9 December 1941, aged 26. Coke had previously served with No. 257 Squadron during the Battle of Britain, being slightly wounded and forced to crash-land his Hurricane on 12 August 1940. His DFC was awarded for an action in November 1941, when he attacked transport on the El Adem–Acroma road, successfully blocking this vital supply route.

286. A total of seventy-five DFCs (four with bars) were to be awarded to Etonians during hostilities.

287. By a twist of fate Allsebrook and his crew were brought ashore at Ventnor, where Lucian Ercolani had also landed after his ditching three months earlier.

288. Others who had trained with Henry and survived a tour were now also being 'screened' and posted to training duties. Jean Sauvage had been sent to the Central Flying School, and Lucian Ercolani, awarded the DSO on 6 January for his actions the previous November, was now commanding No. 1483 (Target Towing) Flight, flying Wellingtons for air gunner refresher training and based at Newmarket racecourse. He was to be posted later to the Far East, initially to No. 99 Squadron flying Wellingtons from India; then to No. 355 Squadron equipped with Liberators, back to No. 99 Squadron and finally as officer commanding No. 159 Squadron, now also with Liberators. He survived the war, becoming chairman and joint managing director of the family furniture firm. He died on 13 February 2010, aged 92. Others were less fortunate. Pilot Officer Salazar completed his tour with No. 44 Squadron, being awarded the DFC. Promoted to Flight Lieutenant, he was killed serving as an instructor with No. 14 OTU while boosting numbers for the '*Millennium*' operation against Bremen of 25/26 June 1942.

289. Henry's logbook records this inaccurately as L9835, a Bristol Beaufort serial.

290. Unlike the Lancaster, which at this time had no dual controls, the Manchester could be so equipped, with a seat for the trainee pilot, although instruments were not duplicated.

291. Henry Maudslay, letter to Gwen Maudslay, 4 March 1942.

292. N9835, again recorded in error as L9835.

293. Henry Maudslay, letter to Gwen Maudslay, 14 March 1942. Charles Pilkington had died barely a month after his 20th birthday. He was the youngest of four sons. His brother Mark, a captain in the Life Guards and holder of the Military Cross, would be killed eight months later on 18 November as a member of the Long Range Desert Group in North Africa, aged 24. Another brother was also serving in the Middle East and a third had been taken prisoner of war. By another twist of fate, Joanna Everard had been Peter Pritchard's girlfriend at the time of his death the previous June. A letter from Joanna Everard to Mrs Pritchard written nearly two weeks after Charles Pilkington's death appears in *Last Letters Home*, ed. Tamsin Day-Lewis (London: Pan Books, 1995).

294. John Harley recovered from his wounds, but was to die on 14 September 1943 taking part in the Allied landings at Salerno.

295. Flight Lieutenant Charles McClure, a South African bomb aimer who had previously worked for the Shell Oil Company in South Africa and Rhodesia. Just over a month later he would receive the DFC for his part in the Augsburg raid.

296. There was a further connection between the squadron and the new AOC.-in-C. Major A. T. Harris had commanded No. 44 Squadron between July and December 1919 when the unit was a nightfighter squadron equipped with Sopwith Camels.

297. Henry Maudslay, letter to Gwen Maudslay, 24 March 1942.

298. No trace has been found of the Lancaster or its crew of eight. They are all commemorated on the Runnymede Memorial.
299. AVM Slessor was to relinquish command of No. 5 Group to AVM Alec Coryton on 25 May, subsequently becoming Assistant Chief of the Air Staff (Policy).
300. This aircraft, a Heinkel He IIIH-3 formerly of 5/KG26, had force-landed at Dalkeith, East Lothian, after attack by a Spitfire of 602 Squadron on 9 February 1940. Repaired and given the RAF serial number AW177, it was evaluated by technical experts and passed to No. 1426 Flight.
301. According to Ray Leach in *An Illustrated History of RAF Waddington* (Bognor Regis: Woodfield Publishing, 2003), Henry and Flight Lieutenant 'Happy' Taylor collected Squadron Leader Nettleton's aircraft R5508, KM-B, from Squires Gate and brought it back to Waddington on 18 April – although there is no record of this flight in Henry's logbook.
302. Henry Maudslay, letter to Gwen Maudslay, 23 April 1942. Orde had originally been commissioned by the Air Council to draw 150 members of Fighter Command engaged in the Battle of Britain. Subsequently his commission had been extended to include other members of the RAF.
303. Henry Maudslay, letter to Gwen Maudslay, 23 April 1942.
304. Henry Maudslay, letter to Gwen Maudslay, 23 April 1942. The painting by artist Frank Wooton showed a Hampden standing between two of Waddington's hangars, with the figures of the station commander, Group Captain Boothman, and Wing Commander Misselbrook walking nearby.
305. Henry Maudslay, letter to Gwen Maudslay, 23 April 1942.
306. Henry's logbook records L7385 inaccurately as L7485 – a No. 106 Squardon aircraft that had been lost on 16/17 April.
307. Henry Maudslay, letter to Gwen Maudslay, 29 April 1942.
308. Henry Maudslay, letter to Gwen Maudslay, 29 April 1942.
309. In fact No. 149 Squadron was based at Mildenhall in Suffolk, although Henry may have been referring to it in relation to Gordon's own location with HQ 4/7 Royal Dragoon Guards at Brandon Camp. The unit with which Gordon Barker flew has not been confirmed. The flight is most likely to have been a cross-country navigational exercise rather than an operation.
310. Henry Maudslay, letter to Gwen Maudslay, 29 April 1942.
311. Henry Maudslay, letter to Gwen Maudslay, 7 May 1943.
312. Born in 1900 at Ely (Cardiff), Wing Commander Lynch-Blosse had been educated at Blundell's and joined the RNAS in 1918, relinquishing his commission in 1921. He was granted a commission in the RAF as a Pilot Officer in 1938. At 42 he was well above average age for an operational squadron commander.
313. Flying Officer Ball had flown the first Lancaster bombing operation, against Essen, on 10/11 March 1942. After a spell with the conversion flight he subsequently returned to operations with No. 44 Squadron. He and his crew were lost without trace when their Lancaster failed to return from Essen on 4/5 August 1942.
314. Henry Maudslay, letter to Gwen Maudslay, 17 May 1942.
315. Henry Maudslay, letter to Gwen Maudslay, 30 May 1942.
316. Henry Maudslay, letter to Gwen Maudslay, 30 May 1942.
317. Completing his logbook, Henry recorded his aircraft this night incorrectly as being L7480, which was that flown by Squadron Leader Herring. Having previously served with 25 OTU, this was to be the first (and only) operation for L7430.
318. The flight had been L7480's twentieth (and final) operation, placing it among the top dozen or so operational Manchesters. It was later transferred to No. 1661 CU and struck off charge on 30 April 1943.
319. Flying Officer Halls and his crew are believed to have crashed in the North Sea. Three bodies were washed up on the Dutch coast, but the pilot and the remainder of his crew have no known grave.
320. In Arthur Kerry's House, the Slessors' son would leave Eton this year and join the RAF.
321. Henry Maudslay, letter to Gwen Maudslay, 5 June 1942.
322. Henry Maudslay, letter to Gwen Maudslay, 8 June 1942.
323. On 14 June Pilot Officer Nicholson lost two engines and was forced to ditch his Lancaster 200 miles out. Nothing was heard for several weeks, when members of the Mess were amazed to receive a card from the crew saying that they were safe in North Africa. They had come down near a convoy and been picked up almost immediately, but strict radio silence prevented any message being sent confirming their rescue.
324. Hilary St George Saunders had won the MC with the Welsh Guards during the First World War and

been British Embassy liaison officer at France's Ministry of Information and House of Commons librarian during the inter-war period. He also wrote (in collaboration with his friends) over thirty novels under the pseudonyms 'Francis Beeding', 'David Pilgrim', 'Barum Browne' and 'Cornelius Coffyn'. During hostilities he wrote many propaganda booklets published anonymously by the Ministry of Information. He would become better known post-war for his co-authorship (with Denis Richards) of the official history of the RAF's contribution to the conflict.

325. Hilary St George Saunders, letter 23 June 1942.
326. It was from this operation, piloting a Hampden of No. 14 OTU, that Henry's ex-No. 44 Squadron companion Flight Lieutenant Tristan Salazar, DFC, failed to return.
327. Pilot Officer C. T. Holland was to be promoted to flight officer and was killed along with five of his crew when his No. 44 Squadron Lancaster was shot down by a nightfighter over northern Holland returning from an attack on Bremen, 13/14 September 1942.
328. Squadron Leader Herring was to lose his life subsequently on 4 July 1943 while attached to No. 511 Squadron from No. 104 (Transport) OTU. He was co-pilot aboard Liberator C.II AL523 carrying General Wladyslaw Sikorski, head of the Polish government in exile, which crashed into the sea on take-off from Gibraltar, killing all crew and passengers with the sole exception of the pilot, Flight Lieutenant Edward Prchal. Herring's body was never found, and he is commemorated on the Runnymede Memorial.
329. Henry Maudslay, letter to Gwen Maudslay, 6 July 1942.
330. Henry Maudslay, letter to Gwen Maudslay, 6 July 1942.
331. Derek Mond was serving in the RNVR as a navigation officer. Promoted to temporary lieutenant, he died as a passenger in an aircraft accident while serving with HMS *Philante* on 30 April 1945. He is believed to have been a passenger aboard a Vickers Supermarine Sea Otter amphibian of No. 740 Squadron Royal Naval Air Service flying from Machrihanish on the Mull of Kintyre, to Lochalsh, Argyllshire, where HMS *Philante* was stationed. The aircraft sank after bouncing while making a water landing near Glas Eilean. The bodies of those aboard, including three passengers from HMS *Philante*, were never recovered, and Lieutenant Mond is commemorated on the Plymouth Naval Memorial, Panel 95, Column 3. (In *1939: The Last Season* (London: Thames and Hudson, 1989), Anne de Courcy states erroneously that Derek was in the Fleet Air Arm, possibly either because of the circumstances of his death or because HMS *Philante* was originally a Fleet Air Arm training yacht before becoming an anti-submarine training vessel in 1941.) With his death, succession to the title of Baron Melchett passed to Derek's younger brother, Julian Mond, who entered Eton in 1938 and whose son is the present Lord Melchett, former Executive Director of Greenpeace UK.
332. Pilot Officer Suckling, a New Zealander from Auckland, was fated to be killed almost exactly a month later with his crew, shot down by a nightfighter on the way to attack Kassel on the night of 25/26 August.
333. Conversion units had an establishment of thirty-two aircraft, necessitating two sets of code letters. At the end of October 1942 No. 1654 CU had sixteen Lancasters and sixteen Manchesters.
334. Pilot Officer Harrad was subsequently posted to No. 61 Squadron and was posted missing, presumed killed, when he and his crew failed to return from a shipping patrol west of the Scilly Isles on 20 August 1942. No trace of either crew or aircraft was ever found.
335. Sergeant, Dinning, an Australian who had been studying veterinary science at the University of Queensland before joining the RAAF, was subsequently sent to No. 97 Squadron. He and his crew were killed when a nightfighter shot down their Lancaster over Belgium during an operation against Nuremberg on 28/29 August 1942. He was 23.
336. Sergeant Rickard would be posted to No. 44 Squadron on 11 August on completion of his course.
337. Flight Lieutenant Sweeny, RAAF, was subsequently posted to No. 9 Squadron, which was in the process of converting to the Lancaster.
338. Flight Lieutenant Smyth and his crew had been posted in on 6 July and were to be killed operating with No. 97 Squadron against Cologne on 15 October 1942.
339. Squadron Leader Clyde Smith already held a DFC from his first tour on Wellingtons with No. 218 Squadron in 1941. He was to be posted as a flight commander to No. 9 Squadron on 11 August and took part in the squadron's first Lancaster operation on 10/11 September 1942, against Düsseldorf. He subsequently became a test pilot at the Aeroplane and Armament Experimental Establishment at Boscombe Down and survived the war holding the DSO and DFC.
340. Henry Maudslay, letter to Gwen Maudslay, 9 August 1941. Sergeant William Spooner, aged 21, from Ilkley, was crewed with Sergeant Dinning and had been attached to the CU from No. 97 Squadron

on 14 July. His training completed, he was posted back to No. 97 Squadron on 13 August. He was to be killed, along with his captain, before the month was through.

341. *Kelly's Directory* lists Roland Lee as a herbalist, of 38 Cobden Street, Humberstone Gate, Leicester.

342. Henry Maudslay, letter to Gwen Maudslay, 16 August 1942.

343. Henry Maudslay, letter to Gwen Maudslay, 18 August 1942.

344. These would be *Morning Flight*, first published in 1935, and *Wild Chorus*, published in 1938. Both were illustrated with a number of colour reproductions of Scott's paintings, which had been favourite prints for boys to have in their Eton rooms, and told of the author's love of wild places and adventures in the estuaries and mudflats of East Anglia.

345. Described as a 'Book of Juvenile Verse', this was first published in 1942. Another book purchased at about this time was a copy of Richard Hillary, *The Last Enemy*.

346. Henry Maudslay, letter to Gwen Maudslay, 19 August 1942.

347. Henry's injuries did not require major surgery but a contributing factor in his transfer to St Hugh's may have been the senior consulting surgeon at the hospital. Brigadier Hugh Cairns had performed the autopsy on T. E. Lawrence (Lawrence of Arabia) in 1935 and was conducting a major study of head injuries caused by motorcycle accidents. Cairns's work convinced the authorities that many lives would be saved by crash helmets, leading to a ruling making their use by Service riders compulsory. Between 1940 and 1945 over 13,000 patients with head injuries were treated by staff at St Hugh's. The hospital also pioneered the culture and use of penicillin in conjunction with the Radcliffe Infirmary.

348. Betty Norton-Griffiths was a London socialite who, in February 1941, *Queen* magazine had described as being 'one of the loveliest women in England'.

349. Presumably Paul Gallico, *The Snow Goose* (London: Michael Joseph, 1941). Subtitled 'A Story of Dunkirk', it relates the story of a lonely hunchbacked artist who lives in an old lighthouse in the marshlands of Essex, and his friendship with a young girl who brings him an injured Canada snow goose. Its subject matter would have appealed to Henry, as did the works of Peter Scott (see above).

350. Patients were issued with a dark blue uniform of jacket and trousers to wear with a shirt and tie once they were allowed out of bed.

351. Henry Maudslay, letter to Gwen Maudslay, 25 August 1942.

352. Derek's father. Lord Melchett, owned the Colworth Estate, Sharnbrook. During the war, part of Colworth House became a rest home for nurses, while the cocktail room, lounge and ballroom were used as a safe repository for some of the Imperial War Museum's art collection. Colworth Park was sold in 1947 and is now part of Unilever's UK Research and Development Department.

353. Virginia Cherrill (1908–96) had been discovered by Charlie Chaplin and made her debut as the blind flower girl in *City Lights*. She married Old Etonian George Child Villiers, the Earl of Jersey, in 1937 (her third husband; she had previously been married to Cary Grant). They were divorced in 1946.

354. During the war Virginia Cherrill spent much of her time performing charity work and working for the Red Cross, paying visits to Middleton Park every second Sunday, but there is no record of Henry meeting her. Middleton Park was sold to A. C. J. Wall in 1946. It is now converted into private flats.

355. Henry Maudslay, letter to Gwen Maudslay, 2 September 1942.

356. Henry Maudslay, letter to Gwen Maudslay, 7 September 1942.

357. Almost simultaneously, on 7 October, the unit became redesignated No. 1654 Heavy Conversion Unit.

358. Flying Officer Oakley, DFM, was subsequently awarded the DFC as a flight commander with No. 627 Mosquito Squadron during 1944–45. During 1955–57, as Wing Commander R. G. W. Oakley DSO, DFC, DFM, he commanded No. 138 Squadron, the RAFs first Valiant V-bomber unit.

359. In his war memoirs (published posthumously as *The Everlasting Arms: The War Memoirs of Air Commodore John Searby DSO, DFC* , ed. Martin Middlebrook (London: William Kimber, 1988), John Searby wrote: 'No time had been lost in sending me on my way (from 1654 CU) to Syerston though I heartily welcomed the move; Henry Maudslay and Rupert Oakley were excellent instructors – none better – but I found the atmosphere too restrictive for my taste.'

360. Squadron Leader Avis had been with No. 1506 BAT Flight at Waddington. On completion of his course, Squadron Leader Avis was posted to No. 44 Squadron, inviting Henry to join him for lunch on his first day at Waddington. He subsequently transferred to No. 57 Squadron. Later promoted to wing commander, Avis went on to command No. 150 Squadron at Hemswell from November 1944 until April 1945.

361. Later Wigsley's night-flying accident rate would be such that it became known as 'the cemetery with lights' to add to its colourful soubriquets.
362. Henry Maudslay, letter to Gwen Maudslay, 5 October 1942.
363. Henry Maudslay, letter to Gwen Maudslay, 30 October 1942.
364. As a postscript to his letter to his mother on 23 October, Henry had written: 'Elizabeth Richards has asked me to Queen Charlotte's dance on December 12 with her and Phoebe Cresswell, said yes and how!'
365. Henry Maudslay, letter to Gwen Maudslay, 30 October 1942.
366. Wing Commander K. P. Smales was now CO of No. 44 Squadron.
367. There is no record of this flight in Henry's logbook.
368. Henry Maudslay, letter to Gwen Maudslay, 10 November 1942.
369. Henry Maudslay, letter to Gwen Maudslay, 10 November 1942.
370. Henry Maudslay, letter to Gwen Maudslay, 24 November 1942.
371. Allsebrook arrived on 1 December, from No. 14 OTU, where he had been instructing following completion of his first tour with No. 49 Squadron. Despite this string-pulling, there is no evidence that Henry instructed Allsebrook while he was at Wigsley.
372. Henry Maudslay, letter to Gwen Maudslay, 24 November 1942.
373. Henry Maudslay, letter to Gwen Maudslay, undated but believed to have been written towards the end of November or during the first few days of December 1942.
374. Henry Maudslay, letter to Gwen Maudslay, 17 December 1942.
375. Henry Maudslay, letter to Gwen Maudslay, 19 December 1942. Allsebrook's course had finished on 17 December and he was about to return for a second tour of operations with No. 49 Squadron at Scampton.
376. The unit in question may have been No. 1661 CU, under the command of Squadron Leader Nettleton, VC, formed on 9 November 1942 from Nos 9, 44 and 49 Conversion Flights. It was based initially at Waddington and Scampton, moving to Winthorpe on 1 January 1943. Alternatively, it may have been No. 1662 CU, formed 26 January 1943 at Blyton, Lincs. The former is the more likely, being part of No. 5 Group, while the latter was in No. 1 Group.
377. Henry Maudslay, letter to Gwen Maudslay, 28 December 1942.
378. Henry Maudslay, letter to Gwen Maudslay, 28 December 1942.
379. Lancaster L7575 had previously served as OF-Y with No. 97 Squadron and had been flown on the Augsburg raid, 17 April 1942, by Flying Officer Erenest Deverill, DFM. Badly damaged, it had been repaired and transferred to No. 1654 CU.
380. Henry Maudslay, letter to Gwen Maudslay, 28 December 1942.
381. By coincidence, the same day as Henry arrived, Flying Officer Drew Wyness was posted from No. 50 Squadron to No. 1654 CU where he was to command 'B' Flight. After returning to operations as 'B' Flight commander with No. 57 Squadron, Wyness, now an A/Squadron Leader with the DFC, was posted to No. 617 Squadron as 'C' Flight Commander on 25 August 1944. He was killed in the attack on the Kembs Dam, 7 October 1944, as was Flight Lieutenant Christopher Howard, Henry's contemporary and fellow Wet Bob at Eton.
382. Wing Commander Russell had served his first tour on Hampdens with No. 50 Squadron and was awarded the DFC in June 1941. On 17 October 1942 he had returned to the squadron to take command following a period with No. 1654 CU at Wigsley. From Darlington and a graduate of Clare College, Cambridge, Russell had been a civil engineer before joining the RAFVR. Awarded a bar to his DFC in October 1943, he subsequently went on to serve with, and later command, No. 138 Squadron, flying special operations and supply drops in support of Resistance movements in occupied Europe. On 21 May 1943 he married Section Officer Mary Stoffer, whose previous marriage to Flight Lieutenant Prescott-Decrie's captain had lasted only some three weeks before Pilot Officer Harry Stoffer was killed flying a No.106 Squadron Manchester in an operation against Rostock on the night of 24 April 1942. Her second marriage was to meet a similar fate after almost a year. Squadron Leader Russell was killed on 7/8 May 1944, when his Halifax was shot down over northern France.
383. Squadron Leader Birch was on his second tour and had survived twenty-five operations with No. 207 Squadron's notorious Manchesters, including several hydraulic and turret failures and a Me 110 nightfighter attack during which his aircraft dived to 2,000 feet and his second pilot (on his first operation) baled out before control could be regained. On at least one occasion he had returned

home at low level, his gunners machine gunning a train en route. He may already have met Henry at No. 1654 CU, having been at Wigsley 11–28 October 1942. He survived the war and became a test pilot for Rolls-Royce in Australia.

384. Squadron Leader Birch's logbook adds to the confusion by recording the aircraft for this operation as ED409 'S'. His usual aircraft was VN-S, 'Sammy the Moke', carrying a large stylized outline motif of a braying donkey on the port side of the nose beneath the cockpit.

385. Strangely the official Bomber Command Night Raid Report for this operation states: 'None of the returning bombers reported any kind of nightfighter opposition', although the incident is recorded in the No. 50 Squadron ORB.

386. Squadron Leader Philip Bennett 'Mickey' Moore, DFC and bar, an Australian and excellent leader who had completed two tours of operations with No. 50 Squadron, was posted to No. 30 OTU for instructor duties on 10 January 1943, transferring to 27 OTU on 27 April. At the beginning of 1945 he would join No. 61 Squadron for a third tour of operations. He survived the war.

387. Henry Maudslay, letter to Gwen Maudslay, 9 January 1943.

388. Henry Maudslay, letter to Gwen Maudslay, 9 January 1943.

389. Henry Maudslay, letter to Gwen Maudslay, 17 January 1943, written in pencil owing to shortage of ink.

390. Henry Maudslay, letter to Gwen Maudslay, 17 January 1943.

391. i.e. the Eton Mile Cup.

392. Henry Maudslay, letter to Gwen Maudslay, 26 January 1943.

393. Henry Maudslay, letter to Gwen Maudslay, 26 January 1943.

394. The cause of the crash was never determined. There is an unconfirmed report that the aircraft experienced an engine fire and that the crew were preparing to bale out when it became uncontrollable.

395. Flying Officer Power and his two gunners were killed, but the remaining four crewmen survived as POWs. In 1983 a propeller blade from his aircraft was presented to No. 50 Squadron at Waddington.

396. Henry Maudslay, letter to Gwen Maudslay, 8 February 1943.

397. Henry's prediction was wrong. Squadron Leader Street, aged 29 and who had completed one tour with No. 61 Squadron Hampdens in early 1942, would survive his second with No. 50 Squadron, being awarded a bar to his DFC in November 1943.

398. Henry Maudslay, letter to Gwen Maudslay, 8 February 1943.

399. Henry Maudslay, letter to Gwen Maudslay, 8 February 1943.

400. Henry Maudslay, letter to Gwen Maudslay, 8 February 1943.

401. Neither is believed to have been lost through enemy action. One, from No. 103 Squadron, was hit by incendiaries from an aircraft above; the other, from No. 207 Squadron, suffered an engine fire from overheating engines.

402. Henry Maudslay, letter to Gwen Maudslay, 3 March 1943.

403. Sergeant David Thomas and Pilot Officer Francis Townsend were both shot down over Holland on the outward route. There were no survivors from either crew.

404. Sergeant Lyons had flown previously with Squadron Leader Moore. He was posted to No. 1660 CU on 21 March 1943. Sergeant Cottam's first flight with Henry was an air test on 3 March in preparation for that night's attack on Hamburg.

405. Henry Maudslay, letter to Gwen Maudslay, 3 March 1943.

406. 'Tinsel' was an electronic countermeasure against the German fighter control system. The wireless operator would sweep likely frequencies until he tuned into the Luftwaffe controller's instructions. A microphone installed in one of the engine bays would then be switched on to broadcast engine noise, thus drowning out the controller's voice communication with the fighters.

407. Sergeant Cottam's logbook records the aircraft as ED415, C. (Other records, possibly relating to a later period in the aircraft's life, show it coded as VN-N.) Until 14 March his captain's name is spelt 'Maudsley', after which it is recorded correctly.

408. Seven other aircraft were lost to flak and fighters along the route to and from the target.

409. Subsequently the site of the 1972 Olympic Stadium.

410. Flight Lieutenant Wood would be awarded the DFC in June 1943 on completion of his second tour, the citation making special mention of an earlier event when on 'a low level raid on a target in north west Germany . . . he made five runs over the target before dropping his bombs'.

411. Flight Lieutenant R. H. Avis had served as an observer in the First World War and again in France in 1940, being evacuated at Dunkirk. He flew fifteen operations while with No. 50 Squadron.

412. Henry's logbook records the location with the quaint, Old English spelling of 'Waynfleete'. He may have been influenced by the spelling of the surname of Eton's first headmaster, allegedly William Waynflete.

413. Flight Lieutenant John Sauvage, DFC, was still at No. 27 OTU but about to be posted to No. 1654 CU prior to joining No. 97 Squadron at Woodhall Spa at the end of April. On 20/21 June 1943, while participating in the shuttle raid against Friedrichshaven, his aircraft was badly damaged by flak. His success in landing his aircraft in North Africa resulted in the award of a bar to his DFC. Promoted to A/Squadron Leader, he would be awarded the DSO in November 1943. He survived the war and left the service in 1946.

414. Mrs Maudslay's 'war job' is probably running Fox Hill.

415. Henry Maudslay, letter to Gwen Maudslay, 20 March 1943.

416. Henry Maudslay, letter to Gwen Maudslay, 20 March 1943.

417. While a first tour comprised thirty operations, a second tour was only twenty.

418. Henry Maudslay, letter to Gwen Maudslay, 24 March 1943.

419. Henry was the only member of his crew to hold an award at this time. Sergeant Marriott's DFM would be gazetted on 19 June 1943 and Flying Officer Urquhart and Flying Officer Tytherleigh would each receive a posthumously gazetted DFC on 29 June 1945 (with effect from 16 May 1943) for their service with No. 50 Squadron.

420. Poor conditions during the winter of 1942–43 had emphasized the need for concrete runways at Scampton and No. 49 Squadron had moved out as a precursor to this. The formation of No. 617 Squadron delayed construction, which was started eventually in September 1943.

421. After No.4 ITW Maltby had received his pilot training at Ansty, Cranage and Upper Heyford, before flying operations with Nos 106 and 97 Squadrons.

422. Henry Maudslay, letter to Gwen Maudslay, 30 March 1943. The reference to the flight sergeant from his old squadron is obscure. He may have meant Flight Sergeant Brown, although he and Henry did not serve with No. 44 Squadron at the same time. He may have meant flight lieutenant, in which case this would have been Flight Lieutenant Harold Wilson, who in the event did not participate in the Dams Raid.

423. Sergeant Cottam's logbook records this flight as lasting half an hour.

424. Again there are discrepancies with Sergeant Cottam's logbook, the latter recording a duration of 4.30, in Lancaster R. Flying Officer Urquhart records a flight of 1.50 in aircraft R. (There may have been a late switch of aircraft.)

425. Harry Moyle, *The Hampden File* (Air Britain, 1989), page 182 records that during the summer of 1940 No. 44 Squadron conducted experiments with a similar system fitted to a Hampden, presumably for assisting minelaying. It is not known whether Henry was aware of these trials.

426. Three crews had flown five sorties each, two had only flown one, and another, McCarthy's, had yet to complete an exercise.

427. Probate Newcastle upon Tyne, 6 July 1943, to her brother in law, Edwin Richardson, solicitor. Effects £1,798 11s 3d In her will Kelly stipulated that after her death 'a vein to be opened so that there is no chance of my being buried alive'.

428. Henry Maudslay, letter to Gwen Maudslay, 11 April 1943, posted on 13 April. This letter showed evidence of security monitoring, being opened and resealed by Examiner 1613.

429. Henry Maudslay, letter to Gwen Maudslay, 11 April 1943.

430. Henry Maudslay, letter to Gwen Maudslay, 11 April 1943.

431. The briefing for this operation required crews to identify the target visually, and Allsebrook had dropped down 6,000 feet to ensure his aim. Despite this precaution, nearly all the crews mistook their objective and bombed an asylum building some 7 miles from the target, leaving the factory unscathed.

432. The 4/7 R. D. G. were at Fritton Decoy, near Great Yarmouth, conducting initial trials with 17-ton Valentine (DD) amphibious tanks, including the use of an adapted form of Submarine Escape Apparatus. Victoria Barker would be born on 14 October 1943.

433. Henry Maudslay, letter to Gwen Maudslay, 4 May 1943.

434. Pilot Officer Urquhart's logbook records the aircraft as ED437.

435. Henry's logbook has the serial of this pencilled in as '147', presumably EE147, but, although this aircraft did serve with No. 617 Squadron, coded 'V' it was a brand new aircraft and not delivered until 3 June. The pencilled serials may have been written in at the beginning of June 1943, shortly before the book was sent to the RAF Central Repository. A more likely candidate is ED437,

originally coded AJ-N, which is believed became AJ-V on 2 May when modified Lancaster ED906 was delivered to become AJ-N. This is supported by the entry in Sergeant Cottam's logbook, made by another member of the squadron post-Dams Raid, which records the aircraft as ED437.

436. Later Sir Barnes Wallis, at this time assistant chief designer of Vickers-Armstrong Aviation; a renowned aeronautical engineer, designer of the airship R 100, whose application of geodetic construction had given great strength to the Wellington bomber.

437. Torpex was a mixture of TNT, RDX and aluminium powder.

438. Henry was nearly correct, John Maudslay's 31st birthday occurred on 11 May.

439. There are two portraits of Henry by Cuthbert Orde. Compared to photographs of Henry, the drawing dated 23 April 1942 captures an atypical view, suggesting a squarer head and features, and it is the one of which Mrs Maudslay voiced her disquiet. The second portrait is immediately recognizable as Henry but, although signed, is unfortunately undated and was most probably drawn at a later date. Indeed it bears a striking similarity to a photograph taken at Eton of Henry as a member of Pop. It is possible that after hearing of Mrs Maudslay's reservations, and learning of Henry's death, Orde produced the undated version posthumously from the Eton portrait.

440. Probably with Sanders & Co. (Booksellers and Prints), Salutation House, 104 High Street, Oxford.

441. Henry Maudslay, letter to Gwen Maudslay, 10 May 1943, postmarked Lincoln, 6.45 p.m. 12 May 1943. This is the full text of the letter.

442. The inert Upkeeps were filled with a mixture of aerated concrete to the same density as Torpex.

443. This may not have been the only near miss Henry had when flying too low. On another (unidentified) practice flight he allegedly returned with foliage wrapped around his tailwheel.

444. Minutes of progress meeting on Upkeep and Highball, 13 May 1943.

445. Flying Officer Malcolm Arthurton, squadron medical officer, cited in John Sweetman, *The Dambusters Raid* (London: Arms and Armour Press, 1990), p.75.

446. Until 14 May the intention had been to mount the operation the following week. By 16 May briefing models had been prepared for the Mohne and Sorpe Dams, but that for the Eder was still being made. It was not completed until 17 May. As a result, study of this target was limited to maps and photographs.

447. The navigation log for AJ-N (Pilot Officer Knight) records the use of IFF. This was contrary to the Operation Order, which stated that it was *not* to be used on the outward journey.

448. Flame floats were containers with a calcium phosphate filling. On immersion with seawater, they produced impure phosphine, which burns on contact with the air, thereby creating a datum against which the gunner could align his gun sight and observe drift.

449. Fred Sutherland, letters to author, 25 March 2000 and 8 June 2000.

450. This was the theory, although the weapon on Flight Lieutenant Barlow's Lancaster survived the aircraft's crash and was captured intact to be examined by the Germans. Whether the fusing was faulty, or the bomb aimer had not yet activated the fusing unit, cannot be determined.

451. Fred Sutherland, front gunner with Pilot Officer Knight, maintains that the formation had become separated before reaching the Rhine (letters to author, 25 March 2000 and 8 June 2000).

452. At the time others aboard AJ-N thought that Henry had either turned back, or struck the ground on account of setting his altimeter too low against the spotlights over the North Sea (letters to author, 25 March 2000 and 8 June 2000).

453. Only Hopgood's bomb aimer, Pilot Officer John Fraser, and rear gunner, Pilot Officer Tony Burcher, managed to escape and were taken prisoner, the latter being badly injured.

454. Later reports, borne out by subsequent investigation, claim that Young's Upkeep appears to have caused the wall to begin to collapse before the next weapon exploded.

455. Fred Sutherland maintains that Henry had not reported his arrival at the Mohne. When he called up on reaching the Eder, the crew of AJ-N were most surprised, having thought that Henry had either turned back or crashed en route to the Rhine (letter to author, 8 June 2000).

456. Fred Sutherland, letter to author, 25 March 2000.

457. John Sweetman, *The Dambusters Raid* (London: Cassell, 1982), pp.117–18. This view is supported by official post-raid reports by both Gibson and Shannon.

458. German eyewitnesses report that Shannon's weapon exploded just short of the western end of the dam, damaging the parapet and roadway.

459. This is recorded in the No. 617 Squadron Form 540 (ORB). The only other evidence comes from a sheet of undated pencilled notes, believed to have been written by a Scampton intelligence officer and presumably used in the ORB's compilation, which states: 'Maudslay believed damaged between

Scheldt and Rhine. Something seen hanging.' The name of the aircrew member who made this comment was not recorded.

460. If the observation by Sergeant Grayston that one of the formating aircraft was lower when they tested the spotlights over the North Sea applied to Henry's aircraft, then he should have experienced a repeat scenario to that experienced four days earlier at Reculver, his aircraft being damaged by spray from a low drop. However, there is no suggestion, either from surviving witnesses or from reports, that this was the situation at the Eder. It is possible that Grayston's remarks may have related to Astell's aircraft, but, since this was lost before bombing, such a theory must remain conjecture.

461. Coastal Command's experience with conventional depth charges had shown that, although capable of withstanding the normal impact with water, a Torpex (RDX) filling was liable to detonate if subjected to the shock of a weapon striking a hard target at a high enough velocity.

462. Fred Sutherland, letter to author, 25 March 2000.

463. Guy Gibson, *Enemy Coast Ahead – Uncensored: The Real Guy Gibson.*

464. Pilot Officer Ottley, flying independently as part of the third wave, was directed to attack the Lister Dam, south of the Sorpe. While still outbound, the aircraft strayed slightly south of track in this area and was shot down by flak near Hamm at 0235. All the crew perished, with the exception of the rear gunner, Sergeant Fred Tees, who was blown clear as the aircraft crashed and exploded.

465. *Heimat* or *Homeland* flak batteries were those located within the boundaries of Germany itself, often manned by part-time crews, comprising largely non-combatant local men. The crew composition of those batteries around Emmerich has not been ascertained.

466. ED778 is believed to have been attacked by a night-fighter that killed both gunners before despatching the Lancaster to crash at Netterden. The pilot, Flight Sergeant George Leach, RCAF, and his flight engineer both survived to be taken POW. The remainder of the crew are buried in Gendringen Roman Catholic Cemetery.

467. The remains of the crew were interred at 11.00 a.m. on 19 May. Only Sergeant Marriott and Warrant Officer Cottam were identified positively by the Germans and buried in graves 37 and 38 respectively. The other five crew members, including Henry, were buried in separate graves, 35–41, each recorded as 'Unbekannt Eng. Flieger'. Flight Lieutenant Robert Barlow's crew, which had collided with a high-tension power line near Haldern on their outward flight, were also interred at the same time. A German document dated 19 June 1943 records that, at the Luftwaffe interrogation centre at Dulag Luft, Oberursel, near Frankfurt-am-Main, bomb aimer Pilot Officer John Fraser, one of the two survivors from Flight Lieutenant Hopgood's crew, gave the name of Flying Officer Tytherleigh as being a gunner with Squadron Leader Maudslay. This information occurs at the end of the document and does not relate directly to previous details. It seems possible that the Germans were still trying to identify Z-Zebra's crew.

468. Squadron Leader Young, DFC, died three days before his 28th birthday. For Sergeant Lawrence Nichols the wireless operator, 17 May would have been his 33rd birthday. Subsequently the bodies of Squadron Leader Young and his crew were washed ashore. They are all buried in the coastal cemetery at Bergen aan Zee. The flak battery that brought them down originally misidentified its target as a Handley Page Halifax.

469. In fact three men had survived, Flight Sergeant Fraser and Pilot Officer Burcher, bomb-aimer and rear gunner respectively with Flight Lieutenant Hopgood, and Sergeant Tees from Pilot Officer Ottley's crew.

470. Among the messages received was one from the former AOC of No. 5 Group, now AOC.-in-C. Coastal Command: 'Well done Scampton. A magnificent night's work. Slessor.'

471. This reconstruction has been based on other surviving letters to next of kin of the operation's casualties.

472. In June 2000 a letter purporting to be that sent by Wing Commander Gibson to the parents of Flying Officer Tytherleigh came up for auction in Swindon. This letter stated: 'Your son was front gunner of an aircraft detailed to carry out an attack against the Eder Dam. Contact with this aircraft was lost after the aircraft took off and nothing further was heard from it. . . .The captain of your son's aircraft, Squadron Leader Maudsley [*sic*], was an experienced and able pilot, and would, I am sure, do everything possible to ensure the safety of his crew.' The letter has been challenged subsequently by Flying Officer Tytherleigh's sister, Edith Widdowson of Halifax, as being a forgery.

473. Henry's flying logbook was returned to his mother by registered post from the RAF Central Depository, Colnbrook, on 10 May 1946.

474. ED937, AJ-Z, was formally struck off charge on 26 May 1943, as were the other seven aircraft lost on the Dams Raid. Its Movement Card logs it as having only flown four hours, although this does not include its final flight. The Aircraft Loss Card records the contemporary view: 'Damaged by own store which detonated on parapet of Eder Dam – crash not observed but this damage believed cause of loss.' Over sixty years later the squadron's Tornado GR 4 aircraft again carry the code letters AJ, with individual letters commemorating aircraft that flew on the Dams Raid, GR 4T, ZA549 being AJ-Z. The aircraft also carries a panel beneath the cockpit inscribed 'Squadron Leader H. E. Maudslay DFC'.

475. With the fate of Henry and his crew uppermost in their minds, friends and neighbours were soon to hear of two local incidents that demonstrated the scope of aircrew survival. On 26 May 1943 Whitley LA845 from No. 24 OTU crashed and burnt at Collins Farm, Willersey, after an engine failure on take-off from nearby Honeybourne. Although the pilot was killed, the remainder of the crew survived with minor injuries. Within a week, however, the neighbourhood would witness a tragic example of the crew's possible alternative fate. On 2 June 1943 Whitley Z6639 from the same unit, flying circuits in deteriorating weather, struck rising ground some 200 yards from Broadway Tower, exploding in flames. All the crew were killed instantly, with the exception of the rear gunner, who was rescued from the wreckage, but died shortly afterwards.

476. The Bomber Command Night Raid Report for the operation, dated 28 July 1943, echoed this view: 'Aircraft Z which is missing was damaged by its own mine which detonated on the parapet of the Eder Dam. The crash was not observed but the damage is believed to have brought down the aircraft.'

477. Henry was not president of Pop.

478. Vera Brittain had been a member of the 'Committee for the Abolition of Night Bombing' and later wrote a pamphlet entitled 'Seeds of Chaos: What Mass Bombing Really Means' for the Bombing Restriction Campaign.

479. The meeting is recorded in *Wartime Chronicle: Vera Brittain's Diary 1939–1945*, ed. Alan Bishop and Y. Aleksandra Bennett. John was brother of Shirley Catlin, later Shirley Williams, MP. In the event, Vera Brittain thought Harrow School better suited to her son's abilities.

480. The German source was Totenliste No. 153, a register of enemy casualties supplied to the International Red Cross. The telegram also confirmed the fate of Pilot Officer Whillis, Pilot Officer Gillespie and five unknown members of Flight Lieutenant Barlow's crew and Sergeant Roberts of Squadron Leader Young's crew.

481. A similar telegram, with suitable amendments, omitting reference to the remainder of the crew and stating that Henry's next of kin had been informed, was sent simultaneously to Diana Byrom.

482. Letter from Ralph Allsebrook to Gwen Maudslay, dated 21 August 1943, via Arthur Thorning.

483. Wing Commander the Hon. Maurice Baring, OBE, journalist, author and poet (1874–1945) had been assistant equipment officer to the RFC and subsequently personal secretary to Major General Sir (later Lord) Hugh Trenchard, founding father of the RAF and the first Chief of the Air Staff.

484. Auberon Thomas Herbert, son of the late Hon. Auberon Edward William Molyneux Herbert, also held the title 11th Lord Dingwall. Serving with the Hampshire Yeomanry (Carabiniers), he transferred to the RFC and was flying with No. 22 Squadron at the time of his death. He is buried in the HAC Cemetery, Ecoust-St Mein, Pas-de-Calais. Aged 40, Herbert was considerably older than many of his contemporaries, having previously been a notable politician. It has not been ascertained whether or not he was a distant relative of Gwen Maudslay.

485. Roger Peek had been Henry's patrol second in the Eton College scouts. He was killed in Libya on 23 June 1942 as Rommel's forces pushed east following the fall of Tobruk. Presumably his death had only recently been notified to his old school.

486. A similar letter was also sent to Diana Byrom, referring only to Henry's burial in the North Military Cemetery, Düsseldorf, without giving a grave number (or revealing that his body had not been identified).

487. As a result of the danger and damage caused by bombing. the Registry had relocated from London to Llandudno, in common with a number of government departments, taking refuge in commandeered hotels.

488. The actual will document also listed a third executor, Cecil Montague Jacomb Ellis, solicitor of 17 Albemarle Street.

489. Also published in *Aeroplane*, 17 March 1944. This communiqué listed the remainder of the crew, with the exception of Canadians Flying Officer Urquhart and Sergeant Cottam.

490. For discussion of the inclusion of the fictitious 'Schwelme' Dam, see John Sweetman, *The Dambusters Raid* (Arms and Armour Press, 1990), p.160.

491. At the time the family were unaware of the full details of Henry's attack on the Eder and his subsequent return flight.

492. Colin Richardson had graduated from Balliol College, Oxford, and was commissioned into the Royal Artillery. He was killed in action in Burma on 3 February 1945, a week after being gazetted for the award of the Military Cross.

493. Edward Folkes was a sick berth attendant aboard HM Hospital Ship *Maine*, who died on 7 December 1941 and is buried at Alexandria, Egypt. Flight Lieutenant Kayll was pilot of a Lancaster of No. 156 Squadron (PFF), killed with his crew over Holland during an operation against Essen on 26/27 April 1944 and buried at Zundert. Flight Sergeant Proctor by coincidence served with No. 44 Squadron and was mid-upper gunner in Flight Lieutenant J. Ruddick's crew, who all died when their Lancaster was brought down participating in an attack on Magdeburg, 21/22 January 1944. He rests in the Berlin 1939–45 War Cemetery. His parental home was in Willersey, while his wife and baby daughter lived in Broadway. A report that he was missing appeared in the *Evesham Journal*, 5 February 1944.

494. Danny Danziger, *Eton Voices* (London: Viking, 1988). Bentine himself had served in the Royal Air Force, as a squadron intelligence officer within Bomber and later Fighter Commands.

495. Danziger, *Eton Voices*.

496. Flying Officer Clyde Miles Graham, son of Major General Sir Miles Graham, Montgomery's chief administration officer for D-Day, a navigator with the crew of Flight Lieutenant Geoffrey Stout, DFC, shot down returning from an attack on the Dortmund Ems Canal, 23/24 September 1944, and Henry's rowing contemporary Flight Lieutenant Christopher Howard, killed piloting his Lancaster in a low-level daylight attack against the Kembs Dam on the Upper Rhine, 7 October 1944.

497. The Imperial War Graves Commission was retitled the Commonwealth War Graves Commission in March 1960.

498. Gordon Barker was among those who had advanced through this area. As second in command of the 4/7th RDG with 32-ton Sherman DD (Duplex Drive) amphibious tanks on D-Day, he was among the first British armour ashore. He landed on 'King' section of GOLD beach, west of la Riviere, subsequently fighting his way through France and Belgium. He was involved in the thrust to Nijmegen and the relief of Arnhem, being promoted commander of 4/7th on 20 September 1944. Continuing into Germany, he led the victory parade through Bremerhaven on 8 May 1945 in his Sherman Mons. Awarded the DSO, he remained in the Army until 1950, peacekeeping in Palestine and on staff duties at the War Office, retiring with the rank of lieutenant colonel.

499. Eighteen naval and four miscellaneous graves make up the total of 7,654 burials.

500. Exhumation of the crew from their graves in Düsseldorf Cemetery had taken place on 3 October 1946, conducted by No. 39 Grave Concentration Unit and witnessed by Flight Lieutenant E. F. Herbert. Examination of the coffin taken from Grave No. 40 (which had been marked as 'Eng. Flieger + 17.5.43. 40' and recorded in the cemetery records as 'Unbekannt Eng. Flieger shot down at Emmerich') had revealed a battledress tunic marked with the name 'Maudslay' and an Air Ministry blouse carrying the rank insignia of a squadron leader.

501. Sergeant Marriott had been recommended for a non-immediate DFM on 26 April 1943 for his service with No. 50 Squadron, although the award was not gazetted until 19 June 1943. The awards for Flying Officer Urquhart and Flying Officer Tytherleigh were gazetted posthumously on 29 June 1945 (w.e.f. 16 May 1943).

502. Reichswald Forest Cemetery is also the final resting -place of another Old Beaudeserter, Wing Commander William Graham (1920–41), who was killed on operations in a Wellington of No. 304 (Silesian) (Polish) Squadron against Bremen on the night of 7–8 May 1941. Also buried here is Sergeant Randal Scott, who trained with Henry at 10 SFTS Tern Hill and who was killed along with his crew on 27/28 December 1941 piloting a Whitley of No. 58 Squadron against Düsseldorf.

503. The purchaser was Cyril Burnham Godfrey, acting on behalf of Hubert Edwin Bradley, Edwin Bradley Junior and Lionel Dennis Bradley, building contractors of Okus Quarries, Swindon. In 2012 Fox Hill Manor became part of the Cotswold Conference Centre. A new bedroom courtyard, 'Maudslay Court' was formally opened on 6 October 2012 by Wing Commander Keith Taylor, then officer commanding No. 617 Squadron.

504. Wing Commander Gibson himself was not to survive the war. After a period of administrative duties, he pressed to be allowed to return to operations and was killed on the night of 19/20

September 1944. He failed to return from an operation against München-Gladbach and Rheydt that he had been controlling as 'Master Bomber', flying a Mosquito of No. 627 Squadron. Gibson and his navigator, Squadron Leader James Warwick, DFC, are buried in a joint grave at Steenbergen, Holland. (See Richard Morris, *Guy Gibson* (London: Viking, 1994) for a detailed account of this officer's life.)

505. Sergeant Douglas Creevy was bomb aimer in a No. 12 Squadron Lancaster shot down during an attack on Düsseldorf on 25/26 May 1943. He and the other members of his crew were also buried originally in the Nordfriedhof, Düsseldorf, before being reinterred in Plot 5 Row D of Reichswald Forest Cemetery.

506. Television screenings of the film in some regions since December 1999 have also edited out Nigger's name and the code for breaching the Mohne Dam, prompting an exchange of readers' correspondence in several national newspapers, including the *Daily Telegraph* and *Daily Mail*.

507. Revelations 7: 9–17.

508. Sergeant Anthony Cursett Sutherland was killed flying with No. 61 Squadron during an attack on Frankfurt, 24 August 1942 during which another of Henry's ex-crew members, Sergeant Rickard, was also killed.

509. Sergeant Copsey was a new arrival, having been posted from No. 14 OTU on 12 September 1941. At the end of the following month he transferred to Pilot Officer Southgate's crew.

510. Sergeant Joseph Rickard subsequently flew with Sergeant Nicholson, who as a flying officer later ditched and was taken to North Africa. He was killed flying with this crew as a pilot officer on 24 August 1942 during an attack on Frankfurt.

511. Sergeant Leonard Leggett was killed on 12 December 1941, his DFM being gazetted in October 1942.

512. Sergeant Desmond Skinner was killed on 7 February 1943 during an operation against Lorient.

513. Pilot Officer Stanley Young was killed on 23 November 1942 attacking Stuttgart.

514. Sergeant William Scott was killed on 4 August 1942 attacking Essen.

515. Pilot Officer Cowling was shot down and taken prisoner of war during an attack on Osnabrück, 6/7 October 1942.

516. Sergeant Reginald Gladwish was killed on 9 January 1943 during a mining sortie.

517. Sergeant William Day was killed on 20 September 1942 operating against Munich.

518. Flight Lieutenant Richard Trevor-Roper flew as Wing Commander Gibson's rear gunner on the Dams Raid and was killed flying with No. 97 Squadron on the ill-fated Nuremberg Raid of 30/31 March 1944.

519. Flight Lieutenant Wood was awarded the DFC in June 1943.

520. On completion of his tour, Sergeant Charles Wilfred 'Wilf' Gray would be posted to No. 1485 Bombing & Gunnery Flight as an instructor and awarded the DFC in October 1943.

521. Sergeant Francis McGrath, a pilot, had been posted to No. 50 Squadron from No. 1660 CU on 23 December 1942. He was killed in an attack on Frankfurt, 10/11 April 1943.

522. Sergeant Edward Hough was subsequently commissioned and died as a pilot officer when he failed to return from Duisburg on 12/13 May 1943.

523. Sergeant William Miller was to receive the DFM in April 1943.

Index